# ANCIENT LIGHTS

# ANCIENT LIGHTS:
## THE REAL DEAL ABOUT THE AMERICAN NATION'S BIRTH

How The Race Card Evil Infiltrated And Undermined
The American Government

# CHRISTINE AND HAYWOOD ISAAC

TATE PUBLISHING
AND ENTERPRISES, LLC

Published by Tate Publishing & Enterprises, LLC
127 E. Trade Center Terrace | Mustang, Oklahoma 73064 USA
1.888.361.9473  |  www.tatepublishing.com

Tate Publishing is committed to excellence in the publishing industry. The company reflects the philosophy established by the founders, based on Psalm 68:11,
*"The Lord gave the word and great was the company of those who published it."*

Book design copyright © 2016 by Tate Publishing, LLC. All rights reserved.
*Cover design by Lirey Blanco*
*Interior design by Shieldon Alcasid*

1. History / General
2. History / United States / General
16.09.23

The Creator, however many be Thy Names and Attributes.

Humanity's Ancient Lights, however many be their colors, creeds, and nationalities.

The American Republic's three branches of government: executive, legislative, judicial.

Tate Publishing Company, for having the wisdom and courage to publish this great work.

Mr. Joey Garrett, who discovered the writers of this great work.

Mr. James Isaac Sr. and Mrs. Katie Brown-Isaac (my parents) and their ancestors.

Mr. Herbert Webb Sr. and Mrs. Annie Mae Brown-Webb (my uncle and aunt) and their ancestors.

Ms. Lillie Grade and yours—for being there for us. Thank you and may God bless you!

Messrs. David Sr., David Jr., and Maurice, ditto!

Little Elijah and his generation ("Useful reading and thinking are fundamental").

And the Americans of all ethnicities—Confederate and Union, black, white, other—without whose dedication and fortitude, our Nation would not have survived! We, the authors of *Ancient Lights* wish to say,

> "We thank you and yours, past and present, for the risks taken and sacrifices made to contest the "Race Card Evil." True, the battle between freedom and slavery is an eternal one. But rest assured that whenever and wheresoever the "ancient serpent" rears its head, the "Ancient Lights" will also be there: ever waiting, watching, and standing "United" to take up the gauntlet on behalf of Humanity—as promised by our Creator (2 Sam. 23:1–5, Isa. 61:1–11, Mal. 4:1–6) (KJV).

# Contents

# Introduction

We're baaaaack! In volume one of *Ancient Lights* we said that more than one volume would be needed to tell how the "Race Card Evil" managed to survive and thrive down through the centuries to haunt the modern Western world. Consequently, this volume takes up where the first left off and needs little in the way of introduction. Still, before starting this leg of our journey, we should consider the words of Illinois Representative Isaac N. Arnold to the Thirty-eighth Congress in June of 1864. Said he to the House of Representatives on the issue of passing the US Constitution's Thirteenth Amendment:

> The historian who writes the story of man's progress from slavery and barbarism to Christian civilization and liberty, will find no more interesting page than that which is now being filled with the struggle in which we are engaged; none where the contest between liberty and slavery has been more clearly defined; none upon a grander theater; none where the combatants, by their numbers, genius, ability, and heroism, have given more dignity and sublimity to the contest.

A lot has happened since the publishing of our first volume—some events that we Americans should be proud of and some that we should not. One of the things that we should take pride in is the sincere effort by many Americans to come together as a people to end the "Race Card Evil." Unfortunately, in this effort to do so, many Americans have been misguided by those with a hidden agenda to gain notoriety by "crucifying" the true story about the birth of our nation—a "crucifixion" based either on benign ignorance and inadequate research or malignant disregard of the truth, or a combination of both!

A clear-cut case of this is the unfortunate murders in South Carolina allegedly perpetrated by young Mr. Dylann Roof—a misguided twenty-one-year-old "white" American who sought to ignite a "race war" and took pictures while holding the Confederate battle flag. South Carolina, already embattled over the Battle Flag flying at her state capital, found herself again under attack about the flag issue. To remedy the situation, President Barack Obama suggested that the flag be put in a museum—to prevent people from misusing it to perpetrate acts that only serve to "desecrate" the Confederacy's military (not national) flag. South Carolina's Governor, Ms. Nikki Haley, and the state legislature responded by retiring the battle flag. But this genuine gesture was not enough for some Americans. Now we see the battle flag under attack because businesses sell it or people display it on their license plates, and we witness the same treatment given to venerated statues of US Supreme Court justices (Roger B. Taney in particular) and Confederate war heroes (Robert E. Lee in particular)! When is enough enough? Where does this "madness" end? What, pray tell, is achieved by this?

The story about the American women and men who paved the way for us to enjoy the blessings of liberty, domestic tranquility, and the pursuit of happiness needs to be told through their words—so that none will doubt what they did and did not stand for. We latter-day Americans need to "know" their story in order to truly appreciate what our government's founders bequeathed to us. We need to "understand" their words and deeds during the eras of the: British-American colonies, first and second Continental Congresses, 1781 Confederation Congress, 1789 US Congress, and 1857 US Supreme Court. Only with such knowledge can we truly understand why we have our 1774 Articles of Association, 1776 Declaration of Independence, 1781 Articles of Confederation, 1787 US Constitution, 1863 Emancipation Proclamation, 1865

Thirteenth Amendment, 1866 Civil Rights Act, 1868 Fourteenth Amendment, and 1870 Fifteenth Amendment. Without such background, we can never truly "know" and "understand" what these documents were intended to mean and achieve!

To accomplish our task, we have to journey through a number of important time periods: first Spain's New World Colonization and England's rise to power—New World Colonization Eras; next, America's Colonial, Revolutionary War, Confederation, Constitutional, Civil War, Reconstruction, post-Reconstruction eras; and finally the world's technological era. All told, about ten or so stops along history's highway. By travelling this path, we will unravel where a number of "modern" ideas came from—to determine whether such ideas are true or false, valid, or invalid. When we end our journey, hopefully, we Americans will better respect the rights of fellow Americans and work together to fulfill our joint destiny in America and the World—as fifty-five (55) of our Colonial American "Ancient Lights" intended.

As always, we hope you enjoy and respect the ride. And we hope you will enlighten all Americans that you encounter, young and old, about US—the story of "We the People of the United States." But before we start, we want to remind you about a song sung by an African American group named Harold Melvin and the Blue Notes, which said in part,

> Wake up everybody no more sleepin in bed
>
> No more backward thinkin' time for thinkin' ahead
> The world has changed so very much
> From what it used to be
> There is so much hatred, war, an' poverty
> Wake up all the teachers time to teach a new way
> Maybe then they'll listen to whatcha have to say
> 'Cause they're the ones who's coming up and the world is
> in their hands
> When you teach the children teach 'em the very best you
> can...

Wake up all the builders time to build a new land
I know we can do it if we all lend a hand
The only thing we have to do is put it in our mind
Surely things will work out they do it every time ...
The world won't get no better if we just let it be
The world won't get no better we gotta change it yeah, just
you and me...
Can't do it alone...
Need some help y'all...
Wake up everybody. ("Wake Up Everybody," Harold
Melvin and the Blue Notes)

# 1

# Excusing People from the Table of Nations: Act of God or Peculiar Institution?

> I saw a star fall from heaven…to him was given the key
> to the bottomless pit…he opened the…pit…there came
> out…locusts…And the shapes of the locusts were like
> horses prepared for battle…on their heads were gold-
> like crowns…their faces were as the faces of men…they
> had breastplates…the sound of their wings was as the
> sound of chariots of many horses running to battle…they
> had tails like unto scorpions…there were stings in their
> tails…And they had a king over them…whose name in
> the Hebrew [Aramaic] tongue is A-bad'don [destruction,
> ruin], but in the Greek…A-pol'ly-on [destroyer].
>
> —Rev. 9:1–3, 7–11 (KJV)

AFTER CRISTOFORO COLOMBO (Christopher Columbus) discovered the Carribean area later called Hispaniola, Spain's rulers realized that it differed drastically from the region the Portuguese explorers found when they rounded the Cape of Good Hope. News of this mysterious, serene, tropical land prompted Spanish theologians and thinkers to speculate about whether Colombo had found the biblical Garden of Eden. This, in turn, sparked heated dispute between the thrones of Ferdinand-Isabella (called Aragon-Castile or Spain) and Joao (John) II (Portugal)—one that Pope Alexander VI was asked to resolve to avert war between the two countries (AD 1493–94). These events twentieth century authors Johanna Johnston and James L. Steffensen recounted in the *Universal History of the World Encyclopedia* chapter entitled "A New World and a New Sea." Said they,

> The mystery of Columbus' islands became more puzzling as Portuguese captains returned to Europe with tales of the Indies they had found by sailing around Africa. The lands at the ends of the two sea routes were nothing alike. Perhaps, some people suggested, Columbus had not found the edge of Asia, but the original Garden of Eden. The islands were filled with delicate fruit, berries, and vegetables; brilliantly colored birds and curious animals wandered their forests. Their people, it was said, were handsome *savages* who led a simple, joyful life, lived in grassy huts, and saw no reason to cover themselves with clothes from head to foot—just the sort of people to live in paradise.
>
> Whatever the islands were, many men were eager to share their wealth. Though Columbus had claimed them in the name of the king and queen of Spain, King John of Portugal ordered his admirals to prepare an expedition to explore the same area. The Spaniards, furious, demanded that the Portuguese cancel their plans. The Portuguese refused, and there was talk of war. Finally the matter was put to the pope. He called for a map, then drew a line, north to south, through the Ocean Sea [Atlantic Ocean] at a point just west of the Cape Verde Islands [off Senegal's coast]. All the *heathen* lands west of this line, the pope said, should belong to Spain; all the *heathen* lands east of the line, to Portugal. After some bickering, the two kings agreed to the pope's settlement, although neither of them thought that much land lay to east of the dividing line. A few years later, however, one of King John's captains, sailing down the African coast, veered westward off his

course and sighted land. It was the great eastern bulge of
South America, the territory that one day would be called
Brazil. The captain claimed it for Portugal.

 *Univ. Hist. of the World*, vol. 8 (*Reformation and
Exploration*), 678 (italics ours).

The "Race Card Evil" oriented views of Alexander VI,
Ferdinand-Isabella, and John II made them believe that they
could claim and divide lands amongst themselves that were
inhabited by members of the "seventy" nations whom they called
*savages* and *heathens*. This "condescending" and "egotistical"
attitude was brought to the New World when explorers such as
Hernando Cortez and Francisco Pizarro respectively arrived in
Mexico and Peru during AD 1519 and 1532.

In their chapter entitled "Adventures in the New World:
1519–1620," authors Johnston and Steffensen recounted that
when Cortez encountered Mexico's Aztec civilization he said:

> "I did not come to till the soil like a peasant"…"I came
> to find gold." His words echoed the thoughts of almost
> every Spaniard in the New World. The discovery of the
> sea route to the West had set off a great treasure hunt.
> Colonizing and slaughtering, building and plundering,
> the gold-hungry Spaniards won a Spanish Empire of the
> West. *Conquistadores*, they were called—the conquerors.
>
> None of the treasure-hunters was more cunning or
> ambitious than Hernando Cortez…[On expedition to
> the Central American coast in 1519] Cortez sailed with
> five ships, 500 soldiers, eleven cannon, and fifteen horses.
> The fleet anchored near the coast of the territory called
> Mexico…Mexico was a vast country whose Indians had
> built a highly organized civilization…But he [Cortez] was
> a skillful leader; besides, he had firearms and horses—and
> good luck. Not long after he began his march, a horde of
> Indians swept out of the hills to attack the Spaniards. As
> soon as the Spanish cavalry appeared, the Indians fled to

safety. As one soldier later wrote, the Indians, "who had never before seen a horse, thought that steed and rider were one creature." One tribe after another surrendered. They had been conquered by the people called the Aztecs, and many of them offered to join Cortez in the fight to destroy the Aztec empire. (Ibid., 686)

Significantly, Johnston and Steffensen noted a number of factors that brought about Aztec society's rapid downfall. One was that neighboring tribes were disgruntled because the Aztecs had conquered and enslaved them—thus joined forces with the conquistadors. Another was that the conquistadors possessed a military or technological advantage that overawed the disgruntled tribes and convinced them to join the invaders. And a third was that Aztec religious beliefs proved counter-productive to the longevity of their society. Said they,

> Over the mountains, toward the great central plateau of Mexico, Cortez led his troops…Often the cities were opened to him without a fight. The Aztecs believed that once they had been ruled by a god with a light skin and a beard, a child of the sun. He had left the land, sailing east on the sea, but he had promised to return. Cortez had a light skin and a beard, his armor shone like the sun, and he had arrived by ship from the east. He rode a strange beast and had weapons that thundered. Surely, here was the god returning at last!
>
> The Emperor Montezuma must have soon realized that Cortez was a man and not a god. But he could not say so openly; his people might become angry and rise up against him. When Cortez reached the capital city, Montezuma greeted him as an honored guest. The splendor of the city and its palaces amazed the Spaniards. Secretly visiting some rooms they had not been invited to see, they found them heaped high with treasure. For four days Cortez enjoyed the emperor's hospitality. On the fifth day he quietly made Montezuma his prisoner. (Ibid., 686–87)

For a little while Cortez succeeded in controlling the Aztecs by controlling Montezuma. But eventually, the "Race Card Evil" oriented attitude of Cortez and his men caused friction with the Aztecs that sparked violence. This friction caused the Spaniards to murder a number of Aztec nobles, the Aztecs to revolt against the Spaniards and murder Montezuma for trying to stop it, and Cortez to conquer Mexico city with brute violence. The net effect of Cortez's retaliation was the complete destruction of Aztec Empire by AD 1522, within three years after encountering it—a sad ending for the famed "Halls of Montezuma."

With respect to Pizarro's AD 1532 encounter with Peru's Incan civilization and its impact, Johnston and Steffensen continued:

> Other fortune-seekers plotted against Cortez, and he never won the power and fame he thought he deserved. And when he died in 1540, his deeds had been outdone by the most ruthless of the conquistadors, Francisco Pizarro… from the Indians he had heard tales of the country of the Incas, a country filled with treasure. He persuaded Charles V, the emperor of Spain, to outfit an expedition to South America, and in 1532 he set sail from Panama to the country that would one day be called Peru.
>
> Pizarro's force was small—about a hundred foot soldiers and sixty cavalrymen—but he was sly and clever. He told the natives that he had come with friendly greetings from a far-off king to the Incan emperor, and they pointed out the way to the cities of the Incas…over the mountains called the Andes. But word of him went ahead, and when he reached Incan territory he saw that the Incan emperor had assembled a vast army in a valley.
>
> Pizarro made camp on the heights and invited the emperor to a friendly conference. The emperor accepted. He came with hundreds of his noblemen and servants, and he came unarmed. Pizarro gave a signal to his men, who seized the emperor and attacked his followers. Within half an hour hundreds of the unarmed Indians lay dead; the rest

fled, leaving the emperor a prisoner. He offered to pay for his freedom with enough gold to fill a room, and Pizarro agreed…When the room had been filled, it held more that $9,000,000 worth of treasure. No monarch had ever paid such a huge ransom, but it failed to save the emperor of the Incas. He was killed [strangled] at Pizarro's order.

Pizarro then marched his soldiers higher into the mountains, to Cuzco, the capital city of the Incan Empire… The empire of the Incas was richer than the Aztec Empire Cortez had found in Mexico, and its civilization was even more advanced. Pizarro announced that the empire now belonged to Spain, and officials who refused to cooperate were seized and burned.

The Indians did little at first to defend their cities… But the greed and cruelty of the Spaniards drove the Indians to revolt. While Pizarro struggled to put down the rebels, the Spaniards began to fight among themselves for their share of the riches. Pizarro was murdered by one of the plotters [AD 1541]. During his nine years in the land of the Incas, he had found the greatest treasure discovered in the New World—and now it was left for his enemies to divide among themselves. (Ibid., 688–89)

Undoubtedly, the indigenous inhabitants of the "Eden-like" New World—Caribbean Islanders, Aztecs, and Incans—all learned a costly lesson about interacting with people, like Cortez and Pizarro, infected with venom from that "Ancient Serpent" called the "Race Card Evil." They (as well as Cortez and Pizarro) learned the Old World lesson about exercising "cautious hospitality" when sitting at the Table of Nations to dine with one's fellow man—as cautioned by the writer of *Proverbs* 23:

When thou sittest to eat with a ruler, consider diligently what is before thee. And put a knife to thy throat [be temperate], if thou be a man given to appetite [or inexperience]. Be not desirous of his dainties [or offerings]: for they are [or may be] deceitful meat…Eat thou not the

> bread of [nor interact with] him that hath an evil eye,
> neither desire thou his dainty meats [or offerings]. For as
> he thinketh in his heart [mind], so is he. Eat and drink [or
> interact], saith he to thee; but his heart is not with thee.
> The morsel which thou hast eaten shalt thou vomit up,
> and lose thy sweet words. (Prov. 23:1–3, 6–8, KJV)

The conquistadors had wreaked havoc in the New World with their "Race Card Evil" oriented attitude, but the story was not over. Ten years before Pizarro died, Mexico's Archbishop Zumarraga reported the conquistadors' wanton destruction of some five hundred or so temples of the indigenous people (AD 1531). Six years later, Pope Paul III issued a strong condemnation stating that the Western world's indigenous people were entitled to the rights of life, liberty and property (AD 1537). And fifteen years thereafter, the Spanish writer Las Casas published his account detailing oppressions suffered by the South American Indians (AD 1552). As a result, the conquistadors were criticized by Spain's upper class.

Despite criticism, the Spanish explorers seized what became known as the Philippines in the name of Spain's Philip II (AD 1562). Such action showed that Spain was bent on doing her will in either the Old or New World—simply because she possessed financial and naval "superiority." However, Spain did not figure into her "Spanish superiority" equation a strong-willed English woman named Elizabeth I Tudor—the daughter of King Henry VIII and Anne Boleyn.

About seven years after Henry VIII ascended England's throne, trouble erupted between England and Spain: first, because Henry defected from the Catholic faith to the Prostestant Reformation Movement that Martin Luther started in Germany (AD 1516–1519); second, because philanderer Henry defected from his Catholic Spanish wife, princess Catherine of Aragon; and third, because Pope Julius II refused to give Henry a divorce so that he could marry Anne Boleyn (AD 1526).

Although his reasons for divorce were dishonest, Henry was correct in the fact that he and Catherine were illegally married by Pope Julius II in violation of Church law (but not biblical law—Deut. 25:5–10, KJV)—the Pope doing so knowing that she was formerly married to Henry's deceased younger brother. Thus Pope Julius could not annul the marriage without admitting his own disregard of Church law. And when Clement VII succeeded Pope Julius, he also refused to grant the annulment—mainly because Catherine's nephew, Charles V, was Italy's emperor and more or less held Clement VII prisoner.

Failing to obtain the annulment Henry, retaliated by: recalling his spiritual ambassador Thomas Cranmer from Germany and making him Archbishop of Canterbury; convincing Parliament to pass various anti-Papal Acts (such as abolishing England's obligation to make monetary payments to Rome); and declaring himself supreme head of the Church of England (the Supremacy Act). Henry then had Cranmer annul his marriage to Catherine and then moved her and their daughter, Mary Tudor, to various locales to keep Catherine from informing either Charles V or the Spanish throne. Thereafter, Henry bona fide his marriage to Anne by crowning her England's Queen during the year their daughter, Elizabeth I Tudor, was born (AD 1533). Ironically, after working so hard to obtain Anne, Henry had her beheaded for suspected infidelity (AD 1536).

Henry died in AD 1547, but his religious reforms lived on. However, in AD 1553 his daughter Mary Tudor ascended England's throne. Shortly thereafter, she married Spain's Philip II (both being Catholic) and tried to force England's return to Catholicism by authorizing a number of violent acts that earned her the nickname Bloody Mary, inspired the "Three Blind Mice" rhyme's creation (to ridicule Mary and Philip), and forced her Protestant half-sister Elizabeth I Tudor to feign adherence to Catholicism to escape execution for being "anti-Catholic."

After Mary died, her twenty-five-year-old sister Elizabeth ascended England's throne (AD 1558), resumed the break with the Catholic Church, and repealed Mary's "pro-Catholic" acts. This prompted Philip II to try winning Elizabeth's hand in marriage to keep England "pro-Catholic." However, when that failed, Philip attacked England to force a return to Catholicism. Unfortunately, the attack failed and caused Spain to lose both her "invincible armada" and "naval supremacy." This event midtwentieth century, authors Edith Firoozi and Ira N. Klein recounted in their *Universal History of the World* chapter entitled "England Under the Tudors (1485–1603)." Said they,

> Now there was no chance that a Catholic would succeed to the English throne, and Philip decided to take England by force. He began building a mighty navy, but in April of 1587, before it was complete, [Francis] Drake sailed into the bustling Spanish port of Cadiz…His broadsides smashed twelve of Philip's best galleys to splinters. Drake then rifled and burned twenty-four merchant vessels, and towed away six more ships as prizes.
>
> Learning from his defeat, Philip built a more modern fleet of 130 ships, the largest navy ever to sail the open ocean. It was called the Invincible Armada, and in the spring of 1588 Philip…launched it against England…If the Armada succeeded in invading England, the Dutch revolt and all of European Protestantism would collapse at Philip's feet.
>
> Elizabeth realized how dangerous the Armada was… She brought together her thirty-four fighting ships, hired almost a hundred armed merchant vessels, and engaged the sailors of Cornwall and Devon, who were skilled with ships and war. She made Charles Howard the admiral of her fleet, and Drake the vice-admiral…Through a gray winter and spring the fleet waited impatiently, and then the approaching Armada was sighted…But when the English sailed out to do battle, they found no galleys.

Instead, there were great galleons…There were galleasses as well…with towers and turrets above and great halls and chapels below, where the Spaniards prayed for victory… For four days the Spaniards fought off their rivals and sailed nearer to England…The land battle never came. Shortly before midnight on July 28, Howard and Drake set fire to eight small ships and sent them sailing into the midst of the Spanish fleet…By the time dawn broke, the Spanish fleet had been scattered out of its tight formation.

The English saw that this was their chance… The English forced the Spanish ships east toward the dangerous shoals off the Flemish coast. The fight raged until ten at night…by dawn the Spanish were almost upon the shoals…the Spanish fleet wallowed away from the shoals. The crippled remains of the fleet fled north, leaking, desperate, short of food and water. Wind and storms drove many of the Spanish galleons onto the Irish coast, where the finest of Spain's soldiers were butchered by English soldiers and Irishmen.

In England church bells chimed out at the news of victory, and Elizabeth declared a holiday…and a medal was struck to mark the victory which had saved England, her queen, and her religion. (*Univ. Hist. of the World*, vol. 9 (*The Age of Great Kings*), 704–07 passim.)

Spain never recovered after she lost her Armada—which made England the Eastern Hemisphere's dominating maritime power. In the Western Hemisphere, Spain still controlled her Caribbean and South American colonies. However, about the time Vasco da Gama sailed around Africa to reach India (AD 1497), John Cabot sailed to North America to explore it on behalf of England and establish an outpost to raid Spanish ships (AD 1498). Carefully listening to Cabot's reports, England saw another type of wealth far more important than gold—namely, the natural resources along North America's eastern seaboard that could produce food, textiles (fabrics), and other raw materials to generate wealth.

In an attempt to found England's first New World colony, Sir Walter Raleigh and his business partners financed an expedition to the area called Roanoke, North Carolina (AD 1584). It took two years and two failed attempts to found a stable colony at Roanoke (AD 1585–1587). After doing so, Elizabeth's war with Philip prevented the colony's financiers from visiting it. And by the time a visit was paid to the colony, it had vanished without a clue—except for the words *Cro* and *Croatoan* respectively carved on a nearby tree and post (AD 1590).

Undaunted by this, England founded her Jamestown, Virginia, colony seventeen years later (AD 1607); and twelve years thereafter it was found thriving (AD 1619). This success prompted a group of religious dissenters from Holland and England, called "Puritans," to found England's second colony at Massachusetts Bay (AD 1620). While both colonies were largely made up of British subjects, their reasons for being founded differed—Jamestown for agricultural reasons, Massachusetts Bay (Plymouth) for religious ones. This difference in purpose would drastically affect the socio-political views and practices of the two British colonies.

Whereas the Plymouth colony was comprised of "free people" seeking to escape "religious" persecution, the Jamestown colony was largely composed of "political dissenters" and "white slaves" ("servants") bound to service for a term of years to pay off debts or start a new life. This difference in climatic, geographic, and religious character would determine whether a colony developed "industrially" or "agriculturally," "free" or "slave."

With respect to the Jamestown colony's character, midnineteenth century American statesman and political historian George Bancroft recounted in his *History of the United States*:

> But the distinctions in society were rendered more marked
> by the character of the population of Virginia. Many
> had reached the shores of Virginia as servants; doomed,

> according to the severe laws of that age, to a temporary
> bondage. Some of them, even, were convicts; but it must be
> remembered [that] the crimes of which they were convicted
> were chiefly political…Servants were emancipated, when
> their years of servitude were ended; and the law was
> designed to secure and to hasten their enfranchisement…
> The facility of escape compelled humane treatment of white
> servants, who formed one fifth of the adult population.
>
> George Bancroft, *The History of the United States of
> America: from the Discovery of the Continent*, abridged and
> edited by Russell B. Nye (Chicago: University of Chicago
> Press, 1966), 57–58 passim.

As historian Bancroft noted, most of the "indentured" immigrants who first came to Jamestown were "Whites" hailing from England's unskilled labor class. Twelve years later (AD 1619), a second ship of "indentured" immigrants arrived—this time having laborers of African ("Moorish"), English, Germanic, Irish, and Scottish ancestry. However, within twenty-one years of this second docking, a Jamestown court made two controversial lifetime slavery rulings—one of which allowed the "Race Card Evil" to enter the colony and hatch a diabolical scheme to create and maintain a permanent "cheap-labor" workforce. This was accomplished by eliminating the "indentured servant" status of "dark" Africans, replacing it with a "perpetual slave" status, and classifying them as "Negroes."

While the exact date for hatching this "New World" scheme is uncertain, what is certain is that it originated from "Old World" religious doctrine based on the *Genesis* 9 "Ham cursed" story. Moreover, the doctrine was: legitimized in the *Talmud* by Jewish theologians during the AD 100s–500s; taught by Catholic-Christian theologians to justify invading-controlling-exploiting western Africa during the AD 1400s; modified by German biblical scholar Johan Boemus to elevate European ("Japhethite") and Asian ("Shemite") cultures over African

("Hamite") culture during the AD 1500s; preached by Reformed-Christian theologians to justify enslaving "dark" Africans (or "Moors") for profit during the early AD 1600s; and legalized in the British-American Colonies to maintain a permanent cheap-labor workforce during the mid AD 1600s (c. 1640–1670).

Regardless of the "Ham cursed" story's origin, the New World "cheap-labor" scheme started about AD 1521—after Boemus advanced his theory that "all barbarous peoples descended from Ham, while all civilized peoples descended from Shem and Japheth." About eighty-nine years later—one year prior to the 1611 King James (KJV) Bible's debut—the Boemus-modified theory surfaced after one Reverend Samuel Purchas published volume six of his work entitled *Purchas His Pilgrimes* (AD 1610). Therein he detailed his observation of the slave-trade practiced in Egypt's Hangia village and cited the "Ham cursed" story as the reason for the "dark" African's enslavement. In his book *The Black Man in the Old Testament and its World*, Bishop Alfred G. Dunston, Jr., himself a twentieth century African-American Reverend, recounted that Reverend Purchas said:

> The merchants brought with them many Negroes…These are the descendants of Chus (Cush or Kush), the sonne (son) of cursed Cham (Ham); as are all [people] of that [dark] complexion. Not by reason of their seed [ancestry], nor heat of the [African] climate: nor of the soyle (soil), as some have suppose; for neither haply, will other races in that soyle (soil) proove [prove; become] black, nor that race in other soyles (soils) grow to better [lighter] complexion: but rather from the curse of Noe (Noah) upon Cham (Ham) in the Posteritie [posterity] of Chus (Cush or Kush).
>
> Bishop Alfred G. Dunston, Jr., *The Black Man in the Old Testament and its World* (Trenton: Africa World Press, Inc., 1994), 21–22; on Johan Boemus see George M. Frederickson, *White Supremacy: A Comparative Study in American and South African History* (New York: Oxford University Press, 1981), 10.

Yet, unlike the "Portuguese-Spanish" African Slavery program—which more or less arose from "commercial, ethnic, and religious" conflict (and possibly "malice") between Christian and Muslim countries vying for control of the Mediterranean World's land and sea trade routes—the "British" program was not the result of "religious and ethnic" conflict, but "commercial necessity, financial profit, and academic carelessness." These points Bishop Dunston cited when recounting the history of the 1611 King James Version's writing. Speaking on how the Egyptian word "Kush" ("Cush" in Hebrew) came to be inaccurately translated by the Greek word "Ethiopia" (meaning "burnt face"), and carried into nineteenth century AD literature, Bishop Dunston said:

> The marginal notes of the English Bible always translate the word "Ethiopia" to "Kush" or "Cush," and rightly so… This does not mean that "Cush" is a Hebrew term, for it was not. The name Cush (or Kush) was given by Egypt to her southern neighbor, and the name so appeared in Egyptian records. This and other such marginal references make it appear certain that in pre-Grecian times the Hebrew Scriptures called the land "Cush"; and according to Josephus the Jewish historian, this name was used in all Asia…The same nation that was called Cush by the Egyptians and ancient Hebrews, was called Ethiopia by the Greeks and Nubia by the Christians, after Julian planted the faith there during the sixth century AD.
>
> Islam began its conquest in the area later than AD 700… They called it "Bilad as Sudan," an Arab term meaning "land of the blacks." This name was applied to "the whole vast space of Steppe and Savanna that lies between the Sahara and the forest lands further to [the] south, an area that stretches from the Atlantic at Dakar all the way across Africa to the Red Sea, and covers as much as a thousand miles from North to South."
>
> Later Europeans called the Sudanese people "Negroes," and the term applied to all the then-known people south

of Egypt and the Sahara…It is at this point that the forty-seven active King James translators performed a definite disservice to the Christian church in general, and to the black African and his descendants in particular. Their rendering of this particular area of translation in some sense might have contributed to the continuing scourge of slavery that mars the pages of Western world history, because Western consciences might possibly have reacted differently had the biblical Ethiopians been more closely identified.

The King James Version was completed and presented to the king in the year AD 1611…The English queen Elizabeth [I] [ruled 1558–1603] and some prime businessmen had money invested in the [slave] trade and in the colonies to which they were being carried. By the year 1611, the black presence was part of the English and colonial scene but they were being called Negroes and not Ethiopians.

It could have been fear, or expediency, or a slave-trade mentality that constrained the King James translators to veil in obscurity the true identity of the people whom they called Ethiopians. The king and many captains of industry were involved in trade, and by 1611, England was competing with Portugal and Holland. She was also involved in colonizing the New World, and English planters were using slave labor to produce the sugar and other crops that were on sale in Europe. It could have been these social and economic considerations that constrained the translators to resist the moral and spiritual obligation properly to identify the black folks about whom the Bible is speaking…it is highly conceivable that a more proper [name] or an English term [of] identification of the Cushites might have changed the whole European attitude towards chattel slavery for black people. The myths of savagery, cannibalism, and general debasement would have been reexamined had the Bible reflected the fact that the people under these myths were then being called "Negroes"

in the Western world. The color and geography of the
Cushites would have contributed to a better appreciation
all around, and the most ignorant, rabid racist would not
have pretended to doubt the existence of a soul in any man
about whom he had read in the pages of the Holy Bible...
The question is, [w]ould the Western world have visited
such brutal and debasing treatment as it has done upon a
people whom they knew were written about so favorably
in Holy Writ? Beyond all doubt there would have been no
question about whether or not they had souls, and there
could have been no living myth that black Africa had been
by-passed by civilization and was therefore wallowing in
savagery and debasement.
    *Ibid.*, pp. 14–16 and 18–21 passim.

Unlike the "British" program, the "British-American" African
Slavery program resulted from King George III's need to create
and maintain a "cheap-labor" workforce in Colonial America to
increase personal wealth. This need stemmed from two problems:
first, "Native Americans" (Algonquians) were disinclined to work
for the European "visitors" who came to their land; second, like
the conquistadors, the British colonizers were disinclined to
work for their own people—because it reminded them of the
feudal system that many European societies lived under. Thus,
whenever the opportunity arose, Jamestown's "Native American"
and "White" laborers fled or revolted. In his *History of The United
States*, Mr. Bancroft characterized the "White" indentured servant
mindset and its effect on the colony. Said he:

The insurrection, which was plotted by a number
of servants in 1663, had its origin in impatience of
servitude and oppression. A few bondsmen...were
excited by their own sufferings, and by the nature of life
in the wilderness...From the character of the times, their
passions were sustained by political fanaticism [i.e., by
Richard Cromwell's Roundheads]; but the conspiracy

did not extend beyond a scheme of indented servants to anticipate the period of their freedom. The effort was the work of ignorant men, and was easily suppressed.

*Hist. of the U. S.*, 58.

Indentured Servants fleeing or plotting insurrection were not the only labor problems that Jamestown colony leaders faced. Another was that "White" indentured servants could abscond, change identities, and start new lives undetected. To cure this problem, the colony's leaders felt it best to use "dark-skinned" Africans as a cheap-labor workforce. Thus, the leaders adopted doctrines of "inferiority," "skin-color," and "race" to solve the runaway problem. In volume one of his *Sex and Race*, historian Rogers said:

> Color discrimination began thus. Tobacco and cotton were needed in Virginia for sale to Europe. Tobacco was at one time currency [money] in Virginia. *White serfs* [indentures] were not succeeding very well. *Black men* were then imported. They proved capable and willing workers. The doctrine of upper-class white superiority over lower-class whites, which had been operating alone for thousands of years, suddenly moved then into larger quarters so to speak, and took in the Negro, putting him in the lowest rank [of society] because of the difference in [skin] color. Had the Negro been an incompetent and an unwilling worker, like the Indian, he would never have gotten the very bad name he did. It was his very assimilability, his capacity for progress that caused the slave-holders to invent the doctrine of inferiority in order to keep him down.
>
> Joel A. Rogers, *Sex and Race: Negro-Caucasian Mixing in All Ages and All Lands*, vol. I ("The Old World"), 9th ed. (New York: Helga M. Rogers, 1967), 25 (italics ours).
>
> The first attempt to found a doctrine of race, based on physical appearance, came with the introduction of Negro slavery in Virginia. Prior to that "race" was used chiefly as meaning "a contest." The King James Version of the

Bible uses it only in this sense. Shakespeare also uses it in the sense of "family." But the American slave-holders, finding themselves forced to explain how the teachings of [Jesus the] Christ could be reconciled with the cruelties of slavery set their lackeys, the theologians, who were the "scientists" of that time to find an explanation.
    *Ibid.*, 22.

Combining the *Genesis* 4 ("Land of Nod"), *Genesis* 9 ("Ham cursed"), Johan Boemus ("Ham's descendants uncivilized"), and Portuguese-Spanish ("Negroes from an indefinite region South of the Equator or Sahara") fictions the Jamestown theologians validated the businessman's right to change the status of "dark-skinned" Indentured Africans to "sub-Human" Chattel. And by the early AD 1600s, this religion-sanctioned propaganda served as justification for obtaining a permanent "cheap-labor" workforce based on "ethnicity" or "skin-color." In volume one of *Sex and Race*, Rogers continued:

Turning to the Bible, the leading "scientific" authority of that period, the servile divines [theologians] discovered that Cain had taken a wife from the Land of Nod. Now according to the story of creation, which is Jewish folklore and nothing more, there were then only three people alive on the planet [after Abel's murder], Adam, Eve, and Cain. Who were these people living in the Land of Nod then? They were pre-Adamites! And pre-Adamites could be no other than Negroes, that is, people who had no part or lot in the creation by God...Yes, there could be no doubt, whatever, that the people of the Land of Nod were Negroes.

Other servants of God, searching the "Scriptures," found still more "scientific" things about race. The Bible had also spoken of "a beast," the unknown beast of Revelations. What else could this be, but the Negro? Still another theory that came to be accepted was that Negroes were the descendants of Ham, whose son, Canaan, had been cursed by Noah. "Cursed be Canaan, a servant of servants shall he be unto his brethren" (Gen. [9: 25, 26–27]).

    *Ibid.*, p. 22.

Not being satisfied with the artificial "biblical" redefinition for a segment of the "70" Nations, Jamestown's theologians changed the "6–7 year" temporary "Indentured Slavery" term of service—which derived from biblical stories about Jacob's dealing with his unscrupulous uncle Laban and Joseph's Egyptian enslavement—to a perpetual or lifetime "Chattel Slavery" term. This they did by combining the *Exodus* 21:5–6 and *Deuteronomy* 15:16–17 "voluntary lifetime servitude" passages with the "suspect" *Leviticus* 25:44–46 "involuntary lifetime servitude" passage which respectively stated:

> If, however, the slave declares, 'I am devoted to *my master* and *my wife and children*; I will not go free,' his master... shall pierce his ear...thus keeping him as his slave forever [perpetually]. (Ex 21:5–6) (NAB) (italics ours).

> If, however, he [the slave] tells you [the master] that he does not wish to leave you, because he is devoted to *you and your household*, since he fares well with you...he shall then be your slave forever [perpetually]...(Dt 15:16–17) (NAB) (italics ours).

> Both thy bondmen, and thy bondmaids, which thou shalt have, shall be of *the heathen* that are round about you; of them shall ye buy bondmen and bondmaids.

> Moreover, of *the children of the strangers* [aliens] that do sojourn among you, of them shall ye buy, and of their families that are with you, which they begat in your land: and *they shall be your possession.*

> And *ye shall take them as an inheritance for your children* after you, *to inherit them for a possession*; they shall be your bondmen for ever [perpetually]: but over your brethren

the children of Israel, ye shall not rule one over another with rigor. (Lev. 25:44–46) (KJV) (italics ours).

"Slaves, male and female, you may indeed possess, provided you buy them from among *the neighboring nations.* You may also buy them from among *the aliens* who reside with you and from their children who are born and reared in your land. *Such slaves you may own as chattels*, and leave to your sons *as their hereditary property*, making them perpetual slaves. But you shall not lord it harshly over any of the Israelites, your kinsman ..." (Lv 25:44–46) (NAB) (italics ours).

However, concerning such "Hebrew" practices, Dr. William Smith noted in his *Bible Dictionary* article entitled "Slave":

[I. *Hebrew slaves.*]—The institution of slavery was recognized, though not established, by the Mosaic law with a view to mitigate its hardship and to secure to every man his ordinary rights.

The circumatances under which a Hebrew might be reduced to servitude were—(1) Poverty; (2) The commission of theft [crime]; and (3) The exercise of parental authority...The servitude of a Hebrew might be terminated in three ways: (1) the satisfaction or the remission of all claims against him; (2) by the recurrence of the year of jubilee, Lev. 25:40; and (3) the expiration of six years from the time that his servitude commenenced...If a servant did not desire to avail himself of the opportunity of leaving his [master's] service, he was to signify his intentions in a formal manner before the judges...the master was to...bore his ear through with an awl, Ex. 21:6...A [Hebrew] servant who had submitted to this... remained, according to the law, a servant "forever." These words are, however, interpreted by Josephus and by the rabbinists as meaning until the year of jubilee ...

[II. *Non-Hebrew slaves.*]—The majority of non-Hebrew slaves were war-captives...Besides these, many

were obtained by purchase from foreign slave-dealers, Lev.
25:44, 45; and others may have been resident foreigners who
were reduced to this state by either poverty or crime The
children of slaves remained slaves, being the class described
as "born in the house," Gen. 14:14; 17:12; Eccles. 2:7…That
the slave might be manumitted appears from Ex. 21:26, 27;
Lev. 19:20. The slave is described as the "possession" of his
master, apparently with a special reference to the power
which the latter had of disposing of him to his heirs, as he
would any other article of personal [Chattel] property. Lev.
25:45, 46…A minor personal injury, such as the loss of an
eye or a tooth, was to be recompensed by giving the servant
his liberty. Ex. 21:26, 27.

    *Smith's Bible Dictionary*, Revised and Edited by F.N.
and M.A. Peloubet (sixth printing, 1972), s.v. "Slave."

Although Jamestown's theologians did not officially nullify
the Old Testament's "Indentured Slave Code," they did create a
"religious" precedent validating the "perpetual chattel slavery" scheme
by using biblical passages that contradicted the "equality" and "self-
determination" passages found in the *Genesis* 1:26–28 and 2:18,
20–24 narratives. After doing this, all that remained was to "legalize"
the scheme by passing legislative acts (positive laws) to enforce it.

For example, by the mid-1600s Jamestown's lawmaking
body excluded (disenfranchised) free or bond Africans labelled
"blacks, black-a-moors, coloreds, negroes" from participating in
the political process. In his *History of the United States*, historian
Bancroft said:

Enfranchisement of the colored population was not
encouraged in Virginia; the female slave was not subject
to taxation; the emancipated Negress was "a tithable."
"The death of a slave from extremity of correction was not
accounted felony; since it cannot be presumed," such is
the language of the statute, "that prepensed [aforethought]
malice, which alone makes murther [murder] felony,

should induce any man to destroy his own estate [human property]." Finally, it was made lawful for "persons pursuing fugitive colored slaves to wound, or even to kill them." The master was absolute lord over the Negro. The slave and the slave's posterity [children] were bondmen. As property in Virginia consisted mainly of land and laborers, the increase of Negro slaves was grateful to the pride and to the interests of the large landed proprietors."
 *Hist. of the U.S.*, 59.

And as early as AD 1664, Maryland made a similar legislative move to impede political enfranchisement of "Negroes"—by altering the then existing legal definition of the political status of children born as a result of cohabitation between British ("white") males and African or Moorish ("black") females. Said Mr. Bancroft:

The early Anglo-Saxon [British] rule, interpreting every doubtful question in favor of liberty, declared the children of freemen [males] to be free. Doubts arose if the offspring of an English man by a Negro woman [female] should be bond or free; and the rule of the Roman law prevailed over [over ruled] the Anglo-Saxon [law]. The offspring [legal status] followed the condition [legal status] of the mother. In 1664, Maryland by "the major[ity] vote" of its lower house [of delegates], decided that "the issue [children] of such marriages should serve [in bondage] thirty years.
 *Ibid.*, 58.

By AD 1682, within seventy-five years of Jamestown's founding, other British-American colonies had passed similar laws to permanently enslave Africans labelled "Negroes"—regardless of whether they converted to the "Christian" religion or not. Again Mr. Bancroft recounted:

In 1671, the number of blacks in a population of forty thousand was estimated at two thousand; not above two

> or three ships of Negroes arrived in seven years. The
> statute of the previous year [1670], which declares who
> are slaves, followed an idea, long prevalent through[out]
> Christendom: "All servants, not being Christians,
> imported into this country by shipping, shall be slaves." In
> 1682 it was added: "conversion to the Christian faith doth
> not make free."
> *Ibid.*, 58–59.

Thus, within a two-hundred-year period (AD 1492–1682) the "Race Card Evil" managed to infiltrate and infect the New World with its Old World "ethnic" poison. Masquerading as God's "Word" the "Ancient Serpent" managed to befriend people native to the Americas, characterize them as "heathens" or "savages," and justify exploiting-murdering-oppressing-robbing them for profit's sake. Undoubtedly, this achievement was an impressive feat. But stripping members of the "70" Nations of their "Human" identity, via an artificially created "sub-Human", definition was an ingenious feat—one that would be a first in recorded Human history.

But, retribution for doing such deeds would follow. For example, in AD 1650 an enlightened Englishman named George Fox challenged the permanent "cheap-labor" workforce scheme through the organization he founded called the "Society of Friends" or "Quakers." And after him would come a star-studded list of enlightened people who would follow and combat the evil scheme.

About a century after Mr. Fox, a shot would be fired by thirteen British Colonies planted on America's soil—one that would be heard around the world. It would denounce "The Race Card Evil" oriented "Divine Right of Kings to Rule" and "Perpetual Slavery" programs. On firing the shot, physical and political turmoil would ensue for the Colonies—because those profiting from such programs refused to end them, while those suffering from such programs refused to extend them.

Such programs were founded on the contradictory principle that some had a "God-given" right to oppress or enslave others and a "God-given" right to be free from such. And the world's response to this contradiction, in the British-American Colonies and around the world, would signal a new age—one in which many sectors of Humanity would challenge Old World ways of thinking. On American soil the shot would herald the birth of a new nation, albeit contaminated by "The Race Card Evil." And on American soil, a remarkable battle would be fought to put the ancient evil "in the course of ultimate extinction."

# 2

# Efforts to Exclude the Race Card Evil from the US Government

> Wisdom has built her house, she has set up her seven
> columns.
>
> —Prov 9:1 (NAB)

> Thus says the LORD [YHWH] of Hosts [armies]…
> Listen, O Joshua, high priest! You and your associates…
> are men of good omen…Look at the [select] stone that
> I have placed…one stone with seven facets [eyes]. I will
> engrave its inscription…and I will take away the guilt
> of the land in one day. On that day…you will invite one
> another under your vines and fig trees.
>
> — Zec 3:7–10 (NAB)

FOR ALMOST A century chattel slavery's definition of "Negro" ("black") as a "race," or "subrace," of people was accepted in the British-American Colonies without any genuine scientific evidence to validate it. However, during the mid-1700s, this changed after German anthropologist Johann Friedrich Blumenbach made serious efforts to "scientifically" define the word *race* and classify humanity into distinct "races."

About AD 1775, Mr. Blumenbach published his *Des generis humani varietate nativa* (*On the Natural Varieties of Mankind*)—a book that "classified" Humanity into "five" racial types and colors: caucasian (white), Ethiopian (black), Malayan (brown), Mongolian (yellow), and Native American (red). By AD 1779, this classification became the basis upon which the science called "physical anthropology" and all later classifications of "race" would be built. In volume one of *Sex and Race* historian Rogers noted,

> Interest in the origin of the so-called races arose in the 17th century [AD 1600s] when the white "race" was in the ascendant; hence it was naturally assumed that the white race was the original [man, race], and that the Ham[ite] [Curse] story was true. In the latter part of the 18th century [AD 1700s] however, Blumenbach, a German anthropologist, improved on this theory, declaring...that the white race was the first [original] [man, race].
>
> For the white race, Blumenbach coined the word "Caucasian," and he did it in a manner characteristic of much of what still passes for science in all matters of race. In his collection of skulls was one of a woman found on Mt. Caucasus in Georgia, Asiatic Russia...Blumenbach, thinking it was typical of the white race, dubbed it "caucasian."
>
> Later, this proceeding vastly amused Thomas Huxley, who ranks near to Darwin in his efforts to solve the riddle of Man. "Of all the odd myths that have arisen in the scientific world," said Huxley, "the 'Caucasian mystery' invented quite innocently by Blumenbach, is the oddest. A Georgian woman's skull was the handsomest in his collection. Hence it became his model exemplar of human skulls from which all others might be regarded as deviations; and out of this by some strange intellectual hocus-pocus grew up the notion that the Caucasian man is the proto-typic 'Adamic' man and his country the primitive center of our kind" (*Sex and Race*, vol. I, 24).

However "innocent" or "amusing" Mr. Blumenbach's "racial" theory was viewed by Huxley and some European intellectuals, it was taken quite seriously by others—especially the dealers, financiers, traders, and owners involved in the African slave trade enterprise during the British American Colonial era.

In Colonial American society, many theologians and slave-trade profiteers proudly boasted about the "Ham cursed, Ham uncivilized, whites the original man" theory of social evolution. This theory, casually phrased the "White Man's Burden," proclaimed "the white man a savior for civilizing (enslaving) people of color for their own good." Yet not every Colonial American accepted this excuse to justify exploiting members of the "seventy" nations so that a minority of big-businessmen could profit.

In England, about AD 1650, George Fox founded the Quaker society to condemn both the ritualism that had crept into Christianity during prior centuries and England's involvement in the African slave trade during her commonwealth era (AD 1649–1660). Whereas in America, about the end of the reign of England's James II (son of Charles I), Pennsylvania's Germantown Mennonite community protested England's involvement in the slave trade on 18 February 1688—it being the earliest recorded in the British-American Colonies. In their *Documents of American History*, political historians Henry Steele Commager and Milton Cantor recounted that the Germantown Mennonites said,

> These are the reasons why we are against the traffick of men-bodies…Is there any[one] that would [wish to] be done or handled at [in] this manner?…To be sold or made a slave for all the time of his life?…Now, what is this better done, than Turks [Muslims] do? Yea, rather it is worse for them, which say they are Christians; for we hear that the most part of such negers [negroes] are brought hither [here] against their will and consent, and that many of them are stolen [kidnapped]. Now, though they are black, we cannot conceive [that] there is more liberty to have them as slaves, as it is to have other white

ones. There is a [biblical] saying, that we should do to all men like as we will [have] be done [to] ourselves [Matt. 7:7–12, KJV]; making no difference [because] of what generation, descent, or colour they are. And those who steal or rob men, and those who buy or purchase them, are they not all alike? [Exod. 21:16, Deut. 24:7, KJV] (Henry Steele Commager and Milton Cantor, Eds., *Documents of American History: vol.I to 1898*, 10th ed., Englewood Cliffs, NJ: Prentice-Hall, Inc., 1988, 37)

While the Germantown Mennonites were first to denounce the African slave trade, it is equally true that most of the colonies also denounced the evil. Indeed, about eleven years after the Mennonite protest the colonies entered into controversy with Britain because of the African slavery issue. In his *The Great Conspiracy*, midnineteenth century political historian and statesman John Alexander Logan recounted,

Indeed African Slavery had already in 1620 been implanted on the soil of Virginia before Plymouth Rock was pressed by the feet of the Pilgrim Fathers, and had spread…with greater or less rapidity…to every one of the thirteen Colonies.

But while it had thus spread more or less throughout all the original Colonies, and was, as it were, recognized and acquiesced in by all, as an existing and established institution, yet there were many, both in the South and North, who looked upon it as an evil—an inherited evil— and were anxious to prevent the increase of that evil. Hence it was that even as far back as 1699, a controversy sprung up between the Colonies and the Home Government [Britain], upon the African Slavery question… (John A. Logan, *The Great Conspiracy: Its Origin and History* [New York: A. R. Hart and Co., 1886], 1–2)

Unfortunately, despite the fact that many of the colonists saw African slavery as an "inherited evil," they were unable to eradicate it because the British Parliament held veto power over the legislative acts of its "subject" colonies. This fact of colonial life was made clear during the reign of Britain's King George III (1760–1820), descendant of George I (founder of Germany's House of Hanover and great-grandson of King James I Stuart). In his *History of the United States*, statesman Bancroft said,

> In 1769, George III in council "gave his consent to an act of Georgia, whereby slaves may be declared to be chattels;" and the war of the Revolution made no change in their condition by law. (*Hist. of the U.S.*, 300–01)
>
> George III was the firm friend of the slave-trade; and Thurlow, one of his chancellors, so late as 1799 insisted that the proposal to terminate it was "altogether miserable and contemptible."
>
> So long as the legislation of the several English colonies in America remained subject to the veto of the king, all hope of forbidding or even limiting the importation of negro slaves was made vain by the mother country. (Ibid., 291–92)

In addition to veto power over the colonies' legislative acts, King George III used underhanded political tactics such as fear of difference in "ethnicity, financial position, skin-color, and socio-political status" to intimidate the colonists and deter them from enacting laws counterproductive to the British crown's financial interests. Again, statesman Bancroft recounted,

> On Permitting the increase of Negro slavery, [the colonists'] opinions were nearly equally divided; but England kept slave-marts open at every court-house, as far, at least, as the South-west Mountain: partly to enrich her slave-merchants; partly, by balancing the races, to weaken the power of colonial [political] resistance. (Ibid., 71)

Given such tactics to maintain African slavery—and others such as inciting unrest among Native Americans, taxation without representation, unreasonable searches and seizures, and quartering soldiers during peace time—many of the thirteen British American colonies became fed up with the political antics of King George III by the early 1700s. This dissatisfaction, in turn, caused the colonies to call for individual legislative sessions to appoint representatives to hold legislative conventions to express their grievances to Britain. First among the colonies to call for such was Virginia—whose most notable statesmen believed that the "Race Card Evil's" African slavery scheme was the root of their problems. Said Statesman Bancroft,

> Virginia…many of her statesmen—George Mason, Patrick Henry, [Thomas] Jefferson, [George] Wythe, [Edmund] Pendleton, Richard Henry Lee [cousin to Henry "Light-Horse Harry" and Robert E. Lee]—emulated each other in confessing the iniquity and the expediency of holding men in bondage. We have seen the legislature of colonial Virginia in 1772, in their fruitless battle with the king respecting the [African] slave-trade, of which he [King George III] was the great champion, demand its abolition as needful for their happiness and their very existence. In January, 1773, Patrick Henry threw ridicule on the clergy of Virginia for their opposition to emancipation [of African slaves]. In the same year [1773], George Mason foretold the blight [destruction] that was to avenge Negro slavery. (Ibid., 296)

Not only did Virginia's distinguished statesmen view the African Slavery scheme as a serious "evil" that needed to be put "in the course of ultimate extinction," but various statesmen in the Georgia colony also held similar views and took similar legislative steps to eradicate it. Recounted statesman Logan in *The Great Conspiracy,*

> Prior to 1752, when Georgia surrendered her charter and became a Royal Colony, the holding of slaves within its limits was expressly prohibited by law; and the Darien (Ga.) Resolutions of 1775 declared not only a "disapprobation and abhorrence of the unnatural practice

of [African] Slavery in America" as "a practice founded in injustice and cruelty, and highly dangerous to our liberties (as well as our lives), but a determination to use our utmost efforts for the manumission [emancipation] of our slaves in this colony upon the most safe and equitable footing for the masters and the slaves." (Ibid., p. 2 note)

As could be expected, the colonists' complaints fell on the deaf profit-oriented ears of King George III and Parliament. This "deaf ear" policy made many leading political figures of the colonies suspect that the crown's enactments and vetoes were designed to "enslave" them also. To counter this, throughout the spring and summer of 1774 the legislatures of Massachusetts and Virginia requested a convention comprised of representatives from all the colonies be held at Philadelphia, Pennsylvania to address their joint political plight.

On 5 September 1774, fifty-six men ("55" voting delagates and "1" presiding officer), representing twelve of the thirteen Colonies, met at Philadelphia's Carpenters Hall. Calling themselves a "Continental Congress," the body met for the express purpose of drafting and presenting their collective grievance against King George III and Parliament. On September 27, they agreed "to have no commercial intercourse with (boycott) Great Britain." On October 12, a Committee appointed by the Congress reported its agreement as a "Declaration of Grievances and Resolves." On October 14, Congress unofficially adopted the measure; and on October 18, made it official. As concerns an "attempt to enslave the colonists," Commager and Cantor recounted in their *Documents of American History* that the delegates said,

In the course of our inquiry, we find many infringements and violations of the foregoing rights which…we pass over for the present, and proceed to state such [Intolerable] acts and measures as have been adopted since the last war, which demonstrate a system formed to enslave America. (*Docs. of Amer. Hist.*, 84)

On 20 October 1774, the delegates signed their resolves as an "association" united under a common cause—thereby signifying that the British-American colonies had officially formed a political "Union" to collectively address their grievances against Britain. This "1774 Continental Congress" and its "articles of association" ("informal constitution") signified the start of an "informal government," which would later be "formally" called the "American Union." Noted Commager and Cantor,

> [On] September 27, 1774 the Continental Congress voted non-intercourse with Great Britain…The committee reported on October 12, and the report was adopted on the 18th and signed on the 20[th] [of] October. "The signature of the Association," says [Richard] Hildreth, "may be considered as the commencement of the American Union." (Ibid., note at 84–85)

Although the 5 September 1774 convention's intent was to boycott Britain as a means of ending the slave trade, the 14 October 1774 "Declaration of Grievances" (which was also a "Declaration of Rights") still accepted Parliament's regulation of the colonies' commerce. This fact midtwentieth-century political historian John R. Alden stated in his *Encyclopaedia Britannica* article "The Continental Congress." Said he,

> [On] Oct. 14, the deputies [delegates] adopted a declaration of personal rights, including those of life, liberty, property, [freedom of] assembly and trial by jury [of peers]. The declaration also denounced taxation without representation and the maintenance of the British army in the colonies without their consent. However, the Congress announced cheerful acceptance of Parliamentary regulation of American commerce. (John R. Alden, *Encyclopaedia Britannica*, rev. 14th ed., 1965, s.v. "Continental Congress, The," 420)

However, despite acceptance of Parliament's regulation of commerce, the "1774 Association's" Article 2 contained Congress's "statement of intent" to end the African slavery enterprise controlled by King George III and Parliament. This statement reflected the true purpose for which the "American Union" was formed. In their *Documents of American History*, Commager and Cantor recounted that Article 2 stated,

> We will neither import nor purchase, any slave imported after the first day of December next, after which time, we will wholly discontinue the slave trade, and will neither be concerned [make business] in it ourselves, nor will we hire out vessels, nor sell our commodities or manufactures to those who are concerned in it. (*Docs. of Amer. Hist.*, 85)

And statesman Bancroft, in his *History of the United States*, clarified the signers' "intent" when he addressed an important point regarding their later drafted "1776 Declaration of Independence." Said he regarding the "1774 Association's" Article 2,

> We have seen that the first [Continental] Congress formed an Association "wholly to discontinue the slave-trade" and that the denunciation of the slave-trade and of slavery by [Thomas] Jefferson, in his draft of the Declaration of Independence, was rejected by the [second Continental] Congress of 1776, in deference to [delegates from] South Carolina and Georgia. (*Hist. of the U.S.*, 292)

Before the First Continental Congress adjourned on October 26, it scheduled a second session for 10 May 1775. However, on 19 April 1775 armed conflicts erupted in Massachusetts between British and Colonial forces at both Lexington and Concord—the conflicts resulting in at least ten Colonial fatalities and a number of wounded on both sides. As to who was at fault for these skirmishes went unsolved (each side blamed the other).

Nevertheless, when the Second Continental Congress convened at Carpenters Hall on May 10, it initiated military measures to address the situation and decided it was time to break ties with Britain.

On 6 July 1775, the Congress issued its "Declaration of the Causes and Necessity of Taking up Arms" against Britain. In response, on August 23 Britain issued its "Proclamation of Rebellion" against the colonies. In their *Documents of American History*, Commager and Cantor recounted the important conclusion reached in the "1775 Declaration of Causes." Said the Second Continental Congress:

> We are reduced to the alternative of chusing [choosing] an unconditional submission to the tyranny of irrational ministers [officials], or resistance by force. The latter [course] is our choice. We have counted the cost of this contest, and find nothing so dreadful as voluntary slavery. Honour [sic], justice, and humanity, forbid us tamely to surrender that freedom which we received from our gallant ancestors…We cannot endure the infamy and guilt of resigning succeeding generations to that wretchedness which inevitably awaits them, if we basely entail hereditary bondage upon them. (*Docs. of Amer. Hist.*, 95)

After the Second Continental Congress adjourned, the delegates underwent a year of discussions and preparations to address the grave contest to come. On 7 June 1776, Virginia's Richard Henry Lee introduced to Congress a threefold resolution: one for totally dissolving allegiance to Britain, another for forming commercial and military alliances with foreign governments, and a third for devising plans for a confederation of the "distinct" or "several" thirteen "American" colonies united under a common cause. On June 10, a Congressional Committee was appointed to draft Lee's proposal. On June 11, Congress appointed a Committee to draft the colonies' Articles of Confederation.

Congress reviewed Lee's draft on June 28, adopted it on July 2, and then sent it to the legislatures of the Colonies turned states on July 4. And on July 6, the final draft that called for dissolving ties with Britain was unanimously approved and formally called "The Declaration of Independence."

During the "1776 Declaration's" drafting, most delegates to the Second Continental Congress adamantly opposed the African Slavery scheme and its "color-bias, superiority-inferiority" themes. Unfortunately, at that time the profit-driven businessmen of two of the thirteen colonies—Georgia and South Carolina—championed the evil. Thus, in order to present a united front against Britain, the delegates allowed the two "proslavery" colonies to enter the "American Union" as "Race Card Evil" oriented States. Recounting this unfortunate event for American posterity, statesman Logan said in *The Great Conspiracy*,

> It was this conviction that it [Slavery] was not alone an evil but a dangerous evil, that induced [Thomas] Jefferson to embody in his original draft of that Declaration [of Independence] a clause strongly condemnatory of the African Slave Trade—a clause afterward omitted from it solely, he [Jefferson] tells us, "in complaisance to South Carolina and Georgia, who never attempted to restrain the importation of slaves, and who, on the contrary, still wished to continue it," as well as in deference to the sensitivities of Northern [business] people, who, though having few slaves themselves, "had been pretty considerable carriers of them to others"—a clause of the great indictment of King George III, which, since it was not omitted for any other reason than that just given, shows pretty conclusively that when the [founding] fathers in that Declaration affirmed that "all men are created equal," they included in the Term "Men," black as well as white, bond as well as free… (*The Great Conspiracy*, 2)

Sadly, a minority of Second Continental Congress delegates—acting on behalf of either themselves or profit-driven entrepreneurs

in Human misery—forced the majority to "tailor down" the
"1776 Declaration's" accusative clause in order to conceal from
the world at large a "great conspiracy" to denigrate, differentiate,
and separate a segment of the Adamite race or "seventy" nations
just to profit from the cheap-labor workforce scheme. This fact is
readily seen from a comparison of the two "different" accusative
clauses of the "1776 Declaration" that allegedly pertained to the
same idea.

On the one hand, Senator Logan recounted in *The Great
Conspiracy* that Jefferson's original *anti-* "Race Card Evil"
accusative clause stated,

> "[King George III has] Determined to keep open a market
> where ["dark-skinned" African] Men should be bought
> and sold, he has prostituted his negative [vetoed]…every
> [Colonial] Legislative attempt to prohibit or to restrain
> this execrable [African slavery] commerce. And that this
> assemblage of horrors might want no fact of distinguished
> dye, he is now exciting those very people [slaves] to rise in
> arms among us, and purchase [take] that liberty of which
> he has deprived them, by murdering the people [colonists]
> on whom he has also obtruded [forced it upon] them; thus
> paying off former crimes committed against the liberties
> of our people with crimes which he urges them to commit
> against the lives of another [people]." (Ibid., 2–3)

On the other hand, Commager and Cantor recounted in
*Documents of American History* that Jefferson's tailored *pro* "Race
Card Evil" accusative clause stated,

> "He [King George III] has excited domestic [slave]
> insurrection among us [colonists], and has endeavored
> to bring on the inhabitants of our frontiers, the merciless
> Indian [Algonquian] Savages, whose known rule of
> warfare, is an undistinguished destruction of all ages, sexes,
> and conditions." (*Docs. of Amer. Hist.*, 102)

Not only did the suppressed "1776 Declaration's" condemnation of the African Slavery scheme appease the delegates from Georgia and South Carolina, but jeopardize the colonists' war effort against Britain—because the big-business slaveowners of the two states refused to abolish the evil or offer people of African descent the opportunity to obtain their freedom by enlisting in the colonial army. Recounted statesman Logan in *The Great Conspiracy*,

> During the War of the Revolution following the Declaration of Independence, the half a million of slaves, nearly all of them in the Southern States, were found to be not only a source of weakness, but, through the incitements of British emissaries [agents], a standing menace of peril to the slaveholders. Thus it was that the South was overrun by hostile British armies, while in the North—comparatively free of this element of [slaveholding] weakness—disaster after disaster met them [the British armies]. (*The Great Conspiracy*, 3)

And to Mr. Logan's observation, statesman Bancroft added in his *History of the United States*,

> The question of recruiting the army by the enlistment of black men forced itself on [the] attention [of the Second Continental Congress]. The several [individual] states employed them as they pleased, and the slave was enfranchised [freed and granted citizenship] by the service. Once Congress touched on the delicate subject; and in March, 1779, it recommended Georgia and South Carolina to raise three thousand active, able-bodied negro men under thirty-five years of age; and the recommendation was coupled with a promise of "a full compensation to the proprietors of such negroes for the property." The resolution appears to have been adopted without opposition, North and South Carolina having both been represented in the committee that reported it. But South Carolina refused by great majorities to give effect to the scheme. (*Hist. of the U.S.*, 293–94)

Not only did a selfish minority risk the "greater good" of American society on the eve of the Revolutionary War, just to personally profit from Human misery, but the "1774" agenda to eradicate the "Race Card Evil" oriented African Slavery scheme was put on hold—because the Second Continental Congress had to concentrate on forming a bona fide government to successfully contest the British government and escape capture or execution for treason.

During June 1776, Congress appointed a Committee to draft a better-defined organizing document than that created during October 1774—one that would create a central (federal) governing body to prosecute the war with Britain, raise and organize an army to contest the powerful opponent, and enact treaties with foreign nations more or less hostile toward the opponent. Next, during July 1776, Pennsylvania delegate John Dickinson (a committee member) drafted "Articles of Confederation" aimed at accomplishing such. Then, during November 1776, Congress adopted Dickinson's version and sent it to the legislatures of the thirteen States for their ratification (legal approval). Thereafter, from 1778–1779, the States inspected and ratified the "Articles"—that is to say, all States except Maryland (due to a land boundary annexation question). Finally, on 1 March 1781, Maryland ratified the "Articles" to make the document's acceptance "unanimous" and "effective" (legally operative) for governing the "several" (thirteen independent or sovereign) states "united" under a common cause. The *World Book Encyclopedia's* "Articles of Confederation" recounted,

> The Second Continental Congress drafted the Articles of Confederation. Richard Henry Lee of Virginia first proposed the establishment of a Confederation in the Congress on June 7, 1776. Congress appointed a Committee to draw up a plan of Union. Within a month, John Dickinson of Pennsylvania prepared a first draft. On

November 15, 1777, Congress adopted a final version. By 1779, all the states except Maryland had ratified (approved) it...Maryland approved the Articles on March 1, 1781. The Articles went into effect on that date. (*World Book Encyclopedia*, vol. 1, 1998, s.v. "Articles of Confederation," 759)

To this, Commager and Cantor added in their *Documents of American History*,

> Congress resolved June 11, 1776, that a Committee should be appointed to draw up Articles of Confederation between the Colonies. A plan proposed by John Dickinson formed the basis of the Articles as proposed to Congress and, after some debate and a few changes, adopted, November 15, 1777. Representatives of the States signed the Articles during 1778 and 1779; Maryland alone refused to ratify the Articles until Congress had arrived at some satisfactory solution of the land [annexation] question. (*Docs. of Amer. Hist.*, 111)

In addition to organizing a central governing body, the four-year delay between the adoption and ratification of the Articles of Confederation stemmed from the fact that the Second Continental Congress had to constantly and quickly change location to evade capture by the British. In fact, in his *Encyclopaedia Britannica* article entitled "The Continental Congress," political historian John R. Alden estimated that the government's address changed about ten times over a thirteen-year period—to locales such as: Baltimore, MD (Dec. 20, 1776); Philadelphia, PA (March 4, 1777); Lancaster, PA (Sept. 27, 1777); York, PA (Sept. 30, 1777); Philadelphia, PA (July 2, 1778); Princeton, NJ (June 30, 1783); Annapolis, MD (Nov. 26, 1783); Trenton, NJ (Nov. 1, 1784); New York, NY (Jan.11, 1785); and New York, NY (March 4, 1789) (at which time the "United Sates of America" became governed under the "1787 U.S. Constitution").

*Encyc. Brit.*, rev. 14th ed., s.v. "Continental Congress, The," 420.

Although the Second Continental or Confederation Congress acted as a central government under the "Articles of Confederation," it nevertheless retained the character it had under the First Continental Congress's Articles of Association—namely, that of being a governing body without "genuine central government power" due to "the individual supremacy" or "political sovereignty" possessed by each Colony turned state. This fact twentieth-century political historian Merrill Jensen explained in his *Encyclopaedia Britannica* article entitled "Articles of Confederation." Said he,

> The Articles of Confederation, the first [official] Constitution of the United States, were written in 1776–1777, ratified March 1, 1781, and served until they were replaced by the Constitution of 1787 on March 4, 1789…The Constitution finally adopted by the [Second] Continental Congress in 1777 and sent to the states for ratification provided for a strictly "federal" government, which had no authority over the states or their citizens.
>
> The Articles of Confederation declared specifically that "each state retains its sovereignty, freedom, and independence" and all powers and rights not "expressly delegated to the United States, in Congress Assembled" [Confed. Art. II]. (*Encyc. Brit.*, rev. 14th ed., s.v. "Articles of Confederation," 525–26 passim)

While it was true that the "individual" States needed and created a "central" or "federal" government to prosecute the war against Britain, it was equally true that they feared giving it the power to oppress them—precisely because of the abuses they suffered under British control. Thus, the Confederation Congress created on 15 November 1777, styled "The United States of America," was a government with extremely "limited" powers—as Mr. Jensen explained,

> Congress was denied the power of taxation…the power
> to regulate trade, although it was given exclusive power
> of making [foreign] commercial treaties…The citizens of
> each state were guaranteed the privileges of the citizens
> of any state to which they moved. Provision was made
> for the extradition of criminals fleeing from one state to
> another…It had the sole power of making peace and war…
> It had sole control of diplomatic negotiations…It had the
> sole authority to…manage affairs with Indians not a part
> of any state. (Ibid., 526 passim)

Although the Confederation Congress was granted "exclusive" or "sole" power to accomplish certain projects, the implementation of its decisions depended on a "unanimous" vote by all the Confederated states. This deficiency became a major stumblingblock in Congress's ability to take action on many important issues affecting the new government. This fact Mr. Jensen noted,

> Opposition to granting the taxing power to Congress was
> so overwhelming that it was not debated, but lesser issues,
> which continued to be issues in later Constitutional history,
> were debated fully. One was the question of representation.
> The states with large populations insisted that they should
> have more votes in Congress than the small [population]
> states. The latter, and those leaders fearful of a powerful
> central government, insisted on the equality of the states
> and established the rule that each [state] should have one
> vote [Confed. Art. V, Clause IV]. (Ibid., 526)

Ironically, while the matter of Congressional Representation was thought to have been "a lesser issue," the "number of votes" and "state population size" would become "the major issue" threatening "Union"—since it was the weakest link through which the "Race Card Evil" could infiltrate the government and cause "disunion" in the desired "Union." Indeed, one of the reasons for establishing the "1774 Union" was that of ending

King George III's African slavery scheme. Had the British crown and Parliament made a genuine effort to address the colonists' grievances, they would have "cheerfully accepted British rule." However, the "divine right of kings to rule" theory (a "Race Card Evil" oriented theory) prevented the British crown and Parliament from rationally negotiating with the colonists. This failure provoked armed conflict in Massachusetts, which then caused the colonists to rebel (commit treason) against the crown.

Consequently, when the "1774 Union" pushed for "nation-to-nation" status to contest Britain, created a "national name" (The United States of America), established a "national government" (the Continental-Confederation Congresses) to govern the Colonies turned states, and embarked on war, all such steps were links in one chain aimed at putting the "Race Card Evil," under any of its pseudonyms, "in the course of ultimate extinction." This fact was made clear in the "1776 Declaration of Independence"—which appealed to both "God" and "humanity" (the "seventy" nations) to support a "just" cause. In their *Documents of American History*, Commager and Cantor recounted that the "1776 Declaration" said in part,

> When in the course of Human events, it becomes necessary for one people to dissolve the political bands which have connected them with another, and to assume among the Powers [nations] of the earth, the separate and equal station to which the Laws of Nature and of Nature's God entitle them…We, therefore, the Representatives of the united States of America, in General Congress, Assembled, appealing to the Supreme Judge of the world [God] for the rectitude [moral honesty and uprightness] of our intentions, do…solemnly publish and declare, That these United Colonies are, and of Right ought to be Free and Independent States….And for the support of this Declaration, with a firm reliance on the Protection of Divine Providence [God], we mutually pledge to each other our Lives, our Fortunes and our sacred Honor. (*Docs. of Amer. Hist.*, 100–02 passim)

Despite this noble intent, a minority of delegates hailing from two States (Georgia and South Carolina)—acting on behalf of profit-oriented northern and southern businessmen—*undermined the Colonial effort to become a nation free of "Race Card Evil" influence*. Indeed, prior to the "1776 Revolution" most of the colonies sought to end the African slavery scheme. However, the mood "changed" in favor of upholding the evil both during and after the "1776 Revolution." This "mood change" retarded every Colonial effort to prosecute the war against Britain, create the Confederation, and create the "United States of America." Said statesman Bancroft in his *History of the United States*,

> The antagonism between the northern and southern states, founded on climate, pursuits, and labor, broke out on the first effort to unite them permanently. When members from the North spoke freely on the evils of slavery, a member from South Carolina answered that, "if property in slaves should be questioned, there must be an end of Confederation." In the same month, the vote on taxing persons ["slaves"] claimed as property ["chattel"] laid bare the existence of a territorial division of parties; the states north of Mason and Dixon's [Pennsylvania-Maryland boundary] line voting compactly on the one side, and those south of that line, which were duly represented, [voting compactly] on the other [side].
>
> The clashing between the two sections fastened the attention of reflecting observers. In August, 1778, soon after the reception at Philadelphia of an envoy from France, he reported to Vergennes: "The states of the south and of the north, under existing subjects of division and estrangement, are two distinct parties, which at present count but few deserters. The division is attributed to moral and philosophical causes." He further reported that the cabal against [George] Washington found supporters exclusively in the north. (*Hist. of the U.S.*, 292)

Seeking to create a "more perfect Union" than the "1774 Association," many Second Continental Congress delegates underestimated the important role that "voting" and "representation" shared. However, before long they realized the gridlock they faced by requiring a "unanimous" vote from the "politically sovereign" confederated states to enact any law (Confed. Art. II and Art. V, Clause IV)—especially with respect to ending the African Slavery cheap-labor scheme. Said Statesman Bancroft,

> In the assertion of the sovereignty of each separate state, there was no distinction between North and South. Massachusetts expressed itself [via vote] as absolutely as South Carolina [via vote]. As a consequence, the Confederation could contain no interdict [prohibition] of the slave-trade, and the importation of slaves could therefore remain open to any state according to its choice. (Ibid., 294–95)

After going to so much trouble to form the 1774 Union to "wholly discontinue the slave trade," prosecute the 1776 Revolution against King George III's "divine right of kings to rule" and "chattel slavery" doctrines, and create the 1781 Articles of Confederation's "more perfect Union," the Second Continental Congress delegates compromised their principles to create the 1787 Constitution for the government styled the "United States of America"—knowing that they were going against both Nature and Nature's God, and that there would be Earthly and Divine consequences to follow (Deut. 5:11, 23:21–23, kjv). Said Statesman Bancroft,

> There was no hope of the delivery of the country from slavery by congress. It was but a minority of them who kept in mind that an ordinance of man can never override natural law, and that in the high court of the Eternal Providence [God] justice forges her weapon long before she strikes. (Ibid., 295–96).

By silencing the Confederation Congress on the "Race Card Evil" oriented African slavery issue, the big-business proponents of the cheap-labor scheme were free to exploit and oppress their victims without opposition—contrary to biblical prohibitions against doing such (Exod. 22:21, Lev. 19:33–34, Deut. 10:17–19, cf. Matt. 22:34–40, kjv). And simultaneously, proponents of the scheme omitted from their State Constitutions any language that would reveal their "willful violation" of biblical injunctions against oppression. Said Statesman Bancroft,

> Nowhere was slavery formally established in the organic law [organizing document, constitution] as a permanent social relation; the Courts of Virginia did not recognize a right of property in the future increase of slaves; in no one state did its Constitution abridge the power of its legislature to abolish slavery. In no one Constitution did the words "slave" and "slavery" find a place, except in that of Delaware, and there only by way of a formal and perpetual prohibition. They are found as little in that of South Carolina, which was the champion of Negro bondage, as in that of Massachusetts. (Ibid., 296)

As said, by the time the Confederation Congress was created only a "minority" of its members remained men of "active vocal social conscience" and remembered that "fighting for one's own freedom while keeping another enslaved was hypocritical." Two such "nonvocal" cases were the renowned Thomas Jefferson and George Washington—both of whom belonged to fraternal societies professing belief in God, humanitarianism, and the brotherhood of man; both of whom owned slaves bequeathed to them; both of whom drew fire from national and international critics due to their prominent roles in seeking American freedom from slavery (thralldom) to Britain while simultaneously holding others in slavery; and both of whom wanted the "Race Card Evil" put to rest.

It is uncertain as to how drastically Jefferson and Washington were infected with "Race Card Evil" doctrine (only they and their Creator know for sure). However, what is certain is that the widowed Jefferson—who had some apprehension about "black and white men sharing equal political power"—had an "interracial" affair with his slave sister-in-law Sally Hemmings (daughter of Jefferson's father-in-law and half-sister of Jefferson's wife); and that Washington refused to issue a Masonic Charter to freeman Prince Hall (which prompted Mr. Hall to obtain one from an Irish military lodge atttached to British forces in Boston). Also certain is the fact that the African slavery issue and its "skin-color superiority" doctrine caused these two notable Americans much mental strife. In his *History of the United States*, Statesman Bancroft explained their respective predicaments:

> Even had light broken in on [Thomas] Jefferson's mind through the gloom in which the subject [of securing unconditional emancipation for Virginia's slaves] was involved for him, Virginia would not have accepted from him a plan for making Virginia a free commonwealth; but there is no evidence that he ever reconciled himself to the idea of emancipated black men living side by side with white men as equal sharers in political rights and duties and powers. The result of his efforts and reflections he uttered in these ominous forebodings: "Nothing is more certainly written in the book of fate than that these people are to be free; nor is it less certain that the two races, equally free, cannot live in the same government."
>
> At that time [circa. 1782], [George] Washington was a kind and considerate master of slaves, without as yet a title to the character of an abolitionist. By slow degrees, the sentiment grew up in his mind that to hold men in bondage was wrong; that Virginia should proceed to emancipation by general statute of the state; that, if she refused to do so, each individual should act for his own household. (Ibid., respectively 297, 298)

The "gloom" troubling Jefferson and Washington stemmed from the fact that they and many of their enlightened contempoararies—such as George Mason, Patrick Henry, George Wythe, Edmund Pendleton, and Richard Henry Lee—"knew" from the start of the revolt against Britain that "divine" retribution would be paid to the British-American Colonies; for "invoking God's help" to overthrow the "divine right of kings, perpetual allegiance, thralldom, slavery" evil that they suffered under King George III, while simultaneously forcing the same on other members of the "seventy" nations. This fact Statesman Bancroft noted in his *History of the United States*. Said he concerning Jefferson's gloom,

> In the helplessness of despair Jefferson, so early as 1782, dismissed the [Slavery versus Emancipation] problem from his thoughts with these words:
> "I tremble for my country when I reflect that God is just, [and] that His justice cannot sleep forever. The way, I hope, is preparing, under the auspices of Heaven, for a total emancipation [of those Africans unjustly held as Chattel Slaves]." (Ibid., 298)

There was good reason for Jefferson and many of his contemporaries to tremble—since their contradictory actions was a "mockery" of the God whom they professed belief in. Such would surely cause "divine" retribution—as promised in the biblical books entitled *Malachi* and *Galatians*:

> And I will come near to you to [do] judgement; and I will be a swift witness against…false swearers [perjurers], and against those that oppress [defraud] the hireling [laborer] in [of] his wages, the widow, and the fatherless [orphan], and that turn aside the stranger [foreigner] from his right, and fear not me, saith the LORD [YHWH] of hosts…Will a man rob God? Yet ye have robbed me…Ye are cursed with a curse: for ye have robbed me, even this whole nation. (Mal. 3:5–9 passim, KJV)

> For if a man think himself to be something, when he is nothing, he deceiveth himself…For every man shall bear his own burden…Be not deceived; God is not mocked [played with]: for whatsoever a man soweth [plants], that shall he also reap [harvest]. (Gal. 6:3–7 passim, KJV)

Such biblical "promises" may have appeared to be high-sounding religious rhetoric—spoken to the deaf ears of those profitting from the African slavery "cheap-labor" scheme or those buying into the "ethnic" or "skin-color" superiority-inferiority theory that supported the evil. However, the free American "white" laborer or entrepreneur in slavery who believed such was in for a rude awakening.

Indeed, the invention of power tools and machines during England's Industrial Revolution (circa 1760)—some sixteen years prior to America's 1776 Revolution—had signalled a move from small-scale to large-scale commodity production. This also signalled a move from the need of a large workforce to a small one—an inverse relationship that would negatively impact the "free" laborer in America and around the world, regardless of "ethnicity" or "skin color." Since these events would spawn and fuel the Age of Capitalism (with help from Adam Smith's 1776 book *The Wealth of Nations*)—a "free" enterprise system in which laborers would theoretically negotiate to obtain the ideal fair market price to promote economic growth and prosperity—the "free" person who paid little heed to these "economic changes" would miss the fact that such events really meant that the "Race Card Evil" oriented African slavery scheme would die out wherever industrialism, independence, and capitalism appeared. In short, these three events would cause conflict between the "free" (paid) and "slave" (unpaid) business-labor relationship regardless of "ethnicity" or "skin color."

On the American front, such events did not matter to those profiting from the "unpaid" labor scheme. Indeed, during the industrial independence, capitalistic eras, the New World was an undeveloped region that needed a "cheap-labor" workforce to produce goods, raw materials, and services for profit. Understanding this, the big businesses profiting from the African slavery scheme disguised their personal profit agenda under the banner of "white race pride, white race superiority" and targeted people of "dark skin color" for economic exploitation. Sadly, this banner was championed by every "white" American naive enough to believe that the "cheap-labor" workforce scheme would not negatively affect them because of their "ethnicity" or "skin color." However, about AD 1780, English statesman Edmund Burke saw through the "cheap-labor, skin-color" scheme, realized its true "worldwide" implication, and warned people about the impending crisis to come. In his *History of the United States*, political historian Bancroft recounted,

> In the last quarter of the eighteenth [century AD], the ownership of white men by white men still blighted more than half of Europe. The evil shielded itself under a new plea, where a difference of skin [color] set a visible mark on the victims of commercial avarice, and strengthened the ties of selfishness by the pride of race. In 1780, Edmund Burke tasked himself to find out what laws could check the new form of servitude which wrapt all quarters of the globe in its baleful influences; yet he did not see a glimmering of hope even for an abolition of the trade in slaves, and only aimed at establishing regulations for their safe and comfortable transportation. He was certain that no one of them was ever so beneficial to the master as a freeman who deals with him on equal footing by convention, that the consumer [oppressor] in the end is always the dupe [fool] of his own tyranny and injustice; yet for slave plantations he suggested nothing more than some supervision by the state, and some mitigation of the power of the master to divide families by partial sales. For himself, he inclined to a gradual emancipation; yet his code for the negroes was founded on the conviction that slavery was "an incurable

evil." He sought no more than to make that evil as small as possible, and to draw out of it some collateral good. (*Hist. of the U.S.*, 291)

Try as he might to obtain "some collateral good" out of an "incurable evil," statesman Burke underestimated the "Race Card Evil's" genius—and so did the Confederation Congress. Indeed, during the Articles of Confederation's writing a "comity clause" was agreed upon that allowed "The Race Card Evil" to enter into the American Union. The clause ran:

> The better to secure and perpetuate mutual friendship and intercourse among the people of the different states in this union, the free inhabitants of each of these states, paupers, vagabonds and fugitives from Justice excepted, shall be entitled to all privileges and immunities of free citizens in the several states…and shall enjoy therein all the privileges of trade and commerce, subject to the same duties, impositions and restrictions as the inhabitants thereof respectively, provided: that such restrictions shall not extend so far as to prevent the removal of property imported into any state of which the Owner is an inhabitant…(Confed. Art IV, Cl 1)

On its face Article IV, Clause 1 seemed harmless enough in its intent to protect the "property" rights of those whom the Confederation delegates represented in their respective Colonies-turned-States. However, by classifying slaves as "property" (chattel), large-scale plantation businessmen as "owners" (slaveowners), and threatening to end the colonial effort to unite in order to fight Britain for independence should the "end-of-slavery" issue be raised, the Georgia and South Carolina delegates were able to "blackmail" the Confederation Congress delegates into allowing the "Race Card Evil" to enter the "Union"—contrary to the 1774 Congress's intent.

Indeed, on 17 June 1779, about four years prior to ending the Revolutionary War, the Confederation Congress began discussions on drafting Articles to include in the upcoming September 1783 Versailles, Paris, Peace Treaty between America and Britain. Among the proposed Articles was one ending the African Slavery scheme. However, when Congress brought up the Article, virtually every State voted against it. This sad fact statesman Bancroft noted in his *History of the United States*,

> When on the seventeenth of June, 1779, a renunciation of the power to engage in the slave-trade was proposed as an Article to be included in the [Verailles, Paris] Treaty of Peace, all the states, Georgia alone being absent, refused the concession by the votes of every member [of Congress] except [John] Jay and [Elbridge] Gerry.
>
> Luzern, the French envoy who succeeded Gerard, soon came to the conclusion that the confederacy would run the risk of an early dissolution if it should give itself up to the hatred [over the African slavery issue] which began to show itself between the north and south. (*Hist. of the U.S.*, 295)

Having excluded the African Slave Trade issue from the Peace Treaty negotiations, the Confederation Congresss allowed South Carolina's "absent ambassador," Henry Laurens—a partner in North America's largest slave-trading business called "Austin and Laurens"—to include recognition of the chattel slavery scheme among the Peace Treaty's Articles (Congress had appointed Benjamin Franklin, Henry Laurens, John Adams, John Jay, and Thomas Jefferson to conduct the ppeace talks; but Jefferson did not attend, and Laurens was released from prison too late to attend). Thus when the treaty recognized the thirteen Colonies as "free" and "sovereign" Confederated governments ("thirteen" separate treaties were made), it simultaneously recognized the evil scheme to classify humans as "chattel" or "property" in the American Union. In their *Documents of American History*, Commager and Cantor noted that Articles I and VII of the Peace Treaty between Britain and America stated in part:

1. Art I.—His Britannic Majesty [King George III] acknowledges the said United States…to be free, sovereign and independent States; that he treats with them as such, and for himself, his heirs and successors, relinquishes all claims to the Government, proprietary and territorial rights of the same, and every part thereof.

2. Art VII.—There shall be a firm and perpetual peace between His Britannic Majesty and the said States, and between the subjects of the one and the citizens of the other…and His Britannic Majesty shall, with all convenient speed, and without causing any destruction, or carrying away any *negroes or other property* [chattel] of the American inhabitants, withdraw all his armies, garrisons and fleets from the said United States… (*Docs. of Amer. Hist.*, 117–18, 119, italics ours).

Fortunately, on 30 November 1783, when the peace treaty was officially signed by Britain and the Confederated "United States," its Article VII also recognized that "free people of color" labeled "Negroes" were included among those defined as "citizens of the several states" and "citizens of the United States." This undeniable fact historians Commager, Cantor, and Bancroft all validated in their research on the event.

Recounting the 1781 Confederation Article IV, Clause I's language (the Comity Clause), Commager and Cantor noted in their *Documents of American History*,

3. Art IV. The better to secure and perpetuate mutual friendship and intercourse among the people of the different states in this union, *the free inhabitants of each of*

*these states*, paupers, vagabonds and fugitives from Justice excepted, *shall be entitled to all privileges and immunities of free citizens in the several states*…[Confed. Art IV, Cl I]. (*Docs. of Amer. Hist.*, 111, italics ours)

And recounting the 1783 Versailles Peace Treaty Article VII's language, statesman Bancroft noted in his *History of the United States,*

Thus far, no word in the [Versailles] Convention had, except indirectly, alluded to the existence of slavery in the United States. On the thirtieth [of September], at the demand of [Henry] Laurens, in the engrossed copies of the Convention [treaty] a clause was interlined, prohibiting, on the British evacuation [from American territory], the "carrying away any Negroes or any other property of the inhabitants." So the [Peace Treaty] instrument, which already contained a confession [in Art I] that the United States were not formed into one nation, [also] made known [in Art VII] that in their [United States] Confederacy [that] man could be held as a chattel; *but, as interpreted alike in America and England, it* [the Peace Treaty] *included free Negroes among their* [the Confederation's] *citizens* [compare Confed. Art IV, Cl 1]. (*Hist. of the U.S.*, 363, italics ours)

Thus, along with Britain's 30 November 1783 recognition of American Independence and Citizenship (state and federal)—for "whites," "blacks" ("Negroes"), or "others"—came the incorporation of the "Race Card Evil" oriented African ("chattel") slavery scheme into the new nation in making. However, the incorporation of this great evil into the new government was not the end of the story regarding humanity's war with the "ancient evil." Rather, the battle was only just beginning.

# 3

# The Race Card Evil Dealt into the US Government

Now the serpent [Race Card Evil] was more subtile than
any beast of the field which the LORD God had made And
the LORD God said unto the serpent, Because thou hast
done this, thou art cursed…And I will put enmity [hatred]
between thee and the woman [the Union]…it [the Union]
shall bruise [strike at] thy head [leaders], and thou shalt
bruise [strike at] his [the Union's] heel [founding].

—Gen. 3:1, 14–15 (KJV)

WHEN FREEING THEMSELVES from "servitude" to Britain, the
Colonies turned states had carved out for themselves neighboring
lands formerly claimed by Britain. This excess territory the
Confederation wanted the states to cede (add) to the new
government and expand the new nation's geographical boundary.
Most of the states had done so by the time the peace treaty with
Britain was signed. Virginia, however, possessed a large amount
of western territory that still needed to be annexed.

In 1784, the Confederation Congress appointed a select
committee, chaired by Thomas Jefferson, to oversee the matter
(via Confed. Art IX, Cl 5 and Art X). The committee had to
devise a plan for Virginia's annexation of her western territory to
the United States (via Confed. Art IX, Cl 2). On 23 April 1784,

Jefferson's plan was reported, but did not go into effect because it prohibited the "Race Card Evil" oriented African Slavery scheme from entering "into the ceded territory" and "all other territories to be ceded to the United States." In *The Great Conspiracy*, Senator Logan explained the reason behind Jefferson's plan:

> The lessons of the [Revolutionary] War, touching Slavery, had not been lost upon our statesmen. Early in 1784 Virginia ceded to the United States her claims of jurisdiction and otherwise over the vast territory northwest of the Ohio [River]; and upon its acceptance, Jefferson… reported to the Ninth Continental Congress an Ordinance to govern the territory ceded already, or to be ceded, by individual States to the United States, extending from the 31st to the 47th degree of north latitude, which provided as "fundamental conditions between the thirteen original States and those newly described" as embryo States thereafter to be carved out of such territory ceded or to be ceded to the United States not only that "they shall forever remain a part of the United States of America" [1784 Western Territory Ordinance, Art 1], but also that "after the year 1800 of the Christian era, there shall be neither Slavery nor involuntary servitude in any of the said States"—and that those fundamental conditions were "unalterable but by the joint consent of the United States in Congress Assembled, and of the particular State within which such alteration is proposed to be made" [1784 Western Territory Ordinance, Art 7, Cl 4]. (*The Great Conspiracy*, 3–4; cf. *Docs. of Amer. Hist.*, 121–122)

Thomas Jefferson and most select committee members wanted to prevent the spread of the African Slavery scheme. However, when the measure was voted on it "died in committee." Senator Logan explained why the "1784 Western Territory Ordinance," forerunner of the "1787 Northwest Ordinance," died. Said he,

But now a signal misfortune befell. Upon a motion to strike out the Clause prohibiting Slavery, six States [CT, PA, MA, NH, NY, RI]…voted to retain [keep] the prohibitive Clause, while three States [MD, SC, VA]…voted not to retain it. The vote of North Carolina was equally divided; and while one of the delegates from New Jersey voted to retain it, yet as there was no other delegate present from that State and the Articles of Confederation [Art V, Cls 2 and 4] required the presence of "two or more" delegates to cast the vote of a State, the vote of New Jersey was lost; and, as the same Articles required an affirmative vote of a majority of all the States [9 states during regular sessions, and a "majority" for Committee Commissioners]—and not simply of those present—the retention of the Clause prohibiting Slavery was also lost [DE, GA, and VT being negative, thus making the original 13–States vote: 6 for, 7 against]. Thus was lost the great opportunity of restricting Slavery to the then existing Slave States, and of settling the question peaceably for all time. (*The Great Conspiracy*, 4; cf. *Docs. of Amer. Hist.*, note at 122)

As said, Jefferson's plan died because it contained the clause prohibiting slavery. This much is obvious since a mere three years later, on 13 July 1787, Congress passed a similar measure called "The Northwest Ordinance." This "1787 plan" was chiefly the work of Arthur St. Clair and three lobbyists—Reverend Manasseh Cutler, Samuel Parsons, and General Rufus Putnam—acting on behalf of a group of land speculators connected with the Ohio Company of Associates (called the Society of the Cincinnati) who sought to establish colonies in the Ohio area. And while the "1787 Ordinance" was similar to Jefferson's original plan in some respects, it differed from the "1784 Ordinance" in one chief repect—namely: the "1784 plan" had a "Slavery Prohibition Clause"; whereas the "1787 plan" had what seemed like a prohibition clause, but actually had a "Slavery Authorization Clause." This fact political historians Commager and Cantor showed in their *Documents of American History*. When recounting the language of Article 6, Clause 2 in the "1787 Northwest Ordinance," they noted that it stated,

> There shall be neither Slavery nor Involuntary Servitude in the said territory, otherwise than in punishment of crimes whereof the party shall have been duly convicted; *Provided always*:
>
> That any person [slave] escaping into the same [territory], from whom Labor or Service [slavery] is lawfully claimed in any one of the Original [13] States, such fugitive [slave] may be lawfully reclaimed, and conveyed to the person [master] claiming his or her Labor or Service as aforesaid.
>
> Be it ordained by the authority aforesaid, That the resolutions of the 23rd of April 1784, relative to the subject of this ordinance, be, and the same are hereby repealed and declared null and void. (*Docs. of Amer. Hist.*, 132, italics ours; cf. *The Great Conspiracy*, 4)

Indeed, the "1787 Ordinance" not only spoke in "pro-slavery" language, but also "opened up more US territory" to the African slavery scheme. This fact Senator Logan explained in his *The Great Conspiracy*. Said he,

> But this Ordinance of '87, adopted almost simultaneously with the framing of our present [1787] Federal [US] Constitution, was essentially different from the [1784] [Western Territory] Ordinance of three years previous, in this [respect]:
>
> That while the latter [Jefferson's 1784 plan] included the territory south of the Ohio River as well as that northwest of it, this [Authur St. Clair's 1787 plan] did not; and as a direct consequence of this failure to include in it the territory south of that River, the States of Tennessee [1796], Alabama [1819] and Mississippi [1817], which

were taken [carved] out of it, were subsequently admitted to the Union as Slave States, and thus greatly augmented [increased] their [Slaveholding States'] political power. And at a later period it was this increased political power that secured the admission [into the Union] of still other Slave States—[such] as Florida [1845], Louisiana [1812] and Texas [1845]—which enabled the Slave States to hold the balance of such power against the Original [13] States that had become Free, and the new Free States of the North-West. (*The Great Conspiracy*, 4–5)

Thus, the "1787 Northwest Ordinance" appeared to be a solution to the African Slavery issue—appeared to be a "compromise" designed to appease both "pro" and "anti" Slavery States and promote political harmony in the Union. However, the "1787 Ordinance" was really a slyly devised plan to promote the evil scheme by "increasing the number of Slave States" in order to "monopolize the Congressional Representation (Electoral) Process."

Unfortunately, the Congress that passed the "1787 Ordinance" refused to see that the measure would set the stage for undermining the political harmony sought by the newly formed government. And the Congress refused to see that the attempt to monopolize the Electoral Process, in order to expand the African slavery scheme in the United States, would make the predictions by Jefferson and many First Continental Congress leaders come true and "curse" the nation with terrible future consequences. This Senator Logan also explained. Said he,

Hence, while in a measure quieting the great question of [African] Slavery for the time being, the Ordinance of '87 in reality laid the groundwork for the long series of irritations and agitations touching its [Slavery's] restrictions and extensions, which eventually culminated in the clash of arms [American Civil War] that shook the Union from its center to its circumference. (Ibid., 5)

Undoubtedly, the circumstances surrounding the 1787 Northwest Ordinance's passage involved one of the most controversial political actions taken by the Confederation Congress—one that occurred during the same year that the 1787 US Constitution was framed and was closely connected with its framing.

During September 1786 a committee of states—called a "Meeting of Commissioners to Remedy Defects of the Federal Government"—was scheduled to meet at Annapolis, Maryland to discuss better ways to address the new government's commercial interests. Although nine of the thirteen States sent Commissioners to the meeting, only twelve delegates from five States attended—Delaware, Pennsylvania, New Jersey, New York, and Virginia being in attendance (delegates from MA, NH, NC, and RI arrived late; and CT, GA, MD, and SC sent none). At the meeting's close, the commissioners sent Congress a report calling for another meeting in Philadelphia during May of 1787—this time for "the sole and express purpose of revising the Articles of Confederation" pursuant to Confederation Article XIII. In the 2003 edition of *The Constitution of the United States of America as Amended*, the "Historical Note" therein recounted,

> Despite repeated proposals that the [Second] Continental Congress revise the Articles [of Confederation], the movement for a new national government began outside the Congress. Representatives of Maryland and Virginia, meeting at Mt. Vernon to discuss trade problems between the two States, agreed to invite delegates from all States to discuss commercial affairs at a meeting in Annapolis, Maryland, in September 1786. Although delegates from only five States reached the Annapolis Convention, that group issued a call for a meeting of all States to discuss necessary revisions of the Articles of Confederation. Responding to this call and the endorsement of the Continental Congress, every State except Rhode Island selected delegates for the meeting in the State House

at Philadelphia. (*The Constitution of the United States of America as Amended*, presented by Hon. Robert Ney, Washington, DC: United States Government Printing Office, 2003, p. V)

During 1787, two different Congressional meetings were held—in two different States, at two different times, and with two different agendas. However, both meetings were responsible for producing "one" important counterproductive result for the new nation—namely, that of allowing the "Race Card Evil" oriented African Slavery scheme to become "legalized" in the American government.

On 25 May 1787 the meeting to "revise the Articles of Confederation" took place at Philadelphia, was attended by fifty-five ("55") delegates representing the states, and was presided over by George Washington. The significance of this event was recounted by Commager and Cantor in their *Documents of American History*. They stated,

> Following the recommendation of the [14 September 1786] Annapolis Convention, Congress adopted, February 21, 1787, a Resolution that "it is expedient that on the second Monday in May next [1787] a Convention of delegates who shall have been appointed by the Several States be held at Philadelphia for the sole and express purpose of revising the Articles of Confederation." A Quorum, however, did not assemble at Philadelphia until May 25 [,1787]...The Convention continued its work throughout the summer of 1787 and on September 15th [1787] agreed to the [US] Constitution as reported from the Committee on Style. On the 17th [of] September [1787] the Constitution was signed, and submitted to Congress. By Resolution of September 28th [1787], Congress submitted the Constitution to the States. By June 21, 1788, nine States had Ratified [approved] the Constitution...Congress by Resolution of September 13,

1788, fixed the date for the election of a [US] President and the organization of the new government under the Constitution. (*Docs. of Amer. Hist.*, 138–39)

And to this the "historical note" to *The Constitution of the U.S.A. as Amended* added,

The Delegates who convened at the Federal Convention on May 25, 1787, quickly rejected the idea of revising the Articles of Confederation and agreed to construct a new framework for a national government. Throughout the summer months at the Convention in Philadelphia, delegates from 12 States debated the proper form such a government should take, but few questioned the need to establish a more vigorous government to preside over the union of States. The 39 delegates who signed the Constitution on September 17, 1787, expected the new charter to provide a permanent guarantee of the political liberties achieved in the Revolution [of 1776–1783]. (*Const. of the U.S.A. as Amended*, p. V)

While the "Constitutional Convention" was sitting at Philadelphia's State House from May to September of 1787 (George Washington presiding), the "Ninth Confederation Congress" was sitting at New York's City Hall on 13 July 1787 to enact the "1787 Northwest Ordinance" (Arthhur St. Clair presiding). This Senator Logan noted in *The Great Conspiracy*. Said he,

Meanwhile, as we have seen—while the [Northwest] Ordinance of 1787 was being enacted in the [next to] last Congress of the old Confederation at New York [City Hall] [Cyrus Griffin presided over the 10th or last Confederation Congress that sat at New York City's Fraunces Tavern from Jan. 22, 1788 to Jan. 21, 1789]— the Convention to frame the present [1787] Constitution was sitting at Philadelphia under the Presidency of

George Washington himself. The old Confederation had proved to be "a rope of sand." A new and stronger form of government had become a necessity for National existence. (*The Great Conspiracy*, 5)

Doubtless, the action taken to "rewrite" (not "revise") the 1781 Articles of Confederation was "questionable" according to its Article XIII (a point that would be raised by "pro-slavery" advocate Senator Saulsbury during Lincoln's era). Nevertheless, the seven Articles of the Constitution agreed upon and signed by "39" delegates at Philadelphia on 17 September 1787—and its 10–Amendment "Bill of Rights" (ratified 15 December 1791)—was a political achievement that signaled the extinction of the misused biblical "divine right of kings to rule" doctrine (*Book of Wisdom* 6:1–10, *Romans* 13:1–7, NAB). This fact twentieth-century Supreme Court Chief Justice Warren E. Burger noted in his foreword to *The Constitution of the United States: Bicentennial Edition*. Said he,

The work of 55 men at Philadelphia in 1787 was another step toward ending the concept of the divine right of kings [to rule doctrine]. In place of the absolutism of monarchy the freedoms flowing from this [U.S. Constitution] document created a land of opportunities. Ever since then discouraged and oppressed people from every part of the world have made their way to our shores; there were others too—educated, affluent, seeking a new life and new freedoms in a new land.

This is the meaning of our Constitution. (*The Constitution of the United States: Bicentennial Edition*, Washington, DC: Commission on the Bicentennial of the United States Constitution, US Government Printing Office, 1988)

And to Mr. Burger's view spiritualist John Ballou, when speaking in his *Oahspe* about the 1787 Constitutional event, added for American posterity's enlightenment,

> As Jehovih [the Creator]…bequeathed to the children of Guatama [America] a government unfettered by the name of God or Lord or Savior [via the First Amendment], so Jehovih sanctified the day of the ratification and the signing and sealing of His compact (American Constitution), as the Day Of The Holy Seal…And Jehovih said: Remember this day, and keep it holy [a "holi-day"], to the end of the world, for hereat was the beginning of the liberty [freedom] of man! ("The Book of Inspiration," 15:1–6 passim; "Holy Compact Day," *Oahspe*, 825)

Notwithstanding the 1787 Constitution's end of the "divine right of kings to rule" doctrine, the "new" nation's charter (Constitution) intentionally admitted the "Race Card Evil" into the "new" government—by legalizing "perpetual chattel slavery" in the "perpetual Union." This sad outcome was achieved through a crafty combination of at least six ideas—mostly taken from the 1781 Articles of Confederation and the 1787 Northwest Ordinance—that were incorporated in the 1787 Constitution by means of the Representation and Taxation, Migration and Importation, Removal or Transportation of Property, Fugitive from Justice, Fugitive from Justice Reclamation, and Non-Deprivation of Property clauses. A simple analysis of their intent and application will show this fact.

The Representation and Taxation clause was enacted to give Congress the "taxing power" it lacked under the Continental and Confederation Congresses. The clause applied a "three-fifths" or "60 percent" rule to a state's "total slave population" to give large-scale slaveholders the benefit of a "lesser property tax base," but prevent a state from counting its "total slave population" plus its "total free population" to raise "the number of House seats" allowed. The clause stated,

> Representatives and direct Taxes shall be apportioned among the several States which may be included in this

Union, according to their respective [Census Population] Numbers, Which shall be determined by adding to the whole Number of Free Persons, including those bound to Service for a Term of Years...three-fifths of all other Persons [slaves]. (US Const, Art I, Sec 2, Cl 3)

The "Migration and Importation" Clause was enacted to give big-businesses involved in the "International Slave Trade" a twenty-year grace period to engage therein before declaring it "illegal" by AD 1808. The Clause stated:

The Migration and Importation of such Persons [dlaves] as any of the States now existing shall think proper to admit, shall not be prohibited by the Congress prior to the Year one thousand eight hundred and eight [1808], but a Tax or duty may be imposed on such Importation, not exceeding ten dollars for each Person [slave]. (US Const, Art I, Sec 9, Cl 1)

Also, this same clause referred to the "Removal or Tranportation of Property (slaves) to any state" subclause found in Confederation Article IV, Clause 1 ("Comity of States" clause). The subclause pertaining to the "Right of Interstate Transportation of Property" stated,

The better to secure and perpetuate mutual friendship and intercourse among the people of the different states in this union...the people of each state shall have free ingress and regress to and from any other state, and shall enjoy therein all the privileges of trade and commerce, subject to the same duties, impositions and restrictions as the inhabitants thereof respectively, provided that such restriction shall not extend so far as to prevent the removal of property [slaves] imported into any state, to any other state of which the Owner [slaveowner] is an inhabitant... (Confed. Art IV, Cl 1)

The "Fugitive from Justice Reclamation clause" was originally part of the 1781 Articles of Confederation "Comity of the States" clause. It concerned a person, either "accused" (pretrial) or "convicted" (posttrial) of commiting crime in one State, who fled or escaped to another state to avoid "prosecution" or "incarceration"—and it provided the "general means to have the person returned to the State fled (called the "extradition" process). This item was placed in the 1787 Constitution's "Comity of the States" clause almost verbatim, and the language of the two clauses respectively stated:

> If any Person guilty [posttrial] of, or charged [pretrial] with treason, felony, or high misdemeanor in any state, shall flee from Justice [being prosecuted or serving sentence], and be found in any of the united states, he shall upon demand of the Governor or executive power, of the state from which he fled, be delivered up and removed to the state having jurisdiction of his offence [crime]. (Confed. Art IV, Cl 2)
>
> A Person charged [pre-trial] in any State with Treason, Felony, or other Crime, who shall flee from Justice [prosecution], and be found in another State, shall on Demand of the executive Authority of the State [governor's office] from which he fled, be delivered up, to be removed [extradited] to the State having Jurisdiction of the Crime. (US Const, Art IV, Sec 2, Cl 2)

On comparing the two clauses, it can readily be seen that both have the "Reclamation" or "Extradition" element. However, what may not readily be seen in the Constitution's version is the "guilty of" ("posttrial") or "flight to avoid serving sentence" element found in the Confederation's version. This element was concealed by the "proslavery" states that helped frame the 1787 Constitution—hidden by manipulating the fact that a person "guilty" (convicted) of a crime and sentenced to a term of "imprisonment" (incarcerated) was "held in a condition of service or labor" (involuntary servitude) and could be "reclaimed" by the authorities to complete the sentence!

The "proslavery" states had this element placed in the 1787 Contitution's Article IV, Section 2, Clause 3, next gave the Confederation Article's "Fugitive from Justice Reclamation Clause" the dual meaning of *convict* and *slave*, then gave its terms "governor, executive power, authority" the dual meaning of "state authority" and "slaveowner-master." The language of Article IV, Section 2, Clause 3 stated,

> No Person [convict, slave] held to Service [imprisonment] or Labour [slavery] in one State, under the Laws thereof, escaping into another [State], shall, in Consequence of any Law or Regulation therein, be discharged [freed] from such Service or Labour, but [the Escaped Convict or Fugitive Slave] shall be delivered up [extradited, reclaimed] on Claim of the Party [Penal Authhority, Slave Owner] to whom such Service or Labour may be due. (US Const, Art IV, Sec 2, Cl 3)

Thus, by using "linguistic" chicanery, the 1787 Constitution's framers undermined the 20 October 1774 Association's original intent to put the "Race Card Evil" oriented African slavery scheme "in the course of ultimate extinction." Instead of achieving the original goal, a "reversal"occurred that was no mere accident— judging from the "deliberate" steps taken to prevent discussing abolishment of African slavery in sessions of the Second Continental and 1781 Confederation Congresses, writing the evil into the 30 November 1783 Versailles peace treaty, striking down Jefferson's 23 April 1784 western territory ordinance because it prohibited the evil's inclusion in the territory (or any future territory) acquired by the United States, passing the 13 July 1787 Northwest Ordinance that opened up more US territory to the evil, and changing the 1 March 1781 Articles of Confederation into the 17 September 1787 Constitution that created a "proslavery" central government that "agreed" with the 1787 Northwest Ordinance!

At the risk of being redundant, a side-by-side comparison of the said articles and clauses pertaining to this "goal reversal" will show the truth of this "orchestrated" conspiracy:

> If any [free] Person guilty of, or charged with treason, felony, or other high misdemeanor [crime] in any state, shall flee from Justice…he shall upon demand of the Governor or executive power, of the state from which he fled, be delivered up and removed to the state having jurisdiction of his offence [crime]. (1 March 1781 Confed. Art IV, Cl 2, Fugitive from Justice Extradition-Reclamation Clause)

> On the thirtieth [of September], at the demand of [Henry] Laurens, in the engrossed copies of the [1783 Versailles treaty] Convention a clause was interlined, prohibiting, on the British evacuation [from American territory], the "carrying away any Negroes or any other property of the inhabitants." So the instrument [peace treaty]…made known [in Art VII] that in their [US] Confederacy man could be held as a chattel…(30 September 1783 peace treaty between the United States and Britain, Art. VII, *Docs. of Amer. Hist.*, 119; *Hist. of the U.S.*, 363)

> Early in 1784 Virginia ceded to the United States her claims…over the vast territory northwest of the Ohio [River]…Jefferson…reported to the Ninth Continental Congress an Ordinance to govern the territory ceded already, or to be ceded…extending from the 31st to the 47th degree of north latitude, which provided…that "after the year 1800 of the Christian era, there shall be neither Slavery nor involuntary servitude in any of the said States"—and that those fundamental conditions were "unalterable but by the joint consent of the United States in Congress Assembled…" (23 April 1784 Western Territory Ordinance, Art 7, Cl 4) (*The Great Conspiracy*, 3–4)

> That any person [Slave] escaping into the same [Northwest Territory], from whom Labor or Service [slavery] is lawfully claimed in any one of the Original [13]

States, such fugitive [slave] may be lawfully reclaimed, and conveyed to the person [owner-master] claiming his or her Labor or Service as aforesaid. (13 July 1787 Northwest Ordinance, Art 6, Cl 2; Fugitive Slave Extradition-Reclamation clause)

A [free] Person charged in any State with Treason, Felony, or other Crime, who shall flee from Justice, and be found in another State, shall on Demand of the executive Authority of the State from which he fled, be delivered up, to be removed to the State having Jurisdiction of the Crime. (17 September 1787 Const, Art IV, Sec 2, Cl 2; Fugitive from Justice Extradition-Reclamation clause)

No [slave] Person held to Service or Labour [slavery] in one State, under the Laws thereof, escaping into another [state], shall, in Consequence of any Law or Regulation therein, be discharged [freed] from such Service or Labour [slavery], but shall be delivered up [extradited, reclaimed] on Claim of the Party [owner, master] to whom such Service or Labour may be due. (17 September 1787 Const, Art IV, Sec 2, Cl 3; Fugitive Slave Extradition-Reclamation clause)

Perhaps the circumstances of the times made the Confederation Congress believe that the need to unify against Britain outweighed the danger posed by admitting the "Race Card Evil" oriented "cheap-labor" scheme into the American government. Nevertheless, in seeking to achieve political unity among the thirteen Colonies, the delegates allowed themselves to be "pawns" in an ingenious scheme to enslave both "dark" people of African descent and free "white" working-class Americans to the will of African slavery profiteers. Said Senator Logan in *The Great Conspiracy,*

The situation was one of extreme delicacy. The necessity for [creating] a closer and stronger Union of all the States was apparently absolute, yet this very necessity seemed to place a whip in the hands of a few States, with which to

> coerce the greater number of States to do their bidding.
> It seems that the majority must yield to a small minority
> on even vital questions, or lose everything. (*The Great
> Conspiracy*, 5–6)

As said, once the "British crisis" ended, the need to create a strong central government prompted the Confederation Congress to hold two different meetings that resulted in the desired government's formation and allowed the "Race Card Evil" to be "covertly" written into its organizing charter (the 1787 Constitution)—something the States never allowed to happen in their own individual Constitutions during the 1776 Revolutionary War Era. Again Senator Logan said,

> Thus it was, that instead of an immediate interdiction
> of the African Slave Trade, Congress was empowered to
> prohibit it after a lapse of twenty years [by 1808]; that
> instead of the basis of Congressional Representation
> being the total population of each State, a middle ground
> was conceded, which regarded the Slaves as both persons
> and property, and the basis both of Representation and
> of Direct Taxation was fixed as being the Total Free
> Population "plus three-fifths of all other Persons" in each
> [slave] State; and that there was inserted in the [1787]
> Constitution a similar Clause to that which we have seen
> was almost simultaneously incorporated in the [Northwest]
> Ordinance of '87, touching [on] the reclamation and
> return to their Owners of the Fugitive Slaves from the
> Free States into which they may have escaped. (Ibid., 6)

Although the 1787 Constitution represented a lofty ideal in its aim to create a government wherein people could be "free," a deal had nevertheless been struck with "the devil" to do so. Such a "compromise" was a terrible price to pay. Such "hypocrisy"— paraded before the Creator and the members of the "seventy" nations—could not possibly go unpunished. To appeal to God for help in fighting against someone imposing "hereditary bondage" upon one's self while seeking to impose such upon another would produce dire consequences. This truth the "fifty-five" or so framers of the American Union knew. Yet, they were "intimidated" into doing so by the "cheap-labor" profiteers of their era. This fact Senator Logan reported in *The Great Conspiracy*. Said he,

> The fact of the matter is, that the [1787] Convention that framed our Constitution lacked the courage of its convictions, and was "bulldozed" by the few extreme Southern Slave-holding States—South Carolina and Georgia especially. It [the Convention] actually paltered with those convictions and with the truth itself. Its convictions—those at least of a great majority of its delegates—were against not only the spread, but the very existence of Slavery; yet we have seen what they unwillingly agreed to in spite of those convictions; and they were guilty moreover of the subterfuge of using the terms "persons" and "service or labor" when they really meant "Slaves" and "Slavery." "They did this latter," Mr. [James] Madison says, "because they did not choose to admit the right of property in [owning] man," and yet in fixing the basis of Direct Taxation as well as Congressional Representation at the total Free population of each State with "three-fifths of all other persons [slaves, Art I, Sec 2, Cl 3]," they did admit the right of property in man! As was stated by Mr. [James] Iredell, to the North Carolina Ratification Convention [of the 1787 Constitution], when explaining the Fugitive Slave clause: "Though the word 'Slave' is not mentioned [in Art IV, Sec 2, Cl 3], this is the meaning of it." And he added: "the Northern delegates, owing to their peculiar scruples on the subject of Slavery, did not choose the word 'Slave' to be mentioned." (Ibid., 6–7)

Although the "Race Card Evil" entered the Union during the 1787 Constitution's writing, the document's "Three-Fifths Slave Census Count" provision was neither the result of an attempt to "denigrate" people called "blacks" or "Negroes," nor one to equate "dark skin color" with "race" or "slavery" (that had already been done via nonlegal writings).

The Congressional Representatives of large slave-owning and slave-profitting businesses demanded that the 1787 Constitution include various "slavery-oriented" clauses, then used such to (1) lower their property tax base, (2) monopolize congressional seats, and (3) expand the African slavery cheap-labor workforce scheme throughout the new nation's territory. This can be seen by reviewing the true purpose of the 1787 Constitution's "Legislative Powers Article" as it related to (1) Congressional Representation, Direct Taxes Apportionment, the Three-Fifths Rule, and the First US Census of 1790 with its "Race Classification Listing" (US Const, Art I, Sec 2, Cl 3); and (2) Congressional Power to levy taxes to pay the national debts, raise armies for the common defense, and provide for the general welfare (US Const, Art. I, Sec 8, Cls 1–6 and 10–18).

Firstly, the 1787 Constitution's "Representation-Direct Taxes Apportionment" clause arose from the Second Continental Congress's need to fulfill the closing statement of the 1776 Declaration of Independence to: "mutually pledge to each other our Lives, our Fortunes and our sacred Honor" in order to support the "counted costs involved in declaring independence from Britain." In other words, Congress was faced with the problems of allocating financial costs and raising armies amongst the Colonies-in-Rebellion during the Revolutionary War—problems that gave rise to the creation of the 1790 United States Census. This fact was recounted by early twentieth century American authors Carroll D. Wright (US Labor Commissioner) and William O. Hunt (chief statistician) who, in their work entitled *The History and Growth of the United States Census*, said on behalf of the US government,

> The causes which led to the establishment, in 1790, of the regular periodical enumeration or census had their origin in the desire of the Colonists to find some equitable plan for the distribution of the burdens of the [Revolutionary] war, which

proved to be one of the most perplexing questions which entered into the deliberations of the [Second] Continental Congress. These causes are quite fully considered in the admirable report on the ninth census made by General Garfield January 18, 1870 [in House Reports, Forty-First Congress, Second Session, vol. 1, no. 3], and need not be repeated here at length. It is sufficient for the purposes of this article to trace briefly the origin of the principle which found final expression in the Constitutional provision for the apportionment of Representatives and direct taxes.

The general proposition to use the number of inhabitants as the basis of apportionment for certain purposes was canvassed as early as 1775, when it was proposed to apportion the bills of credit levied to meet the expenses of the war, for the redemption of which the thirteen colonies were pledged [in the Declaration of Independence], according to the number of inhabitants of all ages, including negroes and mulattoes…In seeking to secure this provision of authority in the proposed Articles of Confederation, the basis of apportionment according to population was maintained in the original draft, but the articles as finally agreed upon by Congress provided instead that the charges of war and other expenses incurred for the common defense and general welfare should be defrayed out of a common treasury, to be supplied by the several States in proportion to the value of all land within each State, and that requisitions for the quota of land forces [armies, miltia] to be furnished by each State should be made in proportion to the number of its white inhabitants [See Confedration Articles III, VIII, and IX (Clause 5)]. (Carroll D. Wright and William O. Hunt, *The History and Growth of the United States Census*, Washington, DC: U.S. Government Printing Office, 1900), 11–12)

Secondly, the numerical "three-fifths" or "sixty percent" figure used in the 1787 Constitution was arrived at during the 1783 Continental (Confederation) Congress debates about what number to use in place of the "land valuation" taxation method—since many States purposely "under-reported" or "under-valued" their land holdings to lower their tax base. In their article entitled the "Three-Fifth Compromise," American authors Richard Gilder and Lewis E. Lehrman stated,

> The three-fifths figure was the outgrowth of a debate that had taken place within the Continental Congress in 1783. The Articles of Confederation had apportioned taxes not according to population but according to land values. The states consistently undervalued their land in order to reduce their tax burden. To rectify this situation, a special committee recommended apportioning taxes by population. The Continental Congress debated the ratio of slaves to free persons at great length. Northerners favored a 4–3 ratio, while Southerners favored a 2–1 or a 4–1 ratio. Finally, James Madison suggested a compromise: a 5–to-3 ratio. All but two states—New Hampshire and Rhode Island—approved this recommendation. But because the Articles of Confederation required unanimous agreement, the proposal was defeated. When the Constitutional Convention met in 1787, it adopted Madison's earlier suggestion.
>
> Richard Gilder and Lewis E. Lehrman, "The Three-Fifth Compromise," Digital History: GLC 80, p. 1 (http://www.digitalhistory.uh.edu/disp textbook.cfm?smtlD=3&psid=163 Retrieved 27 March 2013)

Thus, although the 1787 Constitution applied the "three-fifths" rule to a state's "entire slave population"—and thereby introduced the "Race Card Evil" oriented African slavery scheme into the US Government—the number had nothing to do with notions of ethnicity, race, skin color, slavery, or an attempt to make the so-called Negro less than a man. Rather, the number concerned apportioning taxes and allotting representative seats among the states based on their respective populations. In fact,

Gilder and Lehrman noted how the rule was misused to increase congressional representation of "proslavery" Southern states. They said,

> The Three-Fifths Compromise greatly augmented southern political power. In the Continental Congress, where each state had an equal vote, there were only five states in which slavery was a major institution [MD, VA, NC, SC, and GA]. Thus the southern states had about 38 percent of the seats in the Continental Congress. Because of the 1787 Three-Fifths Compromise, the southern states had nearly 45 percent of the seats in the first U.S. Congress, which took office in 1790.
>
> It is ironic that it was a liberal northern delegate, James Wilson of Pennsylvania, who proposed the Three-Fifths Compromise, as a way to gain southern support for a new framework of government. Southern states had wanted representation apportioned by population; after the Virginia Plan was rejected, the Three-Fifths Compromise seemed to guarantee that the South would be strongly represented in the House of Representatives and would have disproportionate power in electing Presidents.
>
> Over the long term, the Three-Fifths Compromise did not work as the South anticipated. Since the northern states grew more rapidly than the South, by 1820, southern representation in the House had fallen to 42 percent. Nevertheless, from [Thomas] Jefferson's election as President in 1800 to the 1850s, the three-fifths rule would help to elect slaveholding Presidents. Southern political power increasingly depended on the Senate, the President, and the admission of new slaveholding states. (Ibid., p. 1)

In their *History and Growth of the United States Census*, Wright and Hunt noted that the "Three-Fifths" rule also concerned fulfilling financial obligations incurred during the Revolutionary War, drafting "free" whites for military duty, and apportioning Congressional Representation Seats based on a State's "total white population" and "three-fifths" of the slaves resident in slave states such as Georgia, Maryland, North Carolina, South Carolina, and Virginia. Such factors prompted the creation of the 1790 Census that compiled "ethnic" facts for use during the 1787 Constitutional Convention. They said,

> This [population] estimate framed the basis of a [census] table used in the Convention of 1787 which framed the present Constitution of the United States, for the purpose of determining provisionally the representation of each State in Congress pending an actual enumeration… This table [used in the 1787 Constitutional Convention] included, for purposes of apportioning representation, all the whites in the various colonies and three-fifths of the Negroes in Maryland, Virginia, the two Carolinas, and Georgia… (*History and Growth of the U.S. Census*, 10–11 passim)
>
> Without considering the efficacy of these provisions for accomplishing the results intended, it is sufficient to state that in 1783 an attempt was made to amend the [A]rticles [of Confederation] so that, in lieu of the apportionment according to the valuation of land, the burden of the war and other expenses incurred for the common defense and general welfare should be borne by the several States "in proportion to the whole number of white and *other free citizens and inhabitants* of every age, sex, and condition, including those bound to servitude [indentured or incarcerated] for a term of years, and three-fifths of all other persons not comprehended in the foregoing description, except Indians not paying taxes, in each State." This proposed [census] enumeration was to be made triennially and be transmitted to Congress in such manner as they should direct, but the amendment did not prevail, and the Articles of Confederation remained intact until superseded by the Constitution of 1787. It will be noticed, however, that the main features of the proposed amendment to the Articles of Confederation

were afterwards embodied in the Constitution in the familiar clause prescribing the manner of apportioning Representatives and direct taxes, out of which came eventually the American census. (Ibid., 12, italics ours)

Thus, the assumption that the 1787 Constitution's "representation, census, and three-fifths" features are "Race Card Evil" oriented is wrong for two chief reasons. First, Wright and Hunt admitted that such "features" originated in the 1783 attempt to amend the Articles of Confederation for tax apportionment purposes which, among other things, took into consideration: the whole number of *whites, other free citizens and inhabitants, those bound to service* for a term of years, *three-fifths of all other persons* (*slaves*), and *untaxed Indians not counted* (*race* unmentioned, aside from the use of the word *white*). Second, Wright and Hunt stated that the motives of the 1787 attempt—which were an offshoot of the 1783 attempt—were "purely political," hence, "not racial." They said,

> This [census] provision was embodied in the [1787] Constitution for political reasons wholly, and with no thought of providing for any systematic collection of statistical data beyond the political necessities of the Government...By this [census] act, which was approved March 1, 1790, the marshals of the several judicial districts of the United States were required to cause the number of the inhabitants within their respective districts to be taken, *omitting Indians not taxed*, and *distinguishing free persons*, including those bound to service for a term of years, *from all others*. This separation in itself was sufficient to meet all the Constitutional requirements of the enumeration, but the act also required the marshals to distinguish the sex and color of free persons and free males of 16 years and upward from those under that age; in the latter case, undoubtedly, for the purpose of ascertaining the military and industrial strength of the country. For the purposes

of this enumeration, which was to commence on the first Monday in August, 1790…*The inquiries in 1790 related to but six items*, and called for the name of the head of the family and the number of persons in each family of the following descriptions: *free white* males of 16 years and upward; *free white* males under 16 years; *free white* females; *all other free persons*; *slaves*. (Ibid., 13–14 passim, italics ours)

On 1 March 1790 Congres enacted the first U.S. Census (according to the 1787 Constitution's Art I, Sec 8, Cl 4). Then, on 26 March 1790 Congress enacted the First Uniform Naturalization Law. By these enactments, it seemed like the new American nation was trying to implement a "uniform code" for introducing new members into its political community according to Judaeo-Christian or Old Testament teachings that said,

> One [uniform] law shall be to him that is homeborn [natural born], and unto the stranger [resident alien] that sojourneth among you. (Exod. 12:49, KJV)

> And if a stranger [resident alien] sojourn with thee in your land, ye shall not vex [oppress] him. But the stranger [resident alien] that dwelleth with you shall be unto you as one [natural] born among you, and thou shalt love him as thyself; for ye were strangers [resident aliens] in the land of Egypt [bondage]. (Lev. 19:33–34, KJV)

> And if a stranger [resident alien] shall sojourn among you, and will keep the Passover…according to the ordinance [law] of the Passover…ye shall have one ordinance [law], both for the stranger [resident alien], and for him that was [natural] born in the land. (Num. 9:14, cf. Deut. 10:17–19, Eph. 2:11–20 passim, Col. 3:1–3, 11, KJV)

Unfortunately, such was not the case. Before the 1790 Naturalization Law's passage, "citizenship" in the thirteen Colonies was acquired by either of three methods practiced during three different time periods. For instance, prior to the 1776 Revolution "British Citizenship"—in Britain or her Colonies—was obtained through Britain's political representatives in accordance with the "jus soli" (birth by land, soil, allegiance, or geopolitical jurisdiction) rule. During the Revolution (1776–1783), "Colonial citizenship" was acquired in the thirteen Colonies according to their individual ("nonuniform") rules as "sovereign states"—but subject to the "jus soli" rule. Whereas after the Revolution (1783–1790), "Union citizenship" was acquired in the Confederation (1781–1789) by Confederation Article IV's "express grant of citizenship" to all "free people" in the "thirteen sovereign states" allied in the Confederation—the exception being people classed as "paupers, vagabonds, and fugitives from justice."

Moreover, while citizenship or naturalization—prior to, during, and after the Revolution—was mostly granted to "twenty-one-year-old free "white" males, with good moral background, who professed allegiance to the political community (state) in which citizenship was sought," such was also granted to 'non-whites' for the selfsame reasons and without regard to "skin color" difference (yet subject to the "jus soli" rule).

However, about the time that German anthropologist Johann Friedrich Blumenbach published his book *Collectio Craniorum Diversarum Gentium* (1790), the "color-race question" was placed on America's first census questionnaire form (1790). Thereafter, America's first Naturalization Law restricted "naturalization" to "whites" immigrating to the country (albeit the 1787 Constitution only mandated "a Uniform Rule of Naturalization," neither a "color neutral" nor "color specific" rule).

Although America's first census may have been innocently undertaken to enumerate her population for "military purposes" (a draft) and "to increase a particular immigrating skin-color type," Blumenbach's book and the 1790 census "color-race question" helped the poison called "skin-color stereotypes" or "scientific racism" to infiltrate the new nation—such doctrines being based on Blumenbach's misapplied theories on humanity's "five" color, cranial, racial types: caucasian (white), Ethiopian (black), Malayan (brown), Mongolian (yellow), and Native American (red). (*Wikipedia*, s.v. "Johann Friedrich Blumenbach"; (http://en.wikipedia.org/wiki/Johann_Friedrich_Blumenbach). Retrieved 26 January 2014)

Following the 1790 Naturalization Law's implementation Congress, on 12 February 1793, enacted a law entitled "An act respecting fugitives from justice, and persons [slaves] escaping from the service of their masters." The passage of this federal "fugitive slave law," authorized by the 1787 Constitution's "Comity Clause" (Art IV, Sec 2, Cl 3), only confirmed the fact that profiteers from the "Race Card Evil" oriented African slavery scheme had won a major battle in the war to "engrave" in the American psyche and sociopolitical infrastructure a "skin-color" bias. However, the war was just beginning.

In 1801 Thomas Jefferson became United States president. About three years later, Mr. Jefferson gave his sixth annual message to Congress—admitting therein that the slaves of African descent called "Negroes" were "the unoffending victims" of "human rights violations." After this admission, enlightened Americans surfaced to formally declare war on the "Race Card Evil" and its "peculiar institution" called "chattel slavery." Chief among those to denounce the evil were literary giants Richard Hildreth and Harriet Beecher-Stowe. Their antislavery writings would signal the dawn of "judgment day"—the day wherein a "plumb line of judgment" would be applied to test the validity of the African slavery "cheap-labor" scheme and its "skin-color, superiority-inferiority" theme. Most importantly, their writings would enlighten and motivate Americans to such a point that they would readily join the fight to put the evil where it rightfully belonged—"in the course of ultimate extinction."

# 4

# Judgment's Plumb Line
# Enter Richard Hildreth
# and Harriet Beecher-Stowe

Thus he showed me…the Lord stood upon a wall made by
a plumbline, with a plumbline in his hand. And the Lord
said…"what seest thou?" And I said, "A plumbline." Then
said the Lord, "Behold, I will set a plumbline in the midst
of my people…I will not again pass by them any more."

—Amos 7:7–8 (KJV)

WHEN THE CONFEDERATION Congress wrote the 1787
Constitution it created the strong central (federal) government
that the new nation needed. However, it also enacted the 1787
Northwest Ordinance, which opened up the new nation's acquired
territory to African Slavery program and its "race-based" doctrine.
The program—called "Chattel Slavery" and "The Peculiar
Institution"—aimed at enslaving "dark-hued" members of the
"70" Nations as a perpetual "cheap-labor" workforce based on the
doctrine that "non-Whites" (Africans, Asians) were "inferior" to
"whites" (caucasians) either by "God's will" or "nature."

The program could only succeed by "legalizing" the big-
business slaveowners' "right" to carry their "cheap-labor"
workforce throughout the nation's newly acquired territory as

the "chattel" or "property" of American Citizens protected by the 1787 Constitution's Comity Clause and Fifth Amendment. However, this "legal" aspect was just another step on the "curse on Ham, Ham uncivilized, whites the original man" ladder that profiteers could climb in order to maximize profits by oppressing "nonwhite" members of the "seventy" nations at the expense of free "white" American wage earners. This truth the Second Continental Congress admitted on 6 July 1775 in its "Declaration of the Causes and Necessity of Taking up Arms" against Great Britain. In their *Documents of American History*, historians Commager and Cantor recounted that the "Declaration" stated,

> If it was possible for men, who exercise their reason to believe, that the divine Author [Creator] of our existence intended a part of the Human Race to hold an Absolute Property in, and an Unbounded Power over others [of the human race], marked out by His infinite goodness and wisdom, as the Objects of a Legal Domination Never Rightfully Resistible, however severe and oppressive, The Inhabitants of These [13] Colonies might at least require from the Parliament of Great Britain some evidence, that this dreadful [Human] Authority over them, has been granted [by the Creator] to that [political] body [of men]. But a Reverence for Our Creator, [the] Principles of Humanity [the Adamite race or "70" nations], and the Dictates of Common Sense, must convince all those who reflect upon the subject, that Government was instituted to Promote the Welfare of Mankind, and ought to be administered for the attainment of that end. (*Docs. of Amer. Hist.*, 92)

Despite this admission, the 1787–1791 Congress framed (wrote) a "Constitution" and "Bill of Rights" that "covertly" contradicted their words; and thereafter passed a 1793 Fugitive Slave Law that "overtly" contradicted Old Testament prohibitions against "kidnapping/enslaving people for profit's sake" and "denying asylum to those who escaped (fled)" from such wrongful imprisonment. Indeed, the biblical prohibitions clearly stated,

> And he that stealeth [kinaps] a man, and selleth him, or if he be found in his [the merchant-owner-trader] hands [as in possessing or receiving stolen goods], he shall surely be put to death. (Exod. 21:16, KJV)

> If a man be found stealing any of his brethren of the children of Israel, and maketh merchandise [commerce] of him, or selleth him, then that thief shall die; and thou shalt put the evil away from among you. (Deut. 24:7, cf. Gen. 37:23–28, 36, KJV)

> Thou shalt not deliver unto his master the servant [slave] which is escaped from his master unto thee: He shall dwell with thee, even among you, in that place which he shall choose in one of thy gates [towns, cities, etc.], where it liketh [suits] him best: thou shalt not oppress him. (Deut. 23:15–16, KJV)

> You shall not hand over to his master a slave who has taken refuge from him with you. Let him live with you wherever he chooses, in any one of your communities that pleases him. Do not molest him. (Deut. 23:16–17, NAB)

> *In any one of your communities*: from this [phrase] it would seem that the slave in question is a fugitive from a foreign country. (NAB note on Deut. 23:17, italics ours)

As said, Congress's "1793 law" contradicted its "1775 Declaration." And the same would be true for the "legal" Acts Congress would later pass in its attempt to end the "international slave trade" enterprise. For example, while it was true that the 1781 Confederation Congress "lacked the power to regulate commerce," such was not true for the 1789 Congress—since the latter had the power "to regulate Commerce with foreign Nations, and among the several States, and with the Indian tribes" (US Const, Art I, Sec 8, Cl 3).

Unfortunately, the 1789 Congress "straddled the fence" when it came to enacting and enforcing laws to end the African slavery evil. This "lack of will power" to end the evil stemmed from the fact that although the Union had declined participation in the "international slave trade" during 1774, and lacked the power to end another nation's participation in it, the 1787 Constitution had admitted the "international" evil into the Union in disguise—and allowed it to function at the State level for almost a quarter of a century (until 1808) (US Const Art I, Sec 9, Cl 1). Thus, the 1789 Congress could only perform "token acts" to "regulate" the evil and found itself passing four Acts prior to 1808 in an effort to end it (during 1794, 1800, 1803, and 1807).

Indeed, on the one hand, Congress upheld the evil for fifteen years with its 1793 Fugitive Slave Act—which law left the matter of catching escaped slaves up to State slaveowners, who paid out-of-pocket for a slave's apprehension and return. On the other hand, Congress tried to suppress the evil for fourteen years with its 1794 International Slave Trade Prohibition Act—which law prohibited (1) "any US ports or shipyards from out-fitting or building ships to introduce slaves into the US", (2) "any US ships from sailing to obtain slaves from Africa or any foreign territory involved in the international slave trade", and (3) "any US ships from having slaves on board" (this would be constantly amended to prohibit people from investing in ships, or serving aboard any domestic or foreign ships, involved in the international trade). These 1793–1794 slavery-related congressional enactments were a few "controversial" mistakes among others that would follow.

For instance, prior to the 1776 Revolution a person born within Britain's "geographical boundary" (the country) or "political sphere of influence" (the Colony) automatically became a natural-born subject (citizen) of the Crown; whereas an immigrant to Britain or her Colonies seeking naturalization (citizenship) needed the Crown's consent. When the "thirteen Colonies" became "Sovereign States" during the 1776–1783

Revolution, in addition to forming their own constitutions some passed their own naturalization laws (CT, GA, NC, NH, and PA did not)—albeit in accordance with Britain's "jus soli" rule. And when the "sovereign states" formed their 1787 Constitution, they gave Congress "exclusive" naturalization power (US Const Art I, Sec 8, Cl 4)—but in accordance with Britain's rule. Unfortunately, because of the African slavery scheme, the rule would cause Congress much controversy.

Indeed, the 26 March 1790 "First Naturalization Law"—called "An act to establish an uniform rule of naturalization"—stated,

> Section 1. *Be it enacted by the Senate and House of Representatives of the United States of America in Congress assembled,* That any alien, being a *free white person,* who shall reside *within the limits and under the jurisdiction* of the United States for the term of two years, *may be admitted to become a citizen* thereof, on application to any common law court of record, in any one of the states wherein he shall have resided for the term of one year at least, and making proof to the satisfaction of such court, that he is a person of good [moral] character, and taking the oath or affirmation prescribed by law, to support the constitution of the United States, which oath or affirmation such court shall administer; and the clerk of such court shall record such application, and the proceedings thereon; and thereupon such person shall be considered *a citizen of the United States.* And the children of such person naturalized, dwelling within the United States, being under the age of twenty-one years at the time of such naturalization, shall also be considered as *citizens of the United States.* And the children of *citizens of the United States,* that may be born beyond [the] sea, or out of the limits of the United States, shall be considered as *natural born citizens* [*of the United States*]:
>
> *Provided,* That the right of [federal, national] citizenship shall not descend to persons whose fathers

have never been resident in the United States[;] *Provided also*, That any person heretofore proscribed by any state, shall be admitted a citizen [of the] aforesaid, except by an act of the legislature of the state in which such person was proscribed. (*1 Statutes At Large* 103, 103–04, Chap. III, Sec. 1, italics ours in part).

On passing this "national" law, the States had to abolish their individual naturalization rules—albeit they retained the right to set "local" residency requirements and "proscribe" or "override" certain individuals for "state" citizenship for good reasons. Unfortunately, Congress made the mistake of structuring the "uniform naturalization rule" statute's language to make a "Race Card Evil" oriented statement—contrary to the Second Continental Congress's 25 June 1778 vote against doing so. This mistake would take more than a century and a half to correct, as noted in the latter-day Supreme Court case entitled *Ozawa v. United States* (1922). Therein it was said:

In 1790, the first naturalization act provided that "[a]ny alien *being a free white person*…may be admitted to become a [US] citizen…" c. 3, 1 Stat. 103. In all of the naturalization acts from 1790 to 1906, the privilege of naturalization was confined to white pe rsons…although the exact wording of the various statutes was not always the same…The language of the naturalization laws from 1790 to 1870 had been uniformly such as to deny the privilege of naturalization to an alien unless he came within the description "free white person." By Sec. 7 of the Act of July 14, 1870, c. 254, 16 Stat. 254, 256, the naturalization laws were "extended to aliens of African nativity and to persons of African descent…" it is urged that we should give to this phrase the meaning which it had in the minds of its original framers in 1790, and that it was employed by them for the sole purpose of excluding the black or African race and the Indians then inhabiting this country.

It may be true that those two races were alone thought of as being excluded, but to say that they were the only ones within the intent of the statute would be to ignore the affirmative form of the legislation. The provision is not that Negroes and Indians shall be *excluded*, but it is, in effect, that only free white persons shall be *included*. The intention was to confer the privileges of citizenship upon that class of persons whom the [founding] fathers knew as white, and to deny it to all who could not be so classified. It is not enough to say that the framers did not have in mind the brown or yellow races of Asia. It is necessary to go farther and be able to say that, had these particular races been suggested, the language of the act would have been so varied as to include them within its privileges.

If it be assumed that the opinion of the framers was that the only persons who would fall outside the designation "white" were Negroes and Indians, this would go no farther than to demonstrate their lack of sufficient information to enable them to forsee precisely who would be excluded by that term in the subsequent administration of the statute. It is not important in construing their words to consider the extent of their ethnological knowledge or whether they thought that, under the statute, the only persons who would be denied naturalization would be Negroes and Indians. It is sufficient to ascertain whom they intended to include, and, having ascertained that, it follows as a necessary corollary that all others are to be excluded. (*Ozawa v. United States*, 260 U.S. 178, 192–96 passim, 1922 "[a]ny" part of text)

Interestingly, the "language" of the 1790 Naturalization Act—inviting "free white aliens or persons" to citizenship, while excluding so-called Negroes ("blacks"), Indians ("reds"), Asians ("browns"), and Orientals ("yellows")—hints that during the Act's construction there existed a "white fear" of being outnumbered by "people of color." This "fear" stemmed from events involving King George III's use of slave marts to intimidate colonists (c. 1699), the French and Indian War (1754–1763), and Ottawa Chief Pontiac's War (1763–66)—events involving people whose labor or land had been usurped. However, the real threat would come from those whom the Act invited to American citizenship—and for five chief reasons!

First, in 1778 an Alliance Treaty was made between America and France against Britain that incurred war debts for both governments. However, when the French Revolution toppled the monarchy (1792–93) and replaced it with a Republic (1789–99), America refused to pay the Republic on the grounds that the treaty had been struck with the monarchy and not the Republic. This sparked hostilities between the two countries.

Second, when America struck the John Jay Treaty with Britain (1794)—which caused her to remain neutral while Austria, Britain, Spain, and other European powers allied against France due to the "Reign of Terror" event (1794)—France felt America violated the 1778 Alliance.

Third, when French privateers seized American merchant ships along the Atlantic Ocean, Carribeans, Indian Ocean, and Mediterranean Sea (1796–97)—apparently in retaliation about the Jay Treaty—this sparked the undeclared naval "quasi war" between America and France (1798–1800) and caused diplomatic talks to cease between the two countries.

Fourth, when prince Charles Maurice de Talleyrand became France's Foreign Minister (July 1797), the John Adams administration sent envoys Charles Pinckney, Elbridge Gerry, and John Marshall to reopen talks with France. However, three French agents suspected of acting on behalf of Mr. Talleyrand—Baron Jean-Conrad Hottinguer (X), Pierre Bellamy (Y), and Lucien Hauteval (Z)—tried to blackmail the envoys into paying over one quarter of a million dollars to resume talks between America and France. This caused diplomatic friction and prompted Talleyrand, who denied any connection with the agents, to personally negotiate with Adams' envoys.

Fifth, not long after America started receiving "free white alien immigrants" from France and Haiti—who fled the political turmoil occurring in both countries—some of them started newspapers to advocate their views and denounce the Adams administration. This aggravated diplomatic friction and suspicion between the two countries.

Outraged by these events (especially the "XYZ Affair"), Congress changed its 1795 Naturalization Act version. About 18 June 1798 the Act—which formerly permitted "free white aliens" who had resided in the United States for five or more years to be admitted to citizenship—was amended to provide that "no white alien" would be admitted state or federal citizenship without first "residing fourteen years in the United States" and "reporting to the local court having jurisdiction to register the individual seeking admission."

Further, taking advantage of the American public's outrage over the "XYZ Affair," the Federalist Party–controlled Congress passed three acts in succession to curb immigrant "expression of political dissent" and "participation in questionable political activity" on penalty of arrest and deportation—namely the Alien (25 June 1798), Alien Enemies (6 July 1798), and Sedition (14 July 1798) Acts.

While these "alien and sedition" acts were allegedly passed to combat "white" French extremist political ideas (called "Jacobinism"), the Federalist Party used them to target and arrest a number of prominent "white" American journalists and writers (mostly of British, French, and Irish descent) who wrote negative critiques about the Adams administration (Aurora news editor Benjamin Franklin Bache, grandson of Benjamin Franklin, being among those arrested). This abuse of the Acts caused a number of American political giants to speak out against such—particularly Thomas Jefferson (then vice president) and James Madison (future president).

In opposition, Mr. Jefferson wrote his "Kentucky Resolution"—a "state's nullification" doctrine (developed by John Calhoun) which asserted that "States could nullify (declare illegal) objectionable federal laws"(Kentucky's legislature passed this); and Mr. Madison wrote his "Virginia Resolution"—a "States Rights" doctrine which asserted that the 1787 Constitution's Tenth Amendment gave States unrestricted "Sovereignty." Although unforeseen at the time, Jefferson and Madison's ideas—written because of a legitimate denouncement of legislative abuse—would become powerful weapons in the arsenal of African Slavery profiteers.

Whether or not Jerfferson had political motives for writing his "Kentucky Resolution" is debatable. What is undebatable is the fact that his Resolution, coupled with the American public's outcry against the abuse of the Alien and Sedition Acts, significantly contributed to his becoming President in 1801 (the year the Acts expired). And about two years thereafter, he concluded a deal with the financially ailing Napoleon Bonaparte to purchase the Louisiana Territory (1803)—which extended US Territory on an east-west axis from the Mississippi River to the Rocky Mountains and on a north-south axis from Canada to the Gulf of Mexico. From this vast territory about eight States would be created by 1867, with seven more States and two Canadian Provinces (Alberta and Saskatchewan) to follow by the early twentieth century.

Like the Northwest Ordinance—which created five "Free" (IL, IN, OH, MI, WI) and three "slave" (AL, MS, TN) states to raise the Union's "free-to-slave" states ratio 12–8—the Louisiana Purchase would create eight states (LA, MO, AR, TX, IA, MN, KS, NB) that would become the battle ground over the inclusion or exclusion of the African Slavery scheme into or out of the Union (the admission of FL, LA, and TX into the Union would play a critical role in the American Civil War a century later, because it would make the "free-to-slave" states ratio 12–11). (*The Great Conspiracy*, 3–5)

Ironically, not long after finalizing the Louisiana Purchase, President Jefferson removed Arthur St. Clair from being the

Northwest Territory's Governor—doing so because he (Jefferson) favored Ohio Statehood, whereas St. Clair opposed it. And about three years later (2 December 1806), Mr. Jefferson gave his Sixth Annual Message to Congress which contained a statement that was counter-productive to proponents of the African Slavery scheme. In their *Documents of American History*, Commager and Cantor recounted that President Jefferson said to Congress, America, and the world:

> "I congratulate you, fellow-citizens, on the approach of the [1808] period at which you may interpose your authority Constitutionally to withdraw the citizens of the United States from all further participation in those violations of Human Rights which have been so long continued on the unoffending inhabitants of Africa." (*Docs. of Amer. Hist.*, 197)

During January 1808, the 1787 Constitution's "international slavery importation prohibition" clause went into effect outlawing the international slave trade. Next, on 2 March 1807, Congress passed its "act to prohibit the importation of slaves" (a parallel to Britain's 1807 Slave Trade Act, passed due to efforts by English Christian abolitionist groups such as George Fox's Quakers and William Wilberforce's Evangelicals). With these prohibitions becoming the "law of the land," many Americans believed the death knell was ringing for the African Slavery "cheap-labor" scheme. However, they were wrong. Once the prohibitions went into effect, the big-business speculators in the evil found ways to get around the laws.

One tactic involved building "clipper ships"—smaller and swifter boats designed to outrun Federal gunboats patrolling to apprehend slave ships and their human cargo; this tactic made Congress pass three Acts after 1808 to end the evil (1818, 1819, and 1820). A second tactic involved starting a "domestic slavery" program—whereby slaves were mated to breed the "cheap-labor" workforce. And a third tactic involved kidnapping unsuspecting "free" people, regardless of skin color or gender, and selling them as "blacks"—alleging that such victims were "escaped slaves" or, if they looked "white," runaway "mulattoes, quadroons, octoroons" (etc.) having "1/4, 1/8, 1/16, 1/32, or 1/64" *Negro* blood.

By 1810 many Americans were fed up with the "Race Card Evil" oriented African Slavery scheme and decided to wage war with it. During that year opponents of the scheme answered both the 1793 Fugitive Slave Law and circumvention of the 1808 Slavery Prohibition Clause by forming the "Underground Railroad System"—a secret organization to help slaves escape and relocate to "free"areas in the United States or bordering countries such as Canada and Mexico. Despite this resistance, in 1818 African Slavery scheme profiteers lobbied for Congress to bring Missouri into the Union as a "slave" state. Congress countered in 1819 by authorizing the president to dispatch armed "African squadrons" to patrol Africa's coastline to stop the illegal-but-still-practiced "international slave trade" at its source (another law parallel to a British Act). Then in 1820 Congress enacted yet another law— citing that Americans caught engaged in the "international" slave trade would be declared "pirates subject to the death penalty."

Unfortunately, during 1820 proponents of the African Slavery scheme won a major victory when Congress passed its "Missouri Compromise" which allowed Misssouri—situated north of the "thirty-six-degree, thirty-minute" latitude slavery prohibition line—to enter the Union as a "slave" state. Next, after hostilities arose between the United States and Mexico when some two hundred Texans were massacred at San Antonio's Alamo Mission during 1836—at a time when Texas was seeking admission into the Union—African slavery proponents won another victory when Texas was admitted as a "slave" state in 1845. Following this, proponents of the "cheap labor" scheme won another victory when war erupted between America and Mexico after Texas was attacked in 1846 due to its admission: Mexico lost the war, was forced to give territory to the Union in 1848, and unwittingly aided American expansionists in extending the "Race Card Evil" oriented agenda disguised as a "Manifest Destiny" program. Said twenty-first-century American historian Mary B. Norton-Alger in *A People and A Nation*,

> The belief that American expansion westward and southward was inevitable, just, and divinely ordained was first labeled manifest destiny by John L. O'Sullivan, editor of the *United States Magazine and Domestic Review*. The annexation of Texas, O'Sullivan wrote in 1945, was "the fulfillment of our manifest destiny to overspread the continent allotted by Providence for the free development of our yearly multiplying millions." Armed with such sentiments, expansionism reached a new fervor in the 1840s.
>
> Since colonial days Americans had hungered for more land. Acquisition of the Louisiana Territory (1803) and Florida (1819) had set the process in motion...As the proportion of Americans living west of the Appalachians grew...both national parties [Democrats and Whigs] joined the popular clamor for expansion. Democrats sought western land to balance urbanization. Enterprising Whigs looked to the new commercial opportunities the West offered. Southerners envisioned the extension of slavery and more slave states.
>
> Fierce national pride spurred the quest for land...In part, racism contributed to manifest destiny as well. The impulse to colonize and develop the West was based on the belief that Euro-Americans could use the land more productively than Native Americans or Hispanics...Euro-Americans viewed Native Americans and Hispanics as inferior peoples, best controlled or conquered. Thus the same racial attitudes that justified discrimination against black people and slavery supported expansion in the West. (Mary Beth Norton-Alger, et. al., *A People and A Nation*: Volume One to 1877, 6th ed., Boston: Houghton Mifflin Co., 2001, 297)

Unknown to Mexico's dictator Antonio Lopez ("Santa Anna"), proponents of the African slavery scheme had a long-range objective of acquiring the territories controlled by both Mexico (Arizona, California, Colorado, Nevada, New Mexico, Texas, Utah, and Wyoming) and Britain (Oregon). These were acquired during President James K. Polk's administration (1845–1849)—by granting Texas statehood (1845), making the Oregon Treaty with Britain (1846), and finally defeating Mexico in war (1846–1848).

At the American-Mexican War's conclusion, Pennsylvania Representative David Wilmot—described as "no friend of black civil and political rights…but a firm supporter of protecting free white men's labor and land ownership across America"—tried to stop slavery's spread into the territories acquired from the Mexico by proposing his "Wilmot Proviso." Although the "Proviso" failed to pass in the House, it gave proponents of the African Slavery scheme the idea to lobby for passage of Congressional acts that would permit the acquired territories to enter the Union as states "with or without slavery" according to the state Constitutions formed.

The "key" to obtaining such Acts was contained in the 1820 Missouri Compromise—since it posed an important legal question concerning the 1787 Constitution and slavery. Indeed, when Missouri first applied for Union statehood, the question arose concerning the Fifth Amemndment right of citizens to own "property"—meaning, whether or not that "right" included "the right to own man as property" ("slaves"). Congress could only answer "yes"—since it had acknowledged such in the 1783 Versailles peace treaty, 1787 Northwest Ordinance, and 1787 Constitution. However, profiteers from the African Slavery scheme were not satisfied with that answer—because the "thirty-six-degree, thirty-minute" slavery prohibition line restricted slavery's northern expansion into the Union. Thus, when Congress passed the bill in 1848 to organize Oregon for statehood based on the 1787 Northwest Ordinance's "slavery prohibition line," and a similar bill in 1849 to organize California with a state constitution "totally prohibiting slavery," Kentucky Representative Henry Clay proposed that Congress pass an act to organize Utah for statehood with a Constitution "with (for) or without (against) slavery" (29 January 1850).

Mr. Clay's proposed act may have been an honest attempt to acquire Utah's statehood in like manner of the Oregon Act. However, his bill contained a number of "questionable" items that upset his proslavery colleagues. Chief among such items were his proposals that Congress abolish African Sslavery in Washington DC and pass a more stringent Fugitive Slave Law for "national" enactment. After wrangling with Clay's proposals during spring and summer, Congress made another controversial "compromise" during fall. On 9 September 1850, Congress admitted California into the Union as a "free" state, but temporarily postponed statehood for New Mexico, Oregon, and Utah. On 18 September 1850, Congress passed Clay's requested Fugitive Slave Law. And finally, on 20 September 1850, Congress abolished the slave trade in Washington DC (effective 1 January 1851)—doing so based on the theory that trafficking ("buying and selling") slaves in the nation's capital was shameful.

In their *Documents of American History*, Commager and Cantor recounted that Congress's "1850 Fugitive Slave Law" did the following

1.) Section 5 made it the duty of all Federal Marshals and Deputy Marshals to "obey and execute all warrants and precepts issued under the provisions of this Act." And:

   a.) Imposed a $1,000 fine on Marshals and Deputy Marshals (federal agents) for failing to enforce the Act.

   b.) Made federal agents subject to civil suit by slavemasters, if the fugitive slave escaped the agent's custody.

   c.) Ordered all citizens to aid and assist in enforcing the Act.

2.) Section 6 used the 1787 Constitution's Article IV, Section 2, Clause 3 to permit slavemasters, or their agents, to cross State lines to apprehend escaped slaves (by obtaining a warrant from local authorities or making a "citizen's arrest").

3.) Section 7 made it a Federal crime for anyone to harbor an escaped slave or prevent-obstruct the slave's apprehension—the violator being civilly liable up to $1,000 or subject to a six-month jail sentence.

4.) Section 10 applied the law to Washington DC.
(*Docs. of Amer. Hist.*, 321–323; Cf. 9 *U.S. Statutes at Large*, 462ff)

Where the "1793 Fugitive Slave Law" only agitated Americans, the "1850 Fugitive Slave Law" infuriated them! While many people did not agree with the African slavery scheme, they ignored the 1793 law because it only affected a state's slaveholding citizens who paid out of pocket for an escaped slave's apprehension and return. However, the 1850 law forced "all" citizens to assist a state-sanctioned cheap-labor workforce scheme for a slaveholding minority's profit—whether or not involved in the slavery business and regardless of religious belief (Christian or secular), political status (free or slave), or region occupied (north or south). Worse, the 1850 Law "criminalized" and "penalized" anyone aiding or harboring an escaped slave—forcing the person to pay "out-of-pocket" costs (fines) for an escaped slave's return to the slaveholder! Consequently, Americans from all walks of life and geographical regions were angered by this "national" sanction of slavery.

Besides this political insult, intelligent "white" Americans were well aware of the potential danger of revolts that resulted from enslaving people—New York's 1712 and 1741 revolts, as well as the 1776 revolt against Britain, being examples of what people disgruntled with "thraldom" would do to be free. And the "revolts" or "conspiracies to revolt" that occurred during the first quarter of the 1800s were other examples: the Gabriel plot (1800), Sancho plot (1802), Mecklenburg plot (1802), Edgefield District plot (1810), Jefferson Parish Revolt (1811), Charleston plot (1822), Denmark Vessey plot (1822), Georgetown District plot (1829), West Feliciana Parish plot (1829), and Nat Turner Revolt (1831) being some that made many uninvolved citizens uneasy about slavery. (*Runaway Slaves*: *Rebels on the Plantation*, 11–13, 274–76, 291)

More important than the fear of slave conspiracies or revolts was the outrage many "white" Americans felt, in both the North and South, about the "Constitutional" rights of proslavery citizens outweighing those of antislavery citizens. And because most slaveholders believed such was the case, they saw nothing wrong with violating the rights of free "whites" who opposed the "Race Card Evil" oriented program. Indeed, examples such as the Alton, Illinois mob-murder of *Alton Observer* editor and slavery abolitionist Elijah P. Lovejoy for his antislavery writings (1837), and the Norfolk, Virginia, arrest-trial-conviction of Mrs. Margaret Douglas for teaching free "black" children to read (1853)—despite the fact that she hailed from a slaveholding family and had slaves herself—seemed to validate the belief that slaveowners' rights were more important than those of non-slaveowners. Undoubtedly, such events alarmed informed free "white" Americans and heightened their agitation over the 1850 Fugitive Slave Act.

Ironically enough, some slave dealers-traders-owners disagreed with Henry Clay's 1850 Compromise and felt that Congress had no power to abolish the slave trade or slavery in the nation's capital without their consent. Nor did they think that the federal government could restrict the "right" to take their "human" property anywhere in the United States—since Congress and the 1787 Constitution sanctioned slavery, and because America belonged to the "people" (citizens). Thus, on 10 June 1850 a Convention of nine states convened at Nashville, Tennessee, to condemn the federal government's efforts to restrict the African slavery scheme. Then on 10 December 1850 a second convention convened at Milledgeville, Georgia, to condemn both Clay's Compromise and the government's attempt to abolish slavery in the capital or anywhere else. Accordingly, both proponents and opponents of the African slavery scheme were discontent with the 1850 compromise.

However, sincere Christians could not agree that a "legal" foundation existed to "justify" enslaving any segment of humanity. Nor could they agree that a "religious" foundation existed in the Bible to prove that "God authorized perpetual slavery"— particularly in light of "questionable" biblical passages ascribed to the Apostle Paul that clearly contradicted those ascribed to Jesus of Nazareth. For instance

> Jesus: No one can serve two masters. He will either hate one and love the other, or be devoted to one and dispise the other. You cannot serve God and mammon [property, wealth]. (Matt. 6:24; cf. Exod. 20:1–6, KJV)

> Jesus: Neither be you called masters: for one is your Master, even Christ. (Matt. 23:10, KJV)

> Paul: Slaves, be obient to your human masters with fear and trembling, in sincerity of heart, as to[ward] Christ, not only when being watched, as currying favor, but as slaves of Christ, doing the will of God from the heart willingly by serving the Lord and not human beings. (Eph. 6:5–7, KJV; cf. Col 3:22, NAB)

> Paul: Slaves, are to be under the control of their masters in all respects, giving them satisfaction, not talking back to them or stealing from them, but exhibiting complete good faith, so as to adorn the doctrine of God [i.e., "Jesus"] our savior in every way. (Tit. 2:9–10, NAB)

> Paul: Slaves, be subject to your masters with all reverence, not only to those who are good and equitable but also to those who are perverse. (1 Pet. 2:18, NAB)

Outraged at the "legal" and "religious" justifications for a minority to blatantly violate of the rights of a majority of Americans for personal profit, the Underground Railroad System stepped up operations in defiance of the 1850 law and ushered onto the American scene an international cast of people to contest the African Slavery scheme: Northern and Southern Americans, British subjects, Canadians, Frenchmen, Hispanics, Native Americans, free-born blacks and whites, slaves and former slaves, business people, doctors, nurses, judges, lawyers, men, women, Abolitionists, Baptists, Congregationalists, Quakers, Reformed Presbyterians, Wesleyans, and writers to name a few; all risking career, family, fortune, freedom, and life to help slaves escape and reach safe havens in America, Canada, Mexico, and abroad. To be sure, war had been officially declared on the "Race Card Evil" oriented scheme by members of the "seventy" nations. And this "revolution" would mark a first in the annals of recorded history—where a united effort by enlightened Western world humanity would be undertaken in the United States to put the evil "in the course of ultimate extinction."

On the American scene appeared literary men and women, wielding the pen's power, to enlighten people about the evil that had infected the new nation. Chief among such literary giants were Richard Hildreth and Harrriet Beecher-Stowe—both of whom were "white," hailed from religious oriented families, had extensive religious and secular educations, and wrote novels aimed at raising public awareness about the evils of the African slavery scheme.

During 1836, twenty-nine-year-old Massachusetts native Richard Hildreth wrote his novel entitled *The Slave, or Memoirs of a Fugitive*—the first book written to present the American antislavery view. Therein Mr. Hildreth expressed a general diapproval of the "peculiar institution" or "slavery" that was characteristic of many Americans of his era. And significantly, he stated a number of "negative" effects produced on people infected or affected by the slavery evil. Indeed, when writing Mr. Hildreth's biographical sketch for the Unitarian Universalist Historical Society, twenty-first-century American author Lynn Gordon Hughes noted,

> Though not the first American novel to express disapproval of slavery, *The Slave* was the first written specifically to present an antislavery argument. The story illustrates the many ways slavery exerted a corrupting influence over the morals of masters and slaves alike. Hildreth was one of the very few white people of his (or any) era free enough from racism to truly imagine what it would be like to be a slave. The slaves he portrays are neither brutes nor saints, but complex human beings doing their limited best to survive in an impossible situation. *The Slave* is remarkably free from the racist assumptions that marred many other antislavery works by white people, even committed abolitionists. In one of the most powerful moments in the book, the hero, Archy, who had felt superior to his fellow slaves because of his "white blood," realizes the extent to which he has been complicit in the racism of his culture when he comes to admire the dark-skinned slave who leads a band of runaways. The abolitionist leader Wendell Philips remarked that *The Slave* "owed its want of success to no lack of genius, but only to the fact that it was born out of due time." (Lynn Gordon Hughes, "Richard Hildreth," Unitarian Universalist Historical Society, 1999, p. 2 of 6, http://www25.uua.org/uuhs/duub/articles/ richardhildreth.html. Retrieved 19 October 2010)

Whereas Mr. Hildreth's antislavery novel was before its time, during 1852 41–year-old Connecticut native Harriet Beecher-Stowe published her antislavery novel, entitled *Uncle Tom's Cabin* or *Life Among the Lowly*, that was right on time. Indeed, not only was her book a timely and groundbreaking serious venture for a "white female writer" to undertake during her era but,on meeting

Honest Abe in 1863, it earned her the Lincoln-given title of being "the little lady who made this big [Civil] War."

When Mrs. Stowe published her book in March 1852, she had no idea that it would sell in record-making numbers by June of the year; nor did she think that her work would seriously impact on the highest levels of American government. However, *Uncle Tom's Cabin* was so realistic of events during Harriet's era that, coupled with the hostilities resulting from attempts to "nationalize" and "spread" the "Race Card Evil" oriented African Slavery scheme, her book helped create the political party that came to be called the "Independent Democrats" and "Republican or Grand Old Party" (GOP)—a party that launched a Whig lawyer named Abraham Lincoln into political stardom and helped enlighten both Americans and the world at large about the true identity of the "Race Card Evil" oriented African slavery scheme agenda.

Indeed, while *Uncle Tom's Cabin* addressed many facets of daily slave-master versus slave life, Harriet's book brilliantly revealed the true character of the African slavery scheme through six chief episodes: a chance encounter between an escaped slave and his former employer, both with different views on slavery; another chance encounter between two priests sailing on the Ohio River, both with different religious views on slavery; and four from a planned encounter (visit) between two cousins, hailing from different areas of the United States (North and South) and having different views on slavery ("anti" vs. "pro"). Undoubtedly, many literate people of Harriet's era were quite impressed, even if angered, by her keen insight into and presentation of slavery's true nature and identity. Nevertheless, her words rang true.

In her first episode, entitled "In Which Property Gets into an Improper State of Mind," Harriet illustrated how both "law" and "biblical scripture" were used (or misused) to validate the "chattel" slavery scheme. This she did through a meeting between two "Kentucky" characters—a "black" runaway slave, George Harris, and his former "White" employer, Mr. Wilson. After George escaped from his owner, he encountered Mr. Wilson aboard a boat and the following verbal exchange took place:

Mr. Wilson: Well, George, I suppose you're running away—leaving your lawful master…Why, to see you, as it were, setting yourself in opposition to the laws of your country.

George: My country! What country have I, but the grave…

Mr. Wilson: Why, George…this way of talking is wicked—unscriptural. George, you've got a hard master…But you know how the Angel commanded Hagar to return to her mistress [Sarah], and submit herself [Gen. 16:7–9, KJV]…and the Apostle [Paul] sent back Onesimus to his master [at Colossae; Philemon 1:10–12, 16, KJV]; cf. [Colossians 4:7–9, KJV].

George: Don't quote Bible at me that way, Mr. Wilson…(Harriet Beecher-Stowe, *Uncle Tom's Cabin* or *Life Among the Lowly*, New York: Random House, Inc., 1996 [originally 1852], 156–57, dialogue form ours).

In her second episode, entitled "Select Incidents of Lawful Trade," Harriet skillfully attacked the *Genesis* 9 story used to validate "chattel" slavery—doing so through a conversation between two priests of differing religious views ("curse on Ham" vs. "Golden Rule"), John a drover, and Haley a slave trader (with Uncle Tom in tow) as they all sailed down the Ohio River:

Priest number 1: It is undoubtedly the intention of Providence [God] that the African race should be servants—kept in a low condition…"Cursed be Canaan; a servant of servants shall he be," the Scripture says [Gen. 9:25, KJV].

Drover John: I say, stranger, is that [there] what that text means?

Priest number 1: Undoubtedly. It pleased Providence, for some inscrutable reason, to doom the race to bondage, ages ago; and we must not set up our opinion against that.

Drover John: Well, then, we'll all go ahead and buy up niggers, if that's the way of Providence—won't we, squire? Yes, we must all be resigned to the decrees of Providence. Niggers must be sold, and trucked around, and kept under [foot]; it's what they's made for. Appears like this here view's quite refreshing, ain't it, stranger?

Trader Haley: I never thought on it. I couldn't have said as much, myself; I [have] no learning [education]. I took up the [slave] trade just to make a living; if [it ain't] right, I calculated [planned] to repent on it in time, [you] know.

Priest number 2: "All things whatsoever ye would that men should do unto you, do ye even so unto them." I suppose that [Matt. 7:12, KJV] is [also] Scripture, as much as "Cursed be Canaan."

Drover John: Well, it seems quite as plain a text, stranger, to poor fellows like us, now. Both them there chaps [are] parsons [priests]? I say, now, there's [a] difference [of opinion] in parsons, ain't there? "Cursed be Canaan" don't seem to go down [well] with this one, does it? (Ibid., 176–78)

In her third episode, taken from the chapter entitled "Miss Ophelia's Experiences and Opinions Continued," Harriet revealed the real purpose of the "Race Card Evil" oriented African slavery scheme. This she did through a conversation between two cousins— Augustine St. Clare (Uncle Tom's second owner who was a Louisiana resident) and Ophelia (a visiting female who was a Vermont resident). When debating about the African Slavery subject, the following exchange ensued:

Ophelia: O' Augustine, you are a sad rattle-brain!

Augustine: Am I? Well, so I am, I suppose; but for once I will be serious…When, in the course of human events, it becomes necessary for a fellow to hold two or three dozen of his fellow-worms in captivity…

Ophelia: I don't see that you are growing more serious.

Augustine: Wait, I'm coming on, you'll hear. The short of the matter is, cousin…[That] on this abstract question of slavery there can, as I think, be but one opinion. Planters who have money to make by it, clergymen who have planters to please, politicians who want to rule by it—[all] may warp and bend language and ethics to a degree that shall astonish the world at their ingenuity; they can press nature and the Bible, and nobody knows what else, into the service [cause]; but, after all, neither they nor the world believe in it one particle the more. It [Slavery] comes from the devil. That's the short of it—and, to my mind, it's a pretty respectable specimen of what he can do in his own line. (Ibid., 330–31)

In her fourth episode, Harriet showed through the cousins' debate the true reason why the African slavery scheme was implemented:

Augustine: This cursed business, accursed of God and man, what is it? Strip it of all its ornaments [theories], run it down to the root and nucleus of the whole, and what is it? Why, because my brother Quashy is ignorant and weak, and I am intelligent and strong, because I know how, and can do it—therefore, I may steal all he has, keep it, and give him only such and so much as suits my fancy. Whatever is too hard, too dirty, too disagreeable, for me, I may set Quashy to doing [it]. Because I don't like to work, Quashy shall work. Because the sun burns me, Quashy shall stay in the sun. Quashy shall earn the money, and I will spend it. Quashy shall lie down in every puddle, [so] that I may walk over dry-shod. Quashy shall do my will, and not his, all the days of his mortal life, and have such chance of getting [in]to heaven, at last, as I find convenient. This I take to be about what slavery is. I defy anybody on earth to read our Slave-Code, as it stands in our law books, and make anything else of it.

Ophelia: I'm sure you've said enough. I never, in my life, heard anything like this, even at [in] the North. (Ibid., 331–32)

Understandably, neither Ophelia nor most people of her era had ever heard such "bare facts" about the African slavery program. Still, Harriet did not stop with this point. In her fifth episode, she allowed her character Augustine to continue his stream of thought in order to make a very important analogy concerning the "Race Card Evil's" true agenda—one that escaped the notice of most people. This analogy involved the haunting "similarity" between ideas expressed in the African slavery scheme and ideas such as "aristocratic rule," "divine right of kings to rule," "extreme capitalism," "imperialism," "manifest destiny," and the "white man's burden" to name a few:

Augustine: I think quite sensibly, that the American planter is only doing, in another form, what the English aristocracy and capitalists are doing by [to] the lower [working] classes; that is, I take it, appropriating [exploiting] them, body and bone, soul and spirit, to their use and convenience…

Ophelia: How in the world can the two things be compared? The English laborer is not sold, traded, parted from his family, whipped.

Augustine: He [the employee] is as much at the will of his employer as if he were sold to him. The slave-owner can whip his refractory slave to death—the capitalist can starve him [the free employee or laborer] to death. As to family security, it is hard to say which [system] is the worst—to have one's children sold, or see them starve to death at home. (Ibid., 340–41)

Finally, in her sixth episode, Harriet allowed Augustine to sum the slavery matter up in "global" terms—with such clarity that her readers had no other alternative than to face the real deal about man in his dealings with his fellow man the world over:

Augustine: I'll say, besides, that ours is the more bold and palpable infringement of human rights; actually buying a man up, like a horse, looking at his teeth, cracking his joints, and trying his paces, and then paying down for him—having speculators, breeders, traders, and brokers in human bodies and souls sets the thing before the eyes of the civilized world in a more tangible form, though the thing done be, after all, in its nature, the same; that is, appropriating one set of human beings to the use and improvement of another [set of human beings] without any regard to their own [well-being].

Ophelia: I never thought of the matter in this light. (Ibid., 341)

About five years after publishing *Uncle Tom's Cabin*, Mrs. Stowe's analysis of the "Race Card Evil's" true agenda, masked as the African slavery scheme, was validated. In 1857, a nine-judge US Supreme Court panel composed of five members hailing from Southern slaveholding States—Benjamin R. Curtis (MA), James M. Wayne (GA), John A. Campbell (AL), John Catron (TN), John McClean (OH), Peter V. Daniel (VA), Robert C. Grier (PA), Roger B. Taney (MD), and Samuel Nelson (NY)— heard a legal case filed on behalf of Dred Scott (originally named "Sam," but took on his older brother's name "Dred"), a person of African American descent held as a "Negro" slave.

The case arose because Mr. Scott was (1) born into slavery to Peter Blow's family in Southampton County, Virginia (about 1799); (2) sold by Peter to St. Louis, Missouri-based US Army Surgeon John Emerson (between 1830–1832, Peter moving there about 1830 and dying in 1832); and (3) taken by Emerson from Jefferson Barracks in Missouri (a slave state) to Fort Armstrong (Rock Island) in Illinois (a free state, 1833), then to Fort Snelling in Wisconsin (a free territory; modern Minnesota, 1836), back to Missouri (1838), back to Wisconsin (1838), and finally to Missouri (1840)— thus twice crossing the "thirty-six-degree, thirty-minute" slavery prohibition line set by Congress's 1820 Missouri Compromise.

Three years after John Emerson died (29 December 1843), Dred and Harriet (Robinson) Scott—seeking to obtain freedom for their daughters Eliza (born 1838) and Lizzie (born 1840)—filed "freedom suits" against Emerson's widow, Mrs. Eliza Irene Sanford-Emerson, in the Circuit Court for St. Loius County, Missouri (*Dred-Harriet Scott v. Irene Emerson*, Cir. Ct. St. Louis Co., MO), (6 April 1846; Francis B. Murdoch, representing the Scotts). The suits—"wrongful enslavement" petitions that both free US territories and slave states allowed slaves to file—were based on the long-used Missouri State Supreme Court rule that said "once free, always free," which meant that "slavery did not reattach, once slavemasters took slaves into free US territories or states and returned to areas where slavery was legal" (*Winny v. Whitesides*, MO Sup. Ct., 1824).

Losing their first jury trial due to grocery store owner Samuel Russell's hearsay testimony about Irene's ownership of them (June 1847), the Scotts' third attorney, Samuel Mansfield Bay (Charles Drake being their second about 10–13 May 1847), motioned for Judge Alexander Hamilton to grant them a new trial based on that technicality, which he did in December (*Scott v. Irene Emerson*, Cir. Ct. St. Louis Co., MO, 30 June 1847; 2 December 1847). In turn, Irene's attorney (George Goode) appealed the ruling to Missouri's Supreme Court; which was heard and denied the following year (*Emerson v. Scott*, MO Sup. Ct., 30 June 1848).

Proceeding with their second trial (Judge Hamilton presiding), the jury ruled in favor of the Scott family seeing as (1) Dred was actually free since December 1833 (via the 1787 Northwest Ordinance) and May 1836 (via the 1820 Missouri Compromise), when Dr. Emerson respectively reported to Fort Armstrong and Fort Snelling; (2) Harriet was free at least since 1835–36, when she was at Fort Snelling and married Dred while a teenage slave of Major Lawrence Taliaferro (the Wisconsin Territory's Indian Agent); (3) Eliza was born free on the *Gipsey* steamer, north of the "thirty-six-degree, thirty-minute" slavery prohibition line (1838);

and (4) Lizzie, although born in Missouri at Jefferson Barracks (1840), was actually born to free parents according to both the 1787 Northwest Ordinance and 1820 Missouri Compromise (*Scott v. Emerson*, 1849–50). However, Mrs. Emerson appealed to Missouri's Supreme Court (*Emerson v. Scott*, 1850)—which denied the Scott family freedom by disregarding Missouri's twenty-eight-year-old *Winny* rule, as well as Congress's 1787 and 1820 slavery prohibition laws (*Scott v. Emerson*, MO Sup. Ct., 22 March 1852).

In view of this outcome the Scott family's attorney(s)—using the fact that Irene's New York-based brother (John F. A. Sanford) claimed ownership of the Missouri-based Scotts, and using the 1787 Constitution's "Diverse Citizenship" and "Supreme Court Appellate Jurisdiction" Clauses (Article III, Section 1 and Section 2 (Clauses 1–2)—then filed suit against Mr. Sanford in Missouri's federal district court (erroneously styled *Scott v. Sandford*, US Dist. Ct., MO, 2 November 1853); which they lost (15 May 1854), and next appealed to the US Supreme Court for resolution (*Dred Scott v. John F. A. Sandford*, 60 U.S. 393) (1856).

"Missouri State Archives: Missouri's Dred Scott Case, 1846–1857," http://www.sos.mo.gov/archives/resources/africanamerican/scott/scott.asp, pp. 1–17. Retrieved 18 January 2015; "The Revised Dred Scott Case Collection: Dred Scott Chronology," http://digital.wustl.edu/dredscott/chronology.html, pp. 1–2. Retrieved 18 January 2015; "The Revised Dred Scott Case Collection: Second Circuit Court Case, 1849–1857," http://digital.wustl.edu/dredscott/circuit2.html, pp. 1–2. Retrieved 18 January 2015; *Wkipedia*, s.v., "Dred Scott," http://en.wikipedia.org/wiki/Dred_Scott, pp. 1–2. Retrieved 18 January 2015; *Wikipedia*, s.v., "Freedom suit," http://en.wikipedia.org/wiki/Freedom_suit, pp. 1, 2. Retrieved 18 January 2015; *Scott v. Sandford*, 60 U.S. 393 (1856), U.S. Supreme Court Syllabus, 6–9, http://supreme.justia.com/cases/federal/us/60/393/. Retrieved 18 January 2015.

At that time the US Supreme Court needed to hear the Scott family's case because it involved (a) the right of decendants of Africans or African slaves to sue in courts as "citizens" of either a state or the United States (hence a "Naturalization" issue); (b) Congress's legal authority to enact the 1787 Northwest Ordinance and the 1820 Missouri Compromise; and (c) either legalizing or outlawing African Slavery to spread or extinguish the "Race Card Evil" oriented scheme throughout the nation's territory.

Although eight separate opinions were filed when the US Supreme Court made its "7 to 2" ruling against the Scott family, most significant among them were those written by Maryland's Roger B. Taney and Massachusett's Benjamin R. Curtis—since their "opinions" addressed the African slavery issue from the standpoint of state and federal "citizenship" for free or slave American-born descendants of people labeled "Negroes." Thus, the 1857 *Dred Scott* decision would launch *Uncle Tom's Cabin*, America's political (civil) history, America's religious (moral) character, and the "Race Card Evil's" true identity into the national and international spotlights just five years after Harriet's book was published.

Ruling against Scott, Chief Justice Roger B. Taney wrote a "majority" court opinion (decision) based on the 1787 Constitution's covert protection of the African slavery program and Congress's 1790 Naturalization Act—the latter which stated "[a]ny alien *being a free white person*…may be admitted to become a citizen." However, Mr. Taney's ruling was based on incorrect (unsound) facts: factually, historically, legally, and politically. Worse, he stacked (loaded) his ruling with "Race Card" oriented views (dogma) derived from the bogus "Ham cursed and Ham the uncivilized black race" doctrines—doing so while ruling that Congress had no authority to pass the 1787 Northwest Ordinance and 1820 Missouri Compromise to exclude, prohibit, or regulate slavery in the Union.

With respect to enslaved Africans labeled "Negroes" in the British-American Colonies or Colonies turned states, Mr. Taney ruled that neither they nor their "American-born" descendants, whether free or not, could become "citizens" of the States or the United States according to the word's meaning as used in the 1787 Constitution. Said he,

> The [legal] Question is simply this: Can a Negro, whose ancestors were imported into this country and sold as slaves, become a member of the political community formed and brought into existence by the [1787] Constitution of the United States…The only matter in issue before the Court, therefore, is, whether the descendants of such slaves, when they shall be emancipated, or who are born of parents who had become free before their birth, are citizens of a State, in the sense in which the word "citizen" is used in the [1787] Constitution of the United States. (*Scott vs. Sandford*, 60 U.S. 393, 403, 1856, Decided March 1857).

According to Mr. Taney, two questions were involved in Mr. Scott's case: (1) whether the 1820 Missouri Compromise "slavery prohibition line" was constitutionally legal, and (2) whether so-called "Negroes" were, or could become, "citizens" in the individual political communities called "the several states"— and thus become national "citizens" in the political community collectively called "the United States" or "America."

On deciding the second question Mr. Taney—reasoning from the "particular case" (the Scott family) to the "general case" (all people called "Negroes")—tried to give the 1787 Constitution's use of the words *citizens* and *people* a mystical and equivalent political meaning not found in its use of the word *person*. Said he,

> The words "People of the United States" and "Citizens" are synonymous terms, and means the same thing. They both describe the political body, who, according to our Republican institutions, form the sovereignty, and who hold the power and conduct the government through their Representatives…The Question before us is, whether the

class of Persons described…compose a portion of this People, and are constituent members of this sovereignty. (Id., 60 U.S. 393, 404)

Mr. Taney then gave his reasons why the "class of people" called "Negroes" or "slaves" under the Constitution's euphemistic term *persons*, could not be "citizens" in either the "state" or "national" (federal) sense. But when doing so, Mr. Taney based his reasoning on the bogus "*Genesis* 9, Johann Boemus-Johann Blumenbach" teachings that were really the same as King George III's "divine right of Kings to Rule-Perpetual Allegiance" doctrines. Said he:

> We [I] think they [blacks, Negroes] are not [citizens], and that they are not included, and were not intended to be included, under the word "Citizen" in the [1787] Constitution…On the contrary, they were at that time [1787] considered as a subordinate and inferior class of beings, who had been subjugated by the dominant [white] race, and whether emancipated or not, yet remained subject [in perpetual allegiance] to their [white] authority, and had no rights or privileges but such as those [whites] who held the power and the government might choose to grant them. (Id., 60 U.S.393, 404–05)

After stating this, Mr. Taney referred to the 1776 Declaration of Independence and 1787 Constitutional Convention eras to support his views—but accused the political leaders of those eras of making the political decision to permanently exclude the alleged "inferior race" from "state" and "federal" citizenship. Said he,

> It is not the province of the Court to decide upon the justice or injustice, the policy or impolicy, of these laws. The decision of that question belonged to the political or lawmaking power, to those who formed the sovereignty and framed the Constitution. The duty of the Court is to

interpret the instrument they have framed with the best lights we can obtain on the subject, and to administer it as we find it, according to its true intent and meaning when it was adopted. (Id., 60 U.S. 393, 405)

It is difficult at this day to realize the state of public opinion in relation to that unfortunate race, which prevailed in the civilized and enlightened portions of the world at the time of the Declaration of Independence, and when the [1787] Constitution of the United States was formed and adopted. But the public history of every European nation displays it in a manner too plain to be mistaken. (Id., 60 U.S. 393, 407)

Knowing that his statements were "nonsense," Justice Taney used the "white man's burden" doctrine to uphold his views about the thoughts and actions he ascribed to the First and Second Continental Congresses. Said he,

They [blacks, Negroes] had for more than a century before [1787] been regarded as beings of an inferior order; and altogether unfit to associate with the white race, either in social or political relations, and so far inferior, that they had no rights which the white man was bound to respect; and that the negro might justly and lawfully be reduced to slavery for his benefit. He [the Negro] was bought and sold, and treated as an ordinary article of merchandise and traffic; whenever a profit could be made by it. This opinion was at that time fixed and universal in the civilized portions of the white race. It was regarded as an axiom in morals as well as in politics, which no one thought of disputing, or supposed to be open to dispute, and men in every grade and position in society daily and habitually acted upon it in their private pursuits, as well as in matters of public concern [business, economics, education, politics, etc.], without doubting for a moment the correctness of this opinion. (Id., 60 U.S. 393, 407)

Yet after giving his factually, historically, legally incorrect (unsound) views to validate what Uncle Tom's Augustine St. Clare character called "the forceful appropriation of Quashy's labor," and after trying to "bend and warp" the political history of America's Colonial, Confederation, and Constitutional eras in an attempt to "exclude" American-born descendants of Africans from "the political community formed during the framing of the [1774–1787] Union," Chief Justice Taney contradictorily admitted,

> It is true [that], every person, and every class and description of persons, who were at the time of the adoption of the [1787] Constitution recognized as Citizens in the Several States, became also Citizens of this new political body [the United States]; but none other; It was formed by them, and for them and their posterity, but for no one else. And the personal rights and privileges guarantied [sic] to Citizens of this new sovereignty were intended to embrace those only who were members of the Several State Communities, or who should afterwards, by [Jus Soli] birthright or otherwise [naturalization], become members according to the provisions of the [1787] Constitution and the principles on which it was founded. It was the union of those who were at that time members of distinct and separate political communities into one political family, whose power, for certain specified purposes, was to extend over the whole territory of the United States. And it gave each Citizen rights and privileges outside of his State which he did not before possess, and placed him in every other State upon a perfect equality with its own Citizens as to rights of person and rights of property; it made him a Citizen of the United States. (Id., 60 U.S. 393, 406–07)

No doubt Mr. Taney found his ruling amusing. Indeed, while little is said about his "personal" views on the "slavery issue," Mr. Taney was said to have (a) frequently stood in line behind his own slaves at Church Communion, (b) freed his own slaves at considerable cost to himself years before giving his 1857 *Dred Scott* Opinion, and (c) admitted that the African slavery scheme was "an evil" and "a blot on the nation's character." Thus, Chief Justice Taney was actually rendering a "majority" court opinion for "political," not "personal," reasons. However, Justice Benjamin R. Curtis refused to "color" the legal issue with false facts.

Associate Justice Curtis wrote a factually, historically, legally correct (sound) "minority" court dissenting opinion that did not "slant" the real deal about America's Colonial, Confederation, and Constitutional eras as they related to Citizenship requirements for "all" Americans. Beginning his dissent by stating the 1787 Constitution's phrase "Citizens of the United States at the time of the adoption of the Constitution," Mr. Curtis then stated that the phrase was found in the Constitution's Article II, Section 1, Clause 5. By stating this, Justice Curtis revealed that Chief Justice Taney (as well as the entire Supreme Court) "knew" about Clause 5 and had "purposely avoided citing it" in his "majority" opinion in order to slant the real deal about the term "Citizen" which the 1787 Constitution used in four chief places:

1.) Article I, Section 2, Clause 2 where the requirements for holding House of Representatives office are: 25 years of age, 7 years "a citizen of the United States," and "an inhabitant of the State in which one seeks office."

2.) Article I, Section 3, Clause 3 where the requirements for holding Senate office are: 30 years of age, 9 years "a citizen of the United States," and "an inhabitant of the State in which one seeks office."

3.) Article II, Section 1, Clause 5 where the requirements for holding U.S. President office are: 35 years of age, "a natural born citizen of the United States" or "a citizen of the United States at the time of the adoption of the [1787] Constitution," and "14 years residence within the United States."

4.) Article IV, Section 2, Clause 1 where the "Comity Clause" guarantees "The citizens of each State shall be entitled to all Privileges and Immunities of Citizens in the several States."

In opposition to Mr. Taney's view about the 1787 Constitution's use of the term *citizen* and its meaing, Justice Curtis said respecting Article II, Section 1, Clause 5:

I dissent from the opinion pronounced by the Chief Justice, and from the judgment which the Majority of the Court think proper to render in this case…The *1st Section* of the *2d Article* of the Constitution uses the language, "a *Citizen* of the United States *at the time of the adoption of the Constitution*." One mode of approaching this Question is to inquire who were *Citizens* of the United States *at the time of the adoption of the Constitution.*

*Citizens* of the United States *at the time of the adoption of the Constitution* can have been no other than *Citizens* of the United States *under the Confederation.* By the [1781] *Articles of Confederation*, a government was organized, the style whereof was, "The United States of America." This [1781] government was in existence when the [1787] Constitutiton was framed and proposed for adoption, and was to be superseded [replaced] by the new government of the United States of America, organized under the [1787] Constitution.

When, therefore, the Constitution speaks of *Citizenship of the United States,* existing at the time of the adoption of the [1787] Constitution, it must necessarily refer to *Citizenship* under the [1781] government which existed prior to and at the time of such [1787] adoption…it may safely be said that the *Citizens of the Several States* were *Citizens of the United States under the* [1781] *Confederation.* (*Scott v. Sandford*, 60 U.S. 393, 564 and 571–72, italics ours)

After defining the phrase "Citizen…at the time of the doption of the Constitution" in terms of "Citizens…under the Articles of Confederation," Justice Curtis next explained the *powers* and *limitations* of the Confederation government—the grants and restrictions that weakened and jeopardized its existence during the 1776–1783 Revolution against Britain. And on explaining the Confederation's abilities and disabilities, Mr. Curtis then explained the political differences between "Citizenship in the [individual] Several States" and "Citizenship in the [united] Confederation." Said he,

> That [1781–1789] government was simply *a Confederacy of the Several States*, possessing a few defined powers over subjects of general concern, each State retaining every power, jurisdiction, and right, not expressly delegated to the United States in Congress Assembled. And *no power was thus delegated to the government* of the Confederation, *to Act on any Question of Citizenship, or to make any rules in respect thereto*. The whole matter was left to stand upon the action of the Several States, and to the natural consequences of such action, that *the Citizens of each State* should be *Citizens of that Confederacy* into which that State had entered, the style whereof was, "The United States of America." (Id., 60 U.S. 393, 572, italics ours)

After stating that *citizenship* was a matter left solely up to the individual state's discretion during the 1781–1789 Confederation era, Justice Curtis then addressed the issue of the "type of people" who were or were not "admitted to citizenship" within the governments of both the individual states and the Confederation. More specifically, he addressed the "question" of whether or not any "American-born descendants of Africans" held as "Negro" slaves were "granted citizenship" in either State or National governments prior to and during the 1787–1789 Constitutional era. Said he,

> To determine whether any free persons, descended from Africans held in Slavery, were Citizens of the United States under the [1781–1789] Confederation,

and consequently at the time of the adoption of the
[1787–1789] Constitution of the United States, it is only
necessary to show whether any such persons were Citizens
of either of the States under the [1781] Confederation at
the time of the adoption of the [1787] Constitution.

Of this there can be no doubt. At the time of the
ratification of the Articles of Confederation, all free
native-born inhabitants of the States of New Hampshire,
Massachusetts, New York, New Jersey, and North
Carolina, though descended from African slaves, were not
only Citizens of those States, but such of them as had the
other necessary qualifications possessed the franchise of
electors on equal terms with other ["white"] Citizens. (Id.,
60 U.S. 393, 572–73)

By his statement Justice Curtis meant that the "Several
States" were "thirteen (13) separate (individual) and sovereign
(politically independent) countries or nations" during the 1776–
1789 era—they having been the "thirteen (13) British-American
Colonies" that formed a political family called "the Union" during
the 1774 Articles of Association era and, on or after 4 July 1776,
had formed their "individual state constitutions" under the larger
political family called the "United States of America."

By this Justice Curtis also meant that although the Colonies
turned states collectively called themselves the "United States of
America," their "sovereign and separate political characters" existed
during (a) the ratification of the 1781 Articles of Confederation,
(b) the signing of the 1783 Versailles peace treaty with Britain,
and (c). the start of the 1787 Constitution's ratification process
(partly completed in 1788, then finally with the Bill of Rights'
inclusion in 1791). However, unrestricted "state" (individual)
sovereignty ceased when the "national" (united) government
(Congress, presidential office, US Supreme Court) officially
started on 4 March 1789. Thus the 1787 Constitution was the
start of "central, strong, united" national government and the end
of "sovereign, weak, individual" state governments.

Accordingly, by his statement Justice Curtis meant that in order to determine whether or not the 1787 Constitution "excluded American-born descendants of African slaves from citizenship," at either the state or national levels of government, one had to examine that Constitution's forerunner, the "1781–1789" Articles of Confederation, to determine the truth or falsity of Justice Taney's "legal" ruling on "citizenship." And by his factual analysis of both governments, Justice Curtis proved that "American-born descendants of African slaves" were granted both state (sovereign, individual) and national (federated, union) Citizenship during the respective "1781–1787" and "1787–1789" eras. During those eras, states still possessed the "sovereign right" to grant "state citizenship" to people seeking admission into the nation. However, this changed after the 26 March 1790 "uniform rule of naturalization" was established throughout the nation.

Indeed, both Justice Taney and Justice Curtis knew that the 1783 Versailles peace treaty between America and Britain said that "some" people labeled "Negroes" were viewed as "citizens" of both "the several states" and "the United States"—just as "some" people labeled "Negroes" were viewed as "chattel" or "property." This truth political historians Commager, Cantor, and Bancroft respectively stated in their *Documents of American History* and *History of the United States*.

When speaking of Articles I and VII in the 1783 Versailles peace treaty Commager and Cantor recounted,

1.  [Art I.] His Britannic Majesty acknowledges the said United States, viz., NH, MA, RI, CT, NY, NJ, PA, DE, MD, VA, NC, SC, and GA, to be free, sovereign and independent States…

2.  [Art VII.] His Britannic Majesty shall, with all convenient speed, and without causing any destruction, or carrying away any *negroes* or *other property* of the American inhabitants, withdraw all His armies…from the said United States. (*Docs. of Amer. Hist.*, 117, 119, italics ours)

And when speaking of the selfsame 1783 Versailles peace treaty articles, Bancroft recounted,

> Thus far, no word in the [Vesailles peace treaty] convention had, except indirectly, alluded to the existence of slavery in the United States...in the engrossed copies...a clause was interlined, prohibiting, on the British evacuation, the "carrying away any negroes or any other property of the inhabitants." So the [treaty] instrument, which already contained a confession that the United States were not formed into one nation, made known that in their confederacy man could be held as a chattel; *but, as interpreted alike in America and England, it* [the treaty] *included free negroes among their citizens.* (*Hist. of the U.S.,* 363, italics ours)

And when speaking about the Confederation Congress's 25 June 1778 discussion of Article IV, Clause 1—forerunner of the 1787 Constitution's Article IV, Section 2, Clause 1—Justice Curtis recounted in his dissenting opinion,

> The 4th of the fundamental Articles of Confederation was as follows: "*the free inhabitants* of each of these States, Paupers, Vagabonds and Fugitives from Justice excepted, shall be entitled to all the privileges and immunities of free Citizens in the Several States."
>
> On the 25th of June, 1778, the Articles of Confederation being under consideration by the Congress, the delegates from South Carolina moved [motioned] to amend this 4th Article, by inserting after the word "*Free,*" and before the word "*inhabitants,*" the word "*white,*" so that the privileges and immunities of general Citizenship would be secured *only to white persons.* Two [2] States voted for the amendment, eight [8] States voted against it, and the vote of one [1] State was divided [the two remaining States apparently casting a "no" or "0" vote]. [Thus,] The language of the [4th] Article stood unchanged, and both its terms

of inclusion, "*Free inhabitants*," and the strong implication from its terms of exclusion, "*Paupers, Vagabonds* and *Fugitives from Justice*," who were alone excepted [remained unchanged]. (*Scott v Sandford.*, 60 U.S. 393, 575)

By revealing Congress's 25 June 1778 vote on the "language" and "meaning" of its then unratified "general citizenship" ("naturalization") clause (Confed. Art IV, Cl 1), Justice Curtis proved that Justice Taney critically erred in his "majority" Court ruling that said descendants of Africans held as "Negro" slaves were not intended to be included in the political communities called "citizens of the several states," "citizens of the states," "we the People of the United States," and "citizens of the United States." Most importantly, Justice Curtis revealed that within twelve years of the 25 June 1778 vote on admission to "national citizenship" or "naturalization" (1778–1790) the following "anomaly" occurred:

1.) "The *free inhabitants* of each of these States…shall be untitled to all the privileges and immunities of the free citizens in the Several States" (1778 unratified Confed. Art IV, Cl 1) ("Comity of States-General Citizenship admission").

2.) "The *free white inhabitants* of each of these States… shall be entitled to all the privileges and immunities of free citizens in the Several States" (1778 proposed change to Confed. Art IV, Cl 1) (Comity of States; General Citizenship admission).

3.) "The *free inhabitants* of each of these States…shall be entitled to all the privileges and immunities of free citizens in the Several States" (1781 ratified Confed. Art IV, Cl 1, Comity of States; General Citizenship admission into Confederation).

4.) "The *Citizens* of each State shall be entitled to all Privileges and Immunities of Citizens in the Several States" (1787–1788 ratified U.S. Const Art IV, Sec 2, Cl 1, Comity of States; General Citizenship admission into 1787–1788 Union).

5.) "[a]ny alien *being a free white person*…may be admitted to become a citizen…" (1790 Naturalization Act; 1 *Statutes At Large* 103, Chap. 3, Sec. 1; in accordance with the 1787–1788 ratified US Const Art I, Sec 8, Cl 4 ).

By honestly interpreting the "ratified" 1787–1788 Constitution's phrases "natural-born citizen" and "a citizen of the United States, at the time of the Adoption of this Constitution" ("presidential office eligibility," US Const Art II, Sec 1, Cl 5), Justice Curtis slyly revealed that the phrase "natural-born citizen" referred to the time-honored British "jus soli" naturalization rule! The learned Justice Curtis knew that since there were both "free-born" Africans and "freed" descendants of African slaves living during America's Colonial to Constitutional eras, then so-called "Negroes" born to such people were born under the "jus soli" rule—which rule operated in both the "thirteen" British-American Colonies and the Colonies turned states!

Undoubtedly, the entire Supreme Court knew about the Rule—King George III's obstruction of it being the "seventh" fact the Colonies complained of in the Declaration of Independence! The court also knew that, during the 1776–1789 Confederation era, the ability of the Colonies turned states to enact individual naturalization procedures was left up to their discretion because they were "sovereign" and "separate"—but based on the rule. And the Court knew that from 1787–1788 and onward, the naturalization power was exclusively delegated to Congress—but still based on the rule implied in the 1787–1788 Constitution and 1791 Bill of Rights, which said,

"The Congress shall have [the] Power...To establish a uniform Rule of Naturalization...throughout the United States" (US Const, Art I, Sec 8, Cls 1 and 4 passim; Art II, Sec 1, Cl 5).

"The powers not delegated to the United States by the Constitution, nor prohibited by it to the States, are reserved to the States respectively, or to the people" (US Const, Amend 10).

By revealing the 25 June 1778 vote to insert the word *white* between *free inhabitants* in Confederation Article IV—eight (8) against, two (2) for, one (1) undecided, and two (2) no vote (0) cast—Justice Curtis proved that the 1781–1789 Confederation Congress—which was mostly comprised of the same delegates from the 1774–1787 Continental Congresses and 1787–1788 Constitutional Congress—"intended" for the American government (the "Union") to be a "colorless, raceless" government into which anyone of "moral integrity" could gain admission. Hence, by his "factually, historically, legally" accurate (sound) "minority court dissenting opinion," Justice Curtis proved Justice Taney's "majority court opinion" and its "America made for the white man" reasoning erroneous and bogus!

Most importantly, by rendering his dissenting opinion, Justice Curtis revealed that Justice Taney's 1857 *Dred Scott* opinion had dealt the "Race Card" to "white" Americans in order to justify a "cheap-labor" scheme that would ultimately put them in the unemployment line so that a "chosen few" big-business speculators in human misery could financially profit! However, all enlightened Americans of the Hildreth-Stowe-Curtis era knew that a "judgment day" was approaching America—because her founding fathers had "invoked God's aid" to end their "thralldom" (slavery) while they placed such on other members of the "seventy" nations (those whom Augustine St. Clare euphemistically called "brother Quashy").

Undoubtedly, Thomas Jefferson clearly stated the matter by saying that he "shuddered" when reflecting that "God's justice would not sleep forever" concerning the introduction of the African Slavery scheme into the Union. However, Delaware Quaker John Woolman summed it up best when he likened the "Race Card Evil" oriented scheme to "a burdensome stone" destined to ruin any builder foolish enough to use it in a building project. Recounted statesman Bancroft in his *History of the United States*,

> John Woolman, a tailor by trade, "stood up like a trumpet, through which the LORD speaks to his people," to make the Negro masters sensible [aware] of the evil of holding the people of Africa in Slavery; and by his testimony at the meetings of Friends [Quakers], recommended that oppressed part of the creation to the notice of each individual and of the society...
>
> "Men having power," he continued, "too often misapply it; though we make slaves of the Negroes, and the Turks [Muslims] make slaves of the Christians, liberty is the natural right of all men equally." "The slaves look to me like a burdensome stone to such who burden themselves with them. The burden will grow heavier and heavier, till times change in a way disagreeable to us." (*Hist. of the U.S.*, 76–77)

The manifold predictions of dire consequences for allowing the "Race Card Evil" to infect America—made by notables such as Edmund Burke, John Woolman, George Mason, George Washington, Thomas Jefferson, Richard Henry Lee, Richard Hildreth, Harriett Beecher-Stowe, and Roger B. Taney to name a few—would soon prove true. About two years after Mr. Taney's *Scott* opinion went public, Americans drew lines for or against playing the "Race Card Evil's" game any longer. Little did they realize that "judgment day" had arrived—signalled by the 1858–1859 presidential candidate debates. During that time a number of people and ideas would make their public debut on the American and world stages. And during that time, important political statements and actions would be made in an ernest effort to put the "Race Card Evil" either in the course of ultimate "expansion" or "extinction."

# 5

# Judgment Day
# The Race Card Evil's True Identity Exposed

> This is the LORD's [the Creator's] message…What are
> you, O Great Mountain? Before Zerubbabel you are but a
> plain. He shall bring out the capstone amid exclamations
> of "Hail, Hail" to it…For even they who were scornful on
> that day of small beginnings shall rejoice to see the select
> stone in the hands of Zerubbabel. These seven facets are
> the eyes of the LORD that range over the whole earth.
>
> —Zec 4:7–10 (NAB)

> The stone the builders rejected has become the
> cornerstone. By the LORD has this been done; it is
> wonderful in our eyes. This is the day the LORD has
> made; let us rejoice in it and be glad.
>
> —Ps 118:22–24 (NAB)

IF EVER A number of events harmoniously combined to produce an explosive situation in America during the 1800s, they were: Congress compromising for Missouri to enter the Union as a Slave State (1820–21); Richard Hildreth publishing his antislavery book *The Slave* (1836); Santa Anna slaughtering Texas residents at the Alamo (1836); an Illinois proslavery mob murdering antislavery publisher Elijah P. Lovejoy (1837);

Congress admitting Texas into the Union as a Slave State (1845); Britain signing the Oregon Treaty adding territory to the Union (1846); Santa Anna attacking Texas-based Union forces sparking the American Mexican War (1846–48); Santa Anna's Guadalupe-Hidalgo Treaty adding Mexican territory to the Union (1848); Congress passing Henry Clay's Compromise and the Fugitive Slave Law inciting heightened underground railroad resistance (1850); Harriet Beecher-Stowe publishing her antislavery book *Uncle Tom's Cabin* (1852); Congress passing the Kansas-Nebraska Act sparking the Independent Democratic or New Republican Party's (GOP's) creation (1854); Missouri residents sparking a series of antislavery-proslavery Border Ruffian Wars (1855); the U.S. Supreme Court's anticitizenship-proslavery *Scott v. Sandford* ruling (1857); machinations concerning passing the proslavery Lecompton, Kansas constitution (1857); and Abolitionist John Brown attacking a federal arsenal in Virginia (1859). These events made the perfect mix because they concerned the "Race Card Evil's" oriented African Slavery scheme—its inclusion in or exclusion from States or Territories seeking admission into the Union.

Indeed, during the 1800s hostilities arose between Americans from varying backgrounds and regions because of such events resulting from the big-business scheme to hold humans in bondage for profit at the expense of free "white" immigrant laborers. And while many Americans seethed over such events, they tolerated the African Slavery scheme because the 1820 Missouri Compromise's "36–degree, 30–minute" Slavery Prohition Line was abided by. However, Henry because the string of events reeked of a sly attempt by slavery profiteers to "nullify" the Slavery Prohibition Line, "extend" the evil throughout the Northwest Territory, and "recruit" all Americans in maintaining the evil regardless of economic-political-religious-social position, informed Americans became furious.

For example, the Bill to organize the Kansas-Nebraska Territories for Statehood—introduced 4 January 1854 by

Illinois Senator Stephen A. Douglas (one architech of the 1850 Compromise)—tried to repeal the 1820 Missouri Compromise's "thirty-six-degree, thirty-minute" slavery Prohibition line by seeking "popular sovereignty" for those territories (i.e., the right for residents-settlers-voters of those areas to form constitutions to exclude or include slavery). The politically ambitious Senator Douglas promoted this idea to encourage a northern transcontinental railroad route through Illinois, attract settlers to the Great Plains region, and thereby stimulate Illinois economy. However, Mr. Douglas underestimated underestimated the negative effect the "slavery issue" would have in a region that the evil was barred from for thirty-four years.

Two weeks after Senator Douglas submitted the Bill six notable congressmen, called the Independent Democrats (Charles Sumner and Salmon P. Chase among them), wrote an article in major US newspapers entitled "The Appeal of the Independent Democrats" (19 January 1854). The article attacked the Kansas-Nebraska Bill and called for the creation of an antislavery political party to oppose the Senator and his allies. This new political party—composed of antislavery activists, ex-Free Soilers, ex-Whigs, and modernizers—would later be called the New Republican, or Grand Old Party (GOP).

Warning Americans that a series of conflicts would follow the Bill's passage that would divide the country and spark civil war in the nation, the appeal stated a number of grievances and historical facts that its writers felt the public needed to be made aware of. In their *Documents of American History*, political historians Commager and Cantor recounted that the Independent Democrats said,

> We arraign this [Kansas-Nebreaska] bill as a gross violation
> of a sacred pledge; as a criminal betrayal of precious rights;
> as part and parcel of an atrocious plot to exclude from a
> vast unoccupied region [white] immigrants from the Old
> World and free [white] laborers from our own States, and

convert it into a dreary region of despotism, inhabited by masters and slaves...We beg your attention, fellow-citizens, to a few historical facts:

The original settled policy of the United States, clearly indicated by the Jefferson [Western Territory] proviso of 1784 and the [Northwest] Ordinance of 1787, was non-extension of Slavery.

In 1803 Louisiana was acquired by purchase from France...In 1818...the inhabitants of the Territory of Missouri applied to Congress for authority to form a State constitution, and for admission into the Union. There were, at that time, in the whole territory acquired from France, outside of the State of Louisiana, not three thousand slaves.

*There was no apology*, in the circumstances of the country, *for the continuance of slavery.* The original policy was against it, and not less the plain language of the treaty under which the territory had been acquired from France.

It was proposed, therefore, to incorporate in the bill authorizing the formation of a State government [in Missouri], a provision requiring that the constitution of the new State should contain an article providing for the abolition of existing slavery and prohibiting the further introduction of slaves.

This provision was vehemently and pertinaciously opposed, but finally prevailed in the House of Representatives...In the Senate it was rejected, and—in consequence of the disagreement between the two Houses—the bill was lost.

At the next session of Congress, the controversy was renewed with increased violence. It was terminated at length by a compromise. Missouri was allowed to come into the Union with slavery; but...excluding slavery forever from all the territory acquired from France, not included in the new State, lying north of [latitude] 36 degrees 30 minutes...(*Docs. of Amer. Hist.*, 329–30 passim)

Having recounted that such events involved excluding "ehite"
immigrants and free laborers from the Louisiana Purchase
territory, the Independent Democrats recounted President
Monroe's question to his cabinet on the constitutional validity
or invalidity of the 1820 Missouri Compromise (to which they
said "valid"). Next, they recounted Iowa's admission to Statehood
and Minnesota's organization as a "free" Territory according
to the 1820 slavery prohibition line, the 1850 Utah and New
Mexico Acts that contained proslavery clauses, and compared the
differences between such earlier Acts and the 1854 Nebraska Act.
And having recited this history, the appeal's writers summed the
matter up for the American public. In their *Documents of American
History*, Commager and Cantor recounted that they concluded,

> We appeal to the people. We warn you that the dearest
> interests of freedom and the Union are in imminent
> peril. Demagogues may tell you that the Union can be
> maintained only by submitting to the demands of slavery.
> We tell you that the Union can only be maintained by the
> full recognition of the just claims of freedom and man.
> The Union was formed to establish justice and secure
> the blessings of liberty. When it fails to accomplish these
> ends it will be worthless, and when it becomes worthless it
> cannot long endure.
>
> We entreat you to be mindful of that fundamental
> maxim of Democracy—EQUAL RIGHTS AND
> EXACT JUSTICE FOR ALL MEN. Do not submit
> to become agents in extending legalized oppression and
> systematized injustice over a vast territory yet exempt
> from these terrible evils.
>
> We implore Christians and Christian ministers to
> interpose. Their Divine religion requires them to behold
> in every man a brother, and to labor for the advancement
> and regeneration of the human race.
>
> We shall go home to our constituents, erect anew the
> standard of freedom, and call on the people to come to the

> rescue of the country from the domination of slavery. We
> will not despair; for the cause of human freedom is the
> cause of God. (Ibid., 331)

Taking the appeal seriously, Massachusett Congressman Eli Thayer founded the New England Emigrant Aid Company (5 March 1854). Its objective concerned transporting immigrants to the Kansas Territory to establish the Free State towns called Lawrence, Manhattan, Osawatomie, and Topeka to equalize ballot-power and ensure that the Territory could enter the Union as a Free State. Six days later, this objective was announced at a rally against the Kansas-Nebraska bill (11 March 1854). And nine days later, the New Republican Party held its first unofficial public meeting at Ripon, Wisconsin to declare its agenda against the Bill (20 March 1854). Unfortunately, ten days later, Congress passed the Kansas-Nebraska Act which repealed its 1820 Missouri Compromise Slavery Prohibition Line (30 May 1854) (10 *Satutes at Large* 277, ch. 59). Thereafter, a series of political conflicts arose between antislavery and proslavery factions that proved disastrous for the nation.

First, President Franklin Pierce's proslavery administration appointed Pennsylvania's Andrew H. Reeder Governor over the Kansas Territory (29 June 1854). This caused the New Republican Party to respond by holding its first official convention at Jackson, Michigan to formally state its antislavery agenda (6 July 1854)—summed up by Ohio Senator Salmon P. Chase's slogan "Free labor, free land, free men." In turn, acting on rumors that thousands of Northern antislavery emigrants were coming to Kansas Territory to make it a Free State, thousands of proslavery bullies (chiefly from Missouri) called "Border Ruffians" came into the Territory by the year's end to ensure that it became a Slave State (Nov.–Dec. 1854).

Actually, the Ruffians had nothing to gain by the Territory being made a "Slave" State. Rather, they were mostly impoverished, ill-informed Missouri settlers easily manipulated by big-business profiteers from the "Race Card Evil" oriented cheap-labor scheme. Said the *Wikipedia* article concerning the Ruffians,

The Border Ruffians were pro-slavery activists from the slave state of Missouri, who in 1854 to 1860 crossed the state border into Kansas Territory, to force the acceptance of slavery there. The name was applied by Free-State settlers in Kansas and abolitionists throughout the North. Armed Ruffians interfered in territorial elections, and attacked Free-State settlements. This violence was the origin of the phrase "Bleeding Kansas." The Ruffians contributed to the growing sectional tensions, and helped bring on the American Civil War.

Notably, only a few of the Border Ruffians actually owned slaves; most were too poor, What motivated them was hatred of Yankees and abolitionists, and fear of blacks living nearby. The Ruffians were driven by the rhetoric of leaders such as U.S. Senator David Rice Atchison of Missouri, who called Northerners "negro thieves" and "abolitionist tyrants." He encouraged Misourians to defend their institution "with the bayonet and with blood" and, if necessary, "to kill every…abolitionist in the district." (*Wikipedia*, s.v. "Border Ruffian," http://en.wikipedia.org/wiki/Border_Ruffian, p. 1. Retrieved 13 January 2015)

Having crossed into Kansas, the Ruffians elected John Whitfield as their delegate to Congress. At first, this "Ruffian" presence did not upset Kansas Free-Staters because of a concern for "black" rights, freedom, or slavery—but because it affected free-staters controlling their own political self-determination:

Ironically, the bulk of Free-State men in Kansas were not abolitionists, and opposed the presence of both free blacks and slaves. "We want no slaves and we want no Negroes" was the prevailing sentiment reported by an abolitionist in 1854. (Ibid., p. 2)

However, during November of 1854 the Border Ruffian ballots cast for a proslavery Congressional delegate were suspected of being fraudulent—since their votes outnumbered Free Staters by an abnormal amount. Due to this, prior to spring of 1855, a congressional investigating committee found that a ratio of "1,114" legal resident to "1,729" nonresident votes were cast during the November election; and that one district had "20" resident out of "604" voters in the Kansas Territory, while another had "35" resident out of "226" voters. And when the 30 March 1855 election for the Territory's first Legislature was held, Ruffians again invaded the Territory and cast ballots to elect delegate seats in the Legislature by a ratio of "2" antislavery to "37" proslavery. Since this too was suspected of fraud, and because the question of whether slavery would be allowed was involved, during May of 1855 Governor Reeder voided the results and held a special election to obtain replacements. This too was suspected of fraud, since the antislavery to proslavery ratio was "10" to "29" (Congress, however, did not send a special committee to investgate the voter fraud until 1856—when it would then report that the 30 March 1855 election should have produced a Free State Legislature had only "legal" residents-settlers voted).

During July of 1855, the fraudulently seated proslavery Legislature voided Governor Reeder's May 1855 special election results, re-seated the March 1855 proslavery elected delegates, moved the Territorial Capital to the Shawnee Mission near Missouri's border, and passed proslavery laws. Rejecting the proslavery laws, Kansas' antislavery Free Staters met during August of 1855 and declared their intention to hold their own Constitutional Convention to counter the proslavery territorial legislature. This they did at Topeka's Constitution Hall during the fall season—at which time they drafted their Topeka Constitution (23 Oct.–11 Nov. 1855) and passed their territorial constitution (15 December 1855).

*Wikipedia*, s.v.: "Bleeding Kansas," http://en.wikipedia.org/ wiki/Bleeding_Kansas, pp. 2–3. Retrieved 13 January 2015; "Topeka Constitution," http://en.wikipedia.org/wiki/ Topeka_Constitution, p. 1. Retrieved 13 January 2015.

During summer of 1855, the New England Emigrant Aid Company helped some 900–2000 immigrants move to Kansas Territory to offset Border Ruffian voter fraud; and to offset Ruffian violence, Reverend Henry Ward Beecher (Harriet Beecher Stowe's brother) raised money to purchase and ship arms to Free Staters (euphemistically called "Beecher's Bibles"). During October of 1855, Ohio Abolitionist John Brown—disgruntled about Ruffian treatment of the immigrant settlers and feeling that the Abolitionist Movement was more talk than action—arrived in the territory with a small band of followers.

Things seemed quiet enough on Brown's arrival—although relations were strained between pro and anti slavery proponents. That soon changed after free-stater Charles W. Dow was fatally shot by proslavery settler Franklin N. Coleman over a land dispute (21 November 1855 according to Dow's obituary). Then, about 1,500 border Ruffians led by Douglas, County Sheriff Samuel J. Jones—armed with munitions allegedly stolen from the Liberty, Missouri, federal arsenal—attacked the Free State town named Lawrence, near Topeka (1 December 1855). However, free state settlers led by John Brown and James Lane dissuaded the sheriff from attacking and a truce was made—albeit free-stater Thomas Barber, who had come to defend Lawrence, was a fatality (circa. 6 December 1855). Despite this truce, the short-lived "Wakarusa War" spilled over into the following year due to a series of interconnected events.

*Wikipedia*: s.v.: "New England Emigrant Aid Company," http://en.wikipedia.org/wiki/New_England_Emigrant_Aid_Company," pp. 1, 2. Retrieved 12 January 2015; "Bleeding Kansas," pp. 1, 3; "Charles W. Dow," http://en.wikipedia.org/wiki/Charles_W._Dow, p. 1. Retrieved 15 January 2015; "Henry Ward Beecher," http://en.wikipedia.org/wiki/Henry_Ward_Beecher, p. 1. Retrieved 15 January 2015; "John Brown (abolitionist)," http://en.wikipedia.org/wiki/John_Brown_(abolitionist),

p. 1. Retrieved 15 January 2015; "Border Ruffian," p. 2; "Wakarusa War," http://en.wikipedia.org/wiki/Wakarusa_ War, p. 1. Retrieved 15 January 2015.

During the start of 1856 the Free Staters approved their antislavery Topeka Constitution, elected Charles L. Robinson Governor, then held a Territory-wide election for their Legislature's delegates (15 January 1856). Next they sent their Constitution to the US Congress for acceptance and admission into the Union (the document passed in the House, was held up in the Senate Committee, sent back to Topeka, resubmitted to Congress, with no action taken thereon). Nine days later, President Franklin Pierce condemned the Topeka Constitution and declared the Free State Legislature delegates "insurrectionists" (24 January 1856)—because they refused to accept the 30 March 1855 proslavery Shawnee Mission Territorial Legislature that, according to the later-given 1856 official investigative report regarding voter fraud, "was an illegally constituted body, and had no [lawful] power to pass valid laws."

Four months after President Pierce condemned the antislavery Topeka government, the proslavery Shawnee Mission government sent sheriff Samuel Jones to disarm the Lawrence township and arrest its leaders. Leading a Ruffian posse the sheriff burned the Free State Hotel, destroyed two newspaper offices, and looted homes and stores (Governor Robinson's house included)—events that became known as the "Sack of Lawrence" (21 May 1856), which sparked a series of events that rocked the nation and earned the Territory the nickname Bleeding Kansas.

Just days prior to the sack of Lawrence, Massachusetts, Senator Charles Sumner gave his "The Crime Against Kansas" speech—speaking against the Slave Power, likening its profiteers to "pimps," and disclosing how it affected the Kansas Territory's electoral process (19–20 May 1856). While doing so he used his colleague, South Carolina Senator Andrew Butler, as an example of the mindset characteristic of those defending slavery. Two days later Mr. Sumner was physically assaulted in the Senate by South

Carolina Representative Preston Brooks (Butler's cousin, 22 May 1856), received a concussion that prevented him from attending Senate sessions for months, and suffered lifelong medical consequences therefrom. And while Brooks received gifts and praises from influential Southerners and Southern newspapers for his actions, Abolitionist John Brown felt otherwise.

In retaliation for the sack of Lawrence and the assault on Mr. Sumner, John Brown attacked Franklin County's proslavery Potawatomie settlement—killing at least five settlers (24–25 May 1856). Next he engaged Ruffians at the battles of Black Jack (2 June 1856) and Osawatomie, Kansas (30 August 1856). Thereafter, he crossed the Marais de Cygnes River—in which area Border Ruffians and Free Staters clashed prior to a peace accord (19 May 1858). Finally, Mr. Brown made his way to Virginia—where he attacked the Harper's Ferry federal arsenal (16 October 1859), was captured, and hanged for treason (2 December 1859).

> *Wikipedia*, s.v.: "Bleeding Kansas," pp. 2–3; "Topeka Constitution," pp. 1, 3; "Border Ruffians, p. 2; "John Brown (abolitionist)," p. 1. "Preston Brooks, http://en.wikipedia.org/wiki/Preston_Brooks, p. 2. Retrieved 15 January 2015; "Potawatomie Massacre," http://en.wikipedia.org/wiki/Potawatomie_Massacre, pp. 1–3. Retrieved 14 January 2015; "List of battles fought in Kansas," http://en.wikipedia.org/wiki/List_of_battles_fought_in_Kansas, p. 4. Retrieved 12 January 2015.

While all these events were occurring, the US Circuit Court for the District of Missouri was hearing a case related to the Kansas-Nebraska Bill entitled *Scott v. Emerson*. By May of 1854, a decision was reached for both issues—a positive one for the Bill and a negative one for the Scott case. To many Americans the two issues and outcomes seemed "unrelated." However, the New Republican Party did not think so. Suspecting "Race Card Evil" oriented political intrigues on the part of Senator Douglas and his proslavery allies, the Republican Party selected a Whig lawyer from Springfield, Illinois as their champion to articulate their cause and contest Senator Douglas in the upcoming 1860 Presidential election. History would record his name as Abraham Lincoln.

Prior to the November 1856 Presidential election, the US Supreme Court heard Dred Scott's appeal of the Missouri Circuit Court's denial of his freedom suit. During November James Buchanan won the Presidency and during February of 1857 the Supreme Court reached a decision in Scott's case—but deferred publishing it until after the president-elect was sworn into Office. On 4 March 1857, Mr. Buchanan was sworn in and three days later, on 7 March 1857, the Supreme Court made public its "majority court" ruling against Scott while citing that Congress had no legal Constitutional authority to enact the 1820 Missouri Compromise. This "ruling," by Chief Justice Taney, confirmed the Independent Democrats' suspicion that both the Kansas-Nebraska Act and Supreme Court's *Dred Scott* Decision were part of a greater conspiracy aimed at spreading the "Race Card Evil" oriented African slavery scheme throughout America. In his *The Great Conspiracy*, statesman Logan recounted how the two outcomes were interpreted by the Independent Democrats:

> Now it was, that the meaning of the words, "subject only to the [1787] Constitution," as used in the Kansas-Nebraska Act, began to be discerned. For if the people of a Territory were to be "perfectly free," to deal with Slavery as they chose, "subject only to the [1787] Constitution," they were by this [Dred Scott] Judicial interpretation of that instrument "perfectly free" to deal with Slavery in any way so long as they did not attempt "to exclude" it! The thing [Act] was all one-sided. Mr. [Stephen A.] Douglas's attitude in inventing the peculiar phraseology in the Kansas-Nebraska Act—which to some seemed as if expressly "made to order" for the Dred Scott decision—was criticized with asperity… (*The Great Conspiracy*, 49–50)

The Independent Democrats were not about to allow Senator Douglas and his proslavery allies get away with their scheme. On 16 June 1858, at the Springfield, Illinois Republican Convention, Abraham Lincoln was nominated as the candidate to debate Senator Douglas in a bid for the 1860 Presidency. The following night Mr. Lincoln accepted the nomination and gave his "House Divided" speech that predicted the upcoming contest to be waged with the "Race Card Evil" and its program. In their *Documents of American History*, Commager and Cantor recounted that Lincoln said,

> Mr. President and Gentlemen of the Convention…We are now into the fifth year since a policy was initiated with the avowed object and confident promise of putting an end to the slavery agitation. Under the operation of that policy, that agitation has not only not ceased, but has constantly augmented. In my opinion, it will not cease until a crisis shall have been reached and passed. "A house divided against itself cannot stand" [cf. Matt. 12:22–30, KJV]. I believe this government cannot endure permanently half slave and half free. I do not expect the Union to be dissolved; I do not expect the house to fall; but I do expect it will cease to be divided. It will become all one thing, or all the other. Either the opponents of slavery will arrest the further spread of it, and place it where the public mind shall rest in the belief that it is in the course of ultimate extinction, or its advocates will push it forward till it shall become alike lawful in all the States, old as well as new, North as well as South. (*Docs. of Amer. Hist.*, 345)

Mr. Lincoln next showed how the seemingly "coincidental" and "simultaneous" 1854 Kansas-Nebraska bill's passage and the Missouri US Circuit Court's *Dred Scott* case were part of a diabolical plot involving the 1852 and 1856 Presidential Elections of Pierce and Buchanan, the 1857 proslavery Lecompton Constitution (rejected by Kansas and Congress), and the 1857 US

Supreme Court's *Dred Scott* decision—all designed to convince the American public to accept the spread of the African Slavery scheme. Again Commager and Cantor recounted that "Honest Abe" said,

> Let anyone who doubts, carefully contemplate that now almost complete legal combination—piece of machinery, so to speak—compounded of the Nebreska doctrine and the Dred Scott decision. Let him consider, not only what work the machinery is adapted to do...but also let him study the history of its contruction, and trace, if he can, or rather fail, if he can, to trace the evidence of design, and concert of action, among its chief architects, from the beginning.
>
> The new year of 1854 found slavery excluded from more than half the States by State Constitutions, and from most of the National territory by Congressional prohibition. Four days later [4 January 1854], commenced the struggle which ended in repealing that Congressional prohibition. This opened all the National territory to slavery, and was the first point gained [by proslavery advocates]...
>
> While the Nebraska Bill was passing through Congress, a *law case*, involving the question of a negro's freedom... was passing through the United States Circuit Court for the District of Missouri [November 1853–April 1854]; and both [the] Nebraska Bill and [the] law suit were brought to a decision in the same month of May, 1854. The negro's name was "Dred Scott"...Before the then next Presidential election, the law case came to, and was argued in, the Supreme Court of the United States [October 1856]; but the decision of it was deferred until after the election...The election came, Mr. [James] Buchanan was elected [Nov. 1856], and the indorsement, such as it was, secured. That was the second point gained [by proslavery advocates]...The Presidential inauguration came, and still no decision of the Court; but the incoming President [Buchanan], in his inaugural address [4 March 1857],

fervently exhorted the people to abide by the forthcoming [Dred Scott] decision, whatever it might be. Then, in a few days, came the decision.

The reputed author of the Nebraska Bill [Douglas] finds an early occasion to make a speech at this capital indorsing the Dred Scott decision, and vehemently denouncing all opposition to it. The new President [Buchanan], too, seizes the early occasion…to indorse and strongly construe that decision, and to express his astonishment that any different view had ever been entertained.

At length a squabble springs up between the President and the author of the Nebraska Bill, on the mere question of fact, whether the Lecompton Constitution was or was not in any just sense made by the people of Kansas; and in that quarrel the latter [Douglas] declares that all he wants is a fair vote for the people, and that he cares not whether slavery be voted down or voted up, to be intended by him other than as an apt definition of the policy he would impress upon the public mind…That principle is the only shred left of his original Nebraska doctrine. Under the Dred Scott decision "squatter sovereignty" squatted out of existence, tumbled down like temporary scaffolding… helped to carry an election, and then was kicked to the winds. His [Douglas's] late joint struggle with the Republicans, against the Lecompton Constitution, involves nothing of the original Nebraska doctrine. That struggle was made on a point—the right of a people to make their own constitution—upon which he [Douglas] and the Republicans have never differed. (Ibid., 346)

Having shown the general relationship between the Kansas-Nebraska Bill, *Scott v. Sandford* case, President Buchanan's election, Lecompton Constitution, and Senator Douglas's role in all of it, Mr. Lincoln then explained the particular relationship of the same to the big-business scheme of spreading the African Slavery program throughout the Union. Said he with brilliant logical reasoning,

The several points of the Dred Scott decision, in connection with Senator Douglas's "care not" policy, constitute the piece of machinery, in its present state of advancement. This was the third point gained [by proslavery advocates]. The working points of that machinery are:

*Firstly*, that no negro slave, imported as such from Africa, and no descendant of such slave, can ever be a citizen of any State, in the sense of that term as used in the [1787] Constitution of the United States. This point is made in order to deprive the Negro…of the benefit of that provision of the United States Constitution which declares that "The citizens of each State shall be entitled to all privileges and immunities of citizens in the several States."

*Secondly*, that, "subject to the [1787] Constitution of the United States," neither Congress nor a Territorial Legislature can exclude slavery from any United States Territory. This point is made in order that individual men may fill up the Territories with slaves, without danger of losing them as property, and thus to enhance the chances of permanency to the institution through all the future.

*Thirdly*, that whether the holding a negro in actual slavery in a free State makes him free, as against the [claims of the] [slave]holder, the United States [Federal] Courts will not decide, but will leave to be decided by the [State] courts of any slave State the negro may be forced into by the master. This point is made…to sustain the logical conclusion that what Dred Scott's master might lawfully do with Dred Scott, in the free State of Illinois, every other master may lawfully do with any other one [slave], or one thousand slaves, in Illinois, or in any other free State.

*Auxiliary to all this*, and working hand in hand with it, the Nebraska doctrine, or what is left of it, is to educate and mould public opinion, at least Northern public opinion, not to care whether slavery is voted down or voted up…This shows exactly where we now are; and partially, also, whither we are tending [to go]…(Ibid., 346–47, italics ours)

After explaining the political words and deeds of four men holding key positions in the executive, judicial, and legislative branches of the Federal government—Pierce, Buchanan, Taney, and Douglas—Mr. Lincoln called them the "chief architects" and "four horsemen of the Apocalypse" plotting to spread the African Slavery scheme throughout the Union. Said he,

> Why was the [Lecompton] amendment, expressly declaring the right of the people, voted down? Plainly enough, the adoption of it would have spoiled the niche for the Dred Scott decision. Why was the [Supreme] Court decision held up? Why even a Senator's [Douglas's] individual opinion withheld, till after the Presidential election? Plainly enough, now, the speaking out then would have damaged the "perfectly free" argument upon which the election was to be carried. Why the outgoing President's [Pierce's] felicitation on the indorsement? Why the delay of a reargument? Why the incoming President's [Buchanan's] advance exhortation in favor of the [Dred Scott] decision? These things look like the cautious patting and petting of a spirited horse preparatory to mounting him, when it is dreaded that he may give the rider a fall. And why the hasty after-indorsement of the [Dred Scott] decision by the President and others?
>
> We cannot absolutely know that all these exact adaptations are the result of preconcert. But when we see a lot of framed timbers, different portions of which we know have been gotten out at different times and places and by different workmen—Stephen [Douglas], Franklin [Pierce], Roger [Taney], and James [Buchanan], for instance—and when we see the timbers joined together, and see they exactly make the frame of a house or a mill, all the tenons and mortises exactly fitting…we find it impossible not to believe that Stephen and Franklin and Roger and James all understood one another from the beginning, and all [together] worked on upon a common plan or draft drawn up before the first blow was struck…(Ibid., 347)

With Lincoln having exposed the plot, Senator Douglas went on the defensive when he addressed the audience on 9 July 1858. To evade the Lecompton Constitution issue, Douglas attacked Lincoln's decision to resist the *Scott v. Sandford* ruling that denied Federal and State citizenship to descendants of so-called Negro slaves. Immediately Douglas went off on a "Race Card Evil" oriented tangent that contained as much validity and venom as Taney's unsound "majority court" opinion. In his *The Great Conspiracy*, Senator Logan recounted that Senator Douglas said,

> I am free to say to you that in my opinion this [United States] Government of ours is founded on the White basis. It was made by the White man for the benefit of the White man, to be administered by White men, in such manner as they should determine. It is also true that a Negro, an Indian, or *any other man of inferior race* to a White man, should be permitted to enjoy, and humanity requires that he should have, all the rights, privileges, and immunities which he is capable of exercising consistent with the safety of [White] society. (*The Great Conspiracy*, 54, italics ours; capitalized "white" ours in part).

Continuing, Senator Douglas tried to hide his "Race Card Evil" oriented views behind the "states' rights-sovereignty" doctrine. Yet when accusing Mr. Lincoln of "waging war" with Justice Taney's *Scott v. Sandford* decision, the Senator again advanced his "Race Card" views and proudly dealt them to his audience without any mental hesitation or moral reservation. Senator Logan recounted that Mr. Douglas said,

> My answer is, that each State must decide for itself the nature and extent of these rights [to be given non-Whites]….I assert that Virginia has the same power by virtue of her sovereignty to protect Slavery within her limits, as Illinois has to banish it forever from our own borders. I assert the right of each State to decide for itself on all these

questions…I do not acknowledge that the States must all be Free or must all be Slave. I do not acknowledge any of these doctrines of uniformity in the local and domestic regulations in the different States…Mr. Lincoln goes for a warfare upon the Supreme Court of the United States because of their [Taney's] judicial decision in the Dred Scott case…He objects to the Dred Scott decision because it does not put the Negro in the possession of the rights of citizenship on an equality with the White man. I am opposed to Negro equality…I would extend to the Negro, and the Indian, and to all dependent [nonwhite] races every right, every privilege, and every immunity consistent with the safety and welfare of the White races; but equality they never should have, either political or social, or in any other respect whatever. (Ibid., 54–55)

On 10 July 1858, Mr. Lincoln responded to Senator Douglas's "Race Card" oriented speech. Addressing the "Popular Sovereignty" idea, he showed that it was the same as "Squatter Sovereignty" and defined both as "Sovereignty of the People." Statesman Logan recounted that Lincoln brilliantly said,

"Popular Sovereignty! Everlasting Popular Sovereignty!… What is Popular Sovereignty? We recollect at an early period in the history of this struggle there was another name for the same thing—*Squatter Sovereignty*. It was not exactly Popular Sovereignty, but Squatter Sovereignty. What do those terms mean? What do those terms mean when used now…? Why it is the Sovereignty of the People! What was Squatter Sovereignty? I suppose if it had any significance at all, it was the right of the people to govern themselves, to be sovereign in their own affairs while they were squatted down *in a country not their own…on a Territory that did not belong to them* in the sense that a State belongs to the people who inhabit it, when it belonged to the Nation—such right to govern themselves was called 'Squatter Sovereignty.'" (Ibid., 55, italics ours in part)

Mr. Lincoln next showed that the idea of "Popular Sovereignty" originated from the 1776 Declaration of Independence phrase "governments were instituted by the consent of the governed." Then, while refuting the senator's claim that he (Lincoln) wished to wage war on the Southern Slave States because of the slavery issue, Lincoln formally declared his position on the "Race Card Evil" oriented cheap-labor scheme. Statesman Logan recounted,

> He [Lincoln] denied that he had said, or that it could be fairly inferred from what he had said…that he was in favor of making war by the North upon the South for the extinction of Slavery, "or, in favor of inviting the South to a war upon the North, for the purpose of nationalizing Slavery." Said he [Lincoln]: "I did not even say that I desired that Slavery should be put in the course of ultimate extinction. *I do say so now, however;* so there need be no longer any difficulty about that." (Ibid., 57)

Having made his stand, Lincoln next gave his analysis on the "intent" of the framers of the 1787 Constitution regarding the "Race Card Evil" oriented African Slavery program. Statesman Logan recounted that Lincoln said,

> I am tolerably well acquainted with the history of the Country and I know that it [America] has endured eighty-two years [since 1776] half Slave and half Free. I believe…it has endured, because during all that time, until the introduction of the Nebraska Bill, the public mind did rest all the time in the belief that *Slavery was in [the] course of ultimate extinction.* That was what gave us the rest that we had through that period of eighty-two years; at least, so I believe.
>
> I have always hated Slavery, I think, as much as any Abolitionist…but I have always been quiet about it until this new era of the introduction of the Nebraska Bill began…The great mass of the Nation have rested in the belief that Slavery was in [the] course of ultimate

extinction. They had reason so to believe. The adoption of the [1787] Constitution and its attendant history led the people to believe so, and that such was the belief of the framers of the Constitution itself. Why did those old men about the time of the adoption of the Constitution decree that Slavery should not go into the new territory, where it had not already gone? Why declare that within twenty years [by 1808] the [International] African Slave Trade, by which Slaves are supplied, might be cut off by Congress? Why were all these acts [done]…What were they but a clear indication that the framers of the Constitution intended and expected the ultimate extinction of that institution? (Ibid., 57–58)

Lincoln next addressed Senator Douglas's accusation that he (Lincoln) favored a "general consolidation of all local institutions of the States of the Union." Refuting this charge Lincoln said that, although he did not think holding one-sixth of the nation's population "in a state of oppression and tyranny unequalled in the world" was just, he did not wish to interfere in the "business" of those states allowing the "peculiar institution's" existence. He then spoke on the 1857 *Dred Scott* case and why he and virtually the entire legal profession opposed it, did not follow it as a "true" legal rule of law, and thought the ruling needed to be "reversed" (overturned). Statesman Logan recounted that "lawyer" Lincoln said,

"I have expressed heretofore, and I now repeat, my [professional] opposition to the Dred Scott decision…I do not resist it…all that I am doing is refusing to obey it, *as a poltical rule* [of law]. If I were in Congress, and a vote should come up on a question whether Slavery should be prohibited in a new Territory, in spite of the Dred Scott decision, I would vote that it should. That is what I would do.

"Judge [Stephen A.] Douglas said last night, that before the [Court's]decision [came] he might advance his opinion, and it might be contray to the decision when it was made; but after it was made, he would abide by it until it was reversed. Just so! We let this property abide by the decision, but *we will try to reverse that decision*. We will try to put it where Judge Douglas would not object, for he says he will obey it *until it is reversed*. Somebody has to reverse that decision, since it is made, and *we mean to reverse it*, and we mean to do it *peaceably*…The sacredness that Judge Douglas throws around this decision is a degree of sacredness that has never before been thrown around any other decision. I have never heard of such a thing. Why, decisions apparently contrary to that decision, or that good lawyers thought were contrary to that decision, have been made by that very Court before. It is the first of its kind; it is an astonisher in legal history. It is a new wonder of the world. It is based upon falsehood in the main as to the facts—[the] allegations of facts upon which it stands are not facts at all in many instances; and no decision made on any question…thus placed, has ever been held by the [legal] profession as law, and it has always needed confirmation before the lawyers regarded it as settled law." (Ibid., 60–61)

After stating that Justice Taney's *Scott* Opinion was "factually unsound," "generally opposed," "not followed by the legal profession," and "needed reversal" (overturning), Lincoln explained why reversal was needed. In his *The Great Conspiracy* Senator Logan recounted Lincoln's (and the legal profession's) view on the Courts "purposeful betrayal of its function" in the *Scott* case, the "negative legal consequences" resulting from it, and his intent to remedy (correct) the "contrived failure" by the judicial system's highest court. Said Lincoln,

"What are the uses of decisions of Courts? They have two uses. As [concerns] rules of property they [Court decisions] have two uses. First, they decide upon the question before the Court. They decide in this case that Dred Scott is a Slave [legally defined as "Chattel"]. Nobody resists that [legal point]. Not only that, but [second] they say to everybody else, that persons standing just as Dred Scott stands, are [legally defined] as he is. That is, they say that when a question comes up upon another person [in such a position], it [the case] will be so decided again, unless the Court decides in another way—unless the Court overrules [reverses] its [previous] decision. Well, we mean to do what we can to *have the Court decide the other way.* That is one thing we mean to try to do." (Ibid., 61)

After making clear the problem caused by Justice Taney's misrepresentation of American historical, legal, political facts, Lincoln next related the "Race Card Evil" theme cited in the *Scott* case to the personal or political agendas of those seeking to gain financial profit or political status. More specifically, he used Senator Douglas as an example of a would-be exploiter whose "Race Card Evil" oriented beliefs contradicted the political agenda he backed. Statesman Logan recounted how Lincoln's response to Senator Douglas's "America made for the white man" speech revealed the contradiction. Said Lincoln,

"We were often…in the course of Judge Douglas's speech last night, reminded that this Government was made for white men—that he believed it was made for white men. Well, that is putting it in a shape in which no one [white person] wants to deny it; but the Judge then goes into his passion for drawing inferences that are not warranted. I protest, now and forever, against the counterfeit logic which presumes that because I do not want a Negro woman for a Slave I do necessarily want her for a wife. My understanding is that I need not have her for either; but, as God has made us separate, we can leave one another alone, and do one another much good thereby. There are White men enough to marry all the White women, and enough Black men to marry all the Black women, and in God's name let them be so married. The Judge regales us with the terrible enormities that take place by the mixture of races; that the inferior race bears the superior [race] down. Why, Judge, if we do not let them get together in the Territories, they won't mix there…" (Ibid., 62–63)

Exposing Senator Douglas's "Race Card Evil" oriented logic for the hypocrisy that it was, Lincoln then revealed the true meaning behind the "inferiority-superiority" doctrine advocated by the Senator and his supporters. Senator Logan recounted Lincoln's analogy between the "inferiority-superiority," "divine right of kings to rule," and "perpetual alliegance" doctrines. Said Lincoln,

"Those arguments that are made [by Senator Douglas and others], that the inferior races are to be treated with as much allowance [privileges, rights, etc.] as they are capable of enjoying; that as much is to be done for them as their condition will allow—what are these arguments? They are the arguments that Kings have made for enslaving the People in all ages of the world. You will find that all the arguments in favor of King-Craft were of this class; they always bestrode the necks of the People, not that they [the kings] wanted to do it, but because the People were better off for being ridden! That is their argument, and this argument of the Judge [Douglas] is the same old ["Race Card Evil"] Serpent that says: you work, and I eat; you toil [struggle], and I will enjoy the fruits of it [Gen. 3:19, kjv].

"Turn it whatever way you will—whether it comes from the mouth of a King, [as] an excuse for enslaving the People of his Country, or from the mouth of men of one race as a reason for enslaving men of another race, it is all the same old Serpent; and I hold, if that course of argumentation that is made for the purpose of convincing the public mind that we should not care about this, should be granted, it does not stop with the Negro." (Ibid., 63)

As Lincoln winded down his speech he reminded the audience of some important words contained in the 1776 Declaration of Independence, invited them to seriously reflect on the truth or falsity of those words, and asked whether retaining or omitting them from the document was the best course to follow after deciding their validity or invalidity. Regarding making "exceptions" to the basic level of Human equality cited in the Declaration, Senator Logan recounted that Honest Abe said,

> "I should like to know, taking this old Declaration of Independence, which declares that all men are equal upon principle, and making exceptions to it, where will it stop? If one man says it does not mean a Negro, why not say it does not mean some other man? If that Declaration is not the truth, let us get the Statute Book, in which we find it, and tear it out! Who is so bold as to do it? If it is not true, let us tear it out!"…"Let us stick to it then; let us stand firmly by it then…" (Ibid., 64)

Concluding, Mr. Lincoln reminded his audience of the religious doctrine that they professed to believe in or adhere to—a doctrine closely connected with the 1787 Constitution's framing. Concerning the idea of someone being a "superior man," Senator Logan recounted that Lincoln said,

> "The Saviour [Jesus], I suppose, did not expect that any human creature could be perfect as the Father [God] in Heaven; but he said, 'As your Father in Heaven is perfect, be ye also perfect' [Matt. 5:48, KJV]. He [Jesus] set that up as a standard, and he who did most toward reaching that standard, attained the highest [superior] degree of moral perfection. So I say, in relation to the principle that all men are created equal—let it be as nearly reached as we can. If we cannot give Freedom to every creature, let us do nothing that will impose Slavery upon any other creature. Let us then turn this Government back into the channel in which the framers of the [1787] Constitution originally placed it. Let us stand firmly by each other…Let us discard all this quibbling…unite as one People throughout this Land, until we shall once more stand up declaring that all men are created equal." (Ibid., 64)

Undoubtedly, Lincoln's speech rattled Senator Douglas (who was in the audience). On 16 July 1858, the Senator spoke to a Bloomington, Illinois audience in one last effort to rebut Lincoln. However, not long after starting his speech the Senator returned to the "Race Card" oriented subject he mentioned during July ninth. After accusing Abe of promoting a "War of Sections between the North and South," the Senator addressed Lincoln's opposition to Justice Taney's views cited in the *Dred Scott* case. Senator Logan recounted,

> Then, taking up what he said was "Mr. Lincoln's objection to the Dred Scott decision"…Mr. Douglas contended at some length that this Government was "founded on the White basis" for the benefit of the Whites and their posterity. He did "not believe that it was the design or intention of the signers of the Declaration of Independence or the Framers of the Constitution to include Negroes, Indians, or *other inferior races*, with White men as citizens;" nor that the former "had any reference to Negroes, when they used the expression that all men were created equal," nor to "any other inferior race." He held that, "They were speaking only of the White race, and never dreamed that their language would be construed to apply to the Negro"; and after ridiculing the contrary [Lincoln's] view, [Douglas] insisted that, "The history of the Country shows that neither the signers of the Declaration, nor the Framers of the Constitution, ever supposed that their language would be used in an attempt to make this Nation *a mixed Nation* of Indians, Negroes, Whites, and *Mongrels*." (Ibid., 70–71, italics ours)

Senator Douglas then tried to make his "Race Card Evil" oriented views sound "harmonious" with civil, humanitarian, and religious principles. Senator Logan recounted that Senator Douglas said,

The [founding] Fathers proceeded on the White basis, making the White people the governing race, but conceding to the Indian and Negro, and all *inferior races*, all the rights and all the privileges they could enjoy consistent with the safety of the [white] society in which they lived." "That," said he, "is my opinion now. I told you that humanity, philanthropy, justice, and sound policy required that we [whites] should give the Negro [etc.] every right, every privilege, every immunity consistent with the safety and welfare of the [white] State. The question, then, naturally arises, what are those rights and privileges, and what is the nature and extent of them? My answer is, that that is a question which each State and each Territory must decide for itself...I am content with that position. My friend Lincoln is not...He thinks that the Almighty made the Negro his equal and his brother. For my part I do not consider the Negro any kin to me, nor to any other White man; but I would still carry my humanity and my philanthropy to the extent of giving him every privilege and every immunity that he could enjoy, consistent with our own." (Ibid., 71, italics ours)

Concluding his speech, Mr. Douglas admitted that he had championed the 1850 Compromise and appealed to the audience to uphold the African Slavery scheme to preserve "friendly relations" between the Union's Northern and Southern States. Said Senator Douglas,

This Union can only be preserved by maintaining the fraternal feeling between the North and South...by preserving the Sovereignty of the States...to settle its domestic concerns [businesses] for itself...Let that be done, and the Union will be perpetual...and this Republic, which began with thirteen States and which now number thirty-two...may yet expand...and become one vast ocean-bound Confederacy..." (Ibid., 72)

Having stated their cases both Lincoln and Douglas agreed, on 24 July 1858, to a final series of debates to be held in Illinois from August 21 to October 15, 1858—at Ottawa, Freeport, Jonesboro, Charleston, Galesburg, Quincy, and Alton. These debates would be the deciding factor to win the 1860 Presidencial election; and ironically, during these debates Senator Douglas would irreparably damage his public image and improve Mr. Lincoln's.

When the November 1860 Presidential election arrived, it was obvious that Lincoln would win—despite South Carolina's threat to secede from the Union should such occur. When election day ended the Republican Party had succeeded in having its first candidate, "Honest Abe," elected as America's sixteenth President. In view of this outcome, South Carolina withdrew from the Union on 20 December 1860. This move puzzeled the Thirty-sixth Congress—since it had planned,during its upcoming session, to address the African Slavery scheme in a light favoring the Slaveholding States.

To pacify slaveowners, Congress introduced a bill during January 1861 to protect the "vested property rights" that slaveholders believed they were entitled to concerning "owning man" (slave-ownership). On 28 February 1861 the bill passed in the House by the required two-thirds vote; and on 2 March 1861 it passed in the Senate by the same requirement. Since the bill passed in both Houses of Congress by the required number of votes, the President's signature to confirm it was unnecessary Nevertheless, President James Buchanan signed the bill shortly before his term of office expired and Lincoln's began (4 March 1861). The passed bill, entitled the "Thirteenth Amendment," prevented Congress from abolishing or interfering with the African Slavery scheme. The language of this "proslavery" Thirteenth Amendment stated,

> *Resolved by the Senate and House of Representatives of the United States of America in Congress assembled,* That the following article be proposed to the Legislatures of the

several States as an amendment to the Constitution of the United States, which, when ratified by three-fourths of said Legilatures, shall be valid, to all intents and purposes, as part of the said Constitution, viz [namely]:

No amendment shall be made to the Constitution which will authorize or give to Congress the power to abolish or interfere, within any State, with the domestic institutions thereof, including that of persons held to labor or Service ["Chattel" Slavery] by the laws of said States.

"Proposed Amendments to the Constitution not Ratified by the States," *Const. of the U.S. of A. as Amended*, 29–30.

Fortunately, when the Amendment was sent to the States for ratification by their legislatures, it failed to obtain the required "three-fourths of State legislatures vote" cited by the 1787 Constitution's Art I, Sec 7, Cl 2 (Bills) and Art V (Amendments to the Constitution). Hence, the Amendment failed to become part of the 1787 Constitution. Lincoln's election as President, coupled with this failure, angered the big-business slaveholders of Slave States. Thus, between January 9–February 1, 1861 six more States (MS, FL, AL, GA, LA, TX) followed South Carolina and withdrew from the Union to form the Confederate States of America (February 4–8, 1861)—which violated the 1787 Constitution's Art I, Sec 10, Cl 1 and Art IV, Sec 3, Cl 1. And on 12 April 1861, forty-three Confederate ships attacked Fort Sumter federal base situated in Charleston, SC and prompted four more Slave States (VA, NC, TN, AR) to break away from the Union (April 17–May 20, 1861)—which violated the same Constitutional Articles and Art III, Sec 3, Cl 1 ("treason"), ignited America's Confederate-Union ("Civil") War, validated Lincoln's prediction that the "slavery issue" would not be over until "a crisis had been reached and passed," and proved true a long-forgotten biblical prophecy about "Race Card Evil" oriented causes and their effects during any given time era—namely:

> And there appeared…a woman [government] clothed with the sun, and the moon under her feet, and upon her head a crown of twelve stars…she being with [thirteenth] child cried, travailing [laboring] in birth…And there appeared…a great red dragon, having seven heads and ten horns…his tail drew the third part of the stars…and the dragon stood before the woman…to devour her child as soon as it was born…And the woman fled into the wilderness, where she hath [has] a place prepared of [by] God, that they should feed her there [for] a thousand two hundred and threescore days. (Rev.12:1–6, KJV)

Congress's failure to prevent war prompted President Lincoln to entertain other means to preserve the Union. For the remainder of 1861 Lincoln tried to convince the eleven rebel States and four Border States (KY, MD, MO, WV) to accept a government-backed "Compensated Emancipation" plan for their slaves. Unfortunately, the idea fell on arrogant and deaf slaveholders ears. Still, Lincoln refused to abandon his idea of ending the war by peaceful solution.

During December 1861 Lincoln gave his First Message to Congress—advising that the Union must be preserved and all indispensable means must be employed to do so. Next, during March 1862 Lincoln gave his Second Message—advising Congress to seriously entertain his gradual Compensated Emancipation program. Congress responded by adopting a Joint Resolution to enact Lincoln's idea, introducing a bill proposing Emanipation in Washington, DC (11 April 1862), and introducing a bill "to secure Freedom to all persons within the territories of the United States" (19 June 1862). By adopting and enacting such measures, Congress was sending a clear message to the rebel States that it agreed with Lincoln's view that the key to securing Union harmony lie in putting the "Race Card Evil" oriented African Slavery program "in the course of ultimate extinction." However, cheap-labor scheme profiteers were not about to concede defeat.

To prevent Congress from passing legislation to end the evil scheme, slaveowners argued that their Fifth Amendment right to own "property" (slaves) would be violated should such occur. When that failed, they took Lincoln up to the Congressional mount (Capitol Hill) to bribe him with promises of fame—just like the Old Serpent did to Jesus (Matt. 4:1–11) (KJV). In his *The Great Conspiracy*, Senator Logan recounted Kentucky Representative John J. Crittenden's 23 April 1862 House speech which stated in part:

> "Sir," said Mr. [John J.] Crittenden—in one of his most eloquent bursts, in the House of Representatives—"it is not my duty, perhaps, to defend the President of the United States…I voted against Mr. Lincoln, and opposed him honestly and sincerely; but Mr. Lincoln has won me to his side. There is a niche in the Temple of Fame, a niche near to [George] Washington, which should be occupied by the statue of him who shall save this Country. Mr. Lincoln has a mighty destiny. It is for him, if he will, to step into that niche. It is for him to be but President of the People of the United States, and there will be his statue. But, if he choose to be, in these times, a mere sectarian and a Party man, that niche will be reserved for some future and better Patriot. It is in his power to occupy a place next to Washington, the Founder, and the Preserver, side by side. Sir, Mr. Lincoln is no coward. His not doing what the Constitution forbade him to do, is no proof of his cowardice." (*The Great Conspiracy*, 482)

Mr. Crittenden's antislavery colleagues recognized his speech for the proslavery bribe that it was. Among those who noticed was Illinois Representative Owen Lovejoy, brother of the slain Elijah P. Lovejoy, who countered with his own House speech on 24 April 1862. Mr. Lovejoy replied in part,

"The gentleman from Kentucky says he has a niche for Abraham Lincoln. Where is it? He pointed upward! But, Sir, should the President follow the counsel of that gentleman, and become the defender and perpetuator of human Slavery, he should point downward to some dungeon in the Temple of Moloch, who feeds on human blood and is surrounded with fires, where are forged mancles and chains for human limbs—in the crypts and recesses of whose Temple, woman is scourged, and man tortured, and outside whose walls are lying dogs, gorged with human flesh, as [the English poet George Gordon] Byron describes them stretched around Stamboul. That is a suitable place for the statue of one who would defend and perpetuate human slavery."…"I, too, have a niche for Abraham Lincoln; but it is in Freedom's Holy Fane, and not in the blood-besmeared Temple of human Bondage; not surrounded by Slaves, fetters and chains, but with the symbols of Freedom; not dark with Bondage, but radiant with the light of Liberty. In that niche he shall stand proudly, nobly, gloriously, with shattered fetters and broken chains and slave-whips beneath his feet. If Abraham Lincoln pursues the path, evidently pointed out for him in the providence of God, as I believe he will, then he will occupy the proud position I have indicated. That is a fame worth living for; ay, more, that is a fame worth dying for, though that death led through the blood of Gethsemane and the agony of the Accursed Tree [Cross]. That is a fame which has glory and honor and immortality and Eternal Life. Let Abraham Lincoln make himself, as I trust he will, the Emancipator, the Liberator, as he has the opportunity of doing, and his name shall not only be enrolled in this Earthly Temple, but it will be traced on the living stones of the Temple which rears itself amid the Thrones and Hierarchies of Heaven, whose top-stone [capstone] is to be brought in with shouting of 'Grace, grace unto it.'" (Ibid., 483–84)

Although Lincoln believed that the African Slavery program was incompatible with the Union's domestic tranquility, he nevertheless refused to interfere with it during the remainder of the spring of 1862. In fact, it was only after Union forces suffered military setbacks along the Potomac River, during June of 1862, that he seriously considered enacting "military emancipation" in order to offset the Confederate army's use of "slave-manpower" in the war. Before doing so, on 12 July 1862 Lincoln decided to try one last appeal to the border states congressmen to accept a government-backed gradual emancipation-compensation program. However, after his third offer was rejected, and being alarmed by reports of Genral McClellan's inability to hold the Union's line at the Potomac, Lincoln made the decision to play his last and highest trump card in the deadly war game—namely military emancipation. Senator Logan recounted Lincoln's wrestling about the decision,

> Harried, and worried…threatened even by the Commander of the Army of the Potomac, it is not surprising, in view of the apparently irreconcilable attitude of the loyal Border-State men to gradual and compensated Emancipation, that the tension of President Lincoln's mind began to feel a measure of relief in contemplating Military Emancipation in the teeth of all such threats.
>
> He had long since made up his mind that the existence of Slavery was not compatible with the preservation of the Union. The only question now was, how to get rid of it? If the worst should come to the worst, despite McClellan's threat, he would have to risk everything on the turn of the die—would have to "play his last card;" and that "last card" was Military Emancipation. Yet still he disliked to play it. The time and necessity for it had not yet arrived—although he thought he saw them coming. (Ibid., 488)

About June of 1862 Lincoln decided to write his Emancipation Proclamation. However, it was between late July and early August when he informed his cabinet and asked its advice on how best to proceed with publishing it. Senator Logan recounted Lincoln's thoughts about the decision,

> And now, it cannot be better told, than in President Lincoln's own words, as given to the portrait-painter Carpenter, and recorded in the latter's "*Six months in the White House*" what followed:
>
> "It had got to be," said he [Lincoln], "midsummer, 1862. Things had gone from bad to worse, until I felt that we had reached the end of our rope on the plan of operations we had been pursuing; that we had about played our last card, and must change our tactics, or lose the game!"
>
> "I now determined upon the adoption of the Emancipation Policy; and, without consultation with, or the knowledge of, the Cabinet, I prepared the original draft of the Proclamation, and, after much anxious thought, called a Cabinet meeting upon the subject. This was the last of July, or the first part of the month of August, 1862" (The exact date he did not remember).(*Ibid.*, 492)

By early September of 1862 Lincoln had prepared the final draft of his Emancipation Proclamation, but withheld publishing it based on Secretary of State William H. Seward's advice that it should not be done until the Union forces gained a significant victory (so that the measure would not appear as a cry of despair). Such a victory came on 17 September 1862 during the Battle of Antietam near Sharpsburg, Maryland. From dawn to dusk (5:30 a.m.–5:30 p.m.) the bloodiest one-day battle in American history was fought between Union and Confederate forces until Union forces prevailed. Five days later, 22 September 1862, Lincoln published his Preliminary Emancipation Proclamation that would become effective on 1 January 1863. Recounted Senator Logan,

> At last, then, had gone forth the Fiat—telegraphed and read throughout the Land, on that memorable 22d

of September, 1862—which, with the supplemental Proclamation of January 1, 1863, was to bring joy and Freedom to the millions of black bondsmen of the South. (Ibid., 496)

Significantly, President Lincoln's Emancipation Proclamation said in part,

By the President of the United States of America

### A PROCLAMATION

Whereas, on the 22nd day of September, A.D. 1862, a proclamation was issued by the President of the United States, containing, among other things, the following, to wit:

That on the 1st day of January, A.D. 1863, all persons held as slaves within any State or designated part of a State the people whereof shall then be in rebellion against the United States shall be then, thenceforward, and forever free; and the Executive Government of the United States, including the military and naval authority thereof, will recognize and maintain the freedom of such persons... And I hereby enjoin upon the people so declared to be free to abstain from all violence, unless in necessary self-defence; and I recommend to them that, in all case[s] when allowed, they labor faithfully for reasonable wages... upon this act, sincerely believed to be an Act of justice, warranted by the Constitution upon military necessity, I invoke the considerate judgment of mankind and the gracious favor of Almighty God.

In witness whereof, I have hereunto set my hand and caused the Seal of the United States to be affixed. ("Emancipation Proclamation," Antietam National Battlefield Virtual Visitors Center, http://www.nps.gov/ncro/anti/emancipation.html. Retrieved 27 January 2014)

While it is true that President Lincoln's Emancipation Proclamation was the result of his having played his last card in the Union's war effort against Confederate forces, and that it only freed those slaves in the rebel States, it is equally true that he had a larger agenda in mind when he issued the document. This "higher purpose" Senator Logan recounted in *The Great Conspiracy*. Said he,

> His [Lincoln's] great anxiety was to "perpetuate," as well as to save, to the People of the World [the "seventy" nations, humanity], the imperiled [Republican] form of Popular [Democratic] Government, and assure to it a happy and a grand future. (*The Great Conspiracy*, 490)

Moreover, spiritualist John Ballou agreed with Senator Logan's view that Lincoln had a sense of "greater purpose"—saying that the Emancipation Proclamation proved "the pen mightier than the sword" when combatting the "Race Card Evil" oriented cheap-labor scheme. In his *Oahspe* sections respectively entitled "Jehovih Overthroweth Slavery in Guatama [America]" and the "Fallen Swords Day," Mr. Ballou hinted that Lincoln's deed was equivalent to both the "Exodus from Egypt" story and overthrow of the "divine right of kings to rule" doctrine. Recounted Mr. Ballou,

> Es [daughter of the Creator] said: In the olden times, and in the eastern countries, Jehovih [the Creator] began His revelations. The western continent He left for the finishing thereof.
>
> Now, when God looked abroad over Guatama [America], he saw four millions of people in bondage, as slaves; and he saw that they must be liberated...God, then, said...for a season, they [Americans] shall dwell in... darkness.
>
> And this was accomplished, and straightway a [civil] war ensued betwixt the [Southern] owners of the slaves and the [Northern] neighboring states...And, there rose up two million men in arms, pushing on in war on

every side, coursing the rich soil in mortal blood. And yet, neither side had defined its principles, or taken [a] stand *for righteousness sake*...And years went on, and all the people began to perceive that, without righteousness, there would be no end to the war.

Jehovih said: Only death can reach these people, or make them behold my hand. Yet, thou shalt send thy angel hosts over all the north regions and inspire them, to call out for liberty...to a more heavenly stand, to make them see justice and liberty...inspiring mortals day and night to demand freedom for the slaves...Jehovih said...go down to the earth, to Washington [DC], to [Abraham] Lincoln, the president...For he is not bound [up] in doctrine... And it shall come to pass that Lincoln will hear thee, and he shall resolve in his own mind [to lean] unto freedom for the slaves...And, lo and behold, the northern armies ran forth over the [southern] enemy's country as if war were but play; and the southern armies vanished, disarming themselves...The slaves were free!

Jehovih said: Let this be a testimony, that this land [America] is the place of the beginning of the kosmon [spiritual enlightenment] era. There shall be no caste amongst my people. (*Book of Es, Daughter of Jehovih*, 20:1–34 passim (italics ours); *Oahspe*, 770–72.

As Jehovih [the Creator]...delivered into freedom Guatama's [America's] slaves, and thus to general slavery dealt the final blow, so Jehovih blessed that day, and sanctified it...[And] Jehovih said: "Remember the day of proclamation of freedom [1 January 1863], for it is My day, which I bequeathed unto you as a day of freedom in all righteous jollification, which ye shall keep every year, and commemorate, to the end of the world [cf. Ex. 12:1–2, 14, 21–27 and 13:1–10, KJV]." (*Book of Inspiration*, 17:1, 4; *Oahspe*, 825–26)

As could be expected, Lincoln's Proclamation was not well received by the large slaveholding enterprises (North or South) and the political lackeys who represented their "vested property rights" interest in enslaving their fellow man. Hence, Lincoln—recalling the 1861 "Congressionally passed-Presidentially signed-but not State-ratified" proslavery Thirteenth Amendment—believed that his Proclamation should be "Congressionally incorporated" into the 1787 Constitution as an Amendment universally abolishing slavery throughout what would become the Union's thirty-six States. Recounted statesman Logan in *The Great Conspiracy*,

> After President Lincoln had issued his Proclamation of Emancipation, the friends of Freedom clearly perceived—and none of them more clearly than [Lincoln] himself—that until the incorporation of that great Act into the Constitution of the United States itself [was achieved], there could be no real assurance of safety to the liberties of the emancipated; that unless this were done there would be left, even after the suppression of the Rebellion, a living spark of dissention which might at any time again be fanned into the flames of Civil War.
>
> Hence, at all proper times, Mr. Lincoln favored and even urged Congressional action upon the subject. It was not, however, until the following year that definite action may be said to have commenced in Congress toward that end; and, as Congress was slow, he found it necessary to say in his third Annual Message: "while I remain in my present position I shall not attempt to retract or modify the Emancipation Proclamation; nor shall I return to Slavery any person who is Free by the terms of that Proclamation, or by any of the Acts of Congress." (*The Great Conspiracy*, 513)

By fighting to put the African Slavery scheme "in the course of ultimate extinction," and refusing to back down during the ensuing fight, Abe Lincoln had formally declared war on the "Race Card Evil" itself. Moreover, by the end of 1863 Congress also made clear its intent to either completely put the evil to rest or, at the least, remove the "legal" protection it had enjoyed for so many years. Thus both the Executive and Legislative branches of the American government gave notice to "Race Card Evil" oriented champions that a new day was approaching the new nation—one in which a great charter of freedom for all Americans, not just a privileged few, would exist. That day would give working-class Americans the freedom to negotiate wages with employers, raise the quality of their lives according to abilities possessed and efforts expended, and make the pursuit of happiness spoken of in the 1787 Constitution's Preamble a reality. However, people would soon find that the ancient evil was not about to go away quietly into that good night.

# 6

# Death Knell for Slavery
# and the Race Card Evil Game

> And there was war in heaven: Michael and his angels
> fought against the dragon; and the dragon…and his
> angels…prevailed not; neither was their place found any
> more in heaven. And the great dragon was cast out, that
> old serpent, called the Devil, and Satan, which deceiveth
> the whole world…And I heard a loud voice saying in
> heaven, Now is come salvation, and strength, and the
> kingdom of our God, and the power of his Christ: for
> the accuser of our brethren is cast down, which [who]
> accused them before our God day and night. And they
> overcame him by the blood of the Lamb, and by the word
> of their testimony.
>
> —Rev. 12:7–11 (KJV)

BEFORE THE THIRTY-EIGHTH Congress adjourned in December of 1863, chief among the items it needed to address was the rebel states' refusal to recognize the "limited" military emancipation measures Congress and President Lincoln issued from 1861 to 1863. This "arrogant" attitude validated the views of many Congressmen and Lincoln that the 1787 Constitution needed a "general" Emancipation Proclamation written into it—declaring liberty throughout the Union and territories subject to its jurisdiction—to end the "Race Card Evil" oriented African slavery program for all time. Thus, Congress accepted proposed constitutional amendments from Missouri senator John B. Henderson and Ohio Representative James M. Ashley that would be introduced in the upcoming year by Illinois senator Lyman Trumbull and Iowa Representative James F. Wilson (appointed Senate and House judiciary committee chairmans to oversee the proposals).

When Congress resumed in January of 1864, the Senate committee started drafting an antislavery Thirteenth Amendment to replace the 1861 proslavery one. This new version, coauthored by Mr. Trumbull and designated "Senate Bill Number 16" (S. No. 16), outlawed the cheap-labor scheme by using language in the 1787 Northwest Ordinance. In *The Great Conspiracy*, Senator Logan recounted that it stated,

1. <nl>Art XIII, Sec I. Neither Slavery nor Involuntary Servitude, *except as a punishment for crime*, whereof the party shall have been duly convicted, shall exist within the United States, or any place subject to their jurisdiction.</p>

2. Art XIII, Sec II. Congress shall have power to enforce this Article by appropriate legislation.

3. *The Great Conspiracy*, 522; *Congressional Globe*, 38th Congress, 1st Session, 1864, respectively 1313, 1364 (italics ours).

Submitting the proposed amendment for Senate debate on 28 March 1864, Senator Trumbull was first to speak on the need for Congressional legislation to end the African Slavery program. Senator Logan recounted in part,

> Trumbull insisted that Slavery was at the bottom of all the internal troubles with which the Nation had from its birth been afflicted, down to this wicked Rebellion, with all the resulting "distress, desolation, and death;" and that by 1860, it had grown to such power and arrogance that

"its advocates demanded the control of the Nation in its interests, failing in which, they attempted its overthrow." He reviewed, at some length, what had been done by our Government with regard to Slavery, since the breaking out of hostilities…"an indisposition on the part of the Executive Authority [presidential office] to interefere with Slavery"…how…Slaves escaping to our lines, were driven back to their Rebel masters; how the Act of Congress of July, 1861, which gave Freedom to all Slaves allowed by their Rebel masters to assist in the erection of Rebel works and fortifications, had "not been executed," and, said Mr. Trumbull, "so far as I am advised, not a single Slave has been set at liberty under it"…After demonstrating that "any and all these laws and Proclamations…are ineffectual to the destruction of Slavery," and protesting that some more effectual method of getting rid of the Institution must be adopted, he declared, as his judgment, that "the only effectual way of ridding the Country of Slavery, so that it cannot be resuscitated, is by an Amendment of the Constitution forever prohibiting it within the jurisdiction of the United States."

He then canvassed the chances of adoption of such an Amendment by an affirmative vote of two- thirds in each House of Congress, and of its subsequent ratification by three-fourths of the States of the Union, and declared that "it is reasonable to suppose that if this proposed Amendment passes Congress, it will, *within a year*, receive the ratification of the requisite number of States to make it a part of the Constitution." (Ibid., 527–29 passim; *Cong. Globe*, 38th Cong., 1st Sess., 1864, 1313)

On 30 March 1864 a ten-day debate opened in the Senate on the proposed "new" Thirteenth Amendment. At that time the Senate investigated the historical setting in which the "Race Card Evil" oriented scheme was introduced to, and nurtured in, American society—tracing its practice back to the ancient world under the Old Testament's *Genesis* 9 "curse on Ham" and

"Hebrew-Levitical code" accounts, opposition to it under the New Testament's "universal brotherhood" and "Golden Rule" doctrines taught by Jesus of Nazareth, and its maintenance under later-developed American political ideas called "property rights in owning man," "state's rights" (state's sovereignty), and "state's nullification (anullment) of objectionable federal laws."

## Thirteenth Amendment Debate in the Senate

One of the first speakers taking the Senate floor to argue for the African Slavery cheap-labor scheme was Delaware senator Williard Saulsbury Sr. Representing his proslavery constituents, he argued that "Human Slavery" was both "Right" and "a Divinely Sanctioned Institution"—an argument that sounded like Harriet's "Priest #1's" view. *The Great Conspiracy* and 31 March 1864 *Congressional Globe* Journal of Proceedings recounted that Saulsbury, using the *Genesis* 9 "Ham cursed" story as "proof," argued as follows:

> Saulsbury of Delaware, was representative and spokeman of this [proslavery] class, and he took occasion during this very debate to defend Slavery as a Divine Institution, which had the sanction both of the Mosaic [old] and Christian [new] Dispensations [testaments]…Said he:
>
> ["We have grown, Mr. President, vain enough to imagine that had we been the creators of the universe and of all things that exist therein, we could improve upon the workmanship of the Almighty. Had such been the case, no Eve would have plucked the forbidden fruit; no Adam would have been doomed to earn his bread in the sweat of his brow; the earth would not have been so cursed as to bring forth briers and thistles…the food of man would have been manna…No tornado's blast, no earthquake shock would have affrighted or alarmed the world, or destroyed any portion of the human race…nothing but happiness, universal happiness, would have ever existed.

But, sir, we were not the creators of the universe or of existence anywhere, and we must look at questions in a practical light, view them according to the circumstances by which we are surrounded and by the light of current events. In that light I propose to view the (Thirteenth Amendment) question now before the Senate.]

"Slavery had existed under some form or other from the first period of recorded history. It dates back even beyond the period of Abraham, the Father of the Faithful, in whose seed all the ["seventy"] Nations of the Earth were to be blessed. We find that, immediately after the Flood, the Almighty, for purposes inscrutable to us, condemned a whole race to Servitude: *"vayomer orur knoan Efet Afoatim Yeahio Le-echot,"* [meaning] "And he [Noah] said, cursed be Canaan; Slave of Slaves he shall be to his brethren." (Gen. 9:24–25, KJV)

"It continued among all people until the advent of the Christian era. It was recognized in that New [Testament] Dispensation, which was to supersede the Old [Testament]. It has the sanction of God's own Apostle [Paul]; for when Paul sent back Onesimus to Philemon, whom did he send? A Freeman? No, Sir. He sent his… (*doulos,*) a Slave, born as such, not even his *andrapodon*, who was such by captivity in War [cf. Colossians 4:7–9 with Philemon 1:10–19] [KJV]. Among all people, and in all ages, has this Institution, if such it is to be called, existed, and had the countenance of wise and good men, and even of the Christian Church itself, until these modern times, up at least to the nineteenth century [AD]. It exists in this Country, and has existed from the beginning." (*The Great Conspiracy*, 533–34; *Cong. Globe*, 38th Cong., 1st Sess., 1864, 1364–65; text brackets of second paragraph part of *Globe*, other internal brackets ours)

Senator Saulsbury next argued that replacing the 1781 Articles of Confederation with the 1787 Constitution, and the Jefferson-Madison "State's Rights-Nullification" doctrines, all supported the big-business slaveowners' right to withdraw (secede) from the Union rather than free their cheap-labor workforce—even if monetary compensation was offered. Senator Logan recounted,

> Among these "loyal" Democratic opponents of Emancipation, in any shape, or any where, were not wanting men—whether from Loyal Northern or Border States—who still openly avowed that Slavery was right; that Rebellion, to preserve its continuance, was justifiable; and that there was no Constitutional method of uprooting it…He [Saulsbury] also undertook to justify Secession on the singular ground that "we are sprung from a Race of Secessionists," the proof of which he held to be in the fact that, while the preamble to, as well as the body of the [1781] Convention of Ratification of the old Articles of Confederation between the States of New Hampshire, Massachusetts Bay, Rhode Island and Providence Plantations, Connecticut, New York, New Jersey, Pennsylvania, Delaware, Maryland, Virginia, North Carolina, South Carolina, and Georgia, declared that Confederation to be a "Perpetual Union," yet, within nine years thereafter, all the other States Seceded from New York, Virginia, North Carolina, and Rhode Island by ratifying the new [1787] Constitution for "a more perfect Union."
>
> He also endeavored to maintain the extraordinary proposition that "if the Senate of the United States were to adopt this [Thirteenth Amendment] Joint-resolution, and were to submit it to all the States of this Union, and if three-fourths of the States should ratify the Amendment, it would not be binding on any State whose interest was affected by it, if that State protested against it!" (Ibid., 533–35; *Cong. Globe*, 38th Cong., 1st Sess., 1864, 1365)

On concluding, Senator Saulsbury added a silly proslavery view that misapplied both Old and New Testament texts to justify the African slavery scheme. Said he,

"The sinfulness of slavery or the evil of slavery among those with whom it exists is not to be invoked as affording power, in the absence of anything else, to make this proposed [Thirteenth Amendment] change. If that be the source whence is derived the authority to make this amendment to the Constitution it is an authority against which I cannot argue, for the simple reason that I and my antagonist never could agree. In my judgment he advocates a sickly sentiment, I a practical question. He professes to be wiser than the Almighty, under whose providence this system of human bondage has been allowed to exist in all ages of the past; wiser than the Saviour of the world, who when he was on earth never interfered with the law of slavery, although he walked up and down the plains of Judea, where there were slaves, and the law of whose people recognized the existence of slavery—the law that was given to them from Mount Sinai amid lightning and thunder, amid smoke and flame; and recognizing the existence not only of this [slavery] relation but the rightfulness of it. "Thou shalt not covet thy neighbor's wife, his servant (slave), his ox, his ass, nor anything that is his" (Ex. 20:17). What is the meaning of "servant?" Among the people to whom that law was given there were hired servants; there were bondmen and bondmaids. *Efet*, the original in the Hebrew language, which means a slave, means a slave born as such, just as much as *doulos*, in Greek, means a slave born as such. I cannot argue with such an antagonist, because he sets his judgment up against the history of the race and of mankind in all past ages." (*Cong. Globe*, 38th Cong., 1st Sess., 1864, 1366–67)

Saulsbury's "slanted" speech set the stage for a number of rebuttals from his colleagues. First to respond was New Hampshire Senator Daniel Clark, who addressed the issue of why the "Race Card Evil" oriented African slavery program needed legal extinction by means of the Thirteenth Amendment. Said he,

"Here is the issue clearly made up and plainly stated. Slavery says, "I am of God and eternal and absolute right;" Liberty cries, "You are of your father the devil, and his work you do [cf. John 8:44]." Now can these two warring forces exist together, and did not the framers of the [1787] Constitution when they admitted into the charter of free government the idea of human bondage put into it an element of unrest, strife, and death?

"Let us consider. Slavery procures its recognition and admission into the Constitution. It has achieved a great and almost fatal work. It has nestled into the very bosom of the nation's life. It has secured the nation's protection. It has allied with its defense the nation's arms. It has an anchorage-ground from which no political gales can drive it; a fortress where no hostile arm can assault it, and whence it can go forth to secure new triumphs as the nation advances in territorial power. True, her name is not in the Constitution; but alas! She is there—there in vigor and strength—and in the very first Article of that instrument [Constitution] she provides for her representation in Congress, where her voice and her votes have been of signal potency. She gained at a bound the legislative hall, and ever since has sat and hissed and writhed about the nation's limbs. True, again, her name was not in the instrument, but her power was there." (*Cong. Globe*, 38th Cong., 1st Sess., 1864, 1368)

Senator Clark next recounted how African slavery proponents manipulated the 1787 Constitution's framers to circumvent the 1808 international (foreign) slavery prohibition clause. Said he,

"For years before she [slavery] had freighted ships from Africa to these shores, laden with human beings, to endure the tortures of the Middle Passage, and if they escaped those to be forever bondmen and bondwomen. She said these men "have no rights which the white man is bound to respect;" and she demanded in that instrument that this inhuman traffic should not be prohibited to her for twenty years and more, and that she might have leisure and opportunity to fill the land with slaves before any prohibition beyond a nominal tax could be laid upon the trade. Was slavery to die out? So said and so I think believed the [founding] fathers; but why, then, this provision for an unlimited supply of victims for twenty years, upon which she could feed and fatten and increase? True, again, her name was not in the instrument. But see, slaves will runaway. Man, black or white, does not love bondage; God has made him free, and if chains are put upon him, upon opportunity given he will slip them off and escape. Who shall return him? Shall he be free? "In no wise," says the Constitution; "he shall not thereby"—that is, by running away to another State—"be discharged [from] such service or labor, but shall be delivered up on claim of the party to whom such service or labor may be due." Delivered up? By whom? By the United States, said those who interpreted the law. And thus by this Constitution slavery assumed monstrous functions and powers...Such was slavery in and by the Constitution. Such are now its provisions in regard to her, save that the time for her to carry on her cruel foreign slave trade has expired.

"Shall she keep her position? Or shall she be cast out as a demon, and forever prevented from again entering the halls of justice, the Houses of Congress, or the national domain?" (Ibid., 1368)

Senator Clark then levied a multicount indictment against the "Race Card Evil" oriented African Slavery scheme that rivaled those levied by Richard Hildreth, Harriett Beecher-Stowe, and Abraham Lincoln. Recounting the historical setting in which the evil was nurtured in America to ignite the Civil War, Mr. Clark said,

"To determine more fully and clearly this question I propose to examine for a little while the history of slavery in connection with this Government...which may serve to show how carefully she has used the power which she gained by her recognition in the Constitution.

"And here I accuse her of divers and sundry grievous misdoings for which she richly deserves to die, and for which now in the righteous retributions of Providence [God] she must suffer...If all the new States admitted after the formation of the Constitution had been free States, slavery never could have increased as it has, nay, must rather have diminished, and we should have escaped this cruel civil war. But under the Constitution slavery ran a race with freedom to secure a slave State as often as there was admitted a free State; yes, and more; for the first half century of the Government six free States were admitted [VT, OH, IN, IL, ME, MI] and nine slave States [KY, TN, LA, MS, AL, MO, AR, FL, TX].

"Mr. President, I would amend the Constitution and banish slavery from the United States for that [reason alone]. She has spread herself since the formation of the Constitution over millions of square miles and among millions of people. She has excluded from that territory free schools and those institutions of learning which are accessible to the poor, and thus kept the people in comparable ignorance [intellectual darkness]. She has degraded labor and increased poverty and vice. She has reared an aristocracy and trampled down the masses. She has denied oftentimes in those States to citizens of other States their rights under the Constitution. She has shut up to them the liberty of speech and the press. She has assaulted them, imprisoned them, lynched them, expatriated them, for no crime, but because they testified against her. She has debarred from that territory most of the improvements which mark free people. She has perverted knowledge. She has opened in parts of it the foreign slave trade, and obstructed the punishment of the kidnapper and the pirate. In other parts, she has degraded the people to the infamous business of raising negroes for sale, and living upon their increase. She has practiced concubinage, destroyed the sanctity of marriage, and sundered and broken the domestic ties. She has bound men, women, and children, robbed them, beat them, and bruised and mangled them, burned and otherwise murdered them. To their cries she has turned a deaf ear, to their complaints shut the courts, and taken from them the power to testify against their oppressors. She has compelled them to submit in silence and labor in tears. She has forbidden their instruction [enlightenment], and mocked them with the pretense [that] she was Christianizing them through suffering.

"She has devised and set up the doctrine of State rights, denying that her people owed allegiance to the national Government...claimed to nullify the acts of Congress... agreed to...the [slavery prohibition] line of [thiry-six degrees, thirty minutes]...then abrogated [negated] it, and filled Kansas with fraud, violence, and blood...stole into Texas, caused it to rebel against Mexico, and then erected it into a slave State in the Union...made war on Mexico for more territory; and when California, a part of the territory obtained by the war, asked to be admitted as a free State, she refused her assent until appeased by new compromises.

"She went into the [Supreme] Court, and...whispered into the ear of the Chief Magistrate [Taney] that the negro had no "rights which the white man was bound to respect." She caused the Court to deny him the rights of a citizen, and, breaking down the old [legal] landmarks [cf. Deut. 19:14; 27:17; Prov. 22:28; 23:10] [KJV], drive him from the justice-hall a castaway without aid and without hope. Failing to elect a President agreeable to herself [in 1860] , she prepared to revolt...To this end she has waged this war of the rebellion three long years, and will continue to wage it till subdued by superior force and arms.

"Mr. President, this [Civil War] rebellion is slavery [up] in arms; and slavery is the ward if not the child of the Constitution. Right well has the guardian discharged the trust. But the creature thus protected and warmed into life has stolen to the bosom of its protector and aimed its dagger at the life of the Government. Sir, it is time this disastrous relation should cease. Let the letters of guardianship be revoked. Reviewing this history and recounting this catalogue of crimes, let Senators, Mr. President, tell me if slavery should longer be tolerated in our Government. Should it not cease to exist? Should not the Constitution be amended so as to entirely forbid and prohibit it?" (Ibid., 1368–69 passim)

In addition to the view that slavery was "right," Senator Saulsbury also said that the time was "not right" to incorporate Emancipation into the 1787 Constitution. Thus, on 5 April 1864, Maryland Senator Reverdy Johnson took the floor to state why the time was "right" for passing the Thirteenth Amendment. Senator Logan recounted in *The Great Conspiracy*,

Reverdy Johnson, of Maryland, however, by his great speech, of April 5th, in the Senate, did much to clear [up] the tangle in the minds of some faltering Union statesmen on this important subject.

He reviewed the question of human Slavery from the time when the [1787] Constitutional Convention was held; showed that at that period, as well as at the time of the Declaration of our Independence "there was but one sentiment upon the [slavery] subject among enlightened Southern statesmen"—and that was, that Slavery "is a great afflicition to any Country where it prevails;" and declared that "a prosperous and permanent Peace can never be secured if the Institution is permitted to survive."
(*The Great Conspiracy*, 536)

Senator Johnson then addressed Saulsbury's argument that abolishing the evil was impossible because it was originally incorporated into the 1787 Constitution—countering that argument by referring to the Constitution's preamble or mission statement,

> Continuing, he [Mr. Johnson] said: "Remember, now, the question is, can that Institution, which deals with Humanity as Property, which claims to shackle the mind, the soul, and the body, which brings to the level of the brute [beast] a portion of the race of Man, cease to be within the reach of the political power of the People of the United States, not because it was not at one time within their power, but because at that time they did not [choose to] exert the power?
>
> "What says the Preamble to the Constitution? How pregnant with a conclusive answer is the Preamble, to the proposition that Slavery cannot be abolished? What does that Preamble state to have been the chief objects that the great and wise and good men had at heart, in recommending the Constitution, with that Preamble, to the adoption of the American People? That Justice might be established; that Tranquility might be preserved; that the common Defense and general Welfare might be maintained; and, last and chief of all, that Liberty might be secured.
>
> "Is there no Justice in putting an end to human Slavery? Is there no danger to the Tranquility of the Country in its existence? May it not interfere with the common Defense and general Welfare? And, above all, is it consistent with any notion, which the mind of man can conceive, of human Liberty?" (Ibid., 536–37; *Cong. Globe*, 38th Cong., 1st Sess., 1864, 1423)

After stating these important principles for which the American Republic's framers founded their government, Senator

Johnson stated what would become a cardinal feature of the American government's character when dealing with members of the "70" Nations. In response to the claim that the enslaved people's "intellectual" and "moral" condition prevented them from being ready to understand or enjoy the meaning of "freedom," he said,

> "Is it to be supposed, because of the present condition of this degraded population, that they are not proper subjects for the enjoyment of human freedom? Are they by nature, and in spite of whatever education tyranny may have left them, so mentally and morally deficient that they do not know what are the blessings of human freedom? What do we see? Wherever the flag of the United States, the symbol of human liberty, now goes, under it from their hereditary bondage are to be found men, women, and children assembling and craving its protection. Is it because they expect greater physical comfort, and that they obtain it? The mere physical condition of the man, in many cases, while under the control of a master, was better than that which he received after coming under the protection of our flag; but in the one [case] the iron [hand] of oppression had pierced his soul, and in the other [case] he is gladdened by the light of liberty. It is idle to deny, [that] we feel it in our own persons, how with reference to that sentiment all men are brethren. Look to the illustrations which the times now afford, how in the illustrations of that sentiment do we differ from the black man? He is willing to incur every personal danger which promises to result in throwing down his shackles and making him tread the earth which God has created for all as a man and not as a slave. It is an instinct of the soul. Tyranny may oppress it for ages and centuries; the pall of despotism may hang over it; but the sentiment is ever there; it kindles into a flame in the very [firey] furnace of affliction, and it avails itself of the first opportunity that offers promising the least chance of escape, and wades

through blood and slaughter to achieve it, and whether it succeeds or fails demonstrates, vindicates in the very effort the inextinguishable right to liberty." (*Cong. Globe*, 38th Cong., 1st Sess., 1864, 1423)

Winding down his speech, Senator Johnson reminded his colleagues of the Golden Rule's true meaning and that it opposed the doctrine that slavery had a divine origin,

To the atrocious pretense that "there was a *right* to make a Slave of any human being"—which he said would have shocked every one of the framers of the [1787] Constitution had they heard it; and, what he termed, the nauseous declaration that "Slavery of the Black race is of Divine origin," and was *intended to be perpetual*; he [Johnson] said:

"The Saviour of Mankind [Jesus] did not put an end to it [Slavery] by physical power, or by the declaration of any existing illegality in word. His mission upon Earth was not to propagate his doctrines by force. He came to save, not to conquer. His purpose was not to march armed legions throughout the habitable Globe, securing the allegiance of those for whose safety he was striving. He warred by other influences. He aimed at the heart, principally. He inculcated his doctrines, more ennobling than any that the World, enlightened as it was before his advent upon Earth, had been able to discover. He taught to Man the obligation of brotherhood. He announced that the true duty of Man was to do to others as he would have others do to him—to all men, the World over; and unless some convert to the modern doctrine that Slavery itself finds not only a guarantee for its *existence*, but for its *legal* existence, in the Scripture, excepts from the operation of the influences which His morality brought to bear on the mind of the Christian world, the Black man, *and shows that it was not intended to apply to Black men*, then it is not true, it cannot be true, that He designed His doctrine not to be equally applicable to the Black and to the White, to the Race of Man as he then existed, or as he might exist in all after-time." (*The Great Conspiracy*, 537–38; *Cong. Globe*, 38th Cong., 1st Sess., 1864, 1423)

Proud of the fact that Maryland had legally and voluntarily abolished slavery prior to the proposed Thirteenth Amendment debate (despite Maryland native Roger B. Taney's *Dred Scott* ruling), Senator Johnson concluded by addressing the claim of possible "mischief" resulting from passing the Amendment and the hypocrisy of proslavery advocates who relied on "Biblical Scripture" to justify the African Slavery program. Said the enlightened senator,

"Terminate it [slavery], and the wit of man will, as I think, be unable to devise any other topic upon which we can be involved in a fratricidal [Cain vs. Abel] strife. God and nature, judging by the history of the past, intend us to be one. Our unity is written in the mountains and the rivers, in which we all have an interest. The very differences of climate [etc.] render each important to the other, and alike important [to self]. That mighty horde which from time to time have gone from the Atlantic imbued with all the principles of human freedom which animated their fathers in running the perils of the mighty deep and seeking liberty here, are now there, and as they have said they will continue to say until time shall be no more: 'We mean that the Government in [the] future shall be as it has been in the past, one, an example of human freedom, for the light and example of the world, and illustrating in the blessings and the happiness it confers the truth of the principles incorporated into the Declaration of Independence, that life and liberty are man's inalienable right.'

"Mischief may be the result of [passing] such a measure; but, as I think, they will be temporary; but mischief must be the result of what has already occurred, the [peculiar] institution is now fatally wounded; it can survive but [only] to fester and to trouble us; and it would be a disgrace to the nation if we could suffer those Africans, whom we are now calling around our standard and asking to aid us in restoring the Constitution and the power of the Government to its rightful authority, to be reduced to bondage again… Terminate whenever the [Civil War] struggle may [end], whatever may be the [educational or moral] condition of this race when it shall terminate…I trust in God it will be a state of freedom that is to be as permanent as is our own freedom. We are to share the same dangers, enjoy according to our power and our means and our ability the same prosperity and when we die, die as men, and not as chattels.

"The only practical mischief of the measure is the condition of the slaves. They are uneducated. If there was nothing in the [biblical] teachings of morality… showing the wickedness of this institution, showing how inconsistent it is with such [moral] principles and with religion, it might be shown by appealing to the conduct of the slave-owners themselves. Why are these poor creatures kept in a state of absolute ignorance? Why is education, the most humble, denied them? Why are the Holy Scriptures kept from their hovels [sheds]? Why? Can there be but one answer: [namely,] that if they knew what knowledge imparts, if they knew what the gospel of our Saviour inculcates [teaches], they would be freemen, or sooner or later die in the effort to obtain it [freedom]?

"Mr. President…I conclude with saying, not a truth which every Senator here does not feel as strongly as I feel, but with saying what is indelibly engraved upon my soul, that we owe it not only to ourselves and to those who are to follow us, but to humanity, to bring this war to a successful result…and when it [the Government] shall be restored…a Government, National and State, in which human bondage has no place, and when we shall be able to say to the world, 'However late we were in carrying out the principles of our [Republican] institutions, we have at last accomplished it. The Union is restored, and slavery is terminated.'" (*Cong. Globe*, 38th Cong., 1st Sess., 1864, 1424; cf. *The Great Conspiracy*, 539)

On 6 April 1864 Iowa Senator James Harlan took the floor to rebut Senator Saulsbury's argument that slavery was a "right" and "divinely ordained" institution. However, while doing so Mr. Saulbury apparently was either not in his seat or paying attention and missed Mr. Harlan's rebuttal of the argument that "the Levitical Code authorized Jews to buy slaves and treat them as 'chattel property' to be inherited by their descendants." Having missed the opportunity to question his colleague about the matter, near the end of Mr. Harlan's rebuttal, Mr. Saulsbury asked,

> Will the Senator from Iowa allow me in this connection to ask him a question? What interpretation does he give to that passage of Scripture in which the Jews are authorized to buy servants of the heathen round about, with their money, and that they should become an inheritance to their children [Lev. 25:44–46]? (*Cong. Globe.*, 38th Cong., 1st Sess., 1864, 1439)

Mr. Harlan declined to answer the late inquiry. However, Senator Logan recounted in the *The Great Conspiracy* that Mr. Saulsbury had missed the following:

> Mr. [James] Harlan's reply to the position of Mr. Saulsbury that Slavery is right, is a Divine Institution, etc., was very able and interesting. He piled up authority after authority, English as well as American, to show that there is no support of Slavery—and especially of the title to services of the adult offspring of a Slave—at Common Law; and, after also proving, by the mouth of a favorite son of Virginia, that it has no legal existence by virtue of any Municipal or Statutory Law, he declared that "the only remaining Law that can be cited for its support is the Levitical Code"—as follows:
>
> "Both thy Bondmen, and thy Bondmaids, which thou shalt have, shall be of the heathen that are round about you; of them shall ye buy Bondmen and Bondmaids.

"Moreover, of the children of the strangers that do sojourn among you, of them shall ye buy, and of their families that are with you, which they begat in your land; and they shall be your possession.

"And ye shall take them as an Inheritance for your children after you, to inherit them for a possession; they shall be your Bondmen forever." [Lev. 25:44–46, KJV] (*The Great Conspiracy*, note at 534 (quotation marks ours); *Cong. Globe*, 38th Cong., 1st Sess., 1864, 1439)

Having stated the dubious "perpetual slavery" passage, Senator Harlan cited the Mosaic law instructing the post-Exodus Israelites to implement a "uniform rule of naturalization" throughout their national borders—a Rule also applicable to non-Israelites seeking admission into the Israelite community:

"I remark," said he [Harlan], "in this connection, that the Levitical Code, or the Hebrew Law, contains a provision for the Naturalization of Foreigners, whether captives of War, or voluntary emigrants. By compliance with the requirements of this law they became citizens, entitled to all the rights and privileges and immunities of native [born] Hebrews." [Exod. 12:43–49; Lev. 19:33–34; Num. 9:14; Deut. 16:1–17, KJV] (*The Great Conspiracy*, 534; *Cong. Globe*, 38th Cong., 1st Sess., 1864, 1439)

To clarify his "uniform naturalization rule" point, Senator Harlan first recited the "Hebrew slave codes" compensation rule found at *Deuteronomy* 15:12–18:

The Hebrew Slave Code, applicable to Enslaved Hebrews, is in these words:

"And if thy brother, an Hebrew man, or an Hebrew woman, be sold unto thee, and serve thee six years, then in the seventh year thou shalt let him go Free from thee."

Here I request the attention of those who claim compensation for Emancipated Slaves to the [Deuteronomy 15] text:

"And when thou sendest him out Free from thee, thou shalt not let him go away empty [impoverished]:

"Thou shalt furnish him liberally out of thy flock, and out of thy floor—which means granaries—and out of thy winepress: of that wherewith the LORD [YHWH] thy God hath blessed thee, thou shalt give unto him…It shall not seem hard unto thee, when thou sendest him away Free from thee, for he hath been worth a double-hired servant to thee, in serving thee six years." (*The Great Conspiracy*, 534; *Cong. Globe*, 38th Cong., 1st Sess., 1864, 1439)

Senator Harlan then interpreted the code's meaning:

These Hebrew Statutes provide that the heathen might be purchased and held as Slaves, and their posterity after them; that under their Naturalization Laws all strangers and sojourners, Bond and Free, have the privilege of acquiring the rights of citizenship; that all Hebrews, natives or naturalized, might assert and maintain their right to Freedom.

At the end of six years a Hebrew Slave thus demanding his liberty, was not to be sent away empty [handed]; the owner, so far from claiming compensation from his neighbors or from the Public Treasury for setting him Free, was bound to divide with the Freedman, of his own possessions: to give him of his flocks, of his herds, of his granary, and of his winepress, of everything with which the Lord Almighty had blessed the master during the years of his Servitude; and then the owner was admonished that he was not to regard it as a hardship to be required to Liberate the Slave, and to divide with him of his substance.

The Almighty places the Liberated Slave's claim to a division of his former master's property on the eternal principles of Justice, the duty to render an equivalent for

an equivalent [Exod. 21:22–25; modified by Matt. 5:38–
42]. The Slave having served six years must be paid for his
Service, must be paid liberally because he had been worth
even more than a hired servant during the period of his
enslavement. (*The Great Conspiracy*, 534–35; *Cong. Globe*,
38th Cong., 1st Sess., 1864, 1439)

On concluding Senator Harlan stated that not only was
the African Slavery scheme wrong in light of the Hebrew-
Levitical slave code's guideline, but Senator Saulsbury's claim
that a slaveowner was entitled to the "free" labor of a slave's adult
offspring was also unjust and unfounded in any law—divine
or secular:

> "If then," continued Mr. Harlan, "the justice of this claim
> [by Saulsbury] cannot be found either in Reason, Natural
> Justice, or the principles of the Common Law, or in any
> positive [legislative] Municipal or Statute regulation of any
> State, or in the Hebrew Code written by the Finger of God
> protruded from the flame of fire on the summit of Sinai, I
> ask whence the origin of the title to the services of the adult
> offspring of the Slave mother? Or is it not manifest that
> there is no just title? Is it not a mere usurpation without
> any known mode of justification, under any existing Code
> of Laws, human or Divine?" (*The Great Conspiracy*, 535;
> *Cong. Globe*, 38th Cong., 1st Sess., 1864, 1439)

Not being content with the arguments raised by Senators
Johnson and Harlan, Senator Saulsbury returned to the floor that
day to address the "sanctity" of the Hebrew-Levitical slave code.
Said Mr. Saulsbury,

> "When I propounded the question to the honorable
> Senator [Harlan] what interpretation he gave to that [Lev.
> 25:44–46] passage of Scripture which told the Jews that
> of the heathen round about them they might buy slaves,
> and they should be an inheritance unto their children after

them, I received no response, except that he had already referred to that passage.

"As an answer to the honorable Senator I will simply cite a passage from the most learned commentator [Dr. Clarke] of his own Church, showing that his [Harlan's] views are not correct; that slavery, slavery for life, and slaves as an inheritance to their children existed among that people. If I show this I show that the proposition of the honorable Senator that there can be no title, no right to this species of property, is in conflict with the command of the Almighty and with the practice of His chosen people. It is no answer to me to say that times have changed, and that what was allowable according to the express commands of the Almighty at a former period is not to be allowed now. I know that in these modern days it has been said by some that we must have an anti-slavery Constitution, an anti-slavery Bible, and an anti-slavery God. I trust that my honorable friend from Iowa…has not found since he has become a Senator that it is necessary to discard the old Bible and the God that his fathers worshipped.

[Saulsbury then spoke on Dr. Clarke's analysis of the *Genesis* 16 "Sarai-Hagar" passage and proceeded:]

"Why, sir, the [Ex. 21:2, Deut. 15:12] passage of Scripture…that [said] the servant should serve six years, and on the seventh should be allowed to go free, refers, and refers exclusively…to those servants who were of Hebrew origin. It is true that by the command of the Almighty a Hebrew was not allowed to hold one of his own race in bondage for a longer period than six years; in the seventh he was commanded to let him go free." (*Cong. Globe*, 38th Cong. 1st Sess., 1864, 1440)

In response, Senator Harlan took the floor and cited the Leviticus 25:44–45 passages using the term *heathen* and phrase "children of strangers that sojourn among you…their families that are with you, which they begat in your land." And noting such as representing a "different class of persons," he then stated,

"This whole passage refers to slaves made of the heathen round about, the captives taken in war, or those that may have sold themselves into slavery. I next stated that in the Levitical or Hebrew Code there was a naturalization law that provided for the incorporation of all strangers, slaves and freemen, into the nation as Hebrew, and that when they became Hebrews by naturalization they acquired there, as they do here [in America] under our naturalization laws, all the rights of citizenship. They must thenceforward be treated as Hebrews, members of that nationality, controlled by the Hebrew Code and entitled to all its rights and privileges. [cf. "One Law" passages at Ex. 12:43–50; Lev. 22:10–13 and 24:22; Num. 9:14 and 15:13–16, 29–31, KJV]

"I next cited the law of slavery in relation to Hebrews or slaves that were made such of the Hebrew nation itself [Ex. 21:1–6ff., Deut. 15:12–18, KJV]…Then the lawgiver [Moses] takes up the subject of compensation…Here is the whole Code on the subject of slavery: first, the heathen reduced to slavery might be held for life, unless he became a Hebrew by conforming to the naturalization laws, and his posterity might be held also…but if he became a Hebrew by conforming to the naturalization laws, the ceremonies of which were a little different from those supplied in this country, yet were really effective in incorporating him into that nationality, then he became entitled to all the rights of a Hebrew, and as a Hebrew he must necessarily be discharged at the end of the sixth year without compensation to the master; and, still more, the master must pay him for his services; he must not think it a hardship that he is required not only to set him free, but to pay him for the labor he has performed.

"This is the whole of the Hebrew Code on that subject, not cited *in extenso*, but fairly cited. I stated that the custom of holding the offspring of a slave mother, and its operation from generation to generation, did maintain in the Hebrew nation as well as in the other old nations; but

> I was inquiring for the title by which they were held and
> the reasonableness of the claim, and the law on which it
> was founded." (Ibid., 1440)

In giving Mr. Saulsbury this reply, Senator Harlan had answered a number of questions that went unnoticed by the average "unlearned" American:

1.) that prohibiting enslaved Africans from converting to the Christian faith was a direct attempt to prevent them from becoming "naturalized citizens" prior to the 1793 U.S. Naturalization Law's adoption;

2.) that generically labeling Africans as "negroes" and "uncivilized, irreligious heathen" was a direct attempt to justify "Perpetual Chattel Slavery" and prevent children born to them from obtaining freedom on reaching adulthood;

3.) that President Thomas Jefferson "hinted" at this early planned conspiracy in his 2 December 1806 Sixth Annual Message To Congress—which stated that the enslaved Africans' were victims of "Human Rights" violations, since they were not "enslaved" as "war captives" ("unoffending"), but "kidnapped" ("stolen") and sold into bondage much like the biblical Joseph;

4.) and that this early conspiracy aimed at relieving slaveowners of the "biblical command" to "liberally compensate" the freed slaves for their services (hence President Lincoln was exceptionally generous in offering slaveowners compensation for emancipating their slaves).

Nevertheless, Mr. Saulsbury refused to agree and, on the same day, again rose to the Senate floor to contest both Senators Harlan's and Johnson's argument that slavery was a sin. Still attempting to validate the notion of "man having property rights in owning man," Senator Saulsbury said,

"I am grateful at the explanation of the honorable Senator [Harlan], although I do not agree to the correctness of any position he has assumed in his remarks...But the explanation...affords me all the basis of an argument that I want, and that is this: he admits that the Almighty did allow, did command the Hebrews to make slaves of the heathen round about them, and that those heathen should be an inheritance to their children. I shall not stop to inquire into the naturalization [process] of the Hebrews according to their law; but the Senator himself admits the principle for which I contend, and denies the principle asserted as I understood in the speech of the honorable Senator [Johnson] from Maryland yesterday, that slavery was a sin. He [Harlan] admits that according to the Mosaic Law a certain species of slaves might be held and be an inheritance to the children of the master. By whose authority were they so held? That [Hebrew, Israelite, Jewish] people derived their law from the Almighty [God], for He was their great Lawgiver. Then we find, even as admitted by the honorable Senator [Harlan] himself, that according to the law which God gave his chosen people it was not a sin under all circumstances at least to hold slaves, but they might be held not only during the lifetime of the master, but as property they might be transmitted to the children of the master.

"And yet, sir, in these days we hear it said everywhere that slavery, under any and all circumstances, is a sin; and the passions of the people of the entire North (who I do not know are any more pious than people elsewhere, who I have not been taught to believe are more orthodox in Christian faith than people elsewhere) have been inflamed with the idea that away off from them, not in their midst but in other States, there exists an institution called slavery, sinful in itself, and a crusade is invoked for the liberation of the captives in bondage.

"Now, sir, I will show from the same learned commentator [Clarke] of the church to which the honorable Senator [Harlan] belongs that his interpretation even of the law of the Jews is not correct. I will show that it is not correct even under the Christian [New Testament] dispensation, and that the right to property in the slave is recognized in the Christian dispensation...Upon that passage where Paul is said to have returned Onesimus to Philemon, Dr. Clarke comments..."The Christian religion never cancels any civil relations; a slave, on being converted, and becoming a free man of Christ, has no right to claim on that ground emancipation from the service of his master. Justice, therefore, required St. Paul to turn back Onesimus to his master, and conscience obliged Onesimus to agree in the propriety of the measure."

"Dr. Scott...admits that according to the Jewish law there were not only servants for the period of seven years, who were Hebrews, but that there were slaves for life, slaves that descended as an inheritance; and upon this very passage in the New Testament showing that that law under the old [Testament] dispensation was not abrogated by the introduction of the new [Testament] dispensation, he holds that Paul was bound in justice and right to return Onesimus to Philemon. Whom did he return? He returned a slave. He had escaped from his master; he had become converted, had become a believer in the Christian religion, and in that epistle of Paul to Philemon Paul expresses a great desire to have Onesimus with him on account of the comfort it would be to him; but he returned him to Philemon because it was a matter of duty and of right; he was his [Philemon's] property.

"But, sir, I do not propose to enter into this theological argument, and I have only referred to it to show the honorable Senator [Harlan] that even by the standard authority of his own church his positions are not tenable. Why, sir, there was such a thing as the year of Jubilee among the Jews, when all that were held in bondage—I mean of Hebrew origin—returned to their own tribes and to their own inheritance; so that if a man had wasted his property, even if he had become a slave voluntarily, when the year of Jubilee came, he returned to his own tribe and to his own inheritance. Was it ever heard, was it ever contended by any commentator on the Scriptures…that a slave held under the Hebrew Code was admitted to the privilege, upon the return of the year of Jubilee, of entering into the possession of any lands? Not at all. Such an idea has never been advanced by any Chritian writer, unless it has been done in these late days, and the books now published upon such subjects I now never look into, because the children have become so much wiser than their fathers, and the modern Christians so much better than Paul, that I do not trouble myself very much with their teachings or their opinions upon such subjects." (Ibid., 1440–41)

Having cited this "tailored" analysis of the Old and New Testaments to support the "property rights in owning humans" view, Senator Saulsbury next contested Senator Johnson's argument concerning the meaning of the 1787 Constitution and its Preamble in another effort to deny that Congress was empowered to pass the Thirteenth Amendment. With an argument sounding similar to Justice Roger B. Taney and Senator Stephen A. Douglas's "America made for the white man" view, Mr. Saulsbury said,

"The honorable Senator [Johnson] from Maryland seemed to think that this [power to amend the Constitution] might be done because "we, the people," made this Constitution. In one sense "we, the people," did make it. The people of the States united, acting separately, however, did make it. In the language of Mr. [James] Madison, the States are the parties and the only parties, to the Constitution of the United States…It was never submitted to the people *en masse*, or even to a Congress composed of representatives from all the States; but it was proposed to the States separately, and it required the separate ratification of the

States before it became binding as a covenant of union between the States.

"But the honorable Senator [Johnson] from Maryland derived the power to incorporate this [13th Amendment] provision into the Constitution…from the preamble to the Constitution…I shall not enter into any discussion of the question how far the preamble to a written constitution can govern its terms. It may be used, perhaps, in cases of doubt and uncertainty, as explanatory of what the parties meant; but where the terms of the agreement or the constitution are clear as in themselves, the preamble can have no more effect upon the legal interpretation of the instrument than can a preamble in a statute in controlling the express, unequivocal language of the statute itself, where the language is clear and unequivocal.

"But, sir, for whose benefit did the framers of this instrument make it? For the whole world? Did they make it for all the nations of the earth? Had they in contemplation all the people that inhabit the continent of Africa, of Asia, or even of Europe? Had they in contemplation that the object of its establishment was for that servile [Hispanic, Native American] race which was in their own midst? Not at all. I know it may be said that they may have had, to some extent, the people of Europe in their mind because they provided for naturalization. That is true, and so far as they come into consideration in view of the power of naturalization it was established for their benefit. But, sir, what says the preamble to the Constitution on that point?

"Then, sir, I submit, with all due deference to the honorable Senator [Johnson], that because this Constitution was ordained "to form a more perfect Union, to establish justice, insure domestic tranquility, provide for the common defense, promote the general welfare, and secure the blessings of liberty," it does not follow that any such [13th] amendment as this can be made, because the instrument itself shows for whom these blessings were intended to be preserved—to us [Whites] and our posterity.

What connection had the [African, African-American] slave population of the United States with the formation of this Constitution? Did they constitute any part of "us [Whites] and our posterity" in the contemplation of the framers of this instrument? Not at all. Without elaborating this idea, I submit that no just or legitimate argument can be drawn from the preamble of the Constitution that the Congress of the United States have authority to propose this [13th] amendment, or that it would become binding in consideration of the ratification of three-fourths of the States." (Ibid., 1441–42)

Senator Saulsbury next appealed to "God," the bogus *Genesis* 9 "Ham cursed" story, "Mother Nature," and the "indictment of Israel" biblical passages (Isa. 45:9–10; Jer. 18:1–6; Rom. 9:14–20) (KJV) to justify the "property rights in owning man" view. Then, in a final effort to sway both Senate and public opinion against the Thirteenth Amendment's passage, Mr. Saulsbury concluded,

"The honorable Senator [Johnson] asked, is there no justice in [passing] it? Is it not necessary for tranquility? Is it [not] necessary for the common prosperity? My answer is, "no." Whence were we taught...whence do we derive the idea that in this abolition movement there is this great and god-like principle of justice? I profess not to be wiser than the Almighty, or better than the servants He has chosen to proclaim His word and His purposes to men.

"I find that almost since the [Noachian] flood this ["man enslaving man"] relationship has existed upon earth. I have been taught that a just God governs this world; and I choose to consider this relation of life, which takes its origin back to the ["Ham cursed"] denunciation of the Most High through the patriarch Noah, as in the order of God's providence, without being committed to any of the fallacies that might arise out of the argument of some who discuss the question of the "divine institution [of slavery]." I accept it as a fact in animal life, in the life of human beings with immortal spirits, just as I accept the facts in physical nature, where I see inequality and diversity.

"The theory now common seems to be that the law of God's providence is equality and uniformity. Such a law never did pervade or regulate the works of God's providence to man; but the law of His providence is inequality and diversity. I treat of [refer to] this inequality of races, of human beings, precisely as I treat of the inequality which I see in inanimate and physical nature all around me. Why is it [,] it may be asked [?] My answer is plain: I do not know; nor do you know. And who art thou, O man, says the sacred book [Bible], that thou shouldest ask such a question? Shall the clay say to the potter [,] ["Why hast thou made me so?"] [cf. Isa. 45:9; Rom. 9:20, kjv].

"Sir, there is a God who rules over the world. He made it. He had a right to make it as to His own wisdom seemed best, and we finite creatures are not presumptuously to arraign the order of His creation and say this thing is right and that thing is wrong and we could have made it better. In due time it will all perhaps be made manifest. I ask you, sir, instead of asking the Supreme Maker and Ruler over all, why is it that everything that has life is not created with immortal spirits and with the loftier order of intellect? Why do you see the little ant? Why do you see the crawling reptile? Why do you see the least in the chain of being? From the lowest to the highest, the great God could have made them all alike…For purposes of His own He chose not to do so…He did not do so.

"My object in making these remarks is simply to call the attention of the Senate and the country to the great practical question. It is time for us to quit theorizing on this subject and look at things as they are." (Ibid., 1442)

Undoubtedly, Mr. Saulsbury's speech would have made King George III proud—proud to know the senator and those he represented believed that (1) thralldom or slavery was "the natural order of things," (2) "the divine right of kings to rule" doctrine was "divinely ordained" and "correctly applied" (book of Wisdom 6:1–10, Romans 13:1–7, NAB); and the British-American Colonists were happy being viewed and treated as "beings of an inferior intellect and moral order." But King George III would also have been puzzled as to why the the British-American Colonists revolted, if they believed such?

Fortunately, New Hampshire Senator John P. Hale did not agree with Saulsbury's view. After listening to arguments for and against the African Slavery scheme and Thirteenth Amendment's passage, Mr. Hale took the floor and, apparently thinking about the question Pilate asked Jesus regarding the nature of truth, said,

> "Mr. President, permit me to say that this is a day that I and many others have long wished for…It is a day when the nation is to commence its real life or if it is not the day, it is the dawning of the day; the day is near at hand. The day is come when the American people are to wake up to the meaning of the sublime truths which their fathers uttered years ago and which have slumbered dead letters upon the pages of our Constitution, of our Declaration of Independence, and our history—a day when the nation is to be disembarrassed of the inconsistencies which have marked its history and its career, patent [clear] to the world and to ourselves when we have had the courage faithfully, fairly, and bodly to look the truth in the face.
>
> "Sir, what is the truth? We have had upon the pages of our public history, our public documents, and our public records some of the [most] sublimest truths that ever fell from human lips; and there never has been in the history of the world a more striking contrast than we have presented to heaven, and earth between the grandeur and the sublimity of our professions and the degradation and infamy of our practice. That day is to pass away, and to pass away, I trust, right speedily.
>
> "I am glad that the conduct of the theological branch of this discussion has been handed over to a man who can so

ably handle it as my distinguished friend from Iowa [Mr. Harlan]; but let me congratulate him that in conducting that theological discussion very great progress has been made. A little while ago a man who argued this scriptural question had to begin with "cursed be Canaan," at *Genesis*. We have got by that; *Genesis* is laid aside; and we have got so far through the Bible that we have actually finished the reading of the epistle of Paul to Philemon…If my honorable friend takes up that question, and accepts the challenge that is thus made to him, I suppose he will illustrate some differences that may be found in the slavery to which Onesimus was sent back and that which we are about to abolish that are somewhat curious. But I will not dwell upon that subject.

"Mr. President, what is to be cannot be avoided; and if there is any one thing which, it seems to me, the indications from every side everywhere teaches us, it is that the day of this ["Race Card Evil" oriented] power is over; and there is no indication more indicative of it, more satisfactory, more conclusive to my own mind, than the Christian and statesmanlike effort made by the honorable Senator [Johnson] from Maryland yesterday. When from such quarters and from such sources, such exhibitions of true and inevitable consequences are portrayed before the people of this country, there is no great difficulty in understanding the signs of the times or predicting what is speedily to follow. I ask everbody who hears me, do you not rejoice that the day has come? Are you not glad that this nation, blind and deaf so long to the teachings of history and the commands of God, has at length aroused itself from its lethargy, listened to the voices which heaven and earth, God and nature, are proclaiming, and is preparing to put itself in alliance with the Power [the Creator] which cannot be resisted and whose fiat will most surely be executed." (*Cong. Globe*, 38th Cong., 1st Sess., 1864, 1443)

Perhaps Senator Hale recalled Ben Franklin's suggestion that America's Gtreat Seal should depict the Exodus story as an event that held great significance for the Union—albeit the Continental Congress rejected it, probably bearing in mind the Colonies' existing African slavery contradiction. Whatever his thoughts, comparing the African slavery's demise to that of ancient Irael's Egyptian bondage, Mr. Hale concluded,

"But, sir, whenever unconditionally and without equivocation we can come up to the mark and place ourselves on that standard of Christian duty and resolve… place ourselves firmly upon the everlasting rock of duty and our action shall be in accordance with our conscientious convictions, then, and not till then, will that pillar of cloud by day and fire by night which led the chosen people from the house of bondage to the land of promise be ours. Then we shall indeed and in truth be worthy of our genealogy and our history. Then the sublime teachings of the Pilgrim fathers who left everything behind them that they might come hither and plant in this wilderness a temple of liberty and throw wide open its doors for the oppressed of earth to enter and be at rest—then will all that be realized. Then without shame, without reproach, and without apology, we can stand in this nineteenth century, soldiers of the new civilization and of the old Christianity, going forth to battle with every impulse of our hearts and every purpose that we entertain in full accordance with the best wishes and hopes of the good on earth and of the God in heaven; when we take this position and take it firmly and ably, then and not until then shall we see the beginning of the ["Race Card Evil's"] end.

"Sir, I do not read papers very often; but I tell you that yesterday and to-day I, for one individual, have felt more confidence, more hope, more assurance that we were on the right way, that we were on the way to victory, to peace, to honor, to safety, and renown than I ever have since this rebellion commenced.

"Mr. President, let me say one word more, and I shall not detain the Senate longer. When the Saviour of man with the sympathy and pathos with which He loved the chief city of His native land wept over Jerusalem His lamentation was, "if thou hadst known in this thy day the things that belong to thy peace!" Sir, that is what I believe; and by a vigorous prosecution of this [13th Amendment] measure we shall evidence to heaven and earth that we do understand and mean to perform the things which belong to our nation's peace. When we have done that, and not till then, can we look forward with any confident hope to the termination of this ["Race Card Evil" motivated] war." (Ibid., 1444)

On 8 April 1864, judgment day arrived in the Senate for voting on the Thirteenth Amendment's passage. Before voting, however, the Senate was given a pleasant surprise from Massachusetts senator Charles Sumner—who gave one of the most enlightened speeches to ever grace history's pages. And although his speech was untitled, it is only fitting that henceforth it be dubbed "The Visitor"—to honor the New Testament passage which stated, "Be not forgetful to entertain [be hospitable to] strangers [visitors]: for thereby some have entertained angels unawares" (Gen. 18:1–8; 19:1–3; Heb.13:2, KJV). Taking the floor, Mr. Sumner said,

"Mr. President, if an angel from the skies or a stranger [visitor] from another planet were permitted to visit this earth, and to examine its surface, who can doubt that his eyes would rest with astonishment upon the outstretched extent and exhaustless resources of this Republic of the new world, young in years but already rooted beyond any dynasty in history? In proportion as he considered and understood all these things among us which enter into and constitute the national life, his astonishment would increase, for he would find a numerous people, powerful beyond precedent, without a king or a noble, but with the schoolmaster instead. And yet the astonishment…would swell into marvel as he learned that in this Republic… there were four million human beings in abject bondage, degraded to be chattels, under the pretense of property in man, driven by the lash like beasts, despoiled of all rights, even the right to knowledge and the sacred right of family; so that the relation of husband and wife was impossible and no parent could claim his own child; while all were condemned to brutish ignorance. Startled by what he beheld, the stranger would naturally inquire by what authority, under what sanction, and through what terms of law or Constitution, this fearful inconsistency, so shocking to human nature itself, continued to be upheld. But his growing astonishment would know no bounds, when he was pointed to the Constitution of the United States, as the final guardian and conservator of this peculiar and many-headed wickedness.

"'And is it true,' the stranger would exclaim, 'that, in laying the foundation of this Republic, dedicated to human rights, all these wrongs have been positively [legislatively] established?'" He would ask to see that Constitution and to know the fatal words by which the sacrifice was commanded. The trembling with which he began its perusal would be succeeded by joy as he finished it; for he would find nothing in that golden text, not a single sentence, phrase, or word, even, to serve as origin, authority, or apology for the outrage. And then his astonishment... would break forth anew, as he exclaimed, "Shameful and irrational as is slavery, it is not more shameful and irrational than that unsupported interpretation which undertakes to make your Constitution the final guardian and conservator of this terrible and unpardonable denial of human rights.

"Such a stranger as I have decribed, coming from afar, with eyes which no local bias had distorted, and with understanding which no local custom had disturbed, would naturally see the Constitution precisely as it is in its actual text, and he would interpret it in its true sense, without prepossession or prejudice. Of course he would know, what all jurisprudence teaches and all reason confirms, that human rights cannot be taken away by any indirection or by any vain imagining of something that was intended but was not said, and, as a natural consequence, that slavery can exist—if exist it can at all—only by virtue of a *positive text*, and that what is true of slavery is true also of all its incidents [badges, characteristics]; and the enlightened stranger would insist that, in all interpretation of the Constitution, that cardinal principle must never for a moment be out of mind, but must be kept ever forward as guide and master, that *slavery cannot stand on inference*, nor can any support of slavery stand on inference. Thus informed, and in the light of a pervasive principle…he [the visitor] would peruse the Constitution from beginning to end, from its opening preamble to its final amendment, and then the joyful opinion would be given [that the 1787 Constitution does not, and never did, uphold slavery or the usurpation of human rights]." (*Cong. Globe*, 38th Cong., 1st Sess., 1864, 1479)

Having exonerated the 1787 Constitution, Senator Sumner next outlined "three" important facts that stemmed from the wording used in the Constitution, its Preamble, and its Fifth Amendment—wording that proved the "Union" and "Constitution" were never intented to be "proslavery" or "race based" ("color conscious"). Said he,

"There are three things which he [the visitor] would observe: first and foremost, that the dismal words "slave" and "slavery" do not appear in the Constitution; so that if the unnatural pretension of property in [enslaving, owning] man lurk anywhere in that text, it is under a feigned name or an *alias*, which of itself is cause of suspicion, while an imperative rule renders its recognition impossible. Next, he would consider the Preamble, which is the key to open [clarify the meaning of] the whole succeeding instrument; but here no single word can be found which does not open the Constitution to [mean] freedom and close it to [mean] slavery. The object [Mission Statement] of the Constitution is announced to be "in order to form a more perfect Union, establish Justice, insure Domestic Tranquility, provide for the Common Defense, promote the General Welfare, and secure the Blessings of *Liberty* to ourselves and our posterity"; all of which, in every particular, is absolutely inconsistent with slavery. And thirdly, he would observe those time-honored, most efficacious, chain-breaking words in the [Fifth] Amendment: *"No Person shall be Deprived of Life, Liberty, or Property, Without Due Process of Law."* Scorning all false interpretations and glosses which may have been fastened upon the Constitution as a support of slavery, and with these three things before him, he [the visitor] would naturally declare that there was nothing in the original [Constitutional] text on which this hideous wrong could be founded anywhere within the sphere of its operation. With astonishment he would ask again by what strange delusion or hallucination the reason had been so far overcome as to recognize slavery in the Constitution, when plainly it is not there, and cannot be there?" (Ibid., 1479–80, capitalizations ours in part)

Senator Sumner next addressed the proslavery argument that no Constitutional power—executive (presidential), judicial (Supreme Court), or legislative (congressional)—existed that could legally end slavery. Giving examples of valid use that arose from the need to "provide for the common Defense and General Welfare," Mr. Sumner said that "military necessity" empowered the presidential, congressional, and federal court branches to free slaves based on the need to "raise armies and navies" or "draft soldiers"—to fight against the government's foreign (abroad) or domestic (at home) enemies and ensure that the Constitution's "guarantee" of "a Republican form of government" remain intact. Next, Mr. Sumner said that "fear of Slavery" was one such necessity illustrated in the 1776 Declaration of Independence— facts which George Mason and Patrick Henry admitted in the

*Eliot Debates* (respectively vols. 2, p. 327 and 3, p. 595), and which John Adams and James Madison agreed with in their writings. On stating this, Mr. Sumner then revealed some enlightening facts about the Fifth Amendment's "due process of law" clause:

> "But, independent of the [Republican Form of Government] clause of guarantee, there is the [due process of law] clause just quoted, which in itself is a source of [executive, legislative, and judicial] power: "*No Person* shall be deprived of Life, *Liberty*, or Property Without *Due Process of Law*." This was a part of the [10] Amendments to the Constitution proposed by the First [1789] Congresss, under the popular demand for a Bill of Rights. Brief as it [the clause] is, it is in itself alone a whole Bill of Rights. Liberty can be lost only by "Due Process of Law," words borrowed from the old liberty-loving [British] Common Law, illustrated by our master of law, lord Coke, but best explained by the late Mr. Justice Bronson, of New York, in a judicial opinion where he says:
>
>     'The meaning of the [Due Process of Law] section then seems to be, that *no member of the State shall be dis[en]franchised or deprived of any of his rights or privileges* unless the matter shall be adjudged against him upon trial and according to the course of Common Law. The words "Due Process of Law" in this place cannot mean less than a [criminal] Prosecution or [civil] Suit instituted and conducted according to the prescribed forms and solemnities for ascertaining Guilt or determining the Title to property.'" (Ibid., 1480, capitalizations ours in part)

By stating this, Senator Sumner answered the question that Senator Harlan posed to Senator Saulsbury concerning "the [legal] title by which the adult offspring of a slave mother was held, the reaonableness of the [legal] claim, and the [legal rule of] law on which such was founded."

Next, Mr. Sumner revealed that America's founders were not as "dumb" as African Slavery proponents thought they were when the founders sat down with those playing the "Race Card Evil" oriented African Slavery con game. Indeed, in their bid to create the Union, the framers saw the "Race Card" being dealt to them from the deck's bottom. However, they "feigned" ignorance in order to play their own "Raceless Card"—which they knew would win "the game" rather than "a hand." Using legal clarity that would have made Justice Benjamin Curtis and Abe Lincoln proud, Senator Sumner said,

> Such is the protection which is thrown by the Constitution over every "Person," without distinction of race or color, class or condition. There can be no doubt about the universality of the protection. All, without exception, come within its scope. Its natural meaning is plain; but there is an incident of history which makes it plainer still, excluding all possibility of misconception. A [Due Process] clause of this character was originally recommended as an amendment by two slave States, North Carolina and Virginia, but it was restrained [restricted] by them to *Freemen* thus: "No *Freeman* ought to be deprived of his Life, *Liberty*, or Property but by the *Law of the Land*." But when the recommendation came before Congress the word "Person" was substituted for "Freeman," and the more searching phrase "Due Process of Law" was substituted for "Law of the Land." In making this change, rejecting the recommendation of two slave States, the authors of this amendment revealed their [true] purpose, that *No Person* wearing the Human Form should be deprived of *Liberty* without Due Process of Law; and the proposition was adopted by the votes of Congress and then of the States as a part of the [1791 Bill of Rights in the] Constitution. Clearly on its face it is an express Guarantee of Personal Liberty and an express Prohibition against its invasion anywhere [within the jurisdiction of the United States].
>
> In the face of this [Due Process] Guarantee and Prohibition—for it is both—how can any "Person" be held as a Slave? But it is sometimes said that this [Fifth

Amendment] provision must be restrained to places within the exclusive jurisdiction of the national Government. Let me say frankly that such formerly was my own impression…but I never doubted its complete efficacy to render Slavery unconstitutional in all such places, so that "No Person" could be held as a Slave at the National Capital or in any National Territory. Constitutionally Slavery has always been an outlaw wherever that [Fifth Amendment] provision of the Constitution was applicable. Nobody doubted that it was binding on the National [Federal] Courts, and yet it was left unexecuted—a dead letter, killed by the predominant influence of Slavery, until at last Congress was obliged by legislative act to do what the Courts had [willfully] failed to do, and to put an end to Slavery in the National Capital and National Territories. (Ibid., 1480, capitalizations partly ours)

Continuing, Senator Sumner next debunked the proslavery view that neither the federal government nor the 1787 Constitution could interfere with the African slavery scheme:

But there are no words in this Guarantee and Prohibition by which they are restrained to any exclusive jurisdiction. They are broad and general as the Constitution itself; and since they are in support of Human Rights they cannot be restrained by any interpretation. There is no limitation in them, and nobody now can apply any such limitation, without encountering the venerable maxim of law…Impious and cruel is he who does not favor Liberty." Long enough Courts and Congress have merited this condemnation. The time has come when they should merit it no longer. The Constitution should become a living letter under the predominant influence of Freedom. It is this conviction which has brought petitioners to Congress, during the present session, asking that the Constitution shall be simply executed against Slavery and not altered.

Ah! Sir, it would be a glad sight to see that Constitution, which we have all sworn to support, interpreted generously, nobly, gloriously for Freedom, so that everywhere within its influence the chains should drop from the Slave. If it be said that this was not anticipated at the adoption of the Constitution, I remind you of the words of Patrick Henry at the time when he said, "the paper speaks to the point."

Mr. President, thus stands the case. There is nothing in the Constitution on which Slavery can rest, or find any the least support. Even on the face of that instrument it is an outlaw; but if we look further at its provisions we find at least four distinct sources of power, which, if executed, must render Slavery impossible, while the Preamble makes them all vital for Freedom: *first*, the power to provide for the Common Defense and the General Welfare; *secondly*, the power to raise armies and maintain navies; *thirdly*, the power to Guarantee to every State a Republican Form of Government; and *fourthly*, the power to secure *Liberty* to every Person restrained without Due Process of Law. But all these provisions are something more than Powers; *they are Duties also*. And yet we are constantly and painfully reminded in this chamber that pending measures against Slavery are unconstitutional. Sir, this is an immense mistake. *Nothing against Slavery can be unconstitutional.* It is only hesitation which is unconstitutional. (Ibid., 1480–81, capitalizations and italics partly ours).

Unwilling to leave his colleagues guessing about the points covered in his analysis of the 1787 Constitution's objective or its framers' intent, Senator Sumner explained why advocates of the African Slavery scheme felt that they had "religious" and "political" support to perpetuate the evil. In plain language that would have made Mrs. Beecher-Stowe's "Augustine St. Clare" character proud, the Senator first said "The answer is humiliating, but it is easy"—and, perhaps with Jesus's denunciation of "tradition" in mind (Matt. 15:1–9, KJV), Mr. Sumner then stated,

People naturally find in texts of [Biblical, Qur'anic, etc] Scripture the support of their own religious opinions or prejudices; and, in the same way, they naturally find in texts of the Constitution the support of their own political opinions or prejudices. And this may not be in either case because Scripture or Constitution, when truly interpreted, supports these opinions or prejudices; but because people are apt to find in texts simply a reflexion of themselves. Most clearly and indubitably, whoever finds any support of Slavery in the Constitution of the United States has first found such support in himself; not that he will hesitate, perhaps, to condemn Slavery in words of approved gentleness, but because from unhappy education or more unhappy insensibility to this wrong he has already conceded to it a certain traditional foothold of immunity, which he straightway transfers from himself to the Constitution. In dealing with this subject, it has not been the Constitution, so much as human nature itself, which has been at fault. Let the people change, and the Constitution will change also; for the Constitution is but the *shadow* [letter of the law], while the people are the *substance* [spirit of the law].

But under the influences of the present struggle for National Life, and in obedience to its incessant exigencies, the people have already changed, and in nothing so much as Slavery. Old opinions and prejudices have dissolved, and that traditional foothold which Slavery once possessed has been gradually weakened until now it scarcely exists. Naturally this change must sooner or later show itself in the interpretation of the Constitution. But it is already visible even there, in the concession of [Executive, Legislative, Judicial] powers over Slavery which were formerly denied. The time, then, has come when the Constitution, which has been so long interpreted for Slavery, may be interpreted for Freedom. This is one stage of triumph. Universal emancipation, which is at hand, can be won only by complete emancipation of the Constitution itself, which has been degraded to wear chains so long that its real character is scarcely known. (Ibid., 1480, capitalizations and italics ours in part)

As Senator Sumner winded down his speech, he condemned the idea of compensating slaveowning enterprises for freeing their "cheap labor" workforce—doing so by making an analogy between the "Race Card Evil," the African slavery sheme, the Bible's "fall of man" and "Nimrod the Mighty Hunter" stories, and John Milton's "Paradise Lost." Said he,

> But the proposition of compensation is founded on the intolerable assumption of property in [owning] man... Impious toward God and insulting toward man, it is disowned alike by the conscience and the reason; nor is there any softness of phrase or augment by which its essential wickedness can be disguised. The fool hath said in his heart that there is no God [Ps. 10:4, 14:1, 36:1, KJV]; but it is kindred folly to say that there is no man. The first is aetheism, and the second is like unto the first.
>
> Foremost of all persons in history who have vindicated human Liberty, and associated their names with it forevermore, stands John Milton, the secretary of Oliver Cromwell and the author of "Paradise Lost." Cradled under a lawless royalty, he helped to found and support the English Commonwealth, while in all that he wrote he pleaded for Human Rights, now in defense of the English people, who beheaded their king, said now in immortal poems which show how wisely and well he loved the cause which he had made his own. Nowhere has this assumption of property in [owning] man been encountered more completely than in the conversation between the archangel [Michael] and Adam, after the former had pictured a hunter [such as Nimrod] whose game was "men, not beasts" ["Paradise Lost," book 12.4.73]:

> O execrable son! So to aspire
> Above his brethren, to himself assuming
> Authority usurped, from God not given:
> He gave us only over beast, fish, fowl,
> Dominion absolute; that [title] right we hold
> By His donation; but man over men
> He made not lord, such title to Himself
> Reserving, human left from human free.

> But every asserter of property in [owning] man puts himself in the very place of this hunter of "men, not beasts," who is described as "execrable son so to aspire." The language is strong; but not too strong. "Execrable" is the assumption; "execrable" wherever made; "execrable" in all its forms; "execrable" in all its consequences; especially "execrable" as an apology for hesitation against slavery. The assumption, where ever it shows itself, must, like Satan himself, in whom it has its origin, be beaten down under our feet. (Ibid., 1481)

Reminding his colleagues that the purpose for holding the debate was to extinguish the legal protection perpetuating the "Race Card Evil" oriented African slavery scheme, Senator Sumner closed by saying,

> Again, we are brought by learned Senators to the [Fifth Amendment of the] Constitution, which requires that there shall be "just compensation" where "private property" is taken…Slavery is but a bundle of barbarous pretensions… At what price shall these pretensions be estimated?… How much shall be paid for the controlling pretension of property in [owning] man? How much shall be allowed for that other pretension to shut the gates of knowledge [to man], and keep the victim from the book of life? How much shall be expended to redeem the pretension to rob a human being of all the fruits of his toil? And, sir, what "just compensation" shall be voted for the renunciation of that

Heaven-defying pretension, too disgusting to picture in its details, which despoils the slave of wife and child, and hands them over to lust or avarice? Let these pretensions be renounced, and slavery ceases to exist; but there can be no "just compensation" for any such renunciation. The human heart, reason, religion, the Constitution itself, rise in judgment against it. As well vote "just compensation" to the hardened offender who renounces his disobedience to the Ten Commandments and promises that he will cease to steal…commit adultery…covet his neighbor's wife. Ay, sir, there is nothing in the Constitution to sanction any such outrage…

Putting aside, then, all objections that have been interposed…the great question recurs, that question which dominates this whole debate, How shall slavery be overthrown? The answer is threefold: *first*, by the courts, declaring and applying the true principles of the Constitution; *secondly*, by Congress, in the exercise of the powers which belong to it; and, *thirdly*, by the people, through an amendment to the Constitution. Courts, Congress, people may all be invoked, and the ocassion will justify the appeal.

Let the appeal be made to the courts. But alas! One of the saddest chapters in our history has been the conduct of judges, who have lent themselves to the support of slavery. Injunctions of the Constitution, guarantees of personal liberty, and prohibitions against its invasion, have all been forgotten. Courts which should have been asylums of liberty have been changed into *barracoons* [slave holding-pens], and the Supreme Court of the United States, by a final decision of surpassing infamy [in *Dred Scott v. Sandford*], became the greatest *barracoon* of all. It has been part of the calamity of the times that, under the influence of slavery, justice…had fled. But now at last, in a regenerated Republic, with the power of slavery waning, and the people rising in judgment against it, let us hope that the judgments of courts may be reconsidered, and that the powers of the Constitution in behalf of liberty may be fully exercised…Sir, no court can afford to do an act of wrong. Its business is justice, it loses those titles to reverence which otherwise are so willingly bestowed…Doubtless the model decision of the American bench, destined to be quoted hereafter with the most honor, because the boldest in its conformity with the great principles of humanity and social order, was that of a Vermont judge, who refused to surrender a fugitive slave *until his pretended master should show a title-deed from the Almighty*. But unhappily the courts will not perform the duty of the hour, and we must look elsewhere. An appeal must be made to Congress…But all these will not be enough. The people must be summoned to confirm the whole work. It is for them to put the cap-stone upon the sublime structure. And whatever may be the judgment of the Senate, I am consoled by the thought that the most homely text containing such a rule will be more beautiful far than any words of poetry or eloquence, and that it will endure to be read with gratitude when the rising dome of this Capitol, with the statue of Liberty which surmounts it, has crumbled to dust. (Ibid., 1481–83 passim, italics partly ours)

Despite all the enlightened and factual speeches, the Democratic proslavery faction of Senators refused to yield to common sense and truth. Seeing that the majority of Senators felt as President Lincoln did about slavery and that the proposed Thirteenth Amendment would be passed in the Senate, the proslavery faction stooped to time-wasting methods to stall its passage.

For instance, from 5 to 8 April 1864, Kentucky's Senators Garrett Davis (Lincoln's friend) and Lazarus Powell offered a number of "obstructive amendments" to hold up the Senate vote. And after these were voted down Delaware's Senator Saulsbury, on 8 April 1864, proposed a "Thirteenth Amendment with twenty Sections"—allegedly as a "peace offering," but actually just another "obstructive tactic" designed to stall voting on the measure. On voting down Saulsbury's "twenty-section" proposal, the Senate closed its debate after hearing California senator James A. McDougall's irrational, misguided, and "Race Card" oriented speech. Senator Logan recounted in *The Great Conspiracy*,

> The Saulsbury substitute being voted down, the debate closed with a speech by Mr. McDougall…[Said he:] "This policy [to free the African Slaves] will ingulf them. It is as simple a truth as has ever been taught by any history. The Slaves of ancient time were not the Slaves of a different Race. The Romans compelled [enslaved] the Gaul and the Celt, brought them to their own Country, and some of them became great poets, and some eloquent orators, and some accomplished wits, and they became citizens of the Republic of Greece, and of the Republic of Rome, and of the Empire.
>
> "This is not the condition of these persons with whom we are now associated, and about whose affairs we undertake to establish administration. They can never commingle with us. It may not be within the reading of some learned Senators, and yet it belongs to demonstrated Science, that the African race and the European [race] are different; and I here now say it as a fact established by science, that the eighth generation of the Mixed race formed by the union of the African and European, cannot continue their species. Quadroons have few children; with Octoroons reproduction is impossible.
>
> "It establishes as a law of nature that the African has no proper relation to the European, Caucasian, blood. I would have them kindly treated…Against all such policy and all such conduct I shall protest as a man, in the name of humanity, and of law, and of truth, and of religion." (*The Great Conspiracy*, 550–52; *Cong. Globe*, 38th Cong., 1st Sess., 1864, 1489–90)

Despite such antifreedom speeches and stalling tactics, a Senate majority voted in favor of passing the Thirteenth Amendment and its "two sections." Senator Logan recounted,

The amendment made, as in Committee of the Whole, having been concurred in, etc., the Joint Resolution, as originally reported by the Judiciary Committee, was at last passed (April 8th)—by a vote of 38 yeas to 6 nays (Messrs. Davis, Hendricks, McDougall, Powell, Riddle, and Saulsbury)—Messrs. Hendricks and McDougall having the unenviable distinction of being the only two Senators, (mis-)representing Free States, who voted against this definitve Charter of American Liberty. (Ibid., 552; *Cong. Globe*, 38th Cong., 1st Sess., 1490)

Undoubtedly, a landmark achievement had been reached by the Senate voting in favor of the Amendment: one that reaffirmed the ideals Jesus of Nazareth taught, the Declaration of Independence signers spoke of, and President Lincoln noted ten days after the debate ended (18 April 1864) on behalf of America and the world. In his *Between Slavery and Freedom*, midtwentieth-century AD legal analyst William L. Westermann recounted Lincoln's view on the Senate vote to put the "Race Card Evil" oriented African slavery program "in the course of ultimate extinction." Said Mr. Lincoln,

"The world has never had a good definition of liberty [freedom], and the American people, just now, are much in need of one. We all declare for liberty; but in using the same word we do not all mean the same thing. With some the word liberty may mean for each man to do as he pleases with himself, and the product of his labor; while with others the same word may mean for some men to do as they please with other men, and the product of other men's labor. Here are two, not only different, but incompatible things, called by the same name, liberty."

William L. Westermann, *Between Slavery and Freedom*, 50 American Historical Review, 213 (1945).

## Thirteenth Amendment Debate in the House

With the Senate voting in favor of the Thirteenth Amendment, one part of the Congressional battle against the "Race Card Evil" was won. The second part now had to be fought and won in the House of Representatives, where Iowa Representative James F. Wilson presided as chairman over the House Judiciary Committee.

When the January 1864 House Session started, Mr. Wilson introduced the proposed Amendment Joint Resolution for debate. On 6 January 1864 Illinois Representative Isaac N. Arnold, Lincoln's friend and biographer, gave an enlightening speech that equated the missions of Jesus of Nazareth and Abraham Lincoln with raising humanity (the "seventy" nations) to a more elevated and universal view of itself. The *Congressional Globe* recounted that Mr. Arnold said:

> Mr. Chairman, in June 1858, a comparatively unknown man uttered in the Statehouse at Springfield, Illinois, a sentiment which is already historical. Its philosophy, its profound sagacity, its prophetic prescience, its unparalleled boldness and honesty, were characteristic of the man, who, then obscure, has become…the foremost character in American history…This, the first [modern] emphatic enunciation of the philosophical fact of the antagonism between liberty and slavery, the eternal and "irrepressible" conflict between them, electrified the country, and made Abraham Lincoln President of the United States.
>
> The moment the fact is recognized that liberty and slavery are antagonistic, and that there can be no peace between them—that our country, all of it, must pass into the dark night of slavery, or all of it emerge into the clear light of freedom—all loyal, patriotic men must become at once anti-slavery men, abolitionists…And as, when in

the palmy day of the Roman republic, the people came to feel…that Carthage must be destroyed [so] that Rome might live, so, to-day, the American people feel that slavery must die that liberty and the Union may live… "Down with slavery" is becoming the motto of every loyal, patriotic American.

"When the Son of God proclaimed *a common Father* and *the universal brotherhood of man*, He enunciated the great moral principle which brought on the irrepressible conflict with [freedom and] slavery [Matt. 6:9, 23:9; Lk. 10:1; Acts 2:1–12; KJV]. It is difficult, it seems to me, for a man to recognize fully the truth of His [Jesus's] teaching, in the light of this rebellion, without becoming an opponent of slavery. Just to the extent that Christianity prevails, slavery will disappear. The glorious light of Christianity must fade from the earth, or slavery [must] cease. It is a relic of a barbarous and a savage age, and, thank God, it is melting away before the light of the nineteenth century.

It would be a most interesting task to retrace the footprints of liberty, amidst the dust and rubbish which have gathered over the history of the past; to follow the oftentimes obliterated pathway by which, since Christ's sermon on the mount, freedom regulated by law has been developed into its present majestic and grand proportions. I hesitate not to affirm that all that there is which is valuable in republican and free institutions has its foundation in the sublime morality and broad humanity of the Bible. The glorious theme of man's struggle, through the ages, for liberty is yet to be written. Historians have told us much of courts and camps, of the changes of dynasties, of battles by land and on the sea; but who among them has traced the history of man's progress, and his struggles, through the ages, for "life, liberty, and the pursuit of happiness?" This history, even as presented by that nation and race most interesting to us—the English—has yet to be fully written…The historian who writes the story of man's progress from slavery and barbarism to Christian civilization and liberty, will find no more interesting page than that which is now being filled with the struggle in which we are engaged; none where the contest between liberty and slavery has been more clearly defined; none upon a grander theater; none where the combatants, by their numbers, genius, ability, and heroism, have given more dignity and sublimity to the contest. (*Cong. Globe,* 38th Congress., 1st Session, 1864, 113–14; italics ours)

Significantly, Mr. Arnold believed that (1) the African Slavery scheme was the source of the Confederate-Union war, (2) once debate began on the proposed Thirteenth Amendment, it was the duty of all Representatives—on behalf of all true American patriots—to wage war on the "Race Card Evil" oriented African Slavery scheme in an ernest effort to put it "in the course of ultimate extinction," and (3) the real war (Jihad) to be waged was a "moral war" fought with weapons of truth, free speech, education, church (religious) sermon, and ballot—not with bullets and bombs. In his words,

When, in 1858, Abraham Lincoln uttered the philosophical truth that freedom and slavery could not permanently exist together—that our country would become all free or all slave—he did not anticipate any[thing] but a moral conflict. The weapons by which he expected freedom to triumph were the weapons of truth and free discussion. Free speech, a free press, reason, the schoolmaster, the sermon, the lecture, the printing-press, the telegraph, the ballot: these were the agencies, the weapons, by which the battle was to be fought. It was with the ballot, and not with bullets, the victory was expected to be won. The victory was won by these peaceful agencies in the election of Abraham Lincoln as President. Slavery, conscious that it could not stand free discussion, that it might be destroyed if free speech and a free press were tolerated, appealed from the ballot-box to the sword, and brought upon the country this terrible war.

Slavery having plunged the nation into this war, it is fit[ting] that it should die by the laws of war. Slavery stands before the world to-day guilty of all the calamities of our country. Every dollar expended, every suffering endured, every drop of blood spilled, every wound, and every death, on every battle-field and in every hospital, is the price we pay for the existence and toleration of American slavery.

It is to-day a rebel and a traitor. Let us declare it an outlaw under our Constitution and laws.

There has never been a day since our existence as a nation when slavery was loyal to the Constitution and the Union. Now an open enemy, striking at the heart of the Republic, it has always been a plotting, stealthy, secret traitor, undermining the Constitution, and sapping the foundations of our liberties. (Ibid., 114)

On 19 March 1864, Chairman Wilson gave an equally enlightening speech that plainly stated that the founding of the American government was for the benefit of all humanity (the "seventy" nations), and not for a particular segment of it; and that such was the true meaning underlying *Leviticus* 25:10. And when referring to the views expressed by Justice Joseph story and Thomas Jefferson, Mr. Wilson said,

"The…most sublime of the objects declared by the people in the ordination of the Constitution is, "to secure the blessings of liberty to ourselves and our posterity."…Let us not overlook that portion of this well-expressed and better-bestowed praise [by Justice Story] which rests upon the fact that the glorious work of the people was for "the sake of all mankind."…Has not slavery denied that this great work of the people was intended for the "safety of all mankind," and brought upon us the just chastisement of God, who intended "these liberties" for all of His creatures? What are the thunders of this [civil] war but the voice of God calling upon this nation to return from the evil paths…to the grand highway of national thrift, prosperity, happiness, glory, and peace, in which He planted the feet of the [founding] fathers? Cannot we hear amid the wild rushing roar of this war storm the voice of Him who rides upon the winds and rules the tempest saying unto us, "You cannot have peace until you secure liberty to all who are subject to your laws?" It has been whispered into the ears of this nation since first we pronounced life, liberty, and the pursuit of happiness to be the inalienable rights of all men [humans], and now it rolls in upon us like the voice of the ocean, tendering peace or war [according] to our election [choice]. Which shall we elect? Shall it be peace? How can it be peace while liberty and slavery dwell together in our midst? These are enemies. These are ideas which cannot dwell together in harmony. How can we have peace? Let slavery die. Let its death be written in our Constitution. Let the Constitution "Proclaim liberty throughout [all] the land to all the inhabitants thereof [Lev. 25:10]." This is the way to peace—firm, enduring peace, embracing all mankind, and reaching to the most distant generations. In this way only can we secure liberty to ourselves and our posterity." (*Cong. Globe*, 38th Cong., 1st Sess., 1202)

Having said this, Chairman Wilson next illustrated how African slavery scheme profiteers were responsible for persecuting people exercising "contitutionally" protected rights—freedom of assembly, press, speech, and religious expression—who opposed the evil scheme:

"The great rights here enumerated [in the First Amendment] were regarded by the people as too sacred and too essential to the preservation of their liberties to be trusted with no firmer defense than the rule that "Congress can exercise no power which is not delegated to it." Around this negative protection was erected the positive barrier of absolute prohibition. Freedom of religious opinion, freedom of speech and press, and the right of assemblage for the purpose of petition belong to every American citizen, high or low, rich or poor, wherever he may be within the jurisdiction of the United States [U.S. Const, Art IV, Sec 2, Cl 1]. With these rights no State may interfere without breach of the bond which holds the Union together [U.S. Const Art VI, Cl 2]. How have these rights essential to liberty been respected in those sections of the Union where slavery held the reigns of local authority and directed the thoughts, prejudices, and passions of the people? The bitter, cruel, relentless persecutions of the Methodists in the South, almost as void of pity as those which were visited upon the Huguenots in France, tell how utterly slavery disregards the right to a free exercise of religion. No religion which recognizes God's eternal attribute of justice and breathes that spirit of love which applies to all men the sublime commandment, "whatsoever ye would that men should do unto you, do ye even so to them [Matt. 7:12, KJV]," can ever be allowed free exercise where slavery curses men and defies God. No religious denomination can flourish or even be tolerated where slavery rules without surrendering the choicest jewels of its faith into the keeping of that infidel power which withholds the Bible from the poor. Religion, "consisting in the performance of all known duties to God and our fellow-men," never has been and never will be allowed free exercise in any community where slavery dwarfs the consciences of men. The Constitution may declare the right [to freedom of religious or academic expression], but slavery ever will, as it ever has, trample upon the Constitution and prevent the enjoyment of the right." (Ibid., 1202)

Chairman Wilson next showed how the African Slavery scheme retarded the American "free laborer's" economic interests—an important point made by President Lincoln during his debates with Senator Douglas—reminding his colleagues of the big-business slaveowners' statement that "Slavery is the natural and normal condition of the laboring man, whether white or black." Said he,

"How much better has free discussion fared at the hands of the black censor who guard the interests of slavery against the expression of the thoughts of freemen? On what road of this Republic cursed by Slavery have men been free to declare their approval of the divine doctrines of the Declaration of Independence? Where, except in the free States of the Union, have the nation's toiling millions been permitted to assert their great protective doctrine, "The laborer is worthy of his hire [1 Tim. 5:18, KJV]?" What member of our great free labor force, North or South, could stand up in the presence of the despotism which owns men and combat the atrocious assertion that "Slavery is the natural and normal condition of the laboring man, whether white or black," with the noble declaration that "Labor being the sure foundation of the nation's prosperity should be performed by free men, for they alone have an interest in the preservation of free government," with any assurance that his life would not be excluded as the price of his temerity? In all this broad land not one could be found…If non-slaveholding whites became alarmed at the bold announcement that "slavery is the natural and normal condition of the laboring man, whether white or black," seeing therein the commencement of an effort intended to result in the enslavement of labor instead of the mere enslavement of the African race, they were not privileged to peacefully assemble and petition the Government in regard thereto, or to discuss the barbarism and to arouse the people in opposition to it. Slavery held political and social power sufficient to crush all such attempts on the part of the injured people. Slavery could hold its assemblages, discuss, resolve, petition, threaten, disregard its Constitutional obligations, trample upon the rights of labor, do anything its despotic despotism might direct; but freedom and free men must be deaf, dumb, and blind. Throughout all the dominion of slavery republican government, Constitutional liberty, the blessings of our free institutions were mere fables. An aristocracy enjoyed unlimited power, while the people were pressed to the earth and denied the inestimable privileges which by right they should have enjoyed in all the fullness designed by the Constitution." (Ibid., 1202)

By stating this, Mr. Wilson revealed that he (like Lincoln and other notables) had reached the same conclusion as statesman Edmund Burke concerning the "Race Card Evil" oriented African Slavery scheme's true agenda—namely, that it had nothing to do with oppressing a certain "skin color" or "ethnicity," but with a minority of speculators "monopolizing a cheap-labor market" at the expense of the "free laborer" (black, white, or other). This fact was validated by various latter-day political researchers on the "Great Debate" era—twenty-first century American legal analyst Alexander Tsesis being one of such.

Indeed, in the introductory note to his July 2009 essay entitled "Interpreting the Thirteenth Amendment," Mr. Tsesis referred to midtwentieth-century American author Joseph G. Rayback's "The American Workingman and the Antislavery Crusade." Therein Rayback recounted Mr. Wilson's statement that the African Slavery scheme actually had its sights set on the American laborer regardless of skin color, religious creed, or political affiliation,

> The Chairman of [the House] Judiciary Committee, Representative James [F.] Wilson of Iowa, pointed out [on 19 March 1864] that, "non-slavingholding whites became alarmed at the bold announcement that 'Slavery is the natural and normal condition of the laboring man, whether white or black,' seeing therein the commencement of an effort intended to result in the enslavement of labor instead of the mere enslavement of the African race." Wilson was referring to an editorial from a South Carolina newspaper. The fuller text bode even more ominously for white laborers: "The great evil of Northern *free society* is that it is burdened with a *servile* class of *mechanics* and *laborers unfit*

*for self-government*, and yet clothed with the attributes and powers of *citizens*. Master and slave is a relation as necessary as that of parent and child; and the Northern States will yet have to introduce it. Slavery is the natural and normal condition of *laboring men* whether *white* or *black*." (Alexander Tsesis, "Interpreting the Thirteenth Amendment," *U. Pa. Journal of Constitutional Law* 11, no. 5 (2009): 1337 n. 3; quoting Joseph G. Rayback's "The American Workingman and the Antislavery Crusade," *Journal of Economic History* 3, (1943): 152, 162. Also see: www.law.upenn.edu/journals/conlaw/articles/vol11/issue5/Tsesis11U.Pa.J. Retrieved 20 January 2014)

As said, Mr. Wilson was not the only one who noticed the "Race Card Evil's" true agenda. Representatives such as Michigan's Francis W. Kellogg and Indigana's George W. Julian—politicians familiar with the proslavery writings of Virginia lawyer George Fitzhugh—also realized that the "African Slavery" scheme actually targeted the free "white" laborer. Comparing the views of Fitzhugh and Julian Mr. Tsesis noted in his essay,

> The most popular proslavery advocate of this view [that slavery was the natural condition for the laborer] was George Fitzhugh who thought a northern worker "who contracts to serve for a term of days, months, or years, is, for such term, the property of his employer"…Historian Eugene D. Genovese has pointed out the classist logic of this point: "The notion that slavery was a proper social system for all labor, not merely for black labor, did not arise as a last-minute rationalization; it grew steadily as a part of the growing self-awareness of the planter class" (See: "The World the Slaveholders Made," (1969), p. 130)
> Representative George [W.] Julian, another advocate of free labor and abolition [of slavery], compared business exploitation with enslavement [in his work entitled *Political Recollections: 1840 to 1872*, (New York: *Negro University Press*, 1970, 1884), 322–23.] [Therein Mr. Julian said:]

> "The rights of men are sacred, whether trampled down
> by Southern slave-drivers, the monopolists of the soil, the
> grinding power of corporate wealth, the legalized robbery
> of a protective tarrif, or the power of concentrated capital
> in alliance with labor-saving machinery." (Ibid., p.1337 n.
> 3; cf. Rep. Francis W. Kellogg's view cited in the *Cong.
> Globe*, 38th Cong., 1st Sess., 1864, 2955)

After stating that the African Slavery scheme was covertly a
general enslavement program targeting free laborers (whites or
non-whites), Mr. Wilson next counted the ways in which the
scheme had disregarded the 1787 Constitution to achieve its
ultimate objective. Said he,

> "Sir, I might enumerate many other Constitutional rights
> of the citizen which slavery has disregarded and practically
> destroyed, but I have enough to illustrate my proposition:
> that Slavery disregards the supremacy of the Constitution
> [Art VI] and denies to the citizens of each State the
> privileges and immunities of citizens in the several States
> [Art IV, Sec 2, Cl 1].
>
> The proposition needs no argument. We all know that
> for many years before the commencement of the gigantic
> rebellion now in progress the supporters of slavery enforced
> this disregard of the supremacy of the Constitution and of
> the privileges and immunities of the citizen by every power
> and influence known to the communities cursed by the
> presence of a slave. Legislatures, courts, Executives, almost
> every person holding political or social power and position
> in the southern States, were all arrayed on the side of slavery,
> and what they could not accomplish was turned over to the
> mob, which, without law, with abuse, indignities, cruelties,
> and hempen halters [lynch ropes], did its work with fearful
> accuracy and terrible exactness. Twenty million free men
> in the free States were practically reduced to the condition
> of semi-citizens of the United States; for the enjoyment
> of their rights, privileges, and immunities as citizens

depended upon a perpetual residence north of Mason and Dixon's [36–degree, 30–minute] line. South of that line the rights which I have mentioned, and many more which I might mention, could be enjoyed only when debased to the uses of slavery. Slaveholders and their supporters alone were free to think and print, to do and say what seemed to them best on both sides of that line. They could think, read, talk, discuss with perfect freedom in each and every State, and fearfully they used this advantage to destroy the liberties of this country. It is quite time, sir, for the people of the free States to look these facts squarely in the face and provide a remedy which shall make the future safe for the rights of each and every citizen. Had slavery not possessed this advantage, civil war, freighted with sorrow, desolation, and death, would not have visited this nation. But since it has come, the people of the free States should insist on ample protection to their rights, privileges, and immunities, which are none other than those which the Constitution was designed to secure to all citizens alike, and see to it that the power which caused the war shall cease to exist, to the end that the curse of civil war may never be visited upon us again, and that the citizen whose home is in the North shall be as free to assert his opinions and enjoy all of his Constitutional rights in the sunny South as he whose roof-tree is the magnolia shall to the same ends be free amid the mountains of New England and the sparkling lakes of the North and the West. An equal and exact observance of the Constitutional rights of each and every citizen, in each and every State, is the end to which we should cause the lessons of this war to carry us." (*Cong. Globe*, 38th Cong., 1st Sess., 1864, 1202–03)

On 15 June 1864, the final day of debate, a number of speeches were given in favor of the Thirteenth Amendment's passage. Significantly, four notable House members—John F. Farnsworth, William D. Kelly, Isaac N. Arnold, and Ebon C. Ingersoll—spoke to contest the proslavery view of Representatives Fernando Woods

(NY), John V. L. Pruyn (NY), and Lewis W. Ross (IL) who argued that man had a "vested property right" in owning man.

First to rebut the view was Representative John F. Farnsworth, who stated that "the Founding Fathers of the American government believed Slavery was at war with the rights of human nature." Senator Logan recounted, in *The Great Conspiracy*, how Mr. Farnsworth brilliantly used the *Genesis* 1:26–28 Creation narrative to destroy the "vested property right in owning man" view while answering the "title" question that Senator Harlan posed to Senator Saulsbury during the Senate debate on passing the Amendment:

> And Farnsworth met this idea—which had also been advanced by Messrs. Ross, Fernando Wood, and Pruyn— by saying: "What constitutes property? I know it is said by some gentlemen on the other side, that *what the statute makes property, is property.* I deny it. What 'vested right' has any man or State in *Property in Man?* We of the North hold property, not by virtue of statute law, not by virtue of [legal] enactments. Our property consists in lands, in chattels, in things. Our property was made property by Jehovah [Allah, Elohim, YHWH, the Creator] when He gave Man dominion over it. But nowhere did He give dominion of Man over Man. Our title extends back to the foundation of the World. That constitutes property. There is where we get our title. There is where we get our 'vested rights' to property.'" (*The Great Conspiracy*, 587; *Cong. Globe*, 38th Cong., 1st Sess., 1864, 2978)

Like Senator Sumner, Representative Farnsworth exonerated the framers of the 1774 Articles of Association, 1776 Declaration of Independence, 1781 Articles of Confederation, and 1787 Constitution of the false claim of wanting the "Race Card Evil" oriented African Slavery scheme included in the American Government. Then, Mr. Farnsworth said in his enlightening rendition best called "The Stranger":

"Mr. Speaker [of the House], at the time of the organization of this Government there were but about fifty thousand slaves within the limits of the United States. When our fathers rose out of the clouds of the Revolution and formed this [1787] Constitution, which I trust we are about to amend, no one of them dreamed that slavery in this land would continue until this time.

"This fact may be gathered from the writings of the men who wrote and from the speeches of the men who spoke in that day. Why, sir, immediately after the Revolution, [the 2nd Continental] Congress issued an address to the people in which occur these memorable words:

"'Let it be remembered, finally, that it has ever been the boast and pride of America that the rights for which she contended are the RIGHTS OF HUMAN NATURE.'

"This language was deliberately adopted and addressed to the people of the United States. This was after the Declaration of Independence, wherein they had declared as self-evident facts that all men were created equal, and endowed with the inalienable rights of life, liberty, and the pursuit of happiness. And when they followed this by the adoption of the [1787] Constitution the greatest care was taken that no words should be incorporated into that instrument which would imply that "men could hold [own] property in man." I use the very language of James Madison, a member of the Convention which framed the Constitution. He objected to incorporating the word "slave" or "slavery" into the Constitution, for the reason, as he said, that he would have nothing put into it which would recognize the right of a man to hold property in man. And you may search through the Constitution from the beginning to the conclusion of it, and no stranger to the fact that slavery has existed in the United States would believe for a moment that slavery could exist under it.

"Let the Constitution go before a court which is a stranger to the fact that slavery has existed here, and let it be construed as courts are required to construe written instruments, by itself, without looking to the facts of contemporaneous history, and no judge thus construing the Constitution would say that slavery could exist under it.

"Our fathers were thus careful in framing the Constitution so that when slavery should be entirely abolished, and when their posterity should come to look in there, they could find nothing to mar its beautiful symmetry. That was the object that when future generations came to look at that sacred instrument they should not find anything in it to indicate or imply that slavery ever existed in this land. Why, sir, they believed that slavery was going to die out speedily. Already steps had been taken in several of the States toward the abolition of slavery, and several of the States abolished it soon afterwards. There were, as I said before, but fifty thousand slaves in the Union. The raising of slaves for market was unprofitable. The old fathers who made the Constitution, the men who fought the battles of the Revolution, fought for the rights of *human nature*, they believed that slavery was at war with the rights of *human nature*. Of course such men, who had just gone through the fires of a seven years' war for their principles, and who framed the Constitution upon such a base, believed that slavery would die, and that speedily. Mr. [Thomas] Jefferson, in his Notes to Virginia, says:

"'In the very first session held under the republican Government the Assembly passed a law for the perpetual prohibition of the importation of slaves. This will in some measure stop the increase of this great *political* and *moral evil*, while the minds of our citizens may be ripening for a COMPLETE EMANCIPATION OF HUMAN NATURE.'" (*Cong. Globe*, 38th Cong., 1st Sess., 1864, 2978)

Being wise enough to realize that American posterity might be "purposely misled" about the cause for which the founders of the American Union risked their "lives, fortunes, and sacred honor," Mr. Farnsworth made clear the meaning of Thomas Jefferson's words in the "Declaration of Independence" and "Notes to Virginia." Speaking on behalf of the "seventy nations, Mr. Farnsworth destroyed the "America Made for the White Man" theory by stating to the House,

> "Why, sir, it has been said by gentlemen over the way... on that side of the House, and by men of that [political] party, that the "human nature" referred to in that address of Congress was not meant to apply to black human nature; that that [statement] only meant white men, Anglo-Saxons—Anglo-Saxon *human nature*! But Mr. Jefferson declares that the abolishing of the importation of *slaves* may prepare the way for the "speedy emancipation of human nature." That [statement] shows what was meant and how those words were understood and used by the good old Democrats of the Revolution. They included every son and daughter of Adam, whether born under a tropical or frigid sky. One of the first things they did was to prohibit slavery in all the territory belonging to the United States. They said, "We will see to it that this great curse shall spread no further." Why, sir, this shows the hearts and heads of our forefathers were imbued with the spirit of freedom, emancipation—abolition, if you please. In the very first Congress under the Constitution of the United States a petition was presented by Benjamin Franklin, as the President of an abolition society of Philadelphia, praying Congress to go to the very verge of the authority vested in them for the abolition of slavery."
> (Ibid., 2978–79)

Mr. Farnsworth then explained that his purpose for revisiting the American Government's early history was to illustrate just how far off the mark his era's generation had strayed by not adhering to the "liberty landmarks" set by the founders—and the resulting consequences for doing so:

"I refer to these things for the purpose of showing the doctrine which prevailed in that day, "in the early and better days of the Republic." But, sir, alas! It happened we took our departure from these landmarks [Deut. 19:14; Prov. 22:28, KJV]. Men became greedy and avaricious. The invention of the cotton-gin, the cultivation of cotton made it profitable to raise men and women for the southern market. The price of a slave was enhanced; from being worth $250 they went up to $1,200 and $1,300. Then the greed for power took possession of the slaveholders, and the avarice of these men overleaped itself and they became clamorous for the extension of slavery. The bounds were too narrow for them. They became ambitious of a nation that should be founded upon the "corner-stone of slavery."

"Then it was, Mr. Speaker, that the slave power got the control of the Government, of the executive, legislative, and judicial departments. Then it was that they got possession of the high places of society. They took possession of the churches. They took possession of the lands. Then it became criminal for a man to open his lips in denunciation of the evil and sin of slaveholding…I need not go further with the history of this subject. We all know how it culminated." (Ibid., 2979)

Representative Farnsworth next illustrated how the "Race Card Evil" oriented African Slavery scheme produced a great regional disparity in "free state vs. slave state" education and economics—which effect he called "a curse to the soil, people, intelligence, and industry; a curse to white men and to black men." Then, he addressed Mr. Ross's statement that passage of the Thirteenth Amendment would give "Negroes political equality" and cause "miscegenation" ("race-mixing"). Poking fun at this argument Mr. Farnsworth said,

"I thank God that the Republic has at last recognized the manhood of the negro. Gentlemen may call us "miscegenists," and they may talk of equal [political]

rights. I do not know of any man in the party to which I belong who is fearful of coming into competition with the negro. I know there are many men of the party of my colleague [Mr. Ross] who spoke last evening, who do feel that the *negro* is their natural competitor and rival, and they do fear, and fear with some reason, too, that the negroes might outstrip them if we give them a fair chance. I have heard gentlemen talk about their fears that negroes might become Representatives on this floor. Well, I am inclined to think that the country would not suffer much by such a change *in some instances*. Oh! They are afraid of "negro equality" and "miscegenation." You must not unchain the slave and allow him the fruits of his own toil and permit him to fight for the Republic for fear of *negro equality and miscegenation*…Mr. Speaker, I am not afraid of "miscegenation." If my colleague over the way is afraid of it, if he requires the restraining influences of a penal statute to keep him and his party from running into miscegenation, I will willingly vote it to them. But we do not want it; we do not practice miscegenation; we do not belong to that school; that is a Democratic institution; that goes hand in hand with slavery. Why, sir, some of the very best blood of the Democracy of Virginia may be found in the [captured black] contraband village at Arlington today; the blood of the Masons, the Hunters, the Garnetts, the Carters, and the Haxalls; their lineal though natural descendants are among the contrabands." (Ibid., 2979)

Having made his jibe at the "miscegenation" claim, Mr. Farnsworth then commended the dedication and valor displayed by "black" troops fighting for the Union. However, his praise prompted Mr. Ross to ask him "whether he thinks the white man is equal to the negro [?]" Mr. Farnsworth concluded his speech by answering,

"Mr. Speaker [of the House], that is a silly question which is useless to answer. I think some white men are better than some other white men. I think some white men are better than some negroes, and [I think] that some negroes are better than some white men…Mr. Speaker, I am in favor of finishing this business entirely and finally now. No child is so simple as not to know that slavery is the cause of this [civil] war; that it is the source of all our woe. Then why not finish it? It has spread the land with weeds and mourning. It has hung the very heavens with black. It has disgraced and dishonored us long enough with the other nations of the earth, and God is now chastising us for the sin." (Ibid., 2980)

Next came Pennsylvania Representative William D. Kelly, who enlightened the House about the views held by many of America's founding fathers during the Revolutionary War and Constitutional eras—insight derived from the 1787 Convention that framed the Constitution as recorded in volume 3 of *Eliot's Debates* (1788). When addressing the 1787 Constitution's "20–year allowance of the Importation of Slaves" (Article I, Section 9, Clause 1), Mr. Kelly revealed that America's founding fathers from Virginia wanted the "Race Card Evil" oriented scheme "put in the course of ultimate extinction" as soon as possible. Said he,

"Mr. Speaker [of the House], madness and despair rave, and I shall consume none of the brief time allotted me… the privilege is not often given to men to perform an act the influence of which will be felt beneficently by the poor, the oppressed, the ignorant, and the degraded of all lands, and which will endure until terminated by the wreck of matter and the crush of worlds…We were asked this morning whether we are wiser than the framers of our Government. I utter no word, I think no thought of disparagement of those great men. They were good men and were wise in their day and generation, but all wisdom did not die with them, and we are expiating in blood and agony and death and bereavement one of their errors—the unwise compromise they made with wrong in providing for the toleration and perpetuation of human slavery. The Convention which framed the [1787] Constitution unwisely compromised with wrong…It was not unknown to many of them that evil must result from their action. They knew and said while in the Convention that right and wrong were in eternal conflict [cf. Gen. 1:1–5, Eph. 5:1–11, and 1 Thess. 5:5, KJV], and that the avenging God was ever on the side of right.

"In proof of this I turn not to the remarks of men from New England, not to those from dear old Pennsylvania, but of those who represented Virginia in that august assemblage. I hold in my hand the third volume of *Eliot's Debates* of the Convention which framed the Constitution of the United States, and I quote from Mr. George Mason of Virginia, when speaking, June 15, 1788, on the first clause of the ninth section of article one of the Constitution:

"'Mr. Chairman,' said he [Mason], 'this is a fatal section, which has created more danger than any other. The first clause allows the importation of slaves for twenty years. Under the royal [British] Government this evil was looked upon as a great oppression, and many attempts were made to prevent it; but the interest of the African merchants prevented its prohibition. No sooner did the [1776] Revolution take place than it was thought of. It was one of the great causes of our separation from Great Britain. Its exclusion has been a principal object of this State [Virginia], and most of the States in the Union. The augmentation of slaves weakens the States, and such a trade is diabolical in itself and disgraceful to mankind [the "70" Nations]; yet by this [1787] Constitution it is continued for twenty years [1808]. As much as I value a union of all the States, I would not admit the southern States into the Union unless they agree to the discontinuance of this disgraceful trade, because it would bring weakness and not strength to the Union. This detestable kind of commerce.'

"As he [Mason] proceded he spoke of "this detestable kind of commerce," and said "I have ever looked upon this as a most disgraceful thing to America. I cannot express my detestation of it."

"Mr. Tyler, of Virginia, in the discussion of the same day [15 June 1788], as I find on the very next page, "warmly enlarged on the impolicy [a word later used by Chief Justice Taney], iniquity, and disgracefulness of this wicked traffic. He thought the reasons urged by gentlemen in defense of it were inconclusive and ill-founded. It was one cause of the complaints against British tyranny that this trade was permitted. The [1776] Revolution had put a period to it; but now it was to be revived. He [Tyler] thought nothing could justify it."

"Thus all the wise and good men of that period denounced the system of unpaid labor and property in [owning] human beings as wicked, infamously wicked, and the trade in men, women, and children as diabolical. We who advocate this [13th] amendment do but propose to consummate that which the wisest and best men of that day wished to do in the [1787] Convention. We do but propose to advise the people to listen to their counsel and perfect their great work." (*Cong. Globe*, 38th Cong., 1st Sess., 1864, 2983–84)

Mr. Kelly next revealed a fact unknown and not communicated to the citizens of the States in rebellion against the Union— namely, that the so-called seceding States were still in the Union and were, in fact, never out of it! While addressing Kentucky Representative Robert Mallory's statement that the time for passing the Thirteenth Amendment was "importune" (unripe), Mr. Kelly said,

"But the gentleman from Kentucky {Mr. Mallory} says the season [for passing the 13th Amendment] is importune. Sir, justice is ever in season, and it is never importune to do right. But he also says that the rebellious States are in the Union, and yet we do not propose to allow them to vote on the [13th Amendment] measure. The people of those States are probably not aware of the fact that they are in the Union. They believe themselves to be out of the Union, and if they only knew as well as the gentleman from Kentucky does that they have a right to be represented here as well as at Richmond, I doubt not they would have their Representatives here to oppose our action on this question. If in the Union, why are their Representatives not here? Who expelled them from this House or the Senate Chamber? If the Constitution be amended by default of their votes there will be no ground for a motion to open or set aside the judgment, as, to say the least, the default is the result of their voluntary absence." (Ibid., 2984, braces part of text)

Having made this political revelation, Mr. Kelly then reminded his colleagues why the need for a "freedom-for-all" law warranted passing the Thirteenth Amendment,

"Let us, I repeat, heed, and, so far as we may, grant that petition [by Ben Franklin for universal freedom]. Who shall complain that the Congress of 1864 responds to the prayer of the men who secured our freedom and elaborated our Constitution? Who shall induce us to pause in this great work?…Sir, what is it that we propose to do? Is it an act of doubtful power? No. It is simply to execute the fifth article of the Constitution of the United States…We propose to submit to the wisdom, patriotism, and humanity of the people of the States of this Union an amendment in accordance with this article, and for that we are denounced by those who in the name of Democracy plead for the perpetuity of slavery…Their love of Democracy and the Constitution finds expression in degrading the laboring man to a thing of sale upon the auction-block, in shutting out [enlightenment] from more than half our territory's schools and churches and civilization in all its aspects, whether it be religion, science, art, or social life.

"Sir, I arraign slavery as the efficient cause of every national evil we have endured. It put the vice with which we are now contending into the Constitution; it commenced a war upon the dignity of labor and the freedom of conscience and thought the very day our Government was organized; it inspired and gives physical power to the rebellion we are crushing at such fearful cost of vigorous life; it is, as it has been, the fruitful source of all our national woes…slavery is the strength of the rebellion, the power that is assailing our country, the only means by which the masses of white men whose toil is their only wealth can be reduced to ignorance and want…(Ibid., 2984–85)

Concluding his speech by answering a question about what the Government planned to do with the freed slaves, Representative Kelly gave a simple statement of confidence in the Creator's wisdom to guide the Union's republican institutions—and added a warning to Americans about again falling victim to "Race Card Evil" oriented ideas:

"What, asks the gentleman [from Kentucky], are you going to do with the freed negroes? I will tell that gentleman a secret confidentially. Above us all there is a God—slave-owners have not generally known the fact—who will take care of His children. I will trust the freed negroes to the care of God, under our beneficent republican institutions. We are told that the cries of the laborer whose hire has been kept back by fraud enter into the ears of the Lord of Sabaoth [Lev. 19:13; Deut. 24:14–15, KJV]; and if the State of Kentucky is to-day desolated by contending armies, it is because the Lord of Sabaoth is avenging the wrongs of His poor children, made dumb and voiceless by the atheistic laws of that State. It is the work of a just and avenging God punishing even in the third and fourth generation the wrongs done by your fathers and which you have not repented [Ex. 20:1–6; 34:1–9, KJV]. And when the iron shall have so entered the soul of the aristocracy of the slave States as to make them feel in their despair that "verily there is a God" who controls the destinies of men and nations, and when they will trust to Him, in His righteous power, the care of His children, this [civil] war will cease and peace again bless our nation. When we break every yoke and let the oppress go free, the broad fields that war has desolated will again blossom as the rose and reward the labor of the husbandman.

"Let us protect our posterity against the possibility of a recurrence of these fearful evils. Let us not be content with crushing this rebellion. Let us not be content with producing all over the country, loyalty to the flag. Let us establish freedom as a permanent institution, and make it universal." (Ibid., 2985)

Next rose Illinois Representative Isaac N. Arnold. Still believing that the Senate and House debates over the Thirteenth Amendment's passage were perhaps the most significant political events in American and World history, Mr. Arnold took the floor to give a brief speech that is best entitled "Shall Slavery Still Live." In *The Great Conspiracy*, statesman Logan recounted,

Touching the ethics of Slavery, Mr. Arnold's speech on the same occasion was also able, and in parts eloquent, as where he said: "Slavery is to-day an open enemy striking at the heart of the Republic. It is the soul and body, the spirit and motive of the Rebellion. It is Slavery which marshals yonder Rebel hosts, which confront the patriot Armies of Grant and Sherman. It is the savage spirit of this barbarous Institution which starves the Union prisoners at Richmond, which assassinates them at Fort Pillow, which murders the wounded on the field of battle, and which fills up the catalogue of wrong and outrage which mark the conduct of the Rebels during all this War.

"In view of all the long catalogue of wrongs which Slavery has inflicted upon the Country, I demand to-day, of the Congress of the United States, the death of African Slavery. We can have no permanent Peace, while Slavery lives. It now reels and staggers toward its last death-struggle. Let us strike the monster this last decisive blow"…he continued: "Gentlemen may flatter themselves with a restoration of the Slave-power in this country. 'The Union as it was!' It is a dream, never again to be realized. The America of the past, has gone forever. A new Nation is to be born from the agony through which the People are now passing. This new Nation is to be wholly Free. Liberty, *Equality before the Law*, is to be the great Corner-stone." (*The Great Conspiracy*, 587–88)

Concluding, Mr. Arnold reminded House members of the real importance underlying the Thirteenth Amendment's passage—namely, that of putting "The Race Card Evil" oriented cheap-labor scheme "in the course of ultimate extinction" in order to make all America "the home of the free":

"Mr. Speaker, I regret that this late day of the session compels an abridgment of discussion upon a subject of such overshadowing importance, yet I cannot let the occasion pass without briefly giving my reasons for voting for this constitutional amendment.

"Slavery is to-day an open enemy striking at the heart of the Republic…The Thirty-Seventh Congress will live in history as the Congress which prohibited slavery in all the Territories of the Union, and abolished it at the national capital. The President of the United States will be remembered as the author of the proclamation of emancipation, as the liberator of a race, the apostle of freedom, the great emancipator of his country. The Thirty-Eight Congress, if we pass this joint resolution, will live in history as that which consummated the great work of freeing a continent from the curse of human bondage.

"Never, since the day when John Adams plead[ed] for the Declaration of Independence, has so important a question been submitted to an American Congress as that upon which you are now about to vote. The signing of the immortal Declaration is a familiar picture in every log cabin and residence all over the land. Pass this resolution, and the grand spectacle of this vote, which knocks off the fetters of a whole race, will make this scene immortal.

"Live a century, nay, a thousand years, and no such opportunity to do a great deed for humanity, for liberty, for peace, and for your country, will ever again present itself. Pass this joint resolution, and you win a victory over wrong and injustice [as] lasting as eternity. The whole world will rise up to do you honor. Every lover of liberty in Germany, France, Italy, Great Britain, the world, will rise up and call you blessed...This constitutional amendment has passed [in] the Senate, long regarded as the citadel of the slave power; how strange if it should fail in the popular branch of Congress! The people and the States are eager and impatient to ratify it. Will those who claim to represent the ancient Democracy refuse to give the people an opportunity to vote upon it? Is this your confidence in the loyal masses?

"The passage of this resolution will strike the rebellion at the heart...The America of the past is gone forever. A new nation is to be born...This new nation is to be wholly free...Mr. Speaker, I thank God and a liberty-loving constituency for the privilege of voting for this constitutional amendment, for universal emancipation throughout our country. Let us now, to-day, in the name of liberty, justice, and of God, consummate this grand revolution. Let us to-day make our country, our whole country, *the home of the free.*" (*Cong. Globe*, 38th Cong., 1st Sess., 1864, 2988–89 passim)

Lastly, Illinois Representative Ebon C. Ingersoll—brother of late Illinois Representative Owen P. Lovejoy (whose seat Ebon occupied)—took the floor and, after paying tribute to his brother, predicted both the modern world's view of America and the "Race Card Evil's" resilience by stating,

"Sir [Speaker of the House], I hope this resolution may pass by the necessary majority to give it validity. All truly honest and philanthropic men throughout the world will have reason to rejoice and will rejoice if it so passes. It will be heralded over the world as another grand step upward and onward in the irresistible march of a Christianized civilization. The old starry banner of our country, as it "floats over the sea and over the land," will be grander and more glorious than ever before. Its stars will be brighter; it will be holier; it will mean more than a mere nationality; it will mean universal liberty; it will mean that the rights of mankind [the "70" Nations], without regard to color or race, are respected and protected. The oppressed and downtrodden of all the world will take new courage; hope will spring afresh in their struggling and weary hearts; and when they look upon that banner in distant lands they will yearn to be here, where they can enjoy the inestimable blessings which are denied them forever on their native shores.

"Mr. Speaker, it would seem that this resolution should be adopted by a unanimous vote. Yet I fear we shall lose it. The slave power has not yet lost all its influence in this Congress. The pock-marks of slavery are plainly visible on the faces of many of the members of the Opposition. They were inoculated and corrupted by it in the days of its wanton power. Its woeful and baneful influence is upon them still. Slavery has been their idol. They worshipped at its shrine in the days of its power, and even now, when it is going to an ignominious grave, they rally around and protect and defend it in all its hideous ghastliness as though it was really divine. We may admire their pluck, but we must condemn their action, their want of patriotism, their inappreciation of liberty, and their entire lack of generous sentiments common to humanity [the Adamite race or "seventy" nations]. They are blinded by prejudice. They are politically corrupt, under an undue desire to regain that power which they so ingloriously lost during the last Democratic administration, or, I should say maladministration. Being the slaves of the slave power, we cannot expect much of them until we have made them free and hewn down their prejudices.

"In my opinion many of the Opposition members would vote for this resolution if they could be convinced that slavery could no longer be made available to them as a political power [tool]. But they know it as certain as fate that if slavery goes down the present Democratic organization goes down with it. Hence their Herculean efforts to save slavery; but they cannot succeed in their unholy and detestable work. The liberty-loving and loyal people of the country have sworn in their hearts that the rebellion and slavery should both go down, and forever. And they will keep that oath. When we have succeeded in bringing the rebellion and slavery to an end, if we could only petrify the pro-slavery Democracy, what a becoming and fitting tombstone it would make to mark the place of their burial." (Ibid., 2988)

Mr. Ingersoll then addressed the proslavery argument that the Thirteenth Amendment's passage would violate the Constitution and be unfair to the States not represented in Congress. Showing that the Constitution's Article V did give Congress the legal authority to propose Constitutional Amendment, Mr. Ingersoll next said that the States not represented had "no standing" to complain in view of their "voluntary withdrawal" from Congress to initiate or support the rebellion:

"It is plain to be seen, then, that this resolution contemplates no violation of the Constitution. Then why this objection to adopting it and submitting the proposed amendment to the Legislatures of the several States not in rebellion? Are you of the Opposition afraid to trust the representatives of the people? In reality I believe you are. You fear, and have good cause to fear, that the necessary majority of States will ratify the proposed amendment, and make it thereby a part of the Constitution. Then slavery will no longer need defenders and protectors in our national Congress…You will go hungry for place and office, and slavery can no longer gratify your unholy ambition…But the Opposition objects to the adoption of the resolution at the present time, because they say Mississippi, South Carolina, and other States in rebellion can have no voice upon the question of its resolution. Why…? It is because they voluntarily entered into the rebellion. Had they not done so they would have had equal right and enjoyed equal privilege with Illinois upon the question. Are we, because a portion of the States inaugurated and still carry on this rebellion, to suspend all legilative action which might affect things or institutions in such States? I say not. Let those who inaugurate and carry on the rebellion take the consequences. (Ibid., 2989)

Thereafter, Mr. Ingersoll brought a railing indicment against the African Slavery scheme—recounting its shameful history in the Republic and illustrating its opposition to universal education or enlightenment:

"That slavery is an evil no sane, honest man will deny. It has been the great curse of this country from its infancy to the present hour…I believe slavery is the mother of this rebellion, that this rebellion can be attributed to no other cause but slavery…Slavery has ever been the enemy of liberal principles. It has ever been the friend of ignorance, prejudice, and all the unlawful, savage, and detestable passions which proceed therefrom. It has ever been domineering, arrogant, exacting, and overbearing. It has claimed to be a polished aristocrat, when in reality it has only been a coarse, swaggering, and brutal boor. It has ever claimed to be a gentleman, when in reality it has ever been a villain. I think it is high time to clip its overgrown pretensions, strip it of its mask, and expose it in all its hideous deformity to the detestation of all honest and patriotic men.

"For eighty years the bogus aristocracy of slavery have left nothing undone to corrupt and demoralize the people and their Representatives. For eighty years they have attempted to clothe this monster in the radiance of divinity ["Ham cursed" story], when in reality it should only be draped in the blackness of its own enormity. In order to maintain their power they had so molded public opinion, even in the grand free States of the North, that many honest but deluded men were willing to concede that slavery, if not divine, was not so bad an institution after all, that "the devil was not so black as he is painted." The North, against its sense of justice and right, for the sake of peace and union, has, time and time again, humiliated itself in its own [eyes] and the eyes of the world by conceding to the unhallowed and ambitious demands of slavery.

"At the formation of our Constitution slavery demanded that a section should be incorporated therein restraining Congress from passing a law prohibiting the importation of negroes prior to the year 1808. The North, in violation of its sense of honor, got down on its knees and consented…thereby conceding the right of this bogus aristocracy to freight its ships with human beings [members of the "seventy" nations] stolen from their native land and consigned to an ignominious slavery only equaled by its cruelty.

"Again, in 1793, they demanded a fugitive slave law; that is to say, that free northern men should be their blood-hounds. The North again assented., and went into the blood-hound business. In 1850 they again demanded more and fiercer blood-hounds. The North, true to its instincts of peace and union, but false to its honor, agreed…Again, in 1820, the same relentless monster demanded of the North more territory for the uses of slavery. The North again got upon its knees and admitted Missouri with its slave constitution…Again, in 1854, they demanded the repeal of the Missouri Compromise [thirty-six- degree, thirty- minute] line. Again, in northern men, whom they had demoralized and corrupted by the contaminating influences of slavery, [in addition] to a corresponding lust for [political] office, they found the willing tools [flunkeys] wherewith to consummate this treachery…Again, in 1857, the slave power brought all its energies to bear to convert this territory, which had been thrown open to it by the repeal of the Missouri Compromise line, into a slave State. To the everlasting infamy of James Buchanan's administration, be it said, with a few honorable exceptions, it lent the whole force and power of its authority to the accomplishment of this foul crime. But, thank God, the people of the North at last had become aroused, and they determined that slavery should no longer be the master of liberty…They declared that Kansas should be free. The slave power swore it should be slave; and then and there this war commenced which is now deluging [flooding] this land with blood. After a long and not a bloodless struggle justice and freedom triumphed, and Kansas to-day is a beaming star of liberty in the western horizon." (Ibid., 2989–90 passim)

Asking House members to pass the Amendment, Mr. Ingersoll concluded by summing up the meaning underlying the "Ancient Lights" doctrine:

"Sir, I am in favor in the fullest sense of personal liberty. I am in favor of the freedom of speech…which guarantees to the citizen of Illinois, in common with the citizen of Masachusetts, the right to proclaim the eternal principles of liberty, truth, and justice in Mobile, Savannah, or Charleston with the same freedom and security as though he were standing at the foot of Bunker Hill monument; and if this proposed amendment to the Constitution is adopted and ratified, the day is not far distant when this glorious privilege will be accorded to every citizen of the Republic. I am in favor of the adoption of this amendment because it will secure to the oppressed slave his natural and God-given rights. I believe that the black man has certain inalienable rights, which are as sacred in the sight of Heaven as those of any other race. I believe he has a right to live, and live in a state of freedom. He has a right to breathe the free air and enjoy God's free sunshine. He has a right to till the soil, to earn his bread by the sweat of his brow, and enjoy the rewards of his own labor [Gen. 3:19, 1 Tim. 5:17–18, KJV]. He has a right to the endearments and enjoyment of family ties; and no white man has any right to rob him of or infringe upon any of these blessings.

"I am in favor of the adoption of this amendment to the Constitution for the sake of the seven millions of poor white people who live in the slave States but who have ever been deprived of the blessings of manhood by reason of this thrice-accursed institution of slavery. Slavery has kept them in ignorance, in poverty, and in degradation. Abolish slavery, and school-houses will rise upon the ruins of the slave mart, intelligence will take the place of ignorance, wealth of poverty, and honor of degradation; industry will go hand in hand with virtue, and propriety with happiness, and a disenthralled and regenerated people will rise up and bless you and be an honor to the American Republic.

"Slavery has shed every drop of blood which has been spilled in this war. It has filled thousands of graves with our heroic dead. It has filled our hospitals with our shattered heroes. It has swept American commerce from the ocean… consequently I am the unyielding and persistent enemy of slavery…It is this demon of slavery which has called from their happy homes in Illinois one hundred and seventy-five thousand of her sons as brave and heroic as ever the sun shone upon…Mr. Speaker, I have already occupied too much time…I implore the House to adopt this resolution." (Ibid., 2990–91)

Unfortunately, as Mr. Ingersoll predicted, despite the enlightened views and accurate historical facts spoken by many of the delegates, on 15 June 1864, the Thirteenth Amendment failed to secure the necessary two-thirds vote to pass in the House. Out of "181" voting House members, the Amendment was defeated because it fell "27" votes short of the "120" needed for passage—the count being "93" for, "65" against, and "23" not voting. In view of this outcome, Ohio Representative James M. Ashley (House floor manager of the Resolution) made a motion the same day to reconsider the vote during the December House Session. Senator Logan recounted in *The Great Conspiracy*:

> It was about 4 o'clock in the afternoon of June 15th, that the House came to a vote on the passage of the Joint Resolution. At first the strain of anxiety on both sides was great, but, as the roll proceeded, it soon became evident that the Resolution was doomed to defeat…That same evening, Mr. Ashley made a motion to reconsider the vote…and the motion was duly entered in the Journal, despite the persistent efforts of Messrs. [Samuel S.] Cox, [William S.] Holman, and others, to prevent it.
>
> On the 28th of June, just prior to the Congressional Recess, Mr. Ashley announced that he had been disappointed in the hope of securing enough votes from the Democratic side of the House to carry the Amendment. "Those," said he, "who ought to have been the champions of this great proposition are unfortunately its strongest opponents. They have permitted the golden opportunity to pass. *The record is made up, and we must go to the Country on this issue thus presented.*" And then he gave notice that he would call the matter up, at the earliest possible moment after the opening of the December Session of Congress. (*The Great Conspiracy*, 590–91; *Cong. Globe*, 38th Cong., 1st Sess., 1864, 2995)

Although the House failed to pass the Thirteenth Amendment at that time, Congress had achieved a great and historic victory. No longer was it the "Race Card Evil's" puppet. During its first session, the Thirty-eighth Congress unleashed the Journals and Notes of America's founding fathers—to instruct American posterity about the truth underlying the nation's founding and its Mission Statement. Out of the "Great Senate and House Debates" also came a working definition of the "Ancient Lights" rule. No longer was it limited to an English rule concerning the "property rights of neighboring landowners." Now it included the God-given rule concerning the "Human rights due all members of the Adamite race."

During its second session the "House of Representatives," acting on behalf of the American nation, would either extend or extinguish the "Race Card Evil" oriented African Slavery scheme. Whatever the case, it was clear that the nation could not continue to exist with a "half-free, half-slave" population. Undoubtedly, the nation's future would be decided for all time to come by the November 1864 presidential election and January 1865 House session.

7

# The Great Charter of Liberty

"And ye shall hallow the fiftieth year, and proclaim
Liberty throughout all the land unto all the inhabitants
thereof."

—(Lev. 25:10) (KJV)

ALTHOUGH THE THIRTEENTH Amendment failed to pass in the
House, the handwriting on history's wall said the day was dawning
for the African Slavery scheme's legal demise on American soil.
In November of 1864 Mr. Lincoln won his second term of
office, and in December Congress began its second session with
Representative Ashley lobbying to change House members' "nay"
votes before the holiday recess began. By the time the January
1865 House session resumed, Mr. Ashley had succeeded and the
House voted in favor of passing the Amendment. And by the
month's end, it was sent to the state legislatures for ratification.
Opponents of the Amendment became nervous, because the
odds favored it becoming the law of the land.

Between February first and twenty-fourth "eighteen" of the
Union's "thirty-six" states, two of which were once part of the 11–
State Cofederacy, ratified the Amendment (IL, RI, MI, MD, NY,
PA, WVA, MO, ME, KS, MA, VA, OH, IN, NV, LA, MN, WI).
Thus, only "nine" more States were needed to secure the "three-
fourths" or "twenty-seven out of thirty-six" states ratification for

the Amendment to become part of the Constitution—the needed "nine" from among the remaining "nine" Confederate states self-exiled from Congress (AL, AR, FL, GA, MS, NC, SC, TN, TX), "seven undecided free states (CA, CT, IA, NH, NJ, OR, VT), and "two" undecided border states (DE, KY). Moreover, on 4 March 1865 antislavery Lincoln would be sworn in to his second term of office and hasten the African Slavery scheme's demise.

Prior to his second inauguration, Mr. Lincoln had reflected on the Civil War's absurdity—a war fought because a selfish minority desired to profit from the "unpaid labor of others." Further, he reflected on how this minority used God's name and religion to justify their oppressive deeds. And, he considered how the phrase "God's will" was historically used by "religious" people (Christian or other) to achieve unjust ends contrary to the messages stated in four chief biblical passages: Genesis 3:19, Psalm19:9, Matthew 7:1, and Matthew 18:7. After comtemplating how such terms were used by the Union Confederate opponents—"Battle Hymn of the Republic" or "Glory of the Lord's Coming" (Union view) versus "Deo Vindice" or "God will Vindicate Us" (Confederate view)—Lincoln wrote a profound statement in one of his journal entries that summed up Man's view of God's purpose in the universe. In his work entitled *Lincoln's Melancholy*, twenty-first-century American political historian Joshua Wolf Shenk recounted that, prior to his 4 March 1865 Inauguration, "Honest Abe" wrote:

> In great contests each party claims to act in accordance with the will of God. Both *may* be [wrong], and one *must* be wrong. God cannot be *for* and *against* the same thing at the same time. In the present civil war it is quite possible that God's purpose is somewhat different from the purposes of either party—and yet the human instrumentalities, working just as they do, are of the best adaptation to effect this. (Joshua Wolf Shenk, *Lincoln's Melancholy* [New York: Houghton Mifflin, 2005], 198.)

By 3 March 1865, the Thirteenth Amendment still had not obtained the required quorum of States to become the national law. However, on that day Congress signalled the shadow of things to come by passing its Freedmen's Bureau act (13 *US Statutes at Large* 507). And on the following day Lincoln was sworn into Office and gave, in his Second Inaugural Address, a simple-but-powerful speech that reflected his thoughts about "the divine will of God." In their *Documents of American History*, Commager and Cantor recounted that Mr. Lincoln said to the posterity of America and humanity:

> "Fellow-Countrymen:…One-eighth of the whole [American] population was colored slaves…These slaves constituted a peculiar and powerful [business] interest. All knew that this interest was somehow the cause of the [Civil] War. To strengthen, perpetuate, and extend this institution was the object for which the insurgents [Rebels] would rend the Union even by War…Neither party expected for the War the magnitude [in cost, death, and destruction] or the duration which it has already attained…Both [sides] read the same Bible and pray to the same God, and each invokes His [God's] aid against the other [side]. It may seem strange that any man should dare to ask a Just God's assistance in wringing [earning] their bread [living] from the sweat [labor] of other men's faces [Gen. 3:19]…The prayers of both [sides] could not be answered. That of neither [side] has been answered fully. The Almighty has His own purposes. "Woe unto the World because of offenses; for it must needs be that offenses come, but woe to that man by whom the offense cometh [Matt. 18:7]." If we shall suppose that American Slavery is one of those offenses which, in the Providence of God, must needs come, but which, having continued through His appointed time, He now wills to remove, and that He gives to both North and South this terrible [Civil] War as a woe due to those by whom the offense came,

> shall we discern therein any departure from those divine attributes which the believers in a living God always ascribe to Him?" (*Docs. of Amer. Hist.*, 442–43 passim)

Undoubtedly, Mr. Lincoln's speech made sense to many of his listeners—especially to many State delegates holding the Thirteenth Amendment's fate in the balance. Not long after his speech two more States, Vermont (9 March 1865) and Tennessee (7 April 1865), voted for the Amendment's passage and raised the total to "twenty" states; and of the two, one had been part of the eleven-state Confederacy. Thus, only "seven" more states were needed to reach the quorum.

On Sunday, 9 April 1865, the Union Confederate War ended when renowned Confederate General Robert E. Lee surrendered to Union General Ulysses S. Grant at the Appomatox, Virginia, Court House. With the war officially over the prospect of rebuilding American society, on a genuinely "undivided basis" of universal freedom, seemed to be on the horizon. Unfortunately on Friday, 14 April 1865, the same day that Arkansas voted for the Amendment's passage (raising the total to "twenty-one," leaving only "six" more states to reach the needed quorum), President Lincoln was mortally shot during the evening while attending a play at Washington DC's Ford Theater. Mr. Lincoln did not immediately die from his wound, but during the early morning hours of 15 April 1865 he did. If the assasination was a last-ditch effort to defeat the Amendment's passage, then it failed.

Between May and July, two more states, Connecticut (4 May 1865) and New Hampshire (1 July 1865), ratified the Amendment to reduce the needed quorum to "four" states. And during fall of 1865 the Amendment received the final "four" States to meet the needed "twenty-seven states" quorum: South Carolina (13 November 1865), Alabama (2 December 1865), North Carolina (4 December 1865), and Georgia (6 December 1865) voting in favor of it; all "four" having been part of the eleven-state Confederacy. With "twenty-seven" states ratifying the Thirteenth Amendment (Oregon doing so on 8 December 1865, to raise the total to "twenty-eight"), the result was declared by the US Secretary of State's proclamation on 18 December 1865. This momentous event the Honorable Robert Ney, twenty-first-century AD Chairman of the Joint Committee on Printing, recounted in the 2003 edition of *The Constitution of the United States of America as Amended*. In a note to the Thirteenth Amendment he said,

> The thirteenth amendment to the Constitution of the United States was proposed to the legislatures of the Several States by the Thirty-eight Congress, on the 31st day of January, 1865, and was declared, in a proclamation of the Secretary State, dated the 18th of December, 1865, to have been ratified by the legislatures of twenty-seven [27] of the thirty-six [36] States [then in the Union]. ("Article XIII," *The Constitution of the United States of America as Amended*, presented by the Hon. Robert Ney (Washington, DC: U.S. Government Printing Office, 2003), p.16 note)

Although Lincoln was cut down in midstream of his effort to emancipate the American people from the "Race Card Evil" and its African Slavery scheme, his fight to put it "in the course of ultimate extinction" would continue through the efforts of all Americans who paid heed to his message. Indeed, after announcing that the Thirteenth Amendment was part of the "supreme law of the land" (the Constitution), more States ratified the measure. Between 19–28 December 1865, two more states, respectively California and Florida, ratified it and raised the number to "thirty." And between 15–23 January 1866 two more states, respectively Iowa and New Jersey, did so and raised it to "thirty-two." Thus within or about one year (1865–1866), "thirty-two" of the Union's "thirty-six" states ratified the Amendment— leaving only "four" to do so: Texas (18 February 1870), Delaware

(12 February 1901), Kentucky (18 March 1976), and Mississippi (16 March 1995).

Throughout the Union Confederate war both President Lincoln and Congress enacted various legislation to permanently end the African slavery evil. However, the measures had minimal success due to the "negative social attitude" that many "white" Americans displayed towards "nonwhite" Americans—an attitude that resulted from many "whites" being "infected" with the unified "Ham cursed, Ham uncivilized whites the original man America built for whites" theory of social evolution. With the Thirteenth Amendment's passage, many Americans thought the antisocial "white" attitude would end. However, people soon discovered otherwise.

During the second half of 1865, the slaves freed by Lincoln's Proclamation faced heightened hostility from many Southern "whites" who refused to recognize them as citizens and denied them employment in "white" businesses. Worse, "Black Codes" were passed to control and restrict the movement of the black-labor market to other locations for better employment. *Wikipedia's* article entitled "Black Codes" stated,

> The Black Codes were laws [enacted] in the United States after the Civil War with the effect of limiting the basic human rights and civil liberties of blacks. Even though the U.S. constitution originally discriminated against blacks (as "other people") and both Northern and Southern states had passed discriminatory legislation from the early 19th century, the term Black Codes is used most often to refer to legislation passed by Southern states at the end of the Civil War to control the labor, migration and other activities of newly-freed slaves…Though varying from state to state, they [the Black Codes] each endeavored to secure a steady supply of cheap labor, and continued to assume the inferiority of the freed slave. The black codes had their roots in the slave codes that had formerly been in effect. The premise behind chattel slavery in America was

that slaves were property, and, as such, they had few, if any, legal rights. The slave codes, in their many loosely-defined forms, were seen as effective tools against slave unrest... All the slave states passed laws banning the marriage of whites and negroes, so-called anti-miscegenation laws, as did several new free states, including Indiana, Illinois and Michigan...After the partial abolition of slavery by the Thirteenth Amendment...all former slave states adopted new Black Codes. During 1865 every Southern state passed Black Codes that restricted the freedmen, who were emancipated but not yet full citizens. While they pursued re-admission to the Union, the Southern states provided freedmen with limited second-class civil rights and no voting rights. Southern plantation owners feared that they would lose their land. Having convinced themselves that slavery was justified, planters feared African Americans wouldn't work without coercion. The Black Codes were an attempt to control them and to ensure they did not claim social equality.

The Black Codes granted African Americans certain rights, such as legalized marriage, ownership of property, and limited access to the courts. But the Black Codes denied them the rights to testify against whites, to serve on juries or in state militias, or to vote, and express legal concern publicly. And, in response to planters' demands that the freed people be required to work on the plantations, the Black Codes declared that those who failed to sign yearly labor contracts could be arrested and hired out to white landowners. Some states limited the occupations open to African Americans and barred them from acquiring land, and others provided that judges could assign African American children to work for their former owners without the consent of their parents...The Black Codes outraged public opinion in the North because it seemed the South was creating a form of quasi-slavery to negate the results of the war. After winning large majorities in the 1866 elections, the Republicans put the South under military rule. They held new elections in which the Freedmen could vote. Suffrage was also expanded to poor whites. The new governments repealed all the Black Codes…The Black Codes of the 1860s are not the same as the Jim Crow laws. The Black Codes were in reaction to the abolition of slavery and the South's defeat in the Civil War. Southern legislatures enacted them in the 1860s. The Jim Crow era began later, nearer to the end of the 19th century (late 1890s) after Reconstruction. (*Wikipedia*, s.v. "Black Codes (United States)," 1–6 passim; http:// en.wikipedia.org/wiki/Black_Codes_(United_States). Retrieved 23 August 2012)

Due to the "white" antisocial attitude displayed against those labeled "Negroes," and to curtail the violence that accompanied attempts to integrate them into mainstream "white" American society after the war closed, Congress planned to hold another session to address the type of legislation needed to provide the former slaves with a better-defined legal platform upon which to stand and develop their economic, political, and social identity within the nation. This platform would begin with a definite statement to "white" Americans that the newly freed people were "citizens of the United States"—since many "white" Americans believed the "Taney-Douglass" propaganda and failed to understand Congress's "intent" by passing the Thirteenth Amendment.

To pacify allegations by some Congressmen that the Amendment only "freed" the slaves, but did not grant them "citizenship," on 5 January 1866 Illinois Senator Lyman Trumbull proposed to the First Session of the Thirty-Ninth Congress a ten-sectioned piece of legislation entitled "An Act to protect all Persons in the United States in their Civil Rights and furnish the Means of their Vindication"—an important piece of legislation more familiarly called the "The Civil Rights Act of 1866." In plain language Section 1 of the Act stated,

Be it enacted by the Senate and House of Representatives
of the United States of America in Congress Assembled,
That all persons born in the United States and not subject
to any foreign power, Indians excepted [due to being then
considered a "foreign sovereign power"], are hereby declared
to be citizens of the United States, and such citizens, of every
race and color, without regard to any previous condition of
slavery or involuntary servitude, except for punishment of
a crime whereof the party shall have been duly convicted,
shall have the same right, in every State and Territory in
the United States, to make and enforce contracts, to sue,
be parties, and give evidence, purchase, lease, sell, hold, and
convey real and personal property, as is enjoyed by white
citizens, and shall be subject to like punishment, pains, and
penalties, and to none other, any law, statute, ordinance,
regulation, or custom, to the contrary notwithstanding. (14
*Statutes at Large* 27, Chap. 31, Sec. 1, April 9, 1866).

Since the Thirteenth Amendment did little to eradicate a
century or more of the "race" indoctrination of many "white"
Americans, who erroneously believed that America was founded
solely for the "white man's" benefit, Congress passed the 1866
Act to conclusively state that the newly freed slaves were "citizens
of the United States," and thus end the argument that the
Amendment only "freed" the slaves.

When speaking to the Senate on the "intent" or "purpose" for
proposing passage of the 1866 Act, Senator Trumbull informed
Congress of the need to destroy the "Black Codes" that promoted
"customs" or "practices" reminiscent of the "Race Card Evil"
oriented African slavery program. Such "customs" or "practices"
Mr. Trumbull collectively phrased as "badges of slavery"—due
to the practice in some Southern cities of requiring slaves to
wear "yellow badges" when traveling about to seek or perform
employment. In their work entitled *Runaway Slaves: Rebels on the
Plantation*, twenty-first-century American historians John Hope
Franklin and Loren Schweninger said of this degrading practice,

> In some cities, hired slaves were supposed to have a ticket or wear a [yellow] badge, and everywhere they were presumed to have been given permission [to work] by their owners. But slaves could forge tickets, acquire false badges, and argue convincingly that their owners, usually located some distance away, had sent them thither [there] to find work. (John Hope Franklin and Loren Schweninger, *Runaway Slaves: Rebels on the Plantation* (New York: Oxford University Press, 1999), 135)

As said, because many "white" Americans failed to understand why the Thirteenth Amendment was passed and some Congressmen questioned whether it did more than free a large group of enslaved people, Senator Trumbull advised his colleagues that additional legislation was needed to define Congress's "intent" when passing the Amendment. The landmark 1968 US Supreme Court fair housing case entitled *Joseph Lee Jones v. Alfred H. Mayer, Company* recounted that Mr. Trumbull said to the Senate,

> "The trumpet of freedom that we have been blowing throughout the land has given an "uncertain sound," and the promised freedom is a delusion. Such was not the intention of Congress, which proposed the [Thirteenth] Constitutional Amendment, nor is such the fair meaning of the Amendment itself…I have no doubt that, under this [1866 Civil Rights Act] Provision…we may destroy all these discriminations in Civil Rights against the black man, and if we cannot, [then] our Constitutional Amendment amounts to nothing. It was for that purpose that the second clause of that Amendment was adopted, which says that Congress shall have the authority, by appropriate legislation, to carry into effect the article prohibiting slavery. Who is to decide what that appropriate legislation is to be? The Congress of the United States, and it is for Congress to adopt such appropriate legislation as it may think proper, so that it be a means to accomplish the end." (*Joseph Lee Jones v. Alfred H. Mayer, Co.*, 392 U.S. 409, 440; 1968).

After serious reflection on the points raised by Senator Trumbull and others, the Senate passed the Civil Rights Act on 2 February 1866 and then waited for the House of Representatives' consideration and vote on the matter. In the House, Pennsylvania Representative Russell M. Thayer was most vocal about the need for the 1866 Act—holding the view that the Act's objective was that of giving real meaning to Congress's "intent" on passing the Thirteenth Amendment. Again, *Jones v. Mayer* recounted that Mr. Thayer said to his colleagues:

> "When I voted for the [Thirteenth] Amendment to abolish slavery...I did not suppose that I was offering...a mere paper guarantee...The [1866] bill which now engages the attention of the House has for its object to carry out and guarantee the reality of that great measure. It is to give to it practical [legal] effect and force. It is to prevent that great [Thirteenth Amendment] measure from remaining a dead letter upon the Constitutional page of this Country...The events of the last four years...have changed [a] large class of people...from a condition of slavery to that of freedom. The practical question now to be decided is whether they shall be, in fact, freemen. It is whether they shall have the benefit of this great Charter of liberty given to them by the American People." (*Id.*, 392 U.S. 409, 433–34)

Since Mr. Thayer's Speech reflected the majority's view, on 13 March 1866 the House passed the Civil Rights Act and sent it to President Andrew Johnson (Lincoln's vice president and successor) for his consideration (US Const, Art I, Sec 7, Cl 2). Unfortunately, President Johnson did not view the 1866 Act in the same light as the Senate and House. On 27 March 1866 Mr. Johnson vetoed the Act because he believed it violated a "States Rights" issue (U.S. Const, Amend 10). In his work entitled *The Political History of the United States of America During the Period of Reconstruction*, midnineteenth century Congressman-Editor-Scholar Edward McPherson recounted that President Johnson said,

By the first section of the [1866] bill all persons born in the United States, and not subject to any foreign power, excluding Indians not taxed, are declared to be citizens of the United States. This provision comprehends the Chinese of the Pacific States, Indians subject to taxation, the people called Gipsies, as well as the entire race designated as blacks, people of color, negroes, mulattoes, and persons of African blood. Every individual of these races, born in the United States, is by the bill made a citizen of the United States. It does not purport to declare or confer any other right of citizenship than federal citizenship. It does not purport to give these classes of persons any status as citizens of States, except that which may result from their status as citizens of the United States. The power to confer the right of State citizenship is just as exclusively with the several States as the power to confer the right of federal citizenship is with Congress. (Hon. Edward McPherson LLD, *The Political History of the United States of America During the Period of Reconstruction (from April 15, 1865 to July 15, 1870)* (New York: Negro University Press, 1969 (originally published 1871)), 74–75.

After finding fault with Section 1 of the 1866 Civil Rights Act, President Johnson went on to find fault with Sections 2 through 9 of the ten-sectioned act. Interestingly enough, when concluding his views Mr. Johnson correctly interpreted the "Race Card Evil" oriented African slavery's "master vs. slave" relationship as one of "capitalist (employer) vs. laborer (employee)." Again, Mr. McPherson recounted that Mr. Johnson said before vetoing the act,

I do not propose to consider the policy of this bill. To me the details of the bill seem fraught with evil. The white race and the black race of the South have hitherto lived together under the relation of master and slave—capital owning labor. Now, suddenly, that relation is changed, and, as to ownership, capital and labor are divorced. They stand now each other master of itself. In this new relation, one being necessary to the other, there will be a new adjustment, which both are deeply interested in making harmonious. Each has equal power in settling the terms, and, if left to the [economic] laws that regulate capital and labor, it is confidently believed that they will satisfactorily work out the problem. Capital, it is true, has more intelligence, but labor is never so ignorant as not to understand its own interests, not to know its own value, and not to see that capital must pay that value. (Ibid., 78)

Not convinced by President Johnson's "reasons" for vetoing the act, Congress responded by overriding his veto and passing its "second" piece of post–Civil War legislation—an event marking a first in American political history. Again, recounted *Jones v. Mayer*,

President Andrew Johnson vetoed the Act on March 27 [1866]…On April 6 [1866], the Senate, and on April 9 [1866], the House, overrode the President's veto by the requisite majorities, and the Civil Rights Act of 1866 became law. (*Jones v. Mayer*, *Co.*, 392 U.S. 409, 435)

Despite the 1866 Act's passage to enforce the Thirteenth Amendment, by declaring the newly freed slaves "American Citizens," problems still resulted—mainly because some "white" Americans or "white-controlled" agencies and businesses on the local and state government levels refused to recognize "nonwhite" Americans as "citizens." Worse, some congressmen questioned whether the 1866 Act could be applied to make people "state citizens" without violating the Tenth Amendment. However, both the thirty-eigth and thirty-ninth Congresses were correct in their intent and action to grant the freed slaves "citizenship"— for a number of reasons that pro African slavery champions "conveniently" forgot, or "willfully" disregarded, to succeed with their cheap-labor workforce scheme. For instance:

1.) During America's Colonial era, and before her 1776 Revolution, the "Naturalization Process" was regulated by British law—which held that anyone "born within the British Empire's jurisdiction" (Colonies included) was considered a "natural born subject." Thus, if a person was either an indentured servant or slave and a child was born to that person "within the Empire's jurisdiction," then that child was actually a "natural born British subject"— albeit born to parents subjected to indentured servitude or slavery (compare Gen. 15:1–3, KJV).

2.) On the eve of America's 1776 Revolution, and at the time the Declaration of Independence was written, one of the chief grievances against King George III was the "misuse" of the "Naturalization Process" by his officials or agents— the Colonies saying of the King that, "He has endeavored to prevent [hinder, stop] the Population of these States [Colonies]; for that Purpose obstructing the Laws of Naturalization of Foreigners; refusing to pass others to encourage their Migration hither [here]" (Declaration of Independence, paragraph 7).

3.) During the Revolution (between 1776–1779) every colonist who supported the American cause (except slaves prevented from doing so by their owners), was automatically considered a "Citizen" in most of the Colonies (since the "American Government" did not formally exist during that time). For example, after adopting her first constitution (circa. 28 September 1776) Pennsylvania wrote in Section 42 of the same: "Every foreigner of good character who comes to settle in this state, having first taken an oath or affirmation of allegiance to the same…after one year's residence, shall be deemed a free denizen [citizen] thereof, and entitled to all the rights of a natural born subject [citizen] of this state, except that he shall not be capable of being elected a representative until after two years residence."

Also, in 1778 Pennsylvania passed a law to upgrade her "Oath of Allegiance" styled "A Further Supplement to The Act, Entitled 'An Act For Further Security of the Government.'" Section VI (6) of the Act stated: "And all strangers from beyond the seas, if otherwise qualified, pursuant to the constitution of this state, shall be entitled to the privileges of freemen upon their respectively taking the oath of affirmation prescribed by the said act of assembly."

(*The Statutes at Large of Pennsylvania*, DCCCXXII [822], Sec VI [6]; See pp. 1 and 4 (n.4) of "Chester County [PA] Archives and Records Services (Naturalization)" (http:// dsf.chesco.org/archives/cwp/view.asp?A=3&Q=618271). Retrieved 31 July 2008.

4.) While it was true that the 1776–1781 creation and adoption of the Articles of Confederation made "Citizens of the individual States" also "Citizens of the United States in Confederation" (the "U.S." not officially recognized as "sovereign" until 30 November 1783), Confederation Article IV clearly stated that "the free inhabitants [not the free 'White' inhabitants] of each of these states…shall be entitled to all [not some] privileges and immunities of free citizens in the several states"—thus declaring that any slave who obtained his or her freedom was entitled to the privilege of becoming a "Citizen" in any of the Union's individual States! Accordingly, children born to slaves in the "Several States" were "within the dominion or jurisdiction" of both the British-American Colonies and the new American nation. In other words, the children born to slave parents were actually "free born Citizens" regardless of "artificial contrivances" by African Slavery scheme profiteers (one can't pick the family one is born into).

5.) When Britain and America acknowledged the "Chattel" Slavery scheme written into the 1783 Versailles Peace

Treaty at Henry Laurens' request, both countries also acknowledged that free people labeled "Negroes" (etc.) were included among the new nation's "Citizens."

These important facts about "American" citizenship (colonial, state, national) were conveniently forgotten or willfully disregarded. Also forgotten or disregarded was Pennsylvania's 1823 *Corfield v. Coryell* case in which Justice Washington asked the important question, "What are the privileges and immunities of citizens in the several states?" To his question he answered,

> We feel no hesitation in confining these expressions to those privileges and immunities which are, in their nature, fundamental; which belong, of right, to the citizens of all free governments; and which have, at all times, been enjoyed by the citizens of the several States which compose this Union...Protection by the Government; the enjoyment of life and liberty, with the right to acquire and possess property of every kind, and to pursue and obtain happiness and safety; subject nevertheless to such restraints as the Government must justly prescribe for the general good of the whole. The right of a citizen of one State to pass through, or to reside in any other State, for purposes of trade, agriculture, professional pursuits, or otherwise; to claim the benefit of the writ of *habeas corpus*; to institute and maintain actions of any kind in the courts of the State; to take, hold and dispose of property, either real or personal; and an exemption from higher taxes or impositions than are paid by the other citizens of the State...(*Corfield v. Coryell*, 6 Federal Cases 546 [no. 3,230], 551–52 [Circuit Court for the Eastern District of Pa., 1823)

By his ruling Justice Washington more or less stated that American Citizenship did not invest a person with any "special rights" other than those "guaranteed" by the 1787 Constitution and its 1791 Bill of Rights—albeit, when differentiating the personal and private rights protected by the 1787 Constitution from the rights that citizens of a particular State share because of the "public patrimony" of a state, he said,

> [We] cannot accede [agree] to the proposition…that…the citizens of the several States are permitted to participate in all the rights which belong exclusively to the citizens of any particular State, merely upon the ground that they are enjoyed by those citizens; much less, that in regulating the use of the common property of the citizens of such [a] State, the legislature is bound to extend to the citizens of all other States the same advantages as are secured to their own citizens. (Id., at 552)

Because the former slaveholding states disregarded all such points, on 9 July 1868 Congress passed its "third" piece of post–Civil War legislation called the Fourteenth Amendment—which stated in part,

> All persons born or naturalized in the United States and subject to the jurisdiction thereof, are citizens of the United States and [citizens] of the State wherein they reside. No State shall make or enforce any law which shall abridge the privileges or immunities of citizens of the United States; nor shall any State deprive any person of life, liberty, or property, without due process of law; nor deny to any person within its jurisdiction the equal protection of the laws. (US Const, Amend 14, Sec. 1, 1868)

Despite the passage of this legislation—designed to positively state the time-honored British "Jus Soli" Rule that defined "Citizenship" according to "the political jurisdiction, soil, or land born in"—Congress soon discovered that some "White" Americans resorted to terroristic activities (crimes) to prevent "non-White" Americans from enjoying the "privileges and immunities" entitled to "all" Americans. Indeed, after receiving information that some individuals or groups interfered with the former slaves' right to vote or participate in the American political process Congress, on 3 February 1870, passed its "fourth" piece of post-Civil War legislation called the 15th Amendment—which stated in part:

> The rights of citizens of the United States to vote shall not be denied or abridged by the United States or by any State on account of race, color, or previous condition of servitude. (US Const., Amend. 15, Sec. 1, 1870)

After passing this law, Congress thought that the issues of "freedom," "citizenship," and "political enfranchisement" (voting, holding office) for the former slaves would be the end of the matter. But not so! About three months after passing the Fifteenth Amendment, Congress found that it had to pass its "fifth" piece of legislation on 31 May 1870—called the "Voting Rights Act" or "Enforcement Act"—because some "white" Americans still resorted to criminal acts to prevent "nonwhite" Americans from voting or running for political office.

Worse, Congress passed its "sixth" piece of legislation on 28 February 1871 called the "Amended Voting Rights Act." Next, Congress passed its "seventh" piece of legislation on 20 April 1871 called the "Ku Klux Act"—to prosecute "ehites" who resorted to "terrorism" to prevent "nonwhites" from participating in the American political process. And four years later, Congress passed its "eighth" and "ninth" pieces of legislation on 1 March 1875 called the "revised statutes" and the "Civil Rights Act of 1875"—to reaffirm Congress's "intent" as contemplated in the 1865–1866 laws.

Counting President Lincoln's Emancipation Proclamation, at least "ten" [10] pieces of legislation were passed by American government leaders in an effort to put the "Race Card Evil" oriented African Slavery scheme "in the course of ultimate extinction." These numerous attempts served to prove President

Andrew Johnson's assumption wrong that "the master-slave relationship turned capitalist-free laborer relationship could satisfactorily work out its problems." On the contrary, the "Race Card Evil" oriented propaganda upon which the cheap-labor scheme was built had corrupted the egos and minds of so many "white" Americans that they refused to recognize any laws passed to secure citizenship, civil liberty, and freedom for "all" Americans. This fact became apparent about eight years after the 1875 Civil Rights Act's passage—when the US Supreme Court, after being "silent" since its *Dred Scott* ruling, opted to address the legality of the 1875 Act in its *1883 Civil Rights Cases* ruling (109 US 3).

Whereas the legislation Congress passed from 1865 to 1870 (called "post–Civil War legislation") concerned obtaining or enforcing "freedom," "citizenship," and "political rights" for the former slaves, its 1875 Civil Rights Act sought to obtain equal "social rights" for them as well by stating that "black-colored Negro" Americans had the right to use the same "public accommodations…facilities…inns…conveyances [transportations] on land or water, [in] theaters, and [at] other places of amusement" as "Caucasian-White" Americans did. This law sparked legal conflict that ultimately reached the US Supreme Court.

In 1883 the court ruled that Sections 1 and 2 of the 1875 Act were unconstitutional because of its "difference in objective"—saying that those Sections attempted to protect a person's "social," rather than "political," rights contrary to the purpose for which the 14th Amendment was designed. Thus when handing down the court's majority opinion, Associate Justice Joseph P. Bradley (from the "Free State" of New Jersey) said,

> When a man has emerged from slavery, and by the aid
> of beneficent legislation has shaken off the inseperable
> concomitants of that state [of existence], there must be
> some stage in the progress of his [political] elevation
> when he takes the rank of a mere citizen, and ceases to be

the special favorite of the laws, and when his rights as a citizen, or a man, are to be protected in the ordinary modes by which other men's rights are protected. (*Civil Rights Cases*, 109 US 3, 25, 1883)

Mr. Bradley's colleague, Associate Justice John Marshall Harlan (from the "Border Slave State" of Kentucky), did not agree with that view. In his Dissenting Opinion, Mr. Harlan reviewed the history behind Congress passing the 1865 to 1870 legislations. After stating a number of facts "disregarded" by the Court and "unknown" to many Americans (black, white, or other), Justice Harlan said,

The opinion in these [Civil Rights] cases, it seems to me, [are] upon grounds entirely too narrow and artificial. I cannot resist the conclusion that the substance and spirit of the recent amendments of the Constitution have been sacrificed by a subtle and ingenious verbal criticism.

"It is not the words [letter] of the law, but the internal sense [spirit] of it that makes the law; the letter of the law is the body; the sense and reason of the law is the soul [spirit]."

Constitutional provisions [Amendments], adopted in the interest of liberty and for the purpose of securing, through national legislation, if need be, rights inhering in a state of freedom and belonging to American citizenship have been so construed as to defeat the ends [that] the people desired to accomplish, which they attempted to accomplish, and which they supposed they had accomplished by changes in their fundamental law...Before considering the language and scope of these amendments, it will be proper to recall the relations subsisting, prior to their adoption, between the national government and the institution of slavery, as indicated by the provisions of the Constitution, the legislation of Congress, and the decisions of this Court. In this mode, we may obtain keys with which to open the minds of the people and discover the thought intended to be expressed. (*Id.*, 109 U.S. 3, 26–28 passim; Justice Harlan's Dissent)

Recalling the historical relationship that the African Slavery program shared with the Executive, Legislative, and Judicial branches of American government, Mr. Harlan referred to the 1787 Constitution's Fugitive Slave Reclamation Clause (Article IV, Section 2) and its use by proslavery advocates to prompt the 1793 Fugitive Slave Law's enactment. And while doing so, he pointed out important facts about the powers of Congress as argued by the Pennsylvania Attorney General in the case styled *Prigg v. Commonwealth of Pennsyvania* (16 Pet. 539; 41 U.S. 539) (1842). Said Justice Harlan,

> Under the authority of this [Art IV, Sec 2] Clause, Congress passed the Fugitive Slave Law of 1793, establishing a mode for the recovery of fugitive slaves and prescribing a penalty against any person who should knowingly and willingly obstruct or hinder the master, his agent, or attorney in seizing, arresting, and recovering the fugitive, or who should rescue the fugitive from him, or who should harbor or conceal the slave after notice that he was a fugitive.
>
> In *Prigg v. Commonwealth of Pennsylvania*...this Court had occasion to define the powers and duties of Congress in reference to fugitives from labor. Speaking by Mr. Justice Story, it laid down these propositions:

1.) A Clause of the Constitution conferring a right should not be so construed as to make it *shadowy* or *unsubtantial*, or leave the citizen without a remedial power adequate for its protection when another construction equally accordant with the words and the sense in which they were used would enforce and protect the right granted;

2.) Congress is not restricted to legislation for the execution of its *expressly granted powers*, but, for the protection of rights guaranteed by the Constitution, may employ such means, not prohibited, as are *necessary and proper*, or such as are appropriate, to attain the ends proposed;

3.) The Constitution recognized the master's right of property in his fugitive slave, and, as incidental thereto, the right of seizing and recovering him, regardless of any State law or regulation or local custom whatsoever; and,

4.) The right of the master to have his slave, thus escaping, delivered up on claim, being guaranteed by the Constitution, the fair implication was that the national government was clothed with *appropriate authority and functions* to enforce it.

    "It would be a strange anomaly and forced construction to suppose that the national government meant to rely for the due fulfillment of its own proper duties, and the rights which it intended to secure, upon State legislation, and not upon that of the Union. *A Fortiori* [all the more it follows logically that], it would be more objectionable to suppose that a power which was to be the same throughout the Union should be confided [left up] to State sovereignty, which could not rightfully act beyond its own territorial limits."

    The Act of 1793 was, upon these grounds, adjudged to be a Constitutional exercise of the powers of Congress. (Id., 28–29, italics ours in part).

Justice Harlan next cited six important points the attorney general raised in the *Priggs* case—hinting that the slaveholding States had actually surrendered their Tenth Amendment "State Sovereignty" claim by: (a). placing the "Right to Property in Owning Man" into the 1787 Constitution's "Three-Fifths Representation and Taxation" Clause (Art I, Sec 2, Cl 3); (b). agreeing to Congress's "Regulation of Commerce among the Several States" Clause (Art I, Sec 8, Cl 3); (c). agreeing that

Congress had the power to implement the "Uniform Rule of Naturalization" Clause (Art I, Sec 8, Cl 4); (d). agreeing that Congress had the power to end the "International Slave Trade" according to the "1808 Migration or Importation of Persons" clause (Art I, Sec 9, Cl 1); (e). placing into the 1787 Constitution the "Fugitive Reclamation" clause (Art IV, Sec 2, Cl 3); and most importantly, (f). using the "Fugitive Reclamation" clause to force the national government to enact the 1793 and 1850 Fugitive Slave laws to help slaveowners catch runaway slaves. Justice Harlan specifically stated:

> It is to be observed from the report of [the] *Prigg's* case that Pennsylvania, by her Attorney General, pressed the argument [that:]

1.) The obligation to surrender fugitive slaves was on the States and for the States, subject to the restriction that they should not pass laws or establish regulations liberating such fugitives [U.S. Const, Art IV, Sec 2, Cl 3 and Art VI, Cl 2];

2.) The Constitution did not take from the States the right to determine the status of all persons within their respective jurisdictions;

3.) It was for the State in which the alleged fugitive was found to determine, through her Courts or in such modes as she prescribed, whether the person arrested was, in fact, a free man or a fugitive slave [U.S. Const, Art IV, Sec 1 and Sec 2, Cl 3];

4.) The sole power of the general government [the Union] in the premises was, by judicial instrumentality [Supreme Court ruling], to restrain and correct, not to forbid and prevent in the absence of hostile State action [;]

5.) For the general government to assume primary authority to legislate on the subject of fugitive slaves, to the exclusion of the States, would be a dangerous encroachment on State sovereignty [U.S. Const, Amend 10].

But to such suggestions, the Court turned a deaf ear, and adjudged that primary legislation by Congress to enforce the [slave] master's right was authorized by the Constitution.

We next come to the Fugitive Slave Act of 1850, the Constitutionality of which rested, as did that of 1793, solely upon the implied power of Congress to enforce the master's rights. The provisions of that Act were far in advance of previous legislation. They placed at the disposal of the master seeking to recover his fugitive slave substantially the whole power of the nation. It invested Commissioners, appointed under the Act, with power to summon the *posse comitatus* for the enforcement of its provisions, and commanded all good citizens to assist in its prompt and efficient execution whenever their services were required as part of the *posse comitatus*. Without going into the details of that Act, it is sufficient to say that Congress omitted from it nothing which the utmost ingenuity could suggest as essential to the successful enforcement of the master's claim to recover his fugitive slave, and this Court, in *Ableman v. Booth*, 21 How. 506 [62 U.S. 506] [(1858)], adjudged it to be "in all of its provisions, fully authorized by the Constitution of the United States." (Id., 29–30)

Having stated these "overlooked" or "unknown" facts, Justice Harlan then addressed the last significant political event that occurred prior to Congress's enactment of the 1865–1870 "post–Civil War" legislations—namely, the 1856–1857 *Dred Scott* case. Revisiting the case, Mr. Harlan said,

The only other case, prior to the adoption of the recent [Constitutional] amendments, to which reference will be made, is that of *Dred Scott v. Sanford* [*Sandford*], 19 How. 393 [60 U.S. 393] (1856). That case was instituted in a Circuit Court of the United States by Dred Scott, claiming to be a citizen of Missouri, the defendant [John F. A. Sanford] being a citizen of another State [NY]. Its object was to assert the title of himself and family to freedom. The defendant [Sanford] pleaded in abatement [to stop the suit] that Scott—being of African descent, whose ancestors, of pure African blood, were brought into this country and sold as [Negro] slaves—was not a citizen. The only matter in issue, said the [Supreme] Court, was whether the descendants of slaves thus imported and sold, when they should be emancipated, or who were born of parents who had become free before their birth, are citizens of a State in the sense in which the word "Citizen" is used in the Constitution of the United States.

In determining that question, the Court instituted an inquiry as to who were citizens of the several States at the adoption of the Constitution and who at that time were recognized as the people whose rights and liberties had been violated by the British government. The result [of that inquiry] was a declaration by this Court, speaking by Chief Justice Taney, that the legislation and histories of the times, and the language used in the Declaration of Independence, showed[:]

"that neither the class of persons who had been imported as slaves nor their descendants, whether they had become free or not, were then acknowledged as a part of the people, nor intended to be included in the general words used in that instrument"…Such were the relations which formerly existed between the government, whether national or state, and the descendants, whether free or in bondage, of those of African blood who had been imported into this Country and sold as slaves…It was said of the case of *Dred Scott v. Sandford* that this Court there overruled the action of two generations, virtually inserted a new clause in the Constitution, changed its character, and made a new departure in the workings of the federal government. (Id., 30–57 passim)

Next, Justice Harlan spoke about the purposes for which the 1865–1870 Congressional legislations were enacted. With respect to the Thirteenth Amendment, the 1866 Civil Rights Act, and the power of Congress to pass legislation on matters concerning American Citizenship for the former slaves the enlightened "Southern" Justice Harlan said,

> The power of Congress, in this mode, to elevate the enfranchised race to national citizenship was maintained by supporters of the act of 1866 to be as full and complete as its power, by general statute, to make the children, being of full age, of persons naturalized in this country, citizens of the United States without going through the process of naturalization. The act of 1866 in this respect was also likened to that [Act] of 1843, in which Congress declared [:]
>
> "that the Stockbridge tribe of Indians [Native Americans], and each and every one of them, shall be deemed to be and are hereby declared to be, citizens of the United States to all intents and purposes, and shall be entitled to all the rights, privileges, and immunities of such citizens, and shall in all respects be subject to the laws of the United States."
>
> If the act of 1866 was valid in conferring national citizenship upon all embraced by its terms, then the colored race, enfranchised by the Thirteenth Amendment, became citizens of the United States prior to the adoption of the Fourteenth Amendment. But, in the view which I take of the present case, it is not necessary to examine this question. (Id., 32–33)

Justice Harlan next addressed the theme that the American government's founders, whatever concessions they made with proponents of the "Race Card Evil" oriented African Slavery scheme, actually founded the government with the members of the "seventy" nations in mind. Said he,

The terms of the Thirteenth Amendment are absolute and universal. They embrace every race which then was, or might thereafter be, within the United States. No race, as such, can be excluded from the benefits or rights thereby conferred. Yet it is historically true that that [Thirteenth] Amendment was suggested by the condition, in this country, of that race which had been declared by this Court to have had…"no rights which the white man was bound to respect," none of the privileges or immunities secured by that instrument to citizens of the United States. It had reference, in peculiar sense, to a people which (although the larger part of them were in slavery) had been invited by an act of Congress to aid in saving from overthrow a government which, heretofore, by all of its departments, had treated them as an inferior race, with no legal rights or privileges except such as the white race might choose to grant them.

These are the circumstances under which the Thirteenth Amendment was proposed for adoption. They are now recalled only that we may better understand what was in the minds of the people when that Amendment was considered, and what were the mischiefs to be remedied and the grievances to be redressed by its adoption. (Id., 33)

Having explained that the people called "blacks, coloreds, Negroes" had been granted "American citizenship" because of the Thirteenth Amendment and 1866 Civil Rights Act, Mr. Harlan next explained the Fourteenth Amendment's real purpose—namely, that of granting "state citizenship" to the said people and entitling them to "all privileges and immunities of citizens in the several states" according to the 1787 Constitution's Article IV, Section 2, clause 1. Said he,

The assumption that this [Fourteenth] Amendment consists wholly of prohibitions upon State laws and State proceedings in hostility to its provisions is unauthorized by its language. The first clause of the first section [stating]— "All persons born or naturalized in the United States, and subject to the jurisdiction thereof, are citizens of the United States, and of the State wherein they reside"—is of a distinctly affirmative character. In its application to the colored race, previously liberated, it created and granted as well citizenship of the United States as citizenship of the State in which they respectively resided. It introduced all of that race whose ancestors had been imported and sold as slaves at once into the political community known as the "People of the United States." They became instantly citizens of the United States and of their respective States [U.S. Const, Art 1, Sec 8, Cl 4]. Further, they were brought by this supreme act of the nation within the direct operation of that provision of the Constitution which declares that "the citizens of each State shall be entitled to all privileges and immunities of citizens in the several States [U.S. Const, Art IV, Sec 2, Cl 1; Amend 14, Sec1]." (Id., 46)

The Fourteenth Amendment's "purpose" clarified, Justice Harlan next explained what the US Constitution's Article IV statement regarding "all privileges and immunities" meant. Said he,

It is therefore an essential inquiry [into] what, if any, right, privilege or immunity was given, by the nation to colored persons when they were made citizens of the State in which they reside? Did the Constitutional grant of State Citizenship to that race, of its own force, invest them with any rights, privileges and immunities whatever? That they became entitled, upon the adoption of the Fourteenth Amendment, "to all privileges and immunities of citizens in the several States," within the meaning of section 2 of article 4 of the [1787] Constitution, no one, I suppose, will for a moment question. What are the privileges and immunities to which, by that clause of the Constitution, they became entitled? To this it may be answered generally, upon the authority of the adjudicated [legal] cases, that they are those [privileges and immunities] which are fundamental in Citizenship in a free republican government, such as are "Common to the Citizens in the latter States under their Constitutions and Laws by virtue of their being Citizens." Of that provision it has been said, with the approval of this Court, that no other one in the Constitution has lended so strongly to constitute the Citizens of the United States [as] one people [See: *Ward v. Maryland*, 12 Wall. 418; 79 U.S. 418 (1870); *Corfield v. Coryell*, 4 Wash. C.C. 371; 6 Federal Cases 546 (E. D. Pa.) (1823); *Paul v. Virginia*, 8 Wall. 168; 75 U.S. 168 (1869); *Slaughterhouse Cases*, 16 Wall. 36; 83 U.S. 36 (1873)].

Although this Court has wisely forborne any attempt by a comprehensive definition to indicate all of the privileges and immunities to which the Citizen of a State is entitled of right when within the jurisdiction of other States, I hazard nothing in view of former adjudications, in saying that no State can sustain her denial to colored Citizens of other States while within her limits, of privileges or immunities fundamental in republican Citizenship upon the ground that she accords such privileges and immunities only to her white Citizens, and withholds them from her colored Citizens. The colored Citizens of other States, within the jurisdiction of that State, could claim, in virtue of section 2 of Article 4 of the Constitution, every privilege and immunity which that State secures to her white Citizens...A colored Citizen of Ohio or Indiana, while in the jurisdiction of Tennessee, is entitled to enjoy any privilege or immunity, fundamental in Citizenship, which is given to Citizens of the white race in the latter State. It is not to be supposed that anyone will controvert this proposition.

But what was secured to colored Citizens of the United States—as between them and their respective States—by the national grant to them of State Citizenship? With what rights, privileges, or immunities did this grant invest them? There is one, if there be no other—exemption from race discrimination in respect of any civil right belonging to Citizens of the white race in the same State. That, surely, is their Constitutional privilege when within the jurisdiction of other States. And such must be their Constitutional right in their own State…It is fundamental in American Citizenship that, in respect of such rights, there shall be no discrimination by the State, or its officers, or by individuals or corporations exercising public functions or authority, against any Citizen because of his race or previous condition of servitude.

   (Id., 47–48)

The "privileges and immunities" issue clarified, Justice Harlan then explained the "purpose" of the Thirteenth, Fourteenth, and Fifteenth Amendments. Admitting that the Fifteenth Amendment was a fairly "new" creation aimed at ending "racial" discrimination in the elective or voting process, he said,

In *United States v. Cruikshank*, 92 U.S. 542 [(1875)], it was said at page 92 U.S. 555, that the rights of life and personal liberty are natural rights of man, and that "the equality of the rights of Citizens is a principle of Republicanism."

"And in *Ex Parte Virginia*, 100 U.S. 334 [339] [(1879)], the emphatic language of this Court is that [:]

"one great purpose of these [13th, 14th, 15th] Amendments was to raise the colored race from that condition of inferiority and servitude in which most of them had previously stood into perfect equality of civil rights with all other persons within the jurisdiction of the States."

"So, in *Strauder v. West Virginia*, 100 U.S. [303] [(1879)], at 100 U.S. 306, the Court, alluding to the Fourteenth Amendment said:

"This is one of a series of Constitutional provisions having a common purpose, namely, securing to a race recently emancipated, a race that, through many generations, had been held in slavery, all the civil rights that the superior race enjoy."

"Again, in *Neal v. Delaware*, [103 U.S. 370 (1880)], [at] 103 U.S. 386, it was ruled that this [14th] Amendment was designed primarily[:]

"to secure to the colored race, thereby invested with the rights, privileges, and responsibilities of Citizenship, the enjoyment of all the civil rights that, under the law, are enjoyed by white persons."

"The language of this Court with reference to the Fifteenth Amendment adds to the force of this view. In *United States v. Cruikshank*, it was said:

"In *United States v. Reese*, 92 U.S. 214 [(1875)], we held that the Fifteenth Amendment has invested the Citizens of the United States with a new Constitutional right, which is exemption from discrimination in the exercise of the elective franchise, on account of race, color, or previous condition of servitude. From this it appears that the right of suffrage is not a necessary attribute of national Citizenship, but that exemption from discrimination in the exercise of that right on account of race, etc., is. The right to vote in the States comes from the States, but the right of exemption from the prohibited discrimination comes from the United States. The first has not been granted or secured by the Constitution of the United States, but the last has been."

"Here, in language at once clear and forcible, is stated the principle for which I contend. It can scarcely be claimed that exemption from race discrimination, in respect of civil rights, against those to whom State Citizenship was granted by the nation, is any less, for the colored race, a new Constitutional right, derived from and secured by the national Constitution, than is exemption from such discrimination in the exercise of the elective franchise. It cannot be that the latter is an attribute of National Citizenship, while the other is not essential in National Citizenship or fundamental in State Citizenship." (Id., 48–50)

Justice Bradley, when closing his opinion, said that there should come a time when a person emerging from slavery ceases to be the special favorite of the law, takes his place as an ordinary citizen, and relies on ordinary legal modes to address legal issues. Justice Harlan, however, did not see that as being the case for those freed from the African Slavery scheme. Thus as Justice Harlan concluded his dissent, he sagely countered,

I agree that government has nothing to do with social, as distinguished from technically legal, rights of individuals. No government ever has brought, or ever can bring, its people into social intercourse against their wishes. Whether one person will permit or maintain social relations with another is a matter with which government has no concern. I agree that if one Citizen chooses not to hold social intercourse with another, he is not and cannot be made amenable to the law for his conduct in that regard; for no legal right of a Citizen is violated by the refusal of others to maintain merely social relations with him, even upon grounds of race. What I affirm is that no State, nor the officers of any State, nor any corporation or individual wielding power under State authority for the public benefit or the public convenience, can, consistently either with the freedom established by the fundamental law, or with that equality of civil rights which now belongs to every Citizen, discriminate against Freemen or Citizens, in their civil rights, because of their race, or because they once labored under disabilities imposed upon them as a race.

It is, I submit, scarcely just to say that the colored race has been the special favorite of the laws…What the nation, through Congress, has sought to accomplish in reference to that race is, what had already been done in every State in the Union for the white race—to secure and protect rights belonging to them as freemen and citizens, nothing more…The one underlying purpose of Congressional legislation has been to enable the black race to take the rank of mere Citizens. The difficulty has been to compel a recognition of the legal right of the black race to take the rank of Citizens, and to secure the enjoyment of privileges belonging, under the laws, to them as a component part of the people for whose welfare and happiness government is ordained.

At every step in this direction, the nation has been confronted with class tyranny, which a contemporary English historian says is, of all tyrannies, the most intolerable, "for it is ubiquitous in its operation and weighs perhaps most heavily on those whose obscurity or distance would withdraw them from the notice of a single despot."

To-day it is the colored race which is denied, by corporations and individuals wielding public authority, rights fundamental in their Freedom and Citizenship. At some future time it may be some other race that will fall under the ban of race discrimination…there cannot be, in this Republic, any class of human beings in practical subjection to another class with power in the latter to dole out to the former just such privileges as they may choose to grant…For the reasons stated, I feel constrained to withhold my assent to the opinion of the Court. (Id., 61–62)

Although Justice Harlan admitted that no government could "force" people to associate with each other, he noted that the real problem the American government faced—during and after passage of its "post–Civil War" laws—was forcing "white" Americans to recognize the legal rights of "non-White" Americans (especially those called "black, colored, Negro"). By this he meant that most of those laws were passed because many "white" Americans refused to recognize the citizenship of "nonwhite"

Americans—not because "nonwhites" were special favorites of the law. And significantly, his analysis and interpretation of the term *citizen* contained the answer for this refusal—one having "Race Card Evil" overtones.

In his dissent, Justice Harlan recalled Chief Justice Taney's 1857 *Dred Scott* Opinion. Referring to that "opinion," he noted that Mr. Taney said that the terms "people of the United States" and "citizens" were equivalent, meant "the political body who held the power, conducted the government, and were the 'sovereign' people." He also noted that Mr. Taney said that the people called "blacks, coloreds, or Negroes" were considered "an 'inferior' race that had been subjugated [actually kidnapped] by the 'superior' [white] race." Most importantly, he noted that Mr. Taney said that the so-called 'inferior' race "had no [legal] rights except those given them by the 'White Man' and had no rights that the 'white man' was bound [legally obligated] to respect."

By recounting this 1857 "legal" view, Justice Harlan implied that many "white" Americans were "indoctrinated" with a "Race Card Evil" oriented view that the rights of "nonwhite" Americans were "insignificant" as compared to their "white" counterparts. And he implied that the 1858 Lincoln-Douglass debates, during which Senator Douglass repeatedly told his "white" audiences that "America was built by and for the white man" reinforced Justice Taney's view. Thus, Justice Harlan implied that many "whites" were "infected" with a sense of "color superiority" because they were "citizens" who were allegedly "superior to" and "sovereign (kings, rulers) over" their "nonwhite" counterparts, and supposedly "conducted (ran) the government through representatives called "public servants."

In effect, Justice Harlan implied that such Taney-Douglass "feel good" rhetoric made many "White" Americans believe that they actually were "better than superior to lord over" their "nonwhite" counterparts—and that those holding public office were mere servants (slaves) whose sole function was to perform the "people's/citizen's" ("white man's") will." Hence, no one holding political office could pass or enforce any law disagreeable to "the people's will" (a variation of "God's will").

Thus Justice Harlan implied that this egoistic mindset of many "white" Americans during the "pre–Civil War" and "Civil War" eras, made all "post–Civil War" era legislation aimed at according citizenship and political rights to the "Black-Colored-Negro" ex-slaves ineffective—because it fell on deaf "white" ears ringing with "feel good" propaganda such as "I'm white, I'm special, I own America, America was built by and for me, and all political appointees (Federal or State) are my servants whom I tell what to do."

However, during 1898—forty-one years after the *Dred Scott Case* and fifteen years after the *Civil Rights Cases*—a U.S. Supreme Court "Citizenship" case arose that vindicated all the courageous Americans who worked so hard to put the "Race Card Evil" oriented Taney-Douglass propaganda "in the course of ultimate extinction." The case involved an American of Chinese descent named Wong Kim Ark—who had been born in the United States, never left the country, but faced deportation because his status as an American Citizen was questioned. In *United States v. Wong Kim Ark*, the Supreme Court recalled the dissenting opinion of Justice Benjamin Curtis in the 1857 *Dred Scott* case and said,

> In *Dred Scott v. Sandford* (1857)...Mr. Justice [Curtis] said: "The 1st Section of the 2d Article of the Constitution uses the language 'a natural-born citizen.' It thus assumes that Citizenship may be acquired by birth. Undoubtedly, this language of the Constitution was used in reference to that principle of law, well understood in this country at the time of the adoption of the Constitution, which referred Citizenship to the place of birth...And to this extent no different opinion was expressed or intimated by any of the

other Judges [in the *Dred Scott* Case]." (*United States v. Wong Kim Ark*, 169 U.S. 649, 662, 1898).

By this statement the *Wong Kim* Court revealed that:

1.) Justice Curtis purposely brought up the 1787 Constitution's Article 2, Section 1, Clause 5 (Qualifications for holding U.S. Presidential Office) because it referred to the British "Jus Soli" Rule concerning citizenship according to the "country, land, soil, or geo-political jurisdiction" a person was born in or subject to (as distinguished from the "Jus Sanguinis" Rule of citizenship according to the "ancestry, blood, or parents" a person was born to).

2.) The *Dred Scott* case Judges, Mr. Taney included, knew the British Rule and avoided it (Mr. Curtis being the exception).

3.) Mr. Taney's "Majority Court" Opinion purposely used the "Jus Sanguinis" Rule (used on the continent of Europe) for descendants of African slaves born in the British-American Colonies (thus born within British jurisdiction).

4.) Mr. Taney "knew" that only one of the two "Citizenship" Rules could be used by a European nation (but not both), and "knew" that the British-American Colonies were under the "Jus Soli" Rule (the Colonists being "subjects of Britain"). Hence, he attempted to simultaneously use the "Jus Soli" Rule as a "White" Rule and the "Jus Sanguinis" Rule as a "non-White" Rule—thereby violating the Judaeo-Christian "One or Uniform Law" Rule stated in the Old Testament (Ex. 12:49; Lev. 24:22; Num. 9:14, KJV).

5.) By being "silent" about the "Jus Soli" Rule outlined in the Constitution's Article 2, Section 1, Clause 5, the Supreme Court Judges "knew" and "admitted" (via the lie of omission) that their "Majority Court" Opinon relayed to the American public was a bogus, "Race Card Evil" oriented, ruling designed to deny Federal and State Citizenship to descendants of African slaves "born in America" while outlawing the 1820 Missouri Compromise in order to expand the African Slavery cheap-labor scheme.

In addition to these points, the *Wong Kim* court stated a number of other important facts to "clarify" Justice Curtis's Dissenting Opinon concerning American State and Federal Citizenship—facts "unknown" to most Americans in 1857, but "known" to the *Scott* case Judges.

With respect to Britain's "Jus Soli" Rule the *Wong Kim* Court said,

> In the *United States v. Rhodes* (1866), Mr. Justice Swayne, sitting in the Cirsuit Court said: "All persons born in the allegiance of the King [Britain] are natural-born subjects, and all persons born in the allegiance of the United States are natural-born citizens. Birth and allegiance go together. Such is the Rule of the [British] Common Law, and it is the Common Law of this Country [America], as well as of England...We find no warrant for the opinion that this great principle of the Common Law has ever been changed in the United States. It has always obtained [been applied] here with the same vigor, and subject only to the same exceptions, since as before the [1776] Revolution." (Id., 662–63)

The *Wong Kim* Court then gave examples of the "exceptions" to the "Jus Soli" or "birth-by-soil" Rule for a child born to parents who were (1) "ambassadors or diplomatic agents" of a Foreign Country; and (2) "alien enemies in hostile occupation of the Land or Country" wherein the child was born. Said the court regarding category 1,

> That all children born within the Dominion of the United States, of foreign parents holding no diplomatic office,

> became citizens at the time of their birth, does not appear
> to have been contested or doubted until more than fifty
> years after the adoption of the [1787] Constitution [the
> *Wong Kim* Court stating, at p. 658, that the Rule was in
> force in all the English Colonies on American soil up
> to the time of the Declaration of Independence, after it,
> and during the 1787 Constitution's adoption], when the
> matter was elaborately argued…and decided [in *Lynch v.
> Clarke*, NY Court of Chancery (1844)]…(Id., 664)

After stating that "children born to foreign parents holding
no diplomatic office" fell under the "Jus Soli" Rule, the *Wong
Kim* Court then explained why "children born to foreign
parents holding diplomatic office" were considered "Aliens" and
fell under the category 1 exception to the Rule—doing so by
referring to famed legal authority Chancellor Kent and his *Kent's
Commentary*. Said the court regarding "aliens" and "natives",

> Chancellor Kent, in his Commentaries, speaking of the
> "general division of the inhabitants of every Country,"
> under the comprehensive title of "Aliens and Natives,"
> says: "Natives are all persons born within the Jurisdiction
> and Allegiance of the United States. This is the Rule of
> the Common Law, without regard or reference to the
> political condition ["slavery" included] or allegiance of their
> parents, with the exception of the children of ambassadors,
> who are in theory born within the allegiance of the Foreign
> Power they [ambassador parents] represent…To create
> allegiance by birth, the party must be born, not only within
> the [geographical] Territory, but within the Ligeance
> [Allegiance] of the government." (Id., 664–65 passim; the
> Court quoting from *2 Kent Commentary*, 6th ed., pp. 39, 42)

Next, the *Wong Kim* Court defined the "legal" meaning of the
terms Ligeance ("Allegiance"), Subject, and *Citizen*, as understood
in England's common law and in America's constitutional and
statute laws. Again referring to *Kent's Commentary* the court said,

And he [Chancellor Kent] elsewhere says: "And if, at Common Law, all human beings born within the Ligeance of the King [political leader representing the government] and under the King's obedience, were natural-born subjects, and not aliens, I do not perceive why this doctrine does not apply to these United States, in all cases in which there is no express Constitutional or Statute declaration to the contrary...."Subject" and "Citizen" are, in a degree, convertible terms as applied to Natives; and though the term Citizen seems to be [appropriate] to Republican free men, yet we are, equally with the inhabitants of all other Countries, Subjects, for we are equally bound by Allegiance and Subjection to the Government [inhabited] and [the] Law of the Land." (Id., 664–65 passim; the Court quoting from *2 Kent Commentary*, 6th ed., p. 258)

Before referring to *Kent's*, the *Wong Kim* Court had shown that various states in the Union did apply the "jus soli" rule to descendants of African slaves born or domiciled (resident) in their geographical boundaries—without regard to the person's or parent's "ancestry," "ethnicity," "skin color," "race," or "previous condition of servitude" (barring the 1781 and 1787 "Comity Clause" exceptions).

First, showing Massachusetts as one "Northern" state that applied the "jus soli" rule, the *Wong Kim* Court stated,

The Supreme Judicial Court of Massachusetts, speaking by Mr. Justice (afterwards Chief Justice) Sewall [in *Gardner v. Ward* (1805)], early held [ruled] that the determination of the question whether a man was a citizen or an alien was "to be governed altogether by the principle of the Common Law," and that it was established, with few exceptions, "that a man born within the Jurisdiction of the Common Law is a citizen of the country wherein he is born. By this circumstance of his birth he is subjected to the duty of allegiance, which is claimed and enforced by the sovereign [political leader or leaders] of his native land, and becomes reciprocally entitled to the protection of that sovereign and to the other rights and advantages which are included in the term 'Citizenship.'" (Id., 663)

Next, showing North Carolina as one "Southern" state that applied the "jus soli" rule, the *Wong Kim* Court stated,

Justice Gaston [in *State v. Manuel*, 4 Dev. and Bat. 20 (1838)], said: "Before our [1776] Revolution, all free persons born within the dominion of the king of Great Britain, whatever their color or complexion, were Native-born British subjects—those born out[side] of his allegiance were aliens...Upon the [1776] Revolution, no other change took place in the laws of North Carolina, than was consequent upon the transition from a Colony dependent on a European king to a free and sovereign State. {Slaves remained slaves. British subjects in North Carolina became North Carolina freemen. Foreigners, until made members of the State, remained aliens. Slaves, manumitted here, became freemen, and therefore, if born within North Carolina, are citizens of North Carolina, and all free persons born within the State are born citizens of the State. The [NC] Constitution extended the elective [voting] franchise to every freeman who had arrived at the age of twenty-one and paid a public tax, and it is a matter of universal notoriety that, under it, free persons, without regard to color, claimed and exercised the franchise until it was taken from free men of color a few years since by our amended [NC] Constitution}...the term 'Citizen,' as understood in our law, is precisely analogous to [the same as] the term 'Subject' in the Common Law, and the change of phrase has entirely resulted from the change of government. The sovereignty has been transferred from one man [the King] to the collective body of the People [the political State or Government]—and he who before was a 'Subject of the king' is now a 'Citizen of the State.'"

(Id., 663–64; cf. *Scott v. Sandford*, 60 U.S. 393, at 573; braces ours to include omitted text cited by Justice Curtis).

The *Wong Kim Ark* Decision undoubtedly proved that the American Government's founders, Justice Benjamin Curtis, Richard Hildreth, Harriett Beecher-Stowe, Abraham Lincoln, and both the Thirty-eighth and Thirty-ninth Congresses were all correct in their assessment of America's "race" problem. It was bad enough that many "whites" had been "infected" with an "anti-social" attitude against "Blacks" prior to the 1776 Revolution—due to the "Ham cursed and uncivilized" propaganda taught to justify the African Slavery cheap-labor scheme. However, the mindset was agitated prior to America's Civil War because of Charles Carroll's 1849 book calling *The Negro a Beast*, Justice Roger B. Taney's 1857 *Dred Scott* ruling that "Negroes had no rights that the 'white man' was bound to respect," and Senator Stephen A. Douglas's 1858 speeches claiming "America was made for the 'white man.'" After the Civil War, the "antisocial" attitude was reinforced by Hinton Rowan Helper's 1867 book *Nojoque: A Question for a Continent*. Using the Taney-Douglas views, Mr. Helper blatantly denigrated "nonwhites" in his book's dedication by stating,

> [Dedicated to] That most enlightened and progressive portion of the people of the New World, who have the far-reaching foresight, and the manly patriotism, to determine irrevocably, by their votes, in 1868–1872...That, after the fourth of July, 1876, (or, at the very farthest, after the first of January, 1900) no slave nor would-be slave, no Negro nor Mulatto, no Chinaman nor unnative Indian, no black nor bi-colored [bi-racial] individual of whatever name or nationality, shall ever again find domicile [residence] anywhere within the boundaries of the United States of America.
>
> [Also dedicated to] All those preeminently sagacious [wise] and good men who are deeply impressed with

the conviction, that even the firmest founded and the noblest vindicated of all Republics [America]…and the best system of government ever yet devised beneath the sun, can never fulfill its promised mission of unexampled greatness and grandeur, until after it shall have been brought under the exclusive occupancy and control of the heaven-descended and incomparably superior white races of mankind. (Hinton Rowan Helper, *Nojoque: A Question for a Continent* (New York: George W. Carleton and Co., 1867).

Obviously, Mr. Helper's book was intended to sway the upcoming vote to respectively pass the Constitution's Fourteenth (1868) and Fifteenth (1870) Amendments. And although his attempt failed, Mr. Helper succeeded in fueling the "anti-social" attitude of many "whites" to such a point that they created vigilante groups in American society—some of which were reputedly responsible for perpetrating terroristic acts against both "whites" and "nonwhites" to uphold the fictitious doctrine of a "pure superior white race." In their *Documents of American History,* Commager and Cantor revealed that one such group was the Reconstruction Era Ku Klux Klan, whose 1867–68 creed and questionnaire (called the *interrogation* or *prescript*) stated in contradiction,

*Creed*: We, the Order…reverentially acknowledge the majesty and supremacy of the Divine Being [the Creator]…And we recognize our relation to the United States Government, the supremacy of the Constitution, the Constitutional Laws thereof, and the Union of States thereunder.

*Interrogations to be asked*: Did you belong to the Federal army during the late [Civil] war, and fight against the South…? Are you opposed to negro equality, both social and political? Are you in favor of a white man's government of this country [America]…of maintaining the Constitutional rights of the South…of the re-enfranchisement and emancipation of the white men of the South…? (*Docs. of Amer. Hist.*, 499–500 passim, "The Ku Klux Klan: Organization and Principles"; italics ours).

Given such "contradictory" statements, the Klan's philosophy perpetuated the "Race Card Evil" mind-set that caused both the 1776 Revolution and 1861 Civil War—and confused the organization's avowed agenda to act as a legitimate neighborhood watch group and relief society for the post–Civil War South. Regarding the organization's "characteristics and objectives," Commager and Cantor noted that the original KKK charter stated,

> This is an institution of *Chivalry, Humanity, Mercy,* and *Patriotism*…its peculiar objects being:
>
> First: To protect the weak, the innocent, and the defenseless, from the indignities, wrongs, and outrages of the lawless, the violent, and the brutal; to relieve the injured and oppressed, to succor [aid] the suffering and unfortunate, and especially the widows and orphans of Confederate soldiers.
>
> Second: To protect and defend the Constitution of the United States, and all laws passed in conformity thereto, and to protect the States and the people thereof from all invasion from any source whatever.
>
> Third: To aid and assist in the execution of all constitutional laws, and to protect the people from unlawful seizure, and from trial except by their peers in conformity to the laws of the land. (Ibid., 500, "The Ku Klux Klan: Character and Objects of the Order," italics ours)

Influenced by pro "white" or anti "nonwhite" writings and speeches of the 1840s–1860s, and disgruntled with the Civil War's outcome and congressional attempts to secure political rights for ex-slaves, the Reconstuction Era Klan lost sight of its agenda and leaned toward practices that earned the organization a bad reputation. Again, Commager and Cantor noted,

> The Ku Klux Klan, one of the two largest of the secret organizations that flourished in the South during Reconstruction, was founded in 1865 at Pulaski, Tennessee. The order grew rapidly in 1867 and 1868; a general organization was perfected in May 1867 at which a constitution was adopted. General Bedford Forrest was the first Grand Wizard of the Order. The Order was effective in frightening the negro out of his unnatural alliance with the Union Leagues, but it was used as a cloak for lawlessness and violence and formally disbanded in 1869. Its activities continued, however, for some time after this date. Congress took cognizance of the Order and similar secret societies such as the Knights of the White Camelia, by passing the Ku Klux Klan Acts of May 31, 1870 and April 20, 1871…A Congressional Ku Klux Klan Committee sat during the summer of 1871 and took thirteen volumes of testimony on conditions in the South.
>
> *Ibid.*, 499 note ("The Ku Klux Klan: Organization and Principles, 1868"). Also see: J. C. Lester and D. L. Wilson, *The Ku Klux Klan*; W. L. Fleming, *Sequel to Appomatox*; W. G. Brown, *The Lower South in American History*; W. A. Sinclair, *The Aftermath of Slavery*.

After two years of official operation (AD 1867–1869), the Reconstruction Era KKK disbanded because of "lawless acts" by persons acting under its banner and name. Unfortunately, disbanding the Klan failed to stop the "antisocial" attitude displayed by many "whites" as a result of some 454 years of "religious" teaching (AD 1415–1869) and eighteen years of alledged "scholarly" writing (AD 1849–1867). Indeed, *Wikipedia's* article entitled "Ku Klux Klan" recounted,

> Six well-educated Confederate veterans from Pulaski, Tennessee created the original Ku Klux Klan on December

24, 1865, during the Reconstruction of the South after the Civil War. The name was formed by combining the Greek *kyklos* [circle] with *clan*…The Ku Klux Klan was one of a number of secret, oath-bound organizations using violence, which included the Southern Cross in New Orleans (1865) and the Knights of the White Camelia (1867) in Louisiana…Former Confederate Brigadier General George Gordon developed the *Prescript*, which espoused white supremacist belief…Confederate General Nathan Bedford Forrest became Grand Wizard, claiming to be the Klan's national leader.

In an 1868 newspaper interview, Forrest stated that the Klan's primary opposition was to the Loyal Leagues, Republican state governments, people like Tennessee governor Brownlow and other "carpetbaggers" and "scalawags"…Despite Gordon's and Forrest's work, local Klan units never accepted the Prescript and continued to operate autonomously…Klan members used violence to settle old feuds and local grudges, as they worked to restore white dominance in the disrupted postwar society…To that end they worked to curb the education, economic advancement, voting rights, and right to keep and bear arms of blacks…launching a "reign of terror against Republican leaders both black and white "…When they killed black political leaders, they also took heads of families, along with the leaders of churches and community groups, because these people had many roles in society…"Armed guerrilla warfare killed thousands of Negroes; political riots were staged; their causes or occasions were always obscure, their results always certain: ten to one hundred times as many Negroes were killed as whites." Masked men shot into houses and burned them, sometimes with the occupants still inside. They drove successful black farmers off their land…Klan violence worked to suppress black voting…Many people not formally inducted into the Klan had used the Klan's costume for anonymity, to hide their identities when carrying out acts of violence. Forrest called for the Klan to disband in 1869, arguing that the Klan was "being perverted from its original honorable and patriotic purposes, becoming injurious instead of subservient to the public peace." Historian Stanley Horn argues that "generally speaking, the Klan's end was more in the form of spotty, slow, and gradual disintergration than a formal and decisive disbandment." ("Ku Klux Klan," *Wikipedia*, http://en.wikipedia.org/wiki/Ku_Klux_Klan, pp. 4–8 passim. Retrieved 10 June 2015)

The Klan lay dormant for almost a half century after its 1869 disbandment. However, when Thomas F. Dixon Jr., a North Carolina Southern Baptist minister, wrote his books entitled *The Leopard's Spots* (1902) and *The Klansman* (1905), they became popular—to such an extent that they were first made into a play (*The Klansman*), then a silent movie (D. W. Griffith's *The Birth of a Nation*), and finally spawned the post Reconstruction or second era Klan's birth after William Joseph Simmons (called "Colonel") viewed the movie during its 1915 debut. *Wikipedia's* articles on the effect produced by *The Klansman* and *The Birth of a Nation* respectively stated,

> Thomas F. Dixon, Jr. was a Southern Baptist minister, playwright, lecturer, North Carolina state legislator, lawyer, and author, perhaps best known for writing *The Clansman*—which was to become the inspiration for D. W. Griffith's film, *The Birth of a Nation* (1915)…Dixon viewed Southern black America with contempt. Later in his life it is possible to view personalized yet contradictory statements in his writings regarding African Americans… His "Trilogy of Reconstruction [novels]" consisted of *The Leopard's Spots* [1902], *The Clansman* (1905), and *The Traitor* (1907). In these best-selling novels, which presented highly imaginative fiction as hard historical fact, Dixon used historical romance to present Negroes as

inferior to whites and to glorify the antebellum American South. While he opposed slavery, he believed in racial segregation…Thomas Dixon's writings are often quoted by White Supremacist organizations today…A common theme found in his novels is violence against [the] white woman, mostly, though not always by a Southern black man…While never abandoning his belief in white supremacy, Dixon was not enthusiastic about the revived second era Ku Klux Klan. He felt it was bigoted and in no way resembled the reconstruction [era] Klan. He called anti-Semitism "idiocy," noting that the mother of Jesus was Jewish and lauded the loyalty and good citizenship of Catholics. He also felt it was the duty of whites to "lift up and help the weaker races." ("Thomas Dixon, Jr.," *Wikipedia*,   http://www.ask.com/wiki/Thomas_Dixon,_ Jr.?qsrc=3044, pp. 1–3 passim. Retrieved 20 May 2015)

"*The Birth* of *a Nation* (originally called *The Clansman*) is a 1915 American silent drama film…The film was a commercial success, but was highly controversial owing to its portrayal of African-American men (played by white actors in blackface) as unintelligent and sexually aggressive towards white women, and the portrayal of the Ku Klux Klan (whose original founding is dramatized) as a heroic force… The film is also credited as one of the events that inspired the formation of the "second era" Ku Klux Klan at Stone Mountain, Georgia, in the same year [1915]. *The Birth of a Nation* was used as a recruiting tool for the KKK. ("The Birth of a Nation," *Wikipedia*, http://en.wikipedia.org/wiki/ The_Birth_of_a_Nation, p. 1. Retrieved 1 April 2014)

Interestingly enough, Mr. Dixon had a "contradictory" character. During the time of the US Supreme Court's 1896 "Separate But Equal Accomodations" ruling (*Plessy v. Ferguson*; 163 U.S. 537), the thirty-two-year-old Reverend Dixon was quoted as saying in a work entitled *Protestantism and Its Causes,*

> "I thank God that there is not today the clang of a single
> slave's chain in this continent. Slavery may have had its
> beneficent aspects, but democracy is the destiny of the
> [Negro] race, because all men are bound together in the
> bonds of fraternal equality with common love." ("Thomas
> Dixon, Jr.," *Wikipedia*, p. 5.)

However, during the very year that *The Clansman* novel was published, the forty-one-year-old Reverend Dixon was quoted as saying to the 19 August 1905 *Saturday Evening Post*:

> "[N]o amount of education of any kind, industrial, classical
> or religious, can make a Negro [into] a white man or bridge
> the chasm of centuries which separate him from the white
> man in the evolution of human nature." (Ibid., p. 5.)

Although Reverend Dixon applauded the "loyalty and good citizenship" of Catholics, saw the 1915 Era Klan as "bigoted," and felt that the organization was "infected" with an "anti-Semitism idiocy," his book *The Clansman* was nevertheless responsible for inspiring the Second Era Klan's creation—which later White Supremacist group was anti "Black-Catholic-Immigrant-Oriental-Semite-etc." *Wikipedia*'s "Ku Klux Klan" article said about the reborn Klan,

> The new Klan was inaugurated in 1915 by William
> Joseph Simmons...It was a small local organization until
> 1921. Simmons said he had been inspired by the original
> Klan's Prescripts, written in 1867...but...never adopted
> by the first Klan...The pamphlet *ABC of the Invisible
> Empire* [1917]...identified the Klan's goals as "to shield
> the sanctity of the home and the chastity of [white]
> womanhood; to maintain white supremacy; to teach and
> faithfully inculcate a high spiritual philosophy through
> an exalted ritualism; and by a practical devotedness to...
> maintain the distinctive institutions, rights, privileges,
> principles and ideals of a pure Americanism."

The second Klan emerged during the nadir [lowest point] of American race relations…its growth was primarily in response to new issues such as urbanization, immigration and industrialization. The massive immigration of Catholics and Jews from eastern and southern Europe led to fears among Protestants about an alien power that seemed to dominate the largest cities… The migration of both African Americans and whites from rural areas to Southern and Midwestern cities increased social tensions…It [the Klan] appealed to new members based on current social tensions, and stressed responses to fears raised by defiance of prohibition and new sexual freedoms. It emphasized anti-Jewish, anti-Catholic, anti-immigrant and later anti-Communist [feelings]… [Kelly J.] Baker argues that Klansmen seriously embraced Protestantism as an essential component of their white supremacist, anti-Catholic, and paternalistic formulation of American democracy and national culture. ("Ku Klux Klan," *Wikipedia*, pp. 10–12 passim. Also see: Brian R. Farmer, *American Conservatism: History, Theory and Practice* (2005); Kathleen M. Blee, *Women of the Klan: Racism and Gender in the 1920s* (2008); Kelly J. Baker, *Gospel According to the Klan: The KKK's Appeal to Protestant America, 1915–1930* (2011).

Sadly, the American Post Reconstruction Era provided an ideal environment in which the "Race Card Evil" could thrive—one that consisted of denigrating Jim Crow practices and hatred towards anyone or idea that was not "Anglo-Saxon," " Protestant," and "white." Undoubtedly, a deadly "WASP" (White Anglo-Saxon Protestant) was hatched in that Era whose sting would produce far-ranging effects. This fact twenty-first-century American author Clarissa M. Harris noted in her 2002 *Smithsonian* article entitled "Against All Odds." While addressing the life and work of Ms. Ida B. Wells, the nineteenth-century African-American political activist, Ms. Harris stated,

Between 1880 and 1930, approximately 3,220 black Americans were reported lynched, along with perhaps 732 whites. The 1880s ushered in a dramatic and prolonged rise in the percentage of African-American victims. These lawless executions [murders], blind to any Constitutional guarantee of due process, often attracted large crowds. Some spectators brought along children and even picnic baskets, as though the horrific murder of another human being constituted entertainment, or worse, edification [as was the case for the 1893 lynching of Henry Smith in Paris, Texas; at which event thousands of whites apparently attended]. It was the brutal lynching of a friend in 1892 that rallied [Ms.] Wells, then 29, to the anti-lynching cause. (Clarissa Myrick Harris, "Against All Odds," *Smithsonian* 33, no. 4 [July 2002]: 72.)

Sadly, this antisocial "white" attitude survived the Jim Crow Era to negatively impact twentieth century American society—to such an extent that US Supreme Court Justice William O. Douglas of West Virginia was moved to say in the 1968 landmark *Jones v. Alfred H. Mayer, Company* "fair housing" case:

> The true Curse of [African Chattel] Slavery is not what it did to the black man, but what it has done to the white man. For the existence of the [peculiar] institution produced the notion that the white man was of superior character, intelligence, and morality. [That] blacks were little more than livestock—to be fed and fattened for the economic benefits they could bestow [on "whites"] through their labors, and to be subjected to ["white"] authority, often with cruelty, to make clear who was master and who slave. (*Jones v. Alfred H. Mayer Co.*, 392 U.S. 409, at 445)

Enlightened members of the "first" and "second" Continental Congresses, the Confederation Congress, as well as the 38th and 39th Congresses all agreed with Lincoln that the African slavery "cheap labor" scheme was nothing more than "the same old serpent" biting at the heel of the Adamite race before and after man's fall from Eden. Worse, during the AD 1865–1905 era, the "serpent" had spun a cocoon and emerged as a "WASP" in AD 1915—in order to thwart the Great Charter of Liberties enacted by the American people, infect (curse) more people with its venom, and engulf more territory with its deadly agenda. Consequently, because the ancient evil underwent such a transformation, the Adamite members of the "seventy" nations would soon discover that they had to unite in a serious effort to put the beast "in the course of ultimate extinction."

# 8

# The Race Card Evil's Modern Metamorphosis

And I beheld another beast coming up out of the earth;
and he had two horns like a lamb, and he spake as a
dragon…and causeth the earth and them which dwell
therein to worship the first beast, whose deadly wound
was healed.

—Rev. 13:11–12 passim (KJV)

WITHIN FOUR GENERATIONS after the 1774 Articles of Association's creation to end the African Slavery program, the Western World witnessed a number of significant events that forever changed the course of Human history: a war between Britain and her Thirteen Colonies that resulted in a new nation's birth ran by a Republican Government; an unofficial naval war with France because the new nation defaulted on its war debt; a major land purchase from debt-ridden France that extended the new nation's territory; a second war between Britain and her ex-Colonies, due to trade related issues and Britain forcing the new nation's merchant sailors to join her Royal Navy; a second major land acquisition, due to hostilities that erupted between Mexico and Texas, that further extended the new nation's territory (creating Arizona, California, western Colorado, Nevada, Utah, and southwestern Wyoming); a Confederate Union War, due to political schemes to expand the

African Slavery program throughout the new nation's territory; a third major land acquisition (the Alaska Land Purchase), that further extended the new nation's territory; and a war between the new nation and Spain, due to the new nation's intervention in Spanish affairs on the Pacific Coast (which sparked the AD 1899–1902 Philippine-American War). Also within the same period, the World saw "The Race Card Evil" repeatedly evolve and expand to incorporate larger segments of the "70" Nations into its "cheap-labor" monopoly agenda (as Sir Edmund Burke correctly predicted during the 1700s).

On the Western Hemisphere's New World front, the "Race Card Evil" originally started out as a "Divine Biblical Curse" and "Christian Duty to Civilize" (1600s). Thereafter, it respectively became a: "Divine Right to Rule" doctrine (1600s–1700s); "Versailles Peace Treaty Clause Recognizing Chattel Slavery in the British-American Colonies" (1783); "Northwest Ordinance Slavery Prohibition Statute" that repealed Jefferson's "1784 Western Territory Ordinance" and opened up all U.S. Territory south of the "36–degree, 30–minute" Slavery Prohibition Line to Chattel Slavery (1787); "Constitutional Clauses" (Articles I, IV, and Amendment V) that protected Chattel Slavery (1787); "Naturalization Statute" that admitted "free white immigrants" into the U.S. (1790); "Fugitive Slave Law" that allowed slaveowners to legally hunt down escaped slaves (1793); "Congressional Compromise" that admitted Missouri into the Union as a Slave State subject to the "thirty-six-degree, thirty-minute" prohibition line (1820); "manifest destiny doctrine" that justified the new nation's westward expansion into Spanish-controlled Native American territory for occupation purposes (1845–1847); "Congressional Compromise" that opened up the territory acquired from the Mexican-American War to the African Slavery program (1850); more stringent "fugitive slave aw" that forced all lAmericans to participate in upholding the African Slavery program (1850); "US Supreme Court decision" that outlawed the 1820 Missouri Compromise with its slavery prohibition line and advocated a "perpetual allegiance, but noncitizenship doctrine" for victims of the African slavery program (1857); "Confederate Union War" to uphold a man-made right for some humans to own others (1861–1865); state-implemented "black codes" legal practice to financially oppress ex-slaves (1865–1877); US Supreme Court "separate but equal Jim Crow decision," that relegated ex-slaves to a skin color bias and second-class citizenship status (*Homer Adolph Plessy v.* [*Judge*] *John Howard Ferguson*, 1896). Lastly, the evil became an American expansion policy called "The White Man's Burden" (titled from English poet Rudyard Kipling's poem)—which aimed at dominating Spanish-controlled areas in the Pacific and sparked the Spanish-American (1898) and Phillipine-American (1899–1902) Wars.

Within four generations (1774–1902) the "Race Card Evil" evolved at least twenty times on the American front, changed geographical locations just as many times, and annihilated, displaced, exploited, dominated "nonwhites" and immigrant or native-born "whites" who opposed the evil as it extended some variation of itself from the Atlantic Coast to reach the Pacific Coast. And horrifically enough, the evil's machinations against the Adamite race did not stop with causing sociopolitical chaos in the Western world during the nineteenth century AD. Rather, at the outset of the twentieth century AD, humanity would discover that the evil underwent a transformation that would prove the worst was yet to come!

On the Eastern Hemisphere's Old World front, the "Race Card Evil" transformed itself into a deadly "chosen one, superior race" program that attacked "all humans" deemed "inferior"—black, white, or other. Indeed, from 1914 to 1919 the First "World" War (WWI) was fought—between the Allied powers (the United States, Great Britain, Russia, France, Italy, and Japan) and Central powers (the Austrian-Hungarian, German, Ottoman Turk, and Bulgarian Kingdoms)—because Austria's Archduke Francis (Franz) Ferdinand

and his wife were assassinated at Sarajevo (28 June 1914); the assassin being a Serbian "nationalist" who wanted "more territory" added to Serbia (now Yugoslavia). Thanks to man's technological advances in weaponry, the war mobilized about "seventy million" military personnel, caused over "nine million" deaths, and was dubbed "the sixth deadliest conflict in human history."

At the war's close, both the League of Nations (Germany, Japan, Italy, and Spain being among its members) and "1919 Versailles Peace Treaty" were created—the league having the goal of maintaining world peace, protecting Europe's minorities, promoting just treatment for indigenous inhabitants of various regions, and promoting global health; the treaty having the goal of assigning accountability to Germany for causing the war. Also during 1919, the National German Workers' Party was founded and joined by Austrian-born Adolf Hitler shortly thereafter. Ironically, these four events would combine and cause the "Nazi" political party to rise in Germany and spark the Second "World" War (WWII)—by promoting a "Race Card Evil" oriented domination program targeting both "White" and "non-White" peoples globally. On the term "Nazi," *Webster's Dictionary* stated,

> Nazi—derived from the German words *National Sozialistische Deutsche Arbeiterpartei* [NSDAP], ["Nazi" is a political] party name designating, of, or characteristic of the German Fascist political party (National Socialist German Worker's Party), founded in 1919 and abolished in 1945: under [Adolf] Hitler it seized control of Germany in 1933, systematically eliminated opposition, and put into effect its program of nationalism, racism, rearmament, [and] aggression [bullyism], etc." (*Webster's New World Dictionary of the American Language*, 2d coll. ed., s.v. "Nazi")

Originally a name connected with the political party that represented German "workers," the "Nazi" party was concerned with securing better "labor" conditions. However, because the

"1919 Versailles Treaty's" imposed of a "thirty-one-billion-dollar" fine on Germany for causing political turmoil between Austria-Hungary and Serbia (thus causing WWI)—a fine many nations thought was too harsh—the cost negatively impacted Germany's economy and laborers.

Taking advantage of the German laborers' disgruntled attitude, Adolf Hitler joined the German Worker's Party, gained popularity, and became its leader by 1921. About two years later, Hitler led an unsuccessful "Munich Beer Hall Revolution" (November 1923), was convicted of treason the following year and received a five-year sentence for the crime (instead of a life sentence) (February 1924), and was released from Landsberg prison within nine months because he had powerful supporters in high political offices. After his release, Hitler had minimal political influence. However, the Great Depression of 1929 changed that by threatening the economies of Germany and other countries—thus providing the financial fear necessary for Hitler's Nazi party to win elective seats in the Reichstag (parliament) from 1929 to 1933.

Seeking appointment as Germany's chancellor, Hitler repeatedly requested President Paul von Hindenburg to do so and was repeatedly denied. Finally, because the Nazi party occupied the most seats in the Reichstag, Mr. Hindenburg did so. Once appointed, Hitler dissolved the Reichstag and ordered a new election held (March 1933)—at which time his party declared him "dictator" despite his "Race Card Evil" oriented program of aggression, nationalism, racism, and rearmament. *Wikipedia's* biography on Hitler recounted in part:

> Adolf Hitler…was an Austrian-born German politician and the leader of the Nazi party…A decorated veteran of World War I, Hitler joined the German Workers' Party, precursor of the Nazi Party, in 1919, and became leader of the NSDAP in 1921. In 1923, he attempted a coup d'etat…The failed coup resulted in Hitler's imprisonment,

during which time he wrote his memoir, *Mein Kampf* (*My Struggle*). After his release in 1924, Hitler gained popular support by attacking the [1919] Treaty of Versailles and promoting Pan-Germanism, anti-Semitism, and anti-Communism with charismatic oratory and Nazi propaganda. After his appointment as Chancellor in 1933, he transformed the Weimar Republic into the Third Reich, a single-party dictatorship based on the totalitarian and autocratic ideology of Nazism [Nazi-ism]. His aim was to establish a new [world] order of absolute Nazi German Hegemony [dominance] in continental Europe.

Hitler's foreign and domestic policies had the goal of seizing *Lebensraum* ("living space") [more territory] for the Germanic people. He directed the rearmament of Germany and the invasion of Poland by Wehrmacht in September 1939, resulting in the outbreak of World War II in Europe…Hitler's supremacist and racially motivated policies resulted in the systematic murder of eleven million people, including an estimated six million Jews, and in the deaths of between 50 and 70 million people in World War II. (*Wikipedia*, s.v. "Adolf Hitler," http://en.wikipedia.org/wiki/Adolf_Hitler. Retrieved 26 January 2014)

Lasting from 1 September 1939 to 2 September 1945, World War II was "the deadliest conflict in human history" and "the most widespread in Earth's history"—one actively fought on three continents and two oceans between at least twenty-six nations allied against Germany and her Axis powers allies (Italy and Japan among them). Moreover, the war's cost was enormous—its major players mobilizing more than one hundred million military personnel and placing their entire economic, industrial, and scientific resources at the war effort's disposal. The war also involved mass civilian participation, caused mass civilian deaths, and resulted in anywhere from fifty to seventy million fatalities.

To be sure, although the threat of "Nazism" was contested, the real opponent of the Allied Nations was the "Race Card

Evil"—since World War II was the stage upon which ancient evil performed to show the world that it had not gone "in the course of ultimate extinction" (Hitler merely being its puppet). In her *Universal History of the World* article entitled "Totalitarianism and the Great Depression," twentieth-century author Edna Ritchie said regarding Hitler's doctrine and agenda,

> Hitler was not a good writer, and he wandered from one subject to another, but certain of his ideas stood out. One was that the Germans were "the highest species of humanity" on Earth, and must be the master race of the world. Hitler said the Germans belonged to what he called the "Aryan" race, and that they must "care for the purity of the blood." In other words, they must not marry "non-Aryans," the members of other races. If the Germans were to be masters, they must have servants. They would be served particularly by the Slavic peoples—the Russians, the Czechs, and the Poles. Some races, particularly the Jews, were not even fit to serve the Germans, and must be wiped out.
>
> And how would the master race remain master? By force, by conquest, by war. "Mankind has grown great in eternal struggle," said Hitler, "and only in eternal peace does it perish." War was a good thing, and only through war could nations achieve greatness." (*Univ. Hist. of the World*, vol. 14, 1167–68)

Hitler's "chosen, pure superior" nation or race destined to "conquer-rule" others doctrine was obviously a remix of the biblical "Israel's conquest of Canaan" theme. Hence, the Jewish-created "chosen one" doctrine was applied centuries later by Hitler to negatively impact Europe's Jewish population—in much the same way that it was used to justify the African Slavery scheme used against Africans labeled "Negroes" resident in Spain and America during the 15th to 19th centuries AD. And although Hitler's plan for Europe's Jews differed somewhat from the African Chattel Slavery scheme, there were a number of similarities between the two plans that imply a "Race Card Evil" pattern.

Indeed, like the Old Testament's "Israel invasion of Canaan" motif, Hitler's plan involved territory occupation, economic exploitation, and wilfull genocide. And like the American antebellum South's African American slavery experience, Hitler's plan forced Jews to undergo a number of humiliating practices such as: publicly wearing "six-pointed yellow stars" (instead of yellow badges), submitting to "physical branding" (instead of negative naming) for identification purposes, working in "labor" camps (instead of prison camps), submitting to experimentation, hiding out in "safe houses" until escape could be made through an underground system (underground resistance vs. underground railroad), and submitting to "ethnic" extermination (shoting or gasing vs. lynching or burning). And, more likely than not, having pretty "Jewish" females entertaining "German" males contrary to Hitler's "purity of race" doctrine (people can be such hypocrites when the occasion calls for it).

Curiously enough, despite his program directed at Europe's Jews, it is a mystery as to how and when Hitler developed his "anti-Semite" attitude. Indeed, *Wikipedia's* biography about him placed the origin of his "extremist racial views" at Vienna, Austria, either during his youthful years or after Germany's WWI defeat. Said the article,

> From 1905, [fourteen-year-old] Hitler lived a bohemian life in Vienna [Austria], financed by orphan's [social service] benefits and support from his mother...In 1909 he lived in a homeless shelter, and by 1910, he had settled into a house [dormitory] for poor working men [in Vienna's Brigittenau district]...At the time Hitler lived there, Vienna was a hotbed of religious prejudice and racism. Fears of being overrun by immigrants [Jews] from the East were widespread, and the populist mayor, Karl

Lueger, exploited the rhetoric of virulent anti-Semitism for political effect. Georg Schonerer's pan-Germanic anti-semitism had a strong following in the Mariahiff district, where Hitler lived. Hitler read local newspapers, such as *Deutsche Volksblatt*, that fanned prejudice and played on Christian fears of being swamped by an influx of eastern Jews…The origin and first expression of Hitler's anti-Semitism have been difficult to locate. Hitler states in *Mein Kampf* that he first became an anti-Semite in Vienna… Several sources provide strong evidence that Hitler had Jewish friends in his hostel and in other places in Vienna. Historian [Sir] Richard J. Evans states that "historians now generally agree that his notorious, murderous anti-semitism emerged well after Germany's [WWI] defeat, as a product of the paranoid 'stab-in-the-back' explanation for the catastrophe [defeat]." (*Wikipedia*, s.v. "Adolf Hitler," http://en.wikipedia.org/wiki/Adolf_Hitler. Retrieved 26 January 2015)

Regardless of the how and when Hitler became infected with "Race Card Evil" views Ms. Ritchie, in her chapter entitled "Germany Under the Nazis," noted that a few years after he became Germany's dictator both the Nuremberg laws (1935) and the "Week of Broken Glass" (1938) occurred. Said she,

In September of 1935, the so-called Nuremberg Laws were passed against the Jews. A Jew was defined as anyone who had more than two Jewish grandparents, and a Jew could not be a German citizen. While Jews no longer had the privileges of citizenship, such as voting and holding office, they still had to obey the laws of the state. Marriages between Germans and Jews, and between Germans and half-Jews, were forbidden. Jews were also barred from a number of professions and businesses, and much of their property was seized by the government and the Nazi leaders.

Unable to make a living, thousands of Jews left Germany. Those who could not get away saw signs going up all around them: "Jews Not Admitted"—"No Jews Allowed"—"Jews Strictly Forbidden in This Town." It became almost impossible for Jews to buy food and medicine. And then, in November of 1938, came what the Nazis later called the "Week of the Broken Glass." A young Jewish refugee had shot and killed a member of the German Embassy in Paris. In revenge for this, the Nazi leaders sent out orders to the police to organize "demonstrations" of Nazi party members and SS men [Hitler's hand-picked, black-shirted "Schutzstaffel" soldiers] against the Jews. They were to destroy Jewish homes and businesses and synagogues, and there was to be no interference from the police. The orders stated that "as many Jews, especially rich ones, are to be arrested as can be accommodated in the existing prisons."

On the night of November 9, these orders were carried out. The windows of thousands of Jewish shops were smashed, and broken glass lay in the streets. The shops were then looted and destroyed. Meanwhile, houses and synagogues were burned to the ground. Thousands of Jews were arrested and hundreds were murdered. On top of this, the Jews of Germany were forced to pay a fine of one million marks. The Nazi government also issued decrees that confiscated most of the property of Jews and closed almost all businesses and professions to them.

There had been persecutions of Jews in Germany before this, and there had been restrictions, such as the Nuremberg laws. But with the Week of Broken Glass, Germany began its real attempt to eliminate Jews from the country and even from the world. This attempt would lead to the horrors of the concentration camps, where men, women, and children were worked and starved and tormented to death. It would lead to the gas chambers, where men, women, and children were put to death by poison gas. It would lead to corpses piled up and burned in furnaces, and tossed in heaps in ditches. It would lead to the death of 6,000,000 Jews. (*Univ. Hist. of the World.*, vol. 14, 1176–77)

The Nazi Era was not only tough on "Jews," it also affected people from varying backgrounds—"German" and "non-German." Indeed, during 1933 not only did Hitler dissolve the German parliament (Reichstag), allow parliament's building torched in order to blame his opposition and outlaw all of Germany's political parties except his own, and encourage mass book-burning events to limit the German people's intellect, but he also authorized the arrest and muder of a number of his own countrymen suspected of opposing him. Concerning the 1933 "Fire in the Reichstag" event, Ms. Ritchie said,

> And so, on February 27 [ in 1933], a cry went up in Berlin: "The Reichstag is on fire!" This was the building where the German parliament met…A group of Nazis, led by [Herman] Goering, rushed to the burning building. "This is a Communist crime against the new government!" Goering shouted. "This is the beginning of the Communist revolution!…We will show no mercy. Every Communist [party] official must be shot where he is found. Every Communist deputy must this very night be strung up [lynched]."
>
> Goering himself had helped plan the fire. It had been set by the Nazis…Hitler was taking advantage of the situation. The day after the fire, he persuaded President Hindenberg to issue an emergency decree that did away with all civil liberties…Hitler sent his stormtroopers to round up, torture, and beat thousands of Communists, Social Democrats, and other opponents…Hitler, Goering, and [Joseph Goebbels] thundered and snarled on the government-owned radio, warning against the Communist menace, attacking liberals and Jews. They played upon the people's fears, promising them a strong, proud, prosperous Germany, a Nazi [kingdom of] heaven on earth. (Ibid., vol. 14, 1173)

Further, Ms. Ritchie recounted the extent to which Hitler went to eliminate any party or person that would potentially interfere with his agenda. Concerning the 1934 "Blood Purge" event, she said,

There was no doubt that the "old era" had ended and that the "New [World] Order," as Hitler called it, had come to Germany…He outlawed all political parties but his own… He wiped out the trade unions…Hitler would decide how Germans lived and worked and worshipped, and even thought…And yet, some Nazis were still not satisfied. Among them was Ernst Roehm, the leader of the storm troopers…Roehm had taken seriously Hitler's socialistic talk. He called for a "second revolution"…Hitler had no intention of replacing the regular army and the aristocrats who led it…Nor did Hitler have any intention of bringing real socialism to Germany…Hitler discovered that Roehm was even doing a little political plotting…Conferring with Goering and [Heinrich] Himmler, Hitler decided to kill Roehm and his closest followers. This would also be a good opportunity for Hitler to kill some other people who might someday prove troublesome. The job would be done by the SS men and special police under the direction of Goering.

On June 30, 1934, they struck in the "blood purge" that shocked the world. Roehm was thrown into a prison cell and, when he refused to take his own life, was shot by two SS officers. General von Schleicher, a former chancellor of Germany, was shot down in the doorway of his own home, as was his wife. Some of the people who died that day were shot in groups, like the 150 storm troopers who fell before a firing squad in Berlin. Some were shot because they knew too much about Hitler's past. One man was even shot by mistake. He was a Munich music critic named Dr. Willi Schmid. He was killed as he was playing the cello in his study, while his wife and two small children were in the next room. He had been mistaken for Willi Schmidt, a storm troop leader…The purge left Hitler stronger than ever. (Ibid., vol. 14, 1174–76 passim)

Undoubtedly, the "purge" showed that "Jews" were not the only "ethnic" group that Hitler's regime wanted to "purify" itself of. Indeed, the regime wanted to "cleanse" its own "ethnicity" of all views that ran afoul of its agenda. This "hints" that Hitler's "Race Card Evil" oriented agenda was nothing more than a "con" designed to elevate or enrich a "chosen few" by controlling and impoverishing "the many" Germans who went along with the "program." Said Ms. Rithchie,

> Nor were the Jews the only ones persecuted. Hitler was determined to wipe out all Communists and Socialists—in fact, anyone who had the slightest objection to the Nazis and what they were doing…It was true that the [German] workers were controlled by Hitler's Labor Front. They had to work where and when they were told. It was also true that, without labor unions, workers had to take whatever pay they were offered. While profits were rising, wages were falling. Still, there were jobs to be had, even if the pay was low. As for civil liberties, Germans had never had much political freedom, except under the Weimar Republic… And so, while their Jewish and anti-Nazi neighbors were dragged off to concentration camps, most Germans were satisfied enough with the Nazis. (Ibid., 1177–78 passim)

Taking such facts into consideration, we should thank Hitler for bringing us face-to-face with the evil that lurks within ourselves—an ancient evil that Man was warned about long before the Nazi era began. In the biblical "Cain vs. Abel" murder story the Creator said to Cain,

> Why are you angry? Why are you dejected? If you act rightly, you will be accepted [honored, uplifted]; but if not, [then] sin lies in wait at the door; its urge is for you, yet you can rule [have dominion] over it. (Gen. 4:6–7, NAB)

Centuries ago, man was warned about entertaining negative thoughts such as anger, envy, greed, and hatred. Yet centuries later Mr. Hitler arrived on Earth to wreak havoc with his "anti-social" attitude. And the scary thing about his era was that Man developed Nuclear Capability! Fortunately Albert Einstein, Berlin Academy of Science's theoretical physicist professor, was visiting the U.S. in 1933. Knowing that Hitler's scientists were attempting to develop "nuclear" weaponry, Einstein decided against returning to Germany, alerted President Franklin D. Roosevelt about the matter, and advised the President to encourage similar research. Mr. Roosevelt took Einstein's advice, authorized the Manhattan Project and, by 1945, American "atomic" weaponry research produced two nuclear fission bombs—the first a uranium fission bomb named Little Boy, and the second a plutonium fission bomb named Fat Man.

Humanity can only speculate on what damage Hitler would have done had he successfully developed such weaponry first (his "Race Card" oriented agenda prevented the world's scientific community from sharing information with Germany just prior to and during WW II). And Humanity can only speculate on whether America would have used such weaponry on Germany, given its location in Europe. In either case, the world will never know—since Germany surrendered on 8 May 1945. However, in the case of Germany's ally Japan—who had not surrendered— the world witnessed an unparalleled technological horror.

Four years prior to Germany's surrender, Japan had bombed the US Pearl Harbor Naval Base at Oahu, Hawaii (7 December 1941). Four years later, the United States answered by dropping Little Boy on Hiroshima (6 August 1945) and Fat Man on Nagasaki (9 August 1945)—forcing Japan's surrender (15 August 1945). Although the United States could have used "conventional" weapons to defeat Japan, a "guinea pig" was needed for "experimental" purposes—and Japan was the best candidate (perhaps partly due to U.S. hostility towards Japan since the *Ozawa v. US* era (1922); also see *Takahashi Fish and Game Commission* (1969).

In any event, the detonation of "nuclear" weaponry over Japan (1945) and then over "Bikini Island" (1946) ushered in the "Atomic Age"—an era wherein Man became capable of annihilating himself from the Earth! And the fact that *seventy* years later, as of 2015, the Federation of American Scientists estimates that there are at least "19,000" nuclear warheads with "4,400" of them "kept in operational status for ready use" by the world's "Nuclear Bomb Club"—the United States, Soviet Union, United Kingdom, France, People's Republic of China, India-Pakistan, North Korea, and Israel (suspect)—makes a convincing argument that "man probably will destroy himself, if he does not come to his senses!" Ironically, stockpiling such deadly weaponry seems to prove Hitler's view right that "only through war can nations achieve greatness." And it was precisely because of this "negative mind-set" that Bertrand Russell and Albert Einstein formulated their "Russell-Einstein Manifesto"—to warn man about the danger of using nuclear weaponry.

Aside from the bloody and scary scenario Hitler demonstrated, there was one good thing he showed us that we should be thankful for. He showed us just how stupid we Humans can be by not critically examining beliefs or ideas handed down to us! And this is especially true when it comes to "Race Card Evil" oriented beliefs or ideas! For example, Hitler always informed his audiences that his objective was to create a "pure and unmixed" Aryan superior race. However, his adoption of the word "Aryan" (ironically meaning "to be good") connected the German people to the name "Persian," "Iranian," or "Indo-Iranian" (a languange group). Thus Hitler was saying that the so-called Aryans were actually an offshoot of Noah's "son" Japheth—and hence the Germans were (and are) a branch of the "One Race" variously called "Adam, Adamite, Human, Man, and the 70–Nations" (Gen. 1:26–27, 5:1–2, 10:1–5; KJV).

In fact, Hitler's adoption of the swastika as Nazi Germany's "symbol" for his "pure race" propaganda—which supposedly represented a "no mixing" of cultures and peoples—was dated back to ancient India and, curiously enough, was found carved in an "Ethiopian" religious structure that dated back to the AD 1000s–1100s centuries; almost a millennium before Hitler was born! This fact twentieth century historian Peter Hinchliff noted in *The Oxford Illustrated History of Christianity* chapter entitled "Africa." In an inset subtitled "Ethiopian Christianity" he noted,

> The church of Biet Mariam (eleventh to twelfth century) hewn from the solid volcanic rock…Its decorations include ancient symbols annexed by the Christians. Alongside one of the porches there are swastika signs allied with crosses; above one of the others is a bas-relief of the "riders of light" pursuing the "beasts of darkness." (Peter Hinchliff, "Africa," *The Oxford Illustrated History of Christianity*, ed. John McManners (New York: Oxford University Press, 1990), 459)

Perhaps the strangest thing about Hitler's agenda to create a "super race" of "blond-haired, blue-eyed" Germans was that a lot of people were willing to kill and be killed to make his "vision" a reality on Earth—yet Hitler was a "brown-haired, brown-eyed, brown-moustached" Austrian who had "adopted" Germany as his country and was clearly the "opposite" of his "super race" doctrine? Apparently, some people forgot that they were taught that a "creator" makes a person "in his or its own image and likeness!" Thus, given such a "hair-raising, eye-opening" contradiction, Hitler undoubtedly proved that modern man needs to thoroughly examine the validity or invalidity of any doctrine believed, followed, or taught (since Hitler almost got away with realizing his agenda)!

Such "facts" say that we should revisit America's slavery story, thoroughly examine what we have been taught about it, and determine whether or not we "know" the "real deal" about that era. Was it really a "black slave, white slavemaster" era? Or did "mixed scenarios" or "shades of gray" exist that tell a different and more realistic story characteristic of any geography, ethnicity, and time era? To be sure, a look at some examples and counterexamples will reveal whether or not our views have been "colored" by "Race Card Evil" oriented "myths" to prevent us from putting the evil "in the course of ultimate extinction."

# 9

## America's Slavery Story
## Fact versus Fiction

False witnesses did rise up; they laid to my charge things
that I knew not. They rewarded me evil for good to the
spoiling of my soul.

—Psalm 35:11–12 (KJV)

A lie travels swifter than an arrow, but the truth travels at
a snail's pace.

—Aesop

THE WORD *MYTH* comes from the ancient Greek *mythos*, which
originally meant "anything uttered by word of mouth." However,
over time the word was used by different Greek personalities (or
schools of thought) to mean different ideas. For example: the poet
Homer (c. 8th century BC) used "myth" to mean "conversation
and narrative, but not fiction"; whereas his *Iliad* and *Odyssey* used
"myth" to mean "telling a [false] story" (because the hero Odysseus
or Ulysses told false stories about himself); and the philosopher
Plato (c. 4th century BC) used "myth" to mean "something not
wholly lacking truth, but mostly fictitious."

Modernly, *myth* is used to mean "a fictitious or untrue story
that conveys some type of truth that, as a rule, concerns creation

and involves supernatural or suprahuman beings" and is often equated with *legend*—a word which twentieth-century editor J. A. Cuddon, in *The Penguin Dictionary of Literary Terms and Literary Theory*, said was originally applied to stories about the lives of saints, but carried the subsidiary meaning of "a narrative or story about a particular person or thing which lies somewhere between historical fact and myth." (J. A. Cuddon, *The Penguin Dictionary of Literary Terms and Literary Theory*, 3d ed., New York: Penguin Books Inc., 1991, s.v. "legend," "myth.")

Moreover, to Mr. Cuddon's view, *Webster's New World Dictionary of the American Language* added,

> Myth—a traditional story of unknown authorship, ostensibly [professed to come] with a historical basis, but serving usually to explain some phenomenon of nature, the origin of man, or the customs, institutions, religious rites, etc., of a people. (*Webster's New World Dict. of the Amer. Lang.*, 2d coll. ed., s.v. *myth*)

A careful analysis of America's Colonial, Revolutionary War, pre-Civil War, and post-Civil War eras will show that his "slavery story" was not the open-and-shut case of "color" exploitation, hatred, oppression that is traditionally believed by Americans. Indeed, as with any given event or idea, there were "shades of gray" that refute the "Race Card Evil" oriented myths that are modernly taught American society by various sources.

For instance, the "superior white race, inferior nonwhite race" myth was an idea taken from the misused researches of German anthropologist-naturalist Johann Friedrich Blumenbach—who believed that the first humans originated in Asia, postulated "five" Races of Man, and innocently assigned "colors" to them (black, brown, red, yellow, and white). Unfortunately, some of Mr. Blumenbach's contemporaries misrepresented his research and created what became known as "scientific racism"—a theory that alleged the superiority of "whites" and the inferiority of "nonwhites." However, Blumenbach did not believe that "nonwhites"—and particularly those of African descent labeled "Negroes"—were "inferior" to any other branch of humanity with respect to artistry, comprehension, creativity, and reasoning. In fact, *Wikipedia's* article entitled *Anthropological Treatises of Johann Friedrich Blumenbach* recounted that, at page 312 (note 5) of his *Treatise*, Mr. Blumenbach stated,

> Finally, I am of [the] opinion that after all these numerous instances I have brought together of negroes of capacity, it would not be difficult to mention entire well-known provinces of Europe, from out of which you would not easily expect to obtain off-hand such good authors, poets, philosophers, and correspondents of the Paris Academy; and on the other hand, there is no so-called savage nation known under the sun which has so much distinguished itself by such examples of perfectibility and original [thinking] capacity for scientific culture, and thereby attached itself so closely to the most civilized nations of the earth, as the Negro. (*Wikipedia*, s.v. "Johann Friedrich Blumenbach: Anthropological Treatise," http://en.wikipedia.org/wiki/ Johann_Friedrich_Blumenbach. Retrieved 26 January 2014.)

As another example, some people may believe the "myth" that the "Africans" who came to the Jamestown colony on a Dutch *Man-of-War* ship in AD 1619 were "slaves." Not so; they were "indentured servants"—a fact *Wikipedia's* article entitled "John Casor" stated:

> The first group of 20 or so Africans were brought to Jamestown in 1619 and treated by the colonists as indentured servants. After working out their contracts for passage money to Virginia and completing their indenture, each was granted 50 acres (20 hectares) of land (headrights). This enabled them to raise their own tobacco or other

crops...Anthony Johnson was an Angolan colonist, one of the original indentured "so and odd negroes" brought to Jamestown after arriving at Cape Comfort in August 1619. By 1623, Johnson had completed his indenture and was a "free Negro." (*Wikipedia*, s.v. "John Casor," http://en.wikipedia.org/wiki/John_Casor. Retrieved 27 January 2014)

During this early period the Jamestown colony neither defined nor practiced "slavery" or "racial slavery"—only "indentured servitude." *Wikipedia's* biographical sketch on Angolan colonist "Antonio the Negro" or "Anthony Johnson" added,

Anthony Johnson was a black Angolan held as an indentured servant by a merchant in the Colony of Virginia in 1620, but later freed to become a successful tobacco farmer and property owner. Notably, he was the first true slave owner, that is, the first to hold a black African servant as a slave in the mainland American colonies...Johnson was captured by Arab traders in his native Angola by an enemy tribe and sold as a slave to a merchant working for the Virginia Company. He arrived in Virginia in 1621 aboard the *James*. At this time he was known in the records as "Antonio, a Negro." Johnson was later sold to a white planter named Bennet to work on his Virginia tobacco farm as an indentured servant...Prior to 1654, all Africans in the Thirteen Colonies were held in indentured servitude and were released after a contracted period [four to seven years] with many of the indentured receiving land and equipment [called freedom dues] after their contracts for work expired...By around 1635 Antonio and Mary [his African wife since 1623] were free, and Antonio changed his name to Anthony Johnson. In the late 1640s he moved to the Pungoteague River in Northampton County, Virginia where he acquired 250 acres (100 hectares) of land on the eastern shore...In 1665, Anthony Johnson and his family moved to Somerset

County, Maryland, and negotiated a lease on a 300–acre (120 hectares) plot of land for ninety-nine years. Johnson used this land to start a tobacco farm which he named Tories Vineyards. (*Wikipedia*, s.v. "Anthony Johnson (colonist)," http://en.wikipedia.org/wiki/Anthony_ Johnson_(colonist). Retrieved 27 January 2014)

According to the PBS (WGBH) television documentary *Africans in America: From Indentured Servitude to Racial Slavery*, during the year that Anthony Johnson purchased his first property (AD 1640) three indentured servants fled from a Virginia plantation. On being caught and returned to their masters, the court sentenced two of them to a four-year indenture extension and the third, an African man named John Punch, "to serve his said master or his assigns for the time of his natural life" (thereby creating "lifetime slavery").

Notably, *Wikipedia's* sketch on Mr. Johnson said that his claim to fame stemmed from being known as the "first slaveowner" in the thirteen colonies—a point that contradicts the generally accepted "myth" that "whites" started the "lifetime slavery" scheme. Indeed, about AD 1654 Johnson—said to be so illiterate that he acknowledged a debt based on a letter forged by unscrupulous white neighbor Edmund Scarborough—initiated a suit against one of his own indentured servants, named John Casor, that produced the same result as the 1640 *Punch* case. Said *Wikipedia's* article on Mr. Johnson,

> By July 1651 Johnson had five indentured servants of his own and he claimed an additional 250 acres (100 hectares) of land based on the headright system. He is recognized in Virginia court documents when he pled for tax relief in 1653 after a fire destroyed much of his plantation, and in a case brought in 1654 in which he contested the freedom suit of a servant, John Casor...When Anthony was released [from servitude] he was legally recognized as a "free Negro" and ran a successful farm. In 1654, it was

time for Anthony to release John Casor, a black indentured servant. Instead Anthony told Casor he was extending his time. Casor left and became employed by the free white man Robert Parker.

Anthony Johnson sued Robert Parker in the Northampton Court in 1654. The court ruled that Anthony Johnson could hold John Casor indefinitely. The court gave judicial sanction for blacks to own slave[s] of their own race. Thus Casor became the first permanent [chattel] slave and Johnson the first [chattel] slave owner.

Whites still could not legally hold a black servant as an indefinite slave until 1670. In that year, the colonial assembly passed legislation permitting free whites, blacks, and Indians the right to own blacks as slaves.

Slavery was established in Virginia in 1655, when Johnson convinced a court that his servant John Casor (also a black man), was his for life. Johnson himself had been brought to Virginia some years earlier as an indentured servant but he had saved enough money to buy out the remainder of his contract and that of his wife. The court ruling in Johnson's favor resulted in Casor becoming the first state-recognized slave in the Colony of Virginia. Slavery in Virginia was officially enacted in state law for free whites, blacks, and Indians in 1661 [via Act CII [102], Laws of Virginia, March 1661–62; *Hening Statutes at Large*, 2:116–17]. ("Anthony Johnson (colonist)"; also see PBS (WGHB) Documentary "Africans in America: from Indentured Servitude to Racial Slavery," http://www.pbs.org/wgbh/aia/part1/1narr3.html. Retrieved 27 January 2014)

In addition to Anthony Johnson's portrait, *Wikipedia's* biography on "John Casor" added,

John Casor…a servant in Northampton County in the Virginia Colony, in 1655 became the first person of African descent in Britain's Thirteen Colonies to be declared by the county court as a slave for life.

In one of the earliest freedom suits, Casor argued that he was an indentured servant who had been forced to serve past his term. In ordering Casor returned to his master Anthony Johnson, a free black, for life, the court sustained the right of free blacks to own slaves…In 1653 John Casor, a Black man employed by Johnson, said that he had been imported as a "seaven or eight yeares" indentured servant and that, after attempting to reclaim his indenture, he had been told by Johnson that he didn't have one. According to the court documents, Casor demanded his freedom. "Anthony Johnson was in a feare [fear]. Upon this his son in law, his wife and his two sonnes [sons] persuaded the said Anthony Johnson to set the said John Casor free."

Casor went to work for Robert Parker, a white colonist who, along with his brother George, later testified that they knew Casor had an indenture. One commentator said that Johnson may have feared losing his headrights land if the case went to court.

Anthony Johnson brought suit in Northampton County court against Robert Parker in 1654 for detaining his "Negro servant, John Casor," saying "Hee [He] never did see any [indenture] but that hee had ye Negro for his life." In the case of *Johnson vs. Parker*, the court of Northampton County upheld Johnson's right to hold Casor as a slave, saying in its ruling of 8 March 1655:

"This daye Anthony Johnson Negro made his complaint to the court against mr. Robert Parker and declared that hee deteyneth [detaineth] his servant John Casor Negro under the pretence that said Negro was a free man. The court seriously considering and maturely weighing the premises, doe fynde that the saide Mr. Robert Parker most unjustly keepeth the said Negro from Anthony Johnson his master… It is therefore the Judgement of the Court and ordered That the said John Casor Negro forthwith returne unto the service of the said master Anthony Johnson, And that Mr. Robert Parker make payment of all charges in the suit."

By sustaining Anthony Johnson's claim to the perpetual service of John Casor in 1655, the court gave judicial sanction (authorization) of free Negroes to own slaves of their own race—thus giving John Casor the distinction of being the first (black) person to be "legally" declared a slave in what became the United States, and Anthony Johnson the first slaveholder (black or white).

In 1665 Anthony Johnson and his wife Mary, his son John and his wife, Susanna, and their "slave" John Casor moved to Somerset County, Maryland. Casor remained Johnson's slave for the rest of his life. And five years later, in 1670, Virginia's colonial assembly passed a law prohibiting free and baptized "Negroes" and "Indians" from purchasing "Christians" (i.e., English or European "Whites")—but allowing them to buy (purchase the indenture contracts) of persons "of their owne nation" and other ("non-White") nations.

Some historians argue that John Punch, an African indentured servant Court-ordered "indentured for life" in 1640, should be considered Virginia's [hence America's] first slave. Punch had escaped along with two white indentured servants who were both sentenced to 30 strokes of the whip and an additional four years of servitude. However, Punch was Court-ordered to serve "the remainder of his life in indentured servitude" as punishment for escaping while an indentured servant. This difference in penalties is considered one of the first cases to make a "racial" distinction between black and white indentured servants. (*Wikipedia*, s.v. "John Casor.")

Another "myth" modernly believed and taught is that, during the 1619–1865 period, only well-to-do "whites" bought, sold, owned "blacks." However, careful research will reveal that a number of "Blacks" also bought-sold-owned "Whites." This fact historian Joel A. Rogers noted in volume one of his *Sex and Race*. Said he,

Fifty-one years after the Negro's [1619] arrival in [Jamestown] Virginia, a law was passed [in Virginia, circa. 1670] to prevent his [the Negro's] buying [Christian] white people [as slaves]. Louisiana passed such a law as late as 1818. (Joel A. Rogers, *Sex and Race: Negro-Caucasian Mixing in All Ages and All Lands*, vol. 1, "The Old World", 9th ed. New York: Helga M. Rogers, 1967, p. 25)

And in volume two of his *Sex and Race*, Rogers said,

During slavery there were several Negroes in the South, especially Louisiana and South Carolina, who would be accounted millionaires today. Most of them were slaveholders...These rich Negroes were treated in nearly every respect like white people. They could mary white wives—at least many did; they could buy white men and women—they did in Maryland and Louisiana until 1818, and in all probability, Florida, too...Negro slaves sometimes rose to high positions in New Orleans and even had free white men working under them...Rich Negroes, as was said, bought white people. Virginia found it necessary three times, in 1670, 1748, and 1792 to prohibit such purchase. For instance, Act IX [9], [in] October 1748, of this state, reads "No Negro, mulatto, Indian, although a Christian, or any Jew, Moor, or Mohammedan [Muslim]...shall purchase any Christian white servants."

On March 20, 1818, [the] Louisiana [legislature] passed a similar law..."they [the legislature] however, permitted white persons of good fame and character to continue the traffic [in purchasing the white stranger]."

Negroes also bought white people in Maryland. E. S. Abdy cites the following from Baltimore in 1818 ; "There arrived this summer a ship addressed to Mr. Graff, one of the richest merchants in this place. A greater part of the passengers had not paid [for] their freight [passage]. Two families were bought by free Negroes of which there is a fairly large number in Maryland. This disgusted the Germans in Baltimore."

Joel A. Rogers, *Sex and Race: A history of White, Negro and Indian miscegenation in the two Americas*, vol. 2 ("The New World") (New York: Self-published by Rogers, 9th printing, 1989 (originally 1942; renewed 1970), 242–46 passim. Rogers citing: *Hening's Statutes of Virginia*, vol. 5,p. 550; J. P. Guild, *Black Laws of Virginia*, 1936, p. 66; New York Public Library Collection, "Slavery Pamphlets," vol. 23, No. 15; XIII [13] *Louisiana Digest of Civil Laws*, 1808; E. S. Abdy, *Journal of a Residence and Tour in the United States*, vol. 2, 1835, p. 56; L. P. Hennighausen, *German Society of Maryland*, 1909, p. 28.

Undoubtedly, passing such "no buying whites" laws says that quite a number of "blacks" were buying "whites" as slaves. This brings up another "myth" modernly taught to African American society by some African American religious leaders or school teachers. The "myth" is popularly called the "Willie Lynch slave controlsSpeech" and is a clear-cut case of reverse "Race Card Evil" propaganda—which can socially "cripple" young African American minds and prevent them from developing adequate academic, social, and vocational skills necessary to thrive in "multicultural" American society.

The story goes that in AD 1712, a "white" West Indian (Caribbean) slaveowner named William "Willie" Lynch was invited to visit Jamestown to lecture "white" slavemasters on how to control "black" slaves. On arriving at the Colony, Mr. Lynch allegedly gave the following speech on the banks of the James River:

Gentlemen:

I greet you here on the banks of the James River in the year of our Lord, one thousand seven hundred and twelve [1712]. First, I shall thank you, the Gentlemen to [of] the [Jamestown] Colony of Virginia, for bringing me here...

Your invitation reached me on my modest plantation in the West Indies where I have experimented with some of the newest and still the oldest methods for control of slaves…In my bag here, I have a fool proof method for controlling your Black slaves…

I have outlined a number of differences among the slaves; and I take these differences and make them bigger. I use fear, distrust and envy for control purposes…On top of my list is "Age"…the second is "Color"…there is intelligence, size [weight], sex, size of plantation, status on plantation, attitude of owners, whether the slaves live in the valley, on a hill, East, West, North, South, have fine hair or coarse hair, or is tall or short…I shall assure you that distrust is stronger than trust, and envy is stronger than adulation, respect or admiration…Don't forget you must pitch the old Black vs. the young Black male…the dark skin slaves vs. the light skin slaves…the female vs. the male…You must also have your White servants and overseers distrust all Blacks, but it is necessary that your slaves trust and depend on us. They must love, respect and trust only us." (Anonymous Author, "How to Keep a Black Man Down: from One White Slave Owner to Another" Baltimore, MD: public school "lesson" found at a bus stop circa. 2006)

At first glance, nothing appears to be wrong or harmful about "Mr. Willie's" speech being an "educational" tool. However, since the speech starts with the caption that "Lynchburg, VA was named after Willie Lynch," serious "inconsistencies" arise that negates any alleged "educational" value to the story. To see this, one can refer to *Webster's Dictionary* where the following is given on "Lynchburg, Virginia" and "Lynch law":

1.) Lynchburg [VA]—named after John Lynch, reputed founder [of a ] city in central Virginia, on the James River…

2.) Lynch Law—[term originating in America] formerly [called] "Lynch's law" [and] named after captain William

Lynch (1742–1820), [who was a] member of a vigilance committee in Pittsylvania, Virginia, in 1780. ["Lynch law" is] the lawless practice of killing by lynching. (*Webster's New World Dict. of the Amer. Lang.*, 2d coll. ed., s.v. "Lynchburg [VA]" and "Lynch Law.")

As seen, two individuals bearing the name "Lynch" are given: (1) John Lynch—the son of landowner Charles Lynch and Quaker mom Sarah Clark-Lynch (she being an active Quaker opposed to slavery)—he reputedly founded "Lynchburg" city, in Central Virginia along the James River, in "1786" AD; and (2) "Captain William Lynch"—a resident of "Pittsylvania [now Halifax, County]" near the Roanoke River in Southwest Virginia—he was born in AD "1742."

These definitions imply that the only "Willie Lynch" validated to exist is "Captain William "Willie" Lynch" (AD 1742)—whose birth occurred "thirty years after" the AD 1712 "Willie Lynch" speech was given (1742—1712 = 30), and whose name could not possibly have been given to the "Lynchburg, Virginia" ascribed to "John Lynch" some "seventy-four years after" the "Willie Lynch" speech of AD 1712 (1786–1712=74). In fact, *Wikipedia's* article entitled "William Lynch (Lynch Law)" stated,

> Captain William Lynch (1742–1820) was a man from Pittsylvania County, Virginia, who claimed to be the source of the terms "Lynch Law" and "Lynching." He is not the Willie Lynch who alledgedly made the William Lynch speech in 1712, as the date on this apocryphal speech precedes Lynch's birth by thirty years. (*Wikipedia*, s.v. "William Lynch [Lynch Law]," http://en.wikipedia. org/wiki/William_Lynch_(Lynch Law). Retrieved 23 March 2011)

Moreover, the "James River" was named the "Fluvanna River" until about AD "1750." Thus, "Willie Lynch" should have given his "Slave Control Speech" on the banks of either the "Fluvanna River" in "1712" AD or the "James River" about "1750" AD. Such is the real deal for the "Willie Lynch Speech" now circulating in modern African American communities.

Next, there is the modern "myth" that "slavery" was mostly a "Southern" practice. In reality, the practice flourished quite well in the "Big Apple" or "New York City" during America's 1600s–1700s Colonial period. This fact was brought to light during a 30 October 2005 interview held between *Baltimore Sun* reporter Michael Hill and University of Maryland (College Park) history professor Ira Berlin. In his article entitled "Forgotten Slaves," Mr. Hill asked the professor about the reasons for creating the New York Historical Society's "Slavery in New York" exhibit. While giving the reasons, professor Berlin dispelled the "myth" by stating,

> New York City in the 17th [1600s] and 18th [1700s] centuries was the largest slave-holding city on the North American continent. There were more slaves in New York than in Charlestown [SC] or New Orleans [LA]. Slaves made up a quarter of New York's population at various times, and probably a third or more of its workforce. Probably nothing moved in or out of New York without a slave touching it at one time or another. The institution is really quite significant in any understanding of the history of New York. (Michael Hill, "Forgotten Slaves," *Baltimore Sun*, 30 October 2005, Ideas, p. 1F)

Another "myth" that some modern Americans (black, white, or other) make much ado about concerns whether or not a person was "free" or "slave" during America's pre-Civil War Era. However, for people to really understand what such terms meant during that period, they must first free themselves of mythical views about "freedom" and "slavery." Indeed, during the mid-1700s both the "Industrial Revolution" and "Capitalism" were getting underway in England, America, and various other European countries: the Industrial Revolution making its debut after the invention of power tools and machines, which replaced hand tools and made large-scale production possible (1760); Capitalism making its debut after Scottish economist Adam Smith published his book *The Wealth of Nations*, which advocated an "ideal relationship" between free laborers and business owners (1776).

Despite their progressive-sounding names, what these two events meant was the disposal of a "large workforce"—free or slave. In turn, this meant that the "free" wage-earner's economic well-being faced hardship and was not the "bed of roses" that many modern Americans equate with the words *citizen* and *free*. Indeed, in their work entitled *The HPAC and V Contractor's Reference Book and License Review*, twentieth-century authors John Gladstone and George Perpich stated exactly what being a "free" worker meant during the early Industrial-capitalistic era. They said,

> In the early days of the Industrial Revolution horses were considerably better cared for than [free] wage-laborers. A horse was a capital investment. As such its owner must take care not to over work it nor allow it to fall into poor health. No one "owned" the [free] wage-laborer. The capitalist had no concern about the [free] worker's health or life. He was expendable. (John Gladstone and George Perpich, *The HPAC and V Contractor's Reference Book and License Review*, 2d ed. (Coral Gables, FL: Engineer's Press, 1991), p. 1.1 note 2)

Given the financial revelation that a "horse" was a "capital investment" that the "owner" had to take care of, then what was the "investment status" of a "slave"? Was not a "slave" also a "capital investment"? If so, then this implies that a "slave" was better cared for than a "free" laborer (however meager the slave was housed, fed, and clothed). Thus, notwithstanding the cases of "slave abuse" modernly reported, people must be careful not to assume that such was the widespread rule—since a "slave" was a "capital investment"!

Another "myth" that needs to be addressed involves George Washington. On the one hand, some modern African Americans believe that Mr. Washington was a "racist"—probably because he was a high-ranking, slave-owning Freemason who, like many of the "white" Masonic brothers of his era, did not think it proper to associate with free "black" people or give them a charter to practice Freemasonry. However, do these facts warrant indicting him as a "racist"? *Wikipedia's* article "George Washington and slavery" gave a biographical sketch that disputes the "racist" attitude ascribed to him. Said the article,

> George Washington...was a slave owner for practically all of his life. Washington was the only major planter among the seven Founding Fathers [Alexander Hamilton, Benjamin Franklin, George Washington, James Madison, John Adams, John Jay, Thomas Jefferson] to emancipate his slaves...At various times in his life, Washington privately expressed strong support for the gradual abolition of slavery.
>
> Although Washington personally opposed the institution of slavery after the American Revolutionary War, as President he authorized emergency financial and military relief to French slave owners in Haiti in 1791 to suppress a slave rebellion. In 1789 Congress passed and Washington signed a law that reaffirmed the previous ban on slavery in the Northwest Territory; it did not free slaves already in the territory...Washington signed the 1793 Fugitive Slave Law, the first to provide for the right of slaveholders to recapture slaves even in free states that had abolished slavery...Washington's slaves worked from dawn until dark unless injured or ill; they could be whipped for running away or for other infractions. They were fed, clothed, and housed as inexpensively as possible...

Before the American Revolution, Washington expressed no moral reservation about slavery, but by 1778 he had stopped selling slaves because he did not want to break up their families. The historian Henry Wiencek speculates that Washington's slave buying…may have initiated a gradual reassessment of slavery. According to Wiencek, his thoughts on slavery may have also been influenced by the rhetoric of the American Revolution, the example of the thousands of blacks who enlisted in the army to fight for independence, the anti-slavery sentiments of his idealistic abolitionist aide John Laurens [Henry Laurens' son], and his knowledge of the ability of the enslaved black poet[ess] Phillis Wheatley, who in 1775 wrote a poem in his honor [entitled "To His Excellency, George Washington," which prompted Washington to invite her to his Mount Vernon home]…(*Wikipedia*, s.v. "George Washington and slavery," http://en.wikipedia.org/wiki/George_Washington_and_slavery. Retrieved 20 January 2014)

Next, there is the "myth" about a "lawn jockey" statue named Jocko and how it originated when George Washington crossed the Delaware River to contest British Hessian forces at Trenton, New Jersey, in 1776. Concisely put, the story goes that a twelve-year-old African American boy named Jocko Graves froze to death during that night while holding either a latern or the reins of Washington's horse. General Washington was said to have been so moved by the incident that he ordered a statue made of the young man, as a national symbol of "patriotism" and placed it on his Mount Vernon residence. (Earl Koger Sr., *Jocko: a legend of the American Revolution*, Englewoods Cliffs, NJ: Prentice-Hall, 1976. Also see: Chester M. Hampton, "Curbstone Jockey Figure Based On Statue Of Real Negro Hero Of Revolutionary War," *The Sunday Oregonian*, 27 September 1979, p. 29.)

However, modern correspondences between Virginia's Mount Vernon and Baltimore's Enoch Pratt Librarians about the "Jocko Graves" story reveal that no such statue was among

Mount Vernon's artifacts and no historical record exist of anyone named Jocko freezing to death during the Delaware Crossing event. Thus, many historians dismiss the "Jocko Graves" story as modern "urban legend." Whatever the case, the "Jocko legend" implies that Mr. Washington had a "sensitive side" to his character and was not the "cruel" slave-owning person that some "moderns" may depict him as. This being said, it is best to clear up a few points concerning the "Jocko statue."

The statue was used in ancient Greek sculptures (circa 500 BC), by America's Underground Railroad System (circa AD 1850s), and in Frenchman Frederic Auguste Bartholdi's Statue of Liberty design (commissioned in 1865, completed 28 October 1886) to honor America's Independence (4 July 1776) and the Thirteenth Amendment's passage (18 December 1865).

Moreover, the icon is depicted in England's the "Leaky Boot Pubmaster" logo and Australia's the "Faithful Groomsman" inside water fountain plumbing fixture. Most importantly, the meaning underlying the Jocko statue—or its Chinaman, Cavalier Spirit, Faithful Groomsman, Leaky Boot, and Wooden Native American Tobacco Store counterparts—is that of "Hospitality, Welcome Home, Horseracing, and Underground Railroad Assistance." ("Lawn Jockey History:1776–1913," http://www.lawnjock.com/lawn jockey_history.html. Retrieved 30 March 2011.)

Despite such rich urban legend and history, the Jocko statue is subject to "Race Card Evil" attack from uninformed "black" and "white" Americans. In fact, *Wikipedia's* "Lawn Jockey" article stated in part,

> A lawn jockey is a small statue of a man in jockey clothes, intended to be placed in yards. Most today are white jockeys, but historically black jockeys were commonplace. The lawn ornament…was a cast replica…of a black man dressed in jockey's clothing and holding up one hand as though taking the reins of a horse. The hand sometimes carried a lantern or a metal ring suitable for hitching a

> horse. Two traditional lawn jockey styles are produced, commonly known as "jocko" and "cavalier spirit." The former is of stockier build, with a hunched posture; the latter is generally slender and erect...The black lawn jockeys often had exaggerated features, such as big eyes with the whites painted in, large red lips, large flat nose and curly hair...with the flesh of the statue a gloss black. These statues are widely considered offensive and racially insensitive and many remaining samples have now been repainted using pink paint for the skin while the original sculpture's exaggerated features remain. (*Wikipedia*, s.v. "Lawn Jockey," http://en.wikipedia.org/wiki/Lawn_Jockey, p. 1. Retrieved 30 March 2011)

Curiously enough, while the statue's "physical form" has often been subject to "racial controversy" in modern American society, the meaning of Jocko's "name" has not. This is unfortunate, because some people may teach the "patriotic" Jocko "legend" without investigating the "name's" origin. This too must be investigated, since it can be subject to "myth" rather than "fact."

In his Essay I, entitled "On the Natural History of the Man-like Apes," Thomas H. Huxley recounted that about AD 1613 one Reverend Samuel Purchas published part one of his book *Purchas his Pilgrimage*—which detailed his adventures exploring Africa's Congo region. Twelve years later, about AD 1625, Purchas published a second part—which detailed the adventures of his neighbor and fellow explorer Andrew Batell. In chapter 3 of the second part, entitled "The Strange Adventures of Andrew Batell," Mr. Purchas recounted that Batell had resided in the Congo for an 18–year period and wrote an account of his discovery of both the great ape and chimpanzee—the two being respectively called in the Congo and Gabon regions "Pongo" and "Engeco, Enche-Eko, Ncheko, N'schego."

In AD 1748, former Jesuit priest Antoine Francois ("Abbe") Prevost translated Batell's account into French under the title *Histoire general des voyages*; and in AD 1766, naturalist Georges

Louis Leclerc (called "Comte de Buffon") did the same. During these successive translations the West African term for *chimpanzee*, "Enche-Eko," was first translated into French by Prevost as "Engeco, Engeko" and later mistranslated by Buffon as "Enjocko, Jocko" when incorporating Prevost's data into his chapter entitled "Les Oran-outangs ou le pongo et le Jocko." Said Huxley in "Essay I,"

> In 1766 Buffon wrote the 14th volume of his work on researches into African Ape species...Buffon found a version of Batell's account of the Pongo and the Engeco, and on attempting to weld together this data in his own chapter...he added a note to the title citing:
>
> "Orang-outang nom de cet animal aux Indes Orientales: Pongo nom de cet animal a Lowando Povince de Congo.
>
> "Jocko, EnJocko, nom de cet animal a Congo que nous avon adopte..." (Thomas H. Huxley, *Man's Place in Nature and other Essays* (New York: E. P. Dutton and Co., 1927), 13, 14)

To this Huxley respectively added in "Essay I" that in the Bongo, Calongo, Mayombe, Manikesoke, and Motimbas provinces,

> [t]he greatest of these two monsters is called Pongo in their languages, and the lesser is called Engeco.
>
> Moreover, at the present day the word Engeco, or N' schego, is applied by the natives of these regions to the smaller of the two great Apes which inhabit them.
>
> The name of "Chimpanzee," by which one of the African Apes is now so well known appears to have come into use in the first half of the eighteenth century [1700s].
>
> Thus it was that Andrew Batell's "Engeco" became metamorphosed into "Jocko" [by Buffon], and the latter shape [term], was spread all over the world, in consequence of the extensive popularity of Buffon's works.
>
> One of the most interesting among the many valuable discoveries made by Dr. Thomas [N.] Savage is the fact

that the natives in the Gabon country of the present day apply to the Chimpanzee a name—"Enche-Eko"—which is obviously identical with the "Engeko" of Batell. (Ibid., 4, 6, 10, 14, and 20)

Such is the origin and meaning of "Jocko's name." In fact, *Webster's Dictionary* defined the terms *Jocko* and *Jockey* as follows:

Jocko—[a] French [word], [derived from the] earlier [word] *engeco* [,which itself is] derived from *ncheko*, the native name in West Africa [for] a chimpanzee or a monkey.
  Jockey—[a word derived from] *Jocky, Jockie,* [the] northern English and Scottish form of *Jacky*...[which came from the AD 1100–1500 Middle English terms] *Jacke, Jake* [and] Old French *Jaque, Jaques* [and] Ecclesiastical [Church] Late Latin *Jacobus, Jacob* and used as a nickname for *John*, and sometimes, for *James* or *Jacob.* (*Webster's New World Dict. of the Amer. Lang.,* s.v. "jocko," "jockey," and "jack" [no.1] respectively [italics partly ours])

Obviously, a big difference exists between the famous Lawn Statue being named "Jocko" (ape, chimp, monkey) and "Jockey" (Jacob, Jake, James, John). And as should be expected, "Race Card" dealers will use the "negative" of meaning of Jocko's name to fool themselves into thinking that it somehow makes them intellectually "superior." Yet they should be careful about doing so—since Mr. Huxley showed that the "Great White Ape" or "Mandrill" was also among the "Pongo-Jocko" discoveries (*Man's Place*, "Essay I," 10–12). Thus anyone of any color or ethnicity can be an "ape-chimp-monkey" or "chump" by playing the "Race Card Evil" game (an ironic twist to the "man originated from monkey" theory).

Another "myth" that needs clearing up involves the American government's founders' purpose in creating the "Great Seal of the United States." During the "Dred Scott" and "Lincoln-Douglas," era some people claimed that America was founded for the "White Man." Although Harriet-Beecher-Stowe, Justice Benjamin Curtis, Abe Lincoln, and a host of congressmen disproved the claim, about a century and a half later (as of 2015) some Americans still cling to and teach this "white man's land" doctrine. And surprisingly, one well-known modern African American leader gave a speech stating that such was true because the Great Seal of the United States was designed to represent six "White" countries that migrated to Colonial America. However, *Wikipedia's* article entitled "Great Seal of the United States" said,

> On July 4, 1776…the [Second] Continental Congress named the first committee to design a Great Seal, or national emblem, for the country…The United States needed an official symbol of sovereignty to formalize and seal (or sign) international treaties and transactions. It took six years, three committees, and the contributions of fourteen men before the Congress finally accepted a design (which included elements proposed by each of the three committees) in 1782.
>
> The first committee consisted of Benjamin Franklin, Thomas Jefferson, and John Adams…they had little experience in heraldry and sought the help of Pierre Eugene du Simitiere, an artist living in Philadelphia… In August [1776], Du Simitiere showed his design…The shield had six sections, each representing "the Countries from which these States have been peopled" (England, Scotland, Ireland, France, Germany, and Holland [the Netherlands]), surrounded by the initials of all thirteen states…On August 20, 1776 the committee presented their report to Congress. The committee members chose Du Simitiere's design…Congress was however not impressed, and on the same day ordered that the report "lie on the table" [be postponed until another time], ending the work of the [first] committee. (*Wikipedia*, s.v. "Great Seal of the United States," http://en.wikipedia.org/wiki/Great_Seal_of_the_United_States#History. Retrieved 7 March 2015)

As shown, it took six years (1776–1782), three committees (1776, 1780, 1782), and ideas from fourteen people to design "The Great Seal of The United States" (first used in 1782 and officially adopted by Congress in 1789)—Du Simitiere's "six nations" idea neither used nor adopted. Thus anyone claiming that "America was made for the White Man, because Six White Nations peopled the Thirteen Colonies" is either unfamiliar with the Great Seal's history or intellectually challenged!

Another area that needs to be "demythologized" is America's pre-Civil War Era—as it related to slavery. For example, in the landmark 1968 U.S. Supreme Court case styled *Jones v. Alfred H. Mayer Co.* Justice William O. Douglas enumerated the disabilities affecting slaves prior to the Civil War by quoting from W. E. B. Dubois' *Black Reconstruction in America* (1964):

> Slaves were not considered men…They could own nothing; they could make no contracts; they could hold no property, nor traffic in property; they could not hire [themselves] out; they could not legally marry nor constitute families; they could not control their children; they could not appeal from their master; they could be punished at will. (*Jones v. Mayer, Co.*, 392 U.S. 409, 444, 1968)

Later in *Jones v. Mayer*, when quoting from the June 1881 *North American Review* article about Frederick Douglass' "The Color Line," Justice Douglas noted that "Without crime or offense against law or gospel, the colored man is the Jean Valjean of American society" (392 US 409, 447). Given such statements, one should ask whether such "badges of slavery" were true across the board during pre–Civil War years? Was slavery the abysmal horror story one modernly hears or reads about? Significantly, concerning slaves being unable to hire themselves out, in "Forgotten Slaves" professor Berlin stated,

> Some of the [New York City] slaves had much more
> freedom because they were "living out." The houses of
> white New Yorkers were so small, [that] slaveholders first
> began stuffing folks away in the attic and basement, and
> then found it easier to give the slave a little money and
> let him find a place to live. Slaves were happy to take the
> offer, which gave them much more freedom of movement,
> a greater chance of getting together for whatever purposes:
> religious, recreational, educational, conspiratorial.
>
> Slavery takes on the characteristics of its environment.
> It is different in different places. It is different in New
> York [Manhattan] than it is out in Brooklyn. Different in
> Queens than it is on Long Island. Urban slavery is a very
> different kind of institution. In cities, you need a different
> system of social control that does, in fact, give blacks a
> bit more elbow room than they have on the plantations.
> ("Fogotten Slaves," p. 3F)

Undoubtedly, professor Berlin's observation about "city" slavery presents a humorous "old woman in the shoe" picture not considered by modern Americans. But the professor also presented a "geo-economic" side of slavery not considered by people when talking about the pre-Civil War era—namely, that slavery was not the one-sided "agrarian Southern slavery vs. industrial Northern freedom" picture often "mythically" painted.

In agreement with Mr. Berlin's view, historians Franklin and Schweninger added that escaping slaves did not always flee "North." Rather, many slaves fled "South"—and their reason for doing so was a matter of "economics." Indeed, when speaking about a female slave named Jane who "frequently ran away from her [cotton planting] master [Charles C. Jones, Sr., of Liberty County, GA] to find work," Franklin and Schweninger stated in their *Runaway Slaves,*

For some runaways freedom lasted only a few months, but for others it was longer if they eventually merged with the free black population. Those who became successful in creating a new identity were usually able to find work. As suggested by the experiences of Jane in Savannah [GA], the demand in southern cities for a wide range of black workers, both skilled and unskilled, remained strong during the nineteenth century [1800s]. Although there were ebbs and flows in the economies of southern cities, there were few periods when hired slaves were not in demand. Wages varied, but black workers could command between $75 and $150 a year in the 1820s and 1830s and up to $20 a month during the 1850s. They worked as laborers, dockhands, domestics, laundresses, gardners, horse tenders, servants, hod carriers [wooden long-handeled troughs to carry bricks, mortar, etc., on the shoulders], bricklayers, stonemasons, carpenters, draymen [heavy load cart drivers]…steamboat stewards, waiters, and cooks. In many urban areas, as competing whites pointed out, slaves dominated certain occupations. (*Runaway Slaves: Rebels on the Plantation*, 124, 134)

And in agreement with professor Berlin's statement about slaves "hiring themselves out," Franklin and Schweninger said,

Although prohibited by law, the practice of permitting slaves to hire [out] their own time was widespread. Primarily urban [i.e., a city practice], self-hire offered advantages to both owner and slave. Bondsmen and women would gain a measure of independence by being permitted to seek out an employer, negotiate wages and working conditions, and pay the owner [master] an agreed-upon sum. Often they [slaves] were permitted to retain a portion of their wages. Owners on the other hand did not have to bother with negotiating hiring agreements and could expect a good income. The comments of Charles C. Jones, Jr. that hundreds of slaves in

Savannah [GA] "never see their masters except at pay day, live out of their yards, hire themselves [out] without written permit" was applicable to most cities in the South. In fact, the demand for black workers—often with no question asked—was so great at times that slaves earned good wages. Perhaps there is no better illustration of this than the protest meeting of Richmond [VA] freedmen following the Civil War. Their earning power, they asserted, was half what it had been as hired slaves!

Many runaways who had fled to towns and cities tried to pass themselves off as self-hired slaves. It took self-confidence and audacity to approach whites, create a fictitious identity, and ask for emploment, but some runaways convinced employers that they had been sent by their owners to find work…In some cities, hired slaves were supposed to have a ticket or wear a badge, and everywhere they were presumed to have been given permission by their owners. But slaves could forge tickets, acquire false badges, and argue convincingly that their owner, usually located some distance away, had sent them thither [there] to find work. (Ibid., 124, 134–35)

In fact, when explaining why slavery did not readily die out in New York after its legal abolishment in 1827, Professor Berlin said concerning the financial, political, cultural, regional character of the peculiar institution,

So the death of the institution of slavery in New York stretched out…after people thought they had put a stake in the heart of slavery, it actually becomes more important in new York because the city becomes the center of the cotton trade. The economy of New York comes to revolve around cotton. New York bankers fund the expansion of slavery in the South. New York manufacturers are making shoes for slaves. The New York textile industry gets its start making cheap clothes for slaves.

Since we know politics follows economics, it is not surprising that New York politicians are much beholden to their Southern counterparts and eager to defend the Institution of slavery. When the South started seceding in 1860, the mayor of New York says he wants to seceed along with it. New York politicians were great opponents of [Abraham] Lincoln and his emancipatory policies.

And since culture follows politics, you see in the antebellum years the great Southern planters coming to New York, meeting their bankers and brokers, being wined and dined, as you would your best customer. Their kids meet, they intermarry, and these great New York merchant families become intertwined with Southern plantation families. ("Forgotten Slaves," pp. 1F-3F passim)

Most importantly, Professor Berlin explained that it took the joint effort of both "blacks" and "whites" to oust slavery from New York prior to Lincoln's era:

The institution [of slavery] had great staying power. There were over 10,000 slaves in New York in the third decade of the 19th century [1830s]. The institution would not have gone away without considerable effort by both blacks themselves and their white abolitionist allies…During this time, New York is also an important site of the movement against slavery. Black and white New York played a large role in [slavery's] abolition. (Ibid., pp. 1F-3F passim)

As said, the biggest "myth" about America's pre-Civil War Era is the "traditionally" taught or believed picture of well-to-do free "Whites" buying-owning-trading enslaved "Blacks." As earlier shown, about a half-century after the 1619 Jamestown landing of "twenty" indentured Africans (labeled "Negroes"), these "oppressed" people were buying up so many "white" slaves that laws were passed to stop it! And as said, the "contradiction" did not end there. In their *Runaway Slaves*, Franklin and Schweninger also noted that a number of free "black" slaveholders flourished during the pre-Civil War Era—many of whom were not very "understanding" about their people's plight and treated them as badly as their "white" counterparts. Said they about these "black" capitalists,

> Free blacks who controlled slaves for profit dealt with runaways in much the same manner as their white counterparts. Eliza Pinckney, a free mulatto, for example, received in 1810 a trust conveyance for "a number of negroes" from Thomas Pickney Jr., a member of one of South Carolina's most prominent families…The largest free black slaveholder in the South, John Carruthers Stanly of North Carolina, faced a number of problems in the 1820s in dealing with the slave labor force on his three Turpentine plantations in Craven County. With a total of 163 slaves, Stanly was a harsh, profit-minded taskmaster, and his field hands would run away. Stanly dealt with this through his two white overseers and with a spy network that included a few trusted slaves…Nor did Stanly have any pangs of conscience about selling children away from their parents or holding free blacks in bondage. (*Runaway Slaves*, 199–200)
>
> Another large free black slaveholder, sugar planter Andrew Durnford of Louisiana, had fewer problems with runaways than his counterpart in North Carolina…A large majority of profit-oriented free black slaveholders resided in the Lower South…Free black slave owners who lived in urban areas—Charleston [SC], Savannah [GA], Mobile [AL], Natchez [KY], and New Orleans [LA]—also faced difficulties with their slave property…Free black slave owners felt few pangs of guilt selling [off] troublesome property [slaves]. (Ibid., 200–01 passim)

In light of such truths, it is easy to see that the real picture of antebellum (pre–Civil War) slavery has been "whitewashed."

Thus, one should also investigate possible "myths" about the roles played by people fighting on either side in America's Civil War—free or not.

On the one hand, Justice Douglas, quoting from *The Life and Writings of Frederick Douglass* (1955), noted in *Jones v. Mayer* that Frederick Douglass said some sixteen years "after" the Civil War ended (c. 1881):

> Of all the races and varieties of men which have suffered from this feeling [of discrimination], the colored people of this country have endured most. They can resort to no disguises which will enable them to escape its deadly aim. They carry in front the evidence which marks them for persecution. They stand at the extreme point of difference from the Caucasian race, and their African origin can be instantly recognized, though they may be several removes [generations] from the typical African race…They are Negroes—and that is enough, in the eyes of this unreasoning prejudice, to justify indignity and violence. In nearly every department of American life they are confronted by this insidious influence…It meets them at the workshop and factory…It meets them at the church, at the hotel, at the ballot box…in the jury box. (*Jones v. Mayer, Co.*, 392 U.S. 409, 446–47; Justice Douglas quoting from *The Life and Writings of Frederick Douglass*, 343–44, 1955).

On the other hand, at the Civil War's start (c. 1861), Frederck Douglass noted that the Confederate army contained a number of "blacks" in its ranks assigned to various duties—some of which were soldier-oriented. This observation twenty-first century American columnist Walter Williams revealed in his January 2000 *Washington Times* article entitled "Overlooked black Confederates." Said he,

> During our [Civil] War of 1861, former slave Frederick Douglass observed, "There are at the present moment,

many colored men in the Confederate Army doing duty not only as cooks, servants and laborers, but as real soldiers, having muskets on their shoulders and bullets in their pockets, ready to shoot down…and do all that soldiers may do to destroy the federal government." (Walter Williams, "Overlooked black Confederates," *Washington Times*, 31 January 2000, Commentary, p. A13)

And should one think that such behavior was a "forced" feeling of loyalty on the part of "victimized" slaves (later called the Stockholm Syndrome), Mr. Williams added,

In April 1861, a Petersburg, VA, newspaper proposed "three cheers for the patriotic free Negroes of Lynchburg" after 70 blacks offered "to act in whatever capacity may be assigned to them" in defense of Virginia.

Erwin L. Jordan's book "Black Confederates and Afro-Yankees in Civil War Virginia" cites eye-witness accounts…Jordan cites one case where a captured group of white slave-owners and blacks were offered freedom if they would take an oath of allegiance to the United States. One free black indignantly replied, "I can't take no such oaf [oath] as dat [that]. I'm a secesh [secessionist]." A slave in the group, upon learning that his master refused to take the oath, said, "I can't take no oath dat massa [master] won't take." A second slave said, "I ain't going out here on no dishonorable terms." One of the slave-owners took the oath but his slave, who didn't take the oath, returning to Virginia under flag of truce, expressed disgust at his master's disloyalty saying, "massa had no principles" (Ibid., p. A13)

Not only did contradictory behavior exist regarding some "blacks" fighting for the Confederate cause; there was similar behavior for some "whites" fighting for the Union cause. Again Mr. Williams noted,

It was not just Southern generals who owned slaves but Northern generals owned them as well. Gen. Ulysses Grant's slaves had to wait [until passage of] the 13th Amendment for freedom. When asked why he didn't free his slaves earlier, Gen. Grant said, "Good help is so hard to come by these days." (Ibid., p. A13)

And when responding to *Washington Times* columnist Armstrong Williams's 19 December 1999 Commentary "Refolding rite for the Confederate flag," Mr. George Still said in the 28 December 1999 *Washington Times* "Columnist misunderstands South Carolina flag fight" article,

By the same token, one need look no further than the family of Ulysses S. Grant for an example of a slave-owning Unionist. Julia Grant (the famous general's wife) owned slaves throughout the war. (George Still, "Columnist misunderstands South Carolina flag fight," *Washington Times*, 28 December 1999, Editorial (Letters), p. A18)

Even famed Confederate General Robert E. Lee's actions and beliefs must be carefully scrutinized before one can pass judgment on him. For instance, he fought for the Southern Cause during America's Civil War and, like Grant, General Lee was also a slaveowner—being designated executor of numerous slaves and large landholdings upon his father-in-law's death in 1857. However, these "facts" are not sufficient to convict Lee of being either "racist" or "pro slavery." Indeed, regarding Robert E. Lee's personal views on slavery, *Wikipedia's* biographical sketch on this son of Revolutionary War Major General Henry (Light Horse Harry) Lee stated in part,

Since the end of the Civil War, it has often been suggested [that] Lee was in some sense opposed to slavery... [Historian Douglas S.] Freeman's analysis [at p. 64 of his book *R. E. Lee, A Biography*] [1934] places Lee's attitude toward slavery and abolition in a historical context:

This [pro-slavery opinion] was the prevailing view among most religious people of Lee's class in the border states. They believed that slavery existed because God willed it and they thought it would end when God so ruled. The time and the means were not theirs to decide, conscious though they were of the ill-effects of Negro slavery on both races. Lee shared these convictions of his neighbors without having come in contact with the worst evils of African bondage. He spent no considerable time in any state south of Virginia from the day he left Fort Pulaski in 1831 until he went to Texas in 1856. All his reflective years had been passed in the North or in the border states. He had never been among the blacks on a cotton or rice plantation…[In his 27 December 1856 letter to his wife, Mary Anna Lee, he said:] "In this enlightened age, there are few I believe, but what will acknowledge, that slavery as an institution, is a moral and political evil in any Country. It is useless to expatiate on its disadvantages. I think it however a greater evil to the white man than to the black race, and while my feelings are strongly enlisted in behalf of the latter ["blacks"], my sympathies are more strong for the former ["whites"]. The blacks are immeasurably better off here than in Africa, morally, socially and physically. The painful discipline they are undergoing, is necessary for their instruction as a race, and I hope will prepare and lead them to better things. How long their subjugation may be necessary is known and ordered by a wise Merciful Providence [God]."

(Robert E. Lee," *Wikipedia*, http://en.wikipedia.org/wiki/Robert_E._Lee, pp. 7–8. Retrieved 3 July 2014)

And regarding Robert E. Lee fighting against the Union, the article said,

Lee privately ridiculed the Confederacy in letters in early 1861, denouncing secession as "revolution" and a betrayal of the efforts of the [government's] founders. Writing to his son William Fitzhugh, Lee stated, "I can anticipate no greater calamity for the country than a dissolution of the Union." While he was not opposed in principle to secession, Lee wanted all peaceful ways of resolving the difference between North and South…and was one of the few to foresee a long and difficult war…[While still a US Army officer] He had earlier been asked by one of his lieutenants if he intended to fight for the Confederacy or the Union, to which Lee replied, "I shall never bear arms against the Union, but it may be necessary for me to carry a musket in the defense of my native state, Virginia, in which case I shall not prove recreant [unfaithful] to my duty." Meanwhile, Lee ignored an offer of command from the Confederate States of America. After Lincoln's call for troops to put down the rebellion, it was obvious that Virginia would quickly secede. Lee on April 18 [,1861] was offered by presidential advisor Francis P. Blair a role as major general to command the defense of Washington. He replied: "Mr. Blair, I look upon secession as anarchy. If I owned the four millions of slaves in the South I would sacrifice [free] them all to the Union; but how can I draw my sword upon Virginia, my native state?"

Lee resigned from the U.S. Army on April 20 and took up command of the Virginia state forces on April 23 [,1861]. (Ibid., p. 9)


Such contradictions should make one ask why did the average American (Northerner or Southerner) fight in a war rife with paradoxes? This question was asked and answered by twenty-first-century American David Mcquiston. Responding to Mr. Armstrong Williams's 19 December 1999 column, Mr. Mcquiston said,

Actually there were many reasons why the Civil War was fought. Slavery was one of them. Only the very richest of Southerners could afford to own a slave. The going rate for a slave was about $1,200, and you could buy a nice farm for about $600. So why did Johnny Reb fight? Was it to preserve his rich neighbor's right to own a slave? I don't think so…So again, why did Johnny Reb fight? His homeland had been invaded [after a federal base was attacked]. For that matter, why did Billy Yank fight? Largely, [because] he got drafted.

"Columnist misunderstands…flag fight" (p. A18)

And to this observation, Mr. George Still added in the "flag fight" column,

More telling is the well-documented story of the ragged Confederate rifleman captured by Union troops. Able to tell by his clothes and hardscrabble manner that he was too poor to afford an extra pair of shoes, let alone a human being [slave], his captors asked him why he fought for the wealthy slave owners. He looked at them and said they missed the point: "I'm fightin' cause you're down here." (Ibid., p. A18)

Indeed, oftentimes many of us do "miss the point"—because we are poorly informed, willfully ignorant, or readily accept "myths" (or lies) about a given idea, person, place, or thing. And one of the best indicators of this truth is the modern controversy over the Confederate flag formerly flown at South Carolina's state capital.

On one side are those who say the Confederate Flag represents African Slavery and treason. This view Armstrong Williams stated in his 19 December 1999 *Washington Times* column. On the other side are those who say the Confederate Flag represents ideas other than African Slavery and treason—ideas embodied in the 1776 Revolution and Southern heritage. On this point George still said,

In his column, which contains a surprising number of statements that suggests a poor familiarity with American history, Mr. Williams makes two statements worth discussing.

He refers to the [Confederate Battle] flag as a commemoration of the "illegal" secession of the [11] Southern states. He also writes that claims that the flag honors any political ideal other than the support of slavery insult the intelligence of every U.S. citizen…To condemn South Carolina for flying a Confederate flag…one must be just as ready to condemn any reverence for any U.S. flags that flew before passage in 1865 of the 13th Amendment, which abolished slavery. (Ibid., p. A18)

And twenty-first century American Martha M. Boltz said,

In one of Mr. Williams' concluding paragraphs, he says, "Let us not blindly defend this flag as a unique symbol of Southern heritage…" Mr. Williams applies this statement to the Confederate flag, totally ignoring the fact that the same words apply to the Stars and Stripes…The Confederate flag should remain as a symbol of a proud Southern spirit, Southern heritage and a positive link with Southerners in a now unified country. To demand its removal diminishes all of us who cherish the past and yet look to the future. (Ibid., p. A18)

And twenty-first century American David McQuiston added,

Chief Justice Roger B. Taney told Lincoln that no treason had been committed. The United States had seceded from England in a similar manner…It was the political left against the political right. We see the same conflict going on today. When this country [America] was founded, it was founded as 13 separate entities…In fact, the [1783 Versailles] Peace [Treaty]…that settled the Revolutionary War reported out 13 separate treaties, one for each sovereign state. The left wing wanted the federal government to be the "super-state," over all the states. (Ibid., p. A18)

Either way one looks at it, the Confederate flag is a "symbol" to people. Thus, before condemning or upholding any symbol people should ask themselves "What is its actual meaning?" In an effort to clear up "fact" from "myth" surrounding the Confederate flag, twentieth-century American political historian Edward Merton Coulter said in his *Encyclopaedia Britannica* article entitled "Confederate States of America",

> The love of the Old Union was reflected not only in copying the Federal Constitution but also in the search for a flag. The [Confederate] Congressional Committee appointed to design a flag received many suggestions for a modification of the Stars and Stripes and even to take over the flag itself. The result was the *Stars and Bars* [4 March 1861], which continued the red, white and blue colours but had only three stripes; the field was blue with 7 white stars. However, this was enough to confuse it with the United States flag. Confederate troops at the first battle of Bull Run had difficulty, in the heat and dust of battle, in distinguishing their own reinforcements from those of the enemy. To prevent a repetition of this a new banner, the *Battle Flag* was designed, its red field crossed diagonally by a blue cross with 13 white stars. Despite its wide use, however, this famous flag was never officially adopted. In May [1,] 1863 the Confederate congress adopted a second national flag, known as the *Stainless Banner*. It was pure white with the Battle Flag in the left corner. Because this flag, when hanging limp, looked too much like a flag of truce, the Confederate congress on March 4, 1865, changed it by placing a broad red bar across its end. This [*Stainless Banner with broad red vertical bar* at outer edge] was the last [official] flag of the Confederacy. (Edward Merton Coulter, "Confederate States of America," *Encyc. Brit.*, rev. 14th ed., 1965, vol. 6, 286, brackets and italics ours).

Thus, the "battle flag" was never the Confederacy's "official" flag—it was simply an "army" flag (the Union Army also had its own flag), and its "purpose" was "to distinguish between Confederate and Union forces" so that a soldier could hopefully stay alive and avoid capture! In other words, the flags at war (to which "allegiance" was pledged) were the US flag (Union Jack) and the Confederate States of America flag (Stars and Bars).

Although the controversy over the unofficial, but media-popularized, Battle Flag may continue until the proverbial cows come home, it is prudent to heed the view given by twenty-first century American columnist Paul Greenberg. In his 31 May 2000 *Washington Times* article entitled "Flag fight fatigue," Mr. Greenberg said,

> Some things must be faced: the old [Battle] Flag does represent slavery. It may inspire some of us, but it offends others…Some things must be faced: The old [Battle] Flag represents more than slavery. It is a universal symbol of Southernness in general, flown by rock bands in Europe without a trace of ill will. It represents soul food and "ma'am and sir" manners, and countless Confederate Memorial Days. It was the banner of the last great, popular army to respect the laws of chivalry: the Army of Northern Virginia…Some things must be faced: A flag can represent more than one thing. Old Glory [the Union Jack], the Flag of freedom, represented something else when it flew over the Trail of Tears. It flew over shameful scenes when a [Native American] people was dispossessed [of their land] and herded into near extinction. There are stains on that Flag too. (Paul Greenberg, "Flag fatigue flap," *Washington Times*, 31 May 2000, Commentary, p. A13)

As should be expected, even the Declaration of Independence's "meaning" is susceptible to "mythical" interpretation. For instance, in his 2 July 2001 *Baltimore Sun* article entitled "The real truth, justice and American way," syndicated columnist Richard Reeves said,

Most of the Declaration of Independence is, in fact, a list of subject grievances against the British crown...But the best stuff, the harnessing of ideas to action, was at the beginning..."We hold these Truths to be self-evident, that all Men are created equal..."

Uh-oh! Those words...are interpreted in many ways today. But in 1776 they were a direct challenge to the "divine right" of kings. "All men are created equal" was not about uplift and the rights or worth of slaves or the poor. Those words meant that the king of England was no better than anyone else.

That represented a fundamental challenge to the established order—and not only in England and North America. It was one thing for a philosopher [John Locke] to write such things. It was another for Jefferson (and Adams and the rest) to endorse them and try to raise an army to win them. The world would never be the same... that is what we celebrate [every July 4th]. (Richard Reeves, "The real truth, justice and American way," *The Baltimore Sun*, 2 July 2001, Editorial, p. 9A)

And with respect to Abe Lincoln, whereas Mr. McQuiston felt that the sixteenth president destroyed the Union rather than saved it, the renowned twentieth century African American historian Lerone Bennett, Jr. apparently accused Lincoln of being a "racist" in his book *Forced Into Glory: Abraham Lincoln's White Dream*. However, in response to a May 2000 *Washington Times* column that addressed Mr. Bennett's book, twenty-first century American Harold Wefald (of Gaithersburg, Maryland) said,

The Washington Times carried a strangely Laudatory review of the book "Forced Into Glory: Abraham Lincoln's White Dream," by Lerone Bennett Jr., executive editor of Ebony Magazine. Mr. Bennett trashes Lincoln as a Racist who never really freed the Slaves...Trashing Lincoln as a Racist is the old story of multi-culturalism—using the progress of America to vilify the men who made that progress possible. (Harold Wefald, "Author Wrong to call Lincoln a Racist," *Washington Times*, 31 May 2000, Editorial, p. A14)

And while Mr. Bennett's view can be deemed as "modern" interpretation, did the African-Americans who lived during Lincoln's era see him as a racist? Apparently not! In response to a March 2000 *Washington Times* article written by twenty-first century American journalist Peter M. Rexford, one reader inquired about the identity of a slave on a stamp commemorating Mr. Lincoln. In response, Reverend Earl K. Holt III of the First Unitarian Church of St. Louis, Missouri, replied to Mr. Rexford's readers,

> The image on the stamp is of "Freedom's Memorial." It was dedicated on April 4, 1876 by President [Ulysses S.] Grant. The 'unidentified black man' on the 13th Amendment stamp...is Archer Alexander..."In brief, the [statue] project was begun by a former ["Black" female] slave who contributed her first earnings as a free woman, five dollars, 'to make a monument to massa Lincoln, the best friend the colored people ever had.'"(Peter M. Rexford, "Slave Shown with Lincoln identified," *Washington Times*, 31 March 2000, Commentary, p. C6)

Given such "myths" and "contradictions," it is critical that Humanity's next generation seriously rethink the American slavery experience in order to put the "Race Card Evil" oriented version "in the course of ultimate extinction."

# 10

# Humanity's Next Generation Rethinking Slavery and the Race Card Evil Game

How long, ye simple ones, will ye love simplicity…and fools hate knowledge?

—Proverbs 1:22 (KJV)

One generation passes and another comes, but the world stays forever.

—Ecclessiastes 1:4 (NAB)

DURING REPORTER HILL'S interview with professor Berlin, the latter made some very important points as their talk drew to a close. Mr. Hill asked, "Do you think the country [America] is beginning to come to terms with its slavery past?" Professor Berlin answered,

There is enormous popular interest in the subject now. This exhibit is one small part of that. You see it in other places. Every major museum…in the movies—Glory, Amistad, Beloved…on TV…the way it has become part of politics, two presidents who have seen fit to go to the coast of Africa, to the slave factory in Goree…You see it in debates about apologies, and the whole question of reparations lurking back there all the time.

All this speaks to a real desire to try to come to terms with slavery, and that, of course, speaks to a desire to come to terms with race. It is not an easy process. Nobody knows exactly how to do it. We—both blacks and whites—don't often do it very well or elegantly. We are often tripping over our ideological shoelaces as we try. People are afraid. I see this in my students, white and black, who are afraid to misspeak, to embarrass themselves or somebody else. But they do want to come to terms with it.

"Forgotten Slaves," p. 3F.

Unfortunately, there lies part of the problem. So many "myths" and "lies" abound about America's slavery story that many modern Americans are "afraid" to misspeak or embarrass themselves or others about it. However, if "modern" Americans sincerely wish to end the country's "race" problem, then they should not fear discussing "past" events in order to distinguish "fact" from "fantasy" and forever close that shameful chapter of history.

A second part of the problem stems from one sector of American society thinking that another sector "owes" actions, apologies, financial reparations to it because of the "Race Card Evil" oriented cheap-labor scheme. This "modern" mind-set is unjust—because it holds others responsible for "past" events that they had nothing to do with! Those who feel that way are either dishonest, misguided, or miss one of the most important biblical principles stated in the Old and New Testaments—namely, the "personal accountability, responsibility" or "sour grapes rule" that said,

> "Fathers shall not be put to death for their children, nor children for the fathers; only for his own guilt shall a man shall be put to death" (Moses, Dt 24:16, NAB).
>
> "In those days they shall no longer say, 'The fathers ate unripe grapes, and the children's teeth are set on edge,' but through his own fault only shall anyone die: the teeth

of him who eats the unripe grapes shall be set on edge" (Jeremiah 31:29, NAB).

"'The fathers…on edge': a proverb used in Israel, expressing the idea that children suffer for the sins of their parents" (cf. Ez 18, 2). "The Israel of the restoration will be characterized instead by personal responsibility and retribution for one's acts" (NAB note on Jer 31:29)

"As I live, says the Lord GOD: I swear that there shall no longer be anyone among you who will repeat this proverb in Israel ["The fathers have eaten sour-green-unripe grapes, thus the children's teeth are on edge"]… only the one who sins shall die…You ask: 'Why is not the son charged with the guilt of his father [or vice versa]?' Because the son has done what is right and just…Only the one who sins shall die. The son shall not be charged with the guilt of his father, nor shall the father be charged with the guilt of his son. The virtuous man's virtue shall be his own, as the wicked man's wickedness shall be his own" (Ezek. 18:1–20, passim, NAB).

"As he [Jesus] passed by he saw a man blind from birth. His disciples asked him, 'Rabbi, who sinned, this man or his parents, that he was born blind?' Jesus answered, 'Neither he nor his parents sinned; it is so that the works of God might be made visible through him'" (Jesus, John 9:1–3, NAB).

Such "biblical" statements clearly say that it is a "divine" sin (crime) to hold a person responsible (answerable, guilty) and accountable (financially liable) for something that the person did not do! Indeed, who among us "moderns" would apologize or pay out of pocket for "past" or "present" personal injuries (trangressions) either done, or allegedly done, by someone else—past or present ancestor? The very idea that people be "paid for labor they did not perform or suffering they did not experience," or that people be paid by others who did not force labor or exact suffering from another is unjust and equivalent to a slavemaster being paid for a slave's labor or suffering—both being an evil that no good will ever come from, since both say, "Let someone else work or suffer and I will benefit (eat, survive) from what that person has worked or suffered for!"

Such a notion contradicts the Fall-from-Eden "personal labor" idea, validates America's "mythical" slavery story and fuels the nation's modern "race" problem (Gen. 3:17–19 and 5:28–29; Heb. 6:1–8, NAB)—especially since none of the other parties involved in the "international" slave trade were held responsible and accountable for their roles in it: African, Black, Catholic, Christian, Dutch, English, Jewish, Moorish, Muslim, Native American, Spanish, and White to name a few! In fact, it may surprise some "African Americans" to learn that some of their "African" kinfolk whose ancestors were involved in the evil are neither ashamed of nor apologize for it. Indeed, in his 14 March 2001 *Wall Street Journal* article entitled "Tangled Roots," reporter G. Pascal Zachary wrote,

> Far from seeing African-Americans as kin, most Ghanaians lump them together with other Americans, calling the whole lot *obruni*, which in the local Twi language means "white" or "foreigner"…"The African role in the slave trade is not an issue in Ghana," says Audrey Gadzekpo, a newspaper columnist in Accra. "People here are totally detached from any guilt or responsibility for their ancestors selling other Africans into slavery. It's like there's some collective amnesia." (G. Pascal Zachary, "Tangled Roots," *The Wall Street Journal*, 14 March 2001, Commentary, pp. A1, A10)

And in her October 2002 *Source* article entitled "Imitation of Life," reporter N. Jamilya Chisolm revealed that when she visited Ghana the women she met did not readily identify with African-Americans—whom the Ghanaians called "white." To Mr. Zachary's observation, she added,

During our talk, Evone and a few of her girlfriends urged me to get out of the sun, warning, "You're going to get black!" I laughed this off, but deep down, I was burnt. I couldn't sun worship without them chuckling and calling me obruni ("white") because I'm medium brown instead of chocolate. Whether I accepted it or not, it was apparent that being a slightly lighter American gave me a different status. While I insisted I wasn't white, Evone's girlfriends made it clear that I wasn't African [black] either. (N. Jamilya Chisolm, "Imitation of Life," *The Source*, October 2002, p. 116)

Moreover, prior to Ms. Chisolm's visit to Ghana in search of her "roots," the country made a "white" Dutchman its king. This interesting fact columnist Anthony Deutsch reported in the 19 January 2000 *Washington Times*. Said he,

A middle-aged, paunchy, unemployed white man plops down on the sofa to watch TV with his children.

Meet King Togbe Korsi Ferdinand Gakpetor II of Ghana.

In Holland, he is Henk Otte, a Dutch construction worker on welfare. In West Africa, he rules part of the lush Volta region, home to tens of thousands of Ewes, who revere him as Togbe, or king.

Mr. Otte, 43, is as Dutch [white] as the Dutch come, born and raised in Amsterdam like his parents...But, while visiting the hometown of his Ghanaian-born [black] wife Mamaa Awo Mepeyo Kpui in 1995, he was identified as the reincarnation of the late chief, his wife's grandfather. (Anthony Deutsch, "Jobless Dutchman finds work as king in Ghana," *Washington Times*, 19 January 2000, p. A1)

Apparently, the underlying message in this "Tale of Two Journalists" is that in Ghana, the "black" or "African American" reporter, Jamilya Chisolm, is considered "white" and "non-African";

whereas the "white" or "German, Dutch, Hollander" construction worker, Henk Otte, is considered "black" and "African." And if one thinks this is contradictory, then consider Mr. Zachary's "Tangled Roots" findings that exposed the returning-to-the-African-motherland "myth," he recounted,

> Kwaku Sintim-Misa, a popular comedian here, likes to tell a joke about the African-American who emigrates to Ghana.
>
> "Brother, I've found my roots!" the African-American crows. A local [resident] shakes his head, wondering why anyone with a coveted United States passport would chose to move to Ghana. "Move to the Motherland?" the Ghanaian cries, "I want to escape the Motherland."
>
> Mr. Sintim-Misa's story gets laughs because it rings true. Last year [AD 2000], the number of Ghanaians applying to legally enter the U.S. tripled…So many skilled and educated Ghanaians have fled that Mr. Sintim-Misa has the impression that "nobody wants to live in Ghana anymore."
>
> Nobody, that is, except African-Americans…Far from seeing African-Americans as kin, most Ghanaians lump them together with other Americans…With better education and deeper pockets, African-Americans strike many Ghanaians as arrogant. "When they get into any situation they want to take over, and we are not like that," says R. William Hrisir-Quaye, an official with Ghana's commission on culture.
>
> Indeed, many black Americans living in Ghana find they aren't particularly welcome—and wonder whether they need a new civil rights movement to secure a place in their adopted home. ("Tangled Roots," p. A1)

Also during her Ghana visit, reporter Chisolm discovered that the slogan "Black is beautiful" was somewhat "mythical." For example, she learned that many Ghanaians (male and female) were practicing "skin bleaching" in order to look "white"—a rite that many African Americans (male and female) practiced, from the 1920s to 1940s, to fade "dark spots, scars, blemishes" and make their skin color "lighter." On inquiring why Ghanaians practiced the rite, Ms. Chisolm was told by one young woman,

> "I'm bleaching because I like [to have a] white color," explained Evone Birikoang, a pretty, shapely 24-year-old Ghanaian…"Some people say Black is beautiful, but white is beauty. People like white," she pointed out. ("Imitation of Life," p. 116)

And on questioning one Rasta[farian] drummer named Aley Baba about the Ghanaian skin-bleaching practice, Ms. Chisolm discovered the existence of a contradictory social attitude similar to that displayed by many African-American males of the 1920s and beyond. On the one hand, Mr. Baba expressed his disapproval of the practice. But on the other hand, Ms. Chisolm explained,

> Although Evone and [twenty-five-year-old] Esta [Obeng] claimed that bleaching made them more attractive to men, I saw quite a few sneer at them and heard several mumble, "Fanta face, Caca-Cola body." Later, a Rasta drummer I met named Aley Baba explained that Fanta is an orange soda and "caca" is slang for [fecal matter].
>
> "We have this saying about 'Fanta face, Caca-Cola body,' because you see the face red and if you look at the legs and the arms, you see a different color," Aley said. "Some men like it. Me, never." He despises the practice so much that he once put hot pepers in his sister's bleaching creams to get her to stop. Of course it burnt her face, but his efforts weren't in vain: she stopped bleaching. "They want to take the Western society [practices]. But sorry, Black is international," he said. "Those who are Black and change their color to be like the white sister, I feel really sorry for them." Ironically, Aley's girlfriend is Greek [White]. (Ibid., pp. 116–17)

Undoubtedly, Mr. Baba's words and deeds "conflicted." And this "behavioral attitude" of the Ghanaians she met made Ms. Chisolm "reevaluate" many things she formerly believed about the "African American slavery experience" and "black pride." She concluded,

> As the first African country to win independence from European colonial powers, Ghana is known for its staunch nationalism: Its first president, Kwame Nkrumah, preached Pan-Africanism; it's where W. E. B. DuBois sought refuge from American racism and where Malcolm X once said he felt at home. But when I got there, I realized that the people in this country were as vulnerable to negative messages about Blackness as we are in America. Just as slavery and racism have marred African Americans, British colonialism has warped Ghana…So I never did encounter Black pride as I imagined it in Accra, but that doesn't mean Ghanaians don't have it. In 2002, after slavery, colonialism, globalization and all of the other things that have shaped people in America and Africa, things are much more complex than my utopian fantasy. But I do take comfort in this: God gave color to creation and no one can be anyone except who they are. (Ibid., pp. 115, 117)

To be sure, Ms. Chisolm's final statement about living in a "utopian fantasy" should be taken to heart by everyone—American or other, "black" or "other"—given her "realization" that "things are more complex than we often think they are." Indeed, careful and well-rounded research is needed before one attempts to speak on the historical role that the "Race Card Evil" played in American society (or any other)—especially if one wants to avoid "misspeaking" or "embarrassing" one's self or another about the subject. This truth was emphasized by twenty-first century *Washington Times* columnist Robert Woodson, Sr., who in his February AD 2000 Black History Month article entitled

"History of black enterprise retraced" said with respect to the next generation of African Americans:

> In this first Black History Month of the [twenty-first] century, let's give our forebears a tribute they deserve. Let's lift the gag rule on discussion of a legacy of black enterprise and innovative economic progress.
>
> Today, much of what passes in academia as "black history" is at best, incomplete and, at worst, revisionist. It focuses almost exclusively on the degradation whites have imposed on blacks and the agenda of the civil rights establishment since the 1960s. (Robert Woodson Sr., "History of black enterprise retraced," *Washington Times*, 15 February 2000, Commentary, p. A19)

If Mr. Woodson's last statement is read correctly, he is saying that the "black" history taught in schools and popular media is "partial," "slanted," and "Race Card Evil" oriented. In effect, he means that "African Americans" have been "hoodwinked" and given a "one-sided, color-coded, white-bashing" view called "black" history. And to explain his statement, Mr. Woodson illustrated the need for "modern" African-American youths to know the "real deal" about their ancestors' industrious activities during America's Colonial, Revolutionary War, Civil War, and Reconstruction Eras. Said he,

> We should let our young people know that, even before the Civil War, many free blacks made their livings as owners of small shops. In the late 1700s, for example, the city of Philadelphia was a community abounding in both small and large enterprises owned by blacks...During this same era, Baltimore was one of the main centers of commerce for black enterprise...
>
> In Cincinnati, blacks owned engineering firms, brick factories, and other small enterprises. Blacks in New York City were also very active in business development between

the Revolutionary and Civil Wars. They owned some of the best restaurants on Wall Street and were known for their expertise in tailoring. Free blacks in Southern cities developed service enterprises, such as catering, which were so superior that they monopolized the field. At the eve of the Civil War, the combined assets of enterprising blacks totaled $50 million—in 1860 currency. Black entrepreneurs included barbers, blacksmiths, grocers, tailors, restauranters, caterers, carpenters and shoemakers.

After the Civil War and the [Thirteenth Amendment] Emancipation, this same determination and will to achieve inspired remarkable economic and educational achievements among blacks who were just emerging from an era of oppression and slavery. (Ibid., p. A19)

Mr. Woodson next cited successful black entrepreneurs such as George Downing (who started the Newport, RI, Sea Girt Hotel and other businesses), John Merrick (who started the Durham, NC, Mutual Life Insurance Company), Henry Allen Boyd (who started a number of prominent Nashville, TN, businesses), James Forten (who started a Philadelphia, PA, sail-making business that made him millions), and John Whitelaw Lewis (who started an elegant black hotel, designed by a black architect and built by black tradesmen)—these entrepreneurs establishing their businesses between the late1700s and early 1900s. And he pridefully noted,

The black entrepreneurs who carved a pathway to success did not possess any special advantages. Nearly half of them had been bought out of slavery by loved ones who had saved enough money to free them...Black progress in the 30 years following slavery surpassed achievements in the 30 years following the civil rights victories of the 1960s. the per-capita income of blacks skyrocketed by 300 percent during the first half-century of freedom. Between 1865 and 1892, the number of black newspapers increased

> from two to 154; attorneys from two to 250; and physicians
> from three to 749…Between 1867 and 1917, the number
> of black enterprises increased from 4,000 to 50,000. (Ibid.,
> p. A19 passim)

However, after giving such inspiring facts, Mr. Woodson sadly noted,

> Neither the *Plessy vs. Ferguson* decision nor the Jim Crow
> laws that were passed to eliminate black entrepreneurs
> and professionals from market competition could stem
> the tide of determined, successful black entrepreneurs…
> Tragically, today—at a time when the inspiration of this
> legacy of enterprise, self-help, and mutual assistance is
> desperately needed by our youth—the history of black
> entrepreneurship has been silenced.
> *Ibid.*, p. A19 (italics ours).

Undoubtedly, Mr. Woodson's recitation of the "past" progressive deeds of African-Americans living during the said eras shows that the "modern" problems faced by the African-American community have nothing to do with what their ancestors went through. And he was thoughtful enough to give a good reason for the "behavioral change" that the "Black" community underwent—doing so by recounting the researches of twenty-first century sociologist John Sibley Butler.

Specializing in documenting the African-American community's "past" and "present" initiatives to excel in business enterprise, Mr. Butler believes that the turn of black academics to a "culture of victimhood" was the cause of "modern" African-American "lack of intiative to excel." Quoting Mr. Butler, Mr. Woodson recounted,

> "After slavery, most of the research on black Americans
> was in the category called 'racial uplift.' This research
> was designed to show the progress of black Americans

in education, institution building and business enterprise. Although there was research on problems associated with black America, it is clear that the racial uplift literature balanced, and indeed outweighed, the literature on the problems. But, around the late 1970s, research on black Americans made a complete shift to the study of failure within a hostile racial society. Like a city covered after an earthquake, most of the success of black America was buried and forgotten." (Ibid., p. A19)

To be sure, Mr. Butler's statement about the ratio of "uplift" to "victimized" literature hints that the "Race Card Evil" was responsible for this "shift in thinking"—a shift that "blamed whites" for "black failure," and was the chief cause of the "economic" and "intellectual" degeneration of at least two generations of "angry" and "misguided" African American youth. And on acknowledging the negative effect produced by the "failure-oriented" literature that bombarded African American society during the 1970s, Mr. Woodson stated,

> Conveniently air-brushed from the portrait of black America are the remarkable accomplishments of black entrepreneurs and mutual-aid societies that were achieved even during eras of the most brutal racial repression and slavery. Lost is the legacy of self-help, personal responsibility, and principle-based entrepreneurship that could provide today's youths with pride in their heritage and an adaptable model that could guide their futures... Documenting racial disparities and discrimination may have been necessary in order to make a case for the protection of our civil rights. But since the 1960s, this focus on grievances has taken on a life of its own. It has dominated the debate and eclipsed the documentation of black successes. Black spokesmen turned away from the rich legacy of a past that was spiritually and economically vibrant and looked, instead, to legislation and politicians

for salvation. Today's statistics regarding the state of our young people provide evidence that solutions lie elsewhere.

In this month…let's turn our attention from the wrongs and racism perpetrated by others and introduce our children to models who have taught, through their lives, that achievement is possible, despite the odds. (Ibid., p. A19)

Ironically, Mr. Woodson's concluding statement about African-Americans turning "our attention from the wrongs and racism perpetrated by others" brings us full circle to the statement made at the outset of our journey (in volume one)—namely, that "many of us have played the Race Card Evil game." However, "we" refuse to see the "man in the mirror" that way. What "we" see are the "wrongs or racism" perpetrated by others and not ourselves. To be sure, for some African American community members, such "one-sided" thinking is plainly a case of "the black sheep crying wolf to whitewash the black sheep's own wool!" And one respondent to Ms. Abigail ("Dear Abby") Van Buren's "Racism is many-sided problem" column also seemed to think so. A registered nurse who called herself "Jeanie, R. N., formerly of Philadelphia (the City of Brotherly Love)," replied,

Dear Abby: As a registered nurse who has worked in a major city hospital in the United States as well as small hospitals, let me tell you—there is racism in the black community no matter what it's labeled. There is racism between blacks and Asians, blacks and whites, , blacks and Hispanics, just as there is among whites and other races in these United States. Racism is not just a white evil. It's an all-pervasive, color-crossing evil that debases us all. (Jeanie, R. N., "Racism is many-sided problem," *Chicago Tribune*, 27 October 1999, Dear Abby: 9)

Ms. Jeanie made an excellent point about the African American community—one that rings true for most communities inhabiting the Earth! For instance, there is "Racism" between: African and African (Rwanda's Belgian-incited Hutu-Tutsi "ethnic cleansing" war), African American and African American ("light" vs. "dark" skinned), African and African American (the latter feeling they need a "civil rights" movement in Ghana), "white" American and "white" American (antebellum Southern slaveowners saying slavery was the proper condition for the free "white" northern laborer), European and European (Hitler's and Sarajevo's "ethnic cleansing" wars), Hindu and Hindu (the India vs. Pakistan struggle Mahatma Ghandi tried to diffuse), Native American and Native American (pick the occasion), as well as Latin American and Latin American ("light" vs. "dark" skinned Hispanics) to name a few. And as surprising as the last mentioned may sound, twenty-first century American reporter Jason Webb uncovered this fact while on assignment for the *Washington Times*. In his 28 December 1999 article entitled "Modern Argentina largely ignores its black ancestry," Mr. Webb said,

> The disappearance of Argentina's black community, which once made up a quarter of the population, has been so complete that it even became a stock gag used by one of the country's best-known comics…In some provinces… half or more of the people were descendants of slaves. But today many Argentines are only vaguely aware that for three centuries of their history, a large part of the population was black.
>
> Schoolbooks hardly mention them, while paintings in the capital's elegant fine-arts museum show stiff upper-class families posing for portraits…Their complexions range from porcelain white to little darker than a rugged tan…In fact, it was the immigration of more than a million people from Italy and Spain starting in the last part of the 19th century that swamped Argentina's black population… Argentines have a reputation today for a superiority complex sometimes tinged with a sense of satisfaction that

their country is not home to a large nonwhite population, as is most of the rest of Latin America.

A type of casual racism which, while rarely aggressive, would cause outrage in more politically correct countries, is hardly blinked at here...But the racial smugness is founded on whitewashed history.

"They needed to construct a European history, a white, immaculate history in which we had always been white. No one wanted to have to accept that his great-grandfather, his great-great-grandfather, was black," said Daniel Schavelzon, head of urban archealogy at the University of Buenos Aires. (Jason Webb, "Modern Argentina largely ignores its black ancestry," *Washington Times*, 28 December 1999, World, p. A14)

Such being Earth's state of affairs, next generation Americans and Humanity need to reevaluate most of the "believed-in" doctrine that was handed down to them by supposedly "wiser" previous generations. Indeed, any hope for Humanity's brighter future rests on the hope that its next generation will not fall victim to errors in thinking that made the "Race Card Evil" so successful in the past. Above all, any hope for Humanity's brighter future rests on people asking themselves what they truly stand for, and thereafter making a definite stand about it. In the twenty-first century and beyond, the most important question for humanity to answer will not be "Who are you?" Rather, it will be "What are you?" This important question was asked and answered by a remarkable twentieth-century African American—variously known as Malcolm Little, Detroit Red, Malcolm X, and El Hajj Malik El Shabazz—as he made his pilgrimage from darkness (ignorance) to light (knowledge) in a gallant effort to combat the "Race Card Evil" and put it "in the course of ultimate extinction."

# 11

# Malcolm X Marks the Spot

And the vision…is become…as the words of a book…
which men delivered to one that is learned [educated],
saying Read this…and he saith, I cannot; for it is
sealed…[and] to him that is not learned [uneducated]…
and he saith, I am not learned."

—Isaiah 29:11–12 (KJV)

Ye hypocrites, well did Esaias [Isaiah] prophesy of you,
saying, This people draweth nigh [near] unto me [the
Creator]…and honoreth me with their lips [mouths];
but their heart [mind] is far [away] from me. But in
vain they do worship me, teaching for doctrines the
commandments of men.

—Matthew 15:7–9 (KJV)

AT AN EARLY date the "Race Card Evil" infected a number of "white" American groups and tricked them into furthering its agenda. One such organization was the group called "Freemasonry." Indeed, although the famous "fraternity" advocated "brotherhood" and "humanitarianism" at the outset of its AD 1717 founding in England, it restricted membership to "twenty-one-year-old free white males." This requirement traveled with Freemasonry into the British American colonies, 1776 Revolutionary War, 1861

Civil War, and 1867–1877 Reconstruction Eras. *Wikipedia's* article entitled "Prince Hall Freemasonry" recounted,

> Prior to the American Revolutionary War, Prince Hall and fourteen other free black men petitiomed for admittance to the white Boston St. John's Lodge. They were turned down. The Masonic fraternity was attractive to free blacks like Prince Hall because freemasonry was founded upon ideals of liberty, equality and peace.
>
> Having been rejected by colonial Freemasonry, Hall and 14 others sought and were initiated into Masonry through Lodge No. 441 of the Grand Lodge of Ireland on March 6, 1775…The Lodge was attached to the British forces stationed in Boston…When black men wished to become Masons in the new nation the white members of the Lodge had to unanimously vote to accept a petitioner to receive Masonic degrees. If one white person voted against the petitioner that person would be rejected. In a letter by General Albert Pike to his brother in 1875 he said, "I am not inclined to mettle [meddle] in the matter. I took my obligations to white men, not to Negroes. When I have to accept Negroes as brothers or leave Masonry, I shall leave it." (*Wikepedia,* s.v. "Prince Hall Freemasonry," http://en.wikipedia.org/wiki/Prince_Hall_Freemasonry, pp. 1–2. Retrieved 10 October 2015)

Being an ex-Confederate officer and high-ranking Masonic scholar, Mr. Pike's "ethnic" statement tarnished American Freemasonry's image as a genuine "benevolent-fraternal-humanitarian" organization, undermined the spiritual purpose of the Masonic society, and made the group a "Race Card Evil" oriented role model after which many succeeding "white" American fraternal groups would be patterned.

The Ku Klux Klan was another "fraternal" group infected by the "Race Card Evil" at an early date. As earlier shown, the Reconstruction Era Klan was primarily concerned with disrupting the "political" alliance between the Union Loyal Leagues and the newly freed slaves. However, because the organization's "name" was used as a cloak for criminal purposes, General Bedford Forrest officially disbanded it in 1869. Unfortunately, about a half century later, William J. Simmons resurrected the KKK's name. Only this time, the "new" Klan had a "Race Card Evil" oriented agenda—one displaying a "religious" and "fraternal" face. *Wikipedia's* article on this organization, which lasted from 1915–1944, stated,

> The Second Klan saw threats from every direction. A religious tone was present in its activities; "two-thirds of the [1915 Klan] national lecturers were Protestant ministers," says historian Brian R. Farmer…The founder of the new Klan, William J. Simmons, joined twelve different fraternal organizations. He recruited for the Klan with his chest covered with fraternal badges, and consciously modeled the Klan after fraternal organizations…It [the New Klan] presented itself as a fraternal, nativist [pro native-born citizens and anti-immigrants] and strenuously patriotic organization…Religion was a major selling point… Their cross was a religious symbol [taken from the 1915 *Klansman* movie], and their ritual honored Bibles and local ministers. No nationally prominent religious leader said he was a Klan member. ("Ku Klux Klan," pp. 10–12 passim)

The "1915" KKK rose to prominence in the 1920s because many criminal "white" immigrants arrived in America during Italy's fascist era (1922–1943)—which era featured belligerent nationalism, militarism, racism, and other "anti-social" ideas. This criminal "Catholic" element wanted a piece of the "New World's" wealth, did whatever it took to get it, and ushered in a lawless period called America's "Prohibition-Roaring Twenties-gangster" era (1920–1933). To address this threat, the "1915" Klan recruited its membership by appealing to a "White Anglo-Saxon

Protestant" (WASP) nationalist mindset. This, in turn, gave birth to a number of "black" American nationalist organizations known as the Garveyite, Moorish Science, and Nation of Islam movements.

Consequently, as strange as it may seem, the "1915" KKK can be viewed as the "father" of the "Black nationalist" groups—because had it not been for the Klan's (and others) "white nationalist" doctrines and actions, then these "Black" groups probably would have never arisen. And while one would think that all these colorful "Black" and "White" groups would have clashed, they never did—because they spoke a common language! What was their common-speak language? To answer this, a short review of the common histories and ideologies of these "black" and "white" nationalist groups is needed.

As is known, most of what is heard about the Klan or other "white supremacist" groups involves the "burning, bombing, lynching, murdering" aspect that clearly speaks to a "hate" agenda. However, their agenda's real cause concerned "blacks" trying to force "whites" to accept them into their community—rather than living in and building up their own. This behavioral attitude the "Race Card Evil" was sure to exploit. Indeed, the Jamaican-born Marcus A. Garvey discovered this truth in 1901 at age fourteen. In his work entitled *Selected Writings and Speeches of Marcus Garvey*, twenty-first century American editor Bob Blaisdell noted that Mr. Garvey said,

> To me, at home in my early days, there was no difference between white and black. One of my father's properties, the place where I lived most of the time, was adjoining that of a white man. He had three girls and two boys; the Wesleyan minister, another white man whose church my parents attended, also had property adjoining ours. He had three girls and one boy. All of us were playmates. We romped and were happy children playmates together. The little girl whom I liked the most knew no better than I did

myself. We were two innocent fools who never dreamed of a race feeling and problem. As a child, I went to school with white boys and girls, like all other Negroes. We were not called Negroes then. I never heard the term Negro used once until I was about fourteen.

At fourteen my little white playmate and I parted. Her parents thought the time had come to separate us and draw the color line. They sent her and another sister to Edinburgh, Scotland, and told her that she was never to write or try to get in touch with me, for I was a "nigger." It was then that I found [out] for the first time that there was some difference in humanity, and that there were different races, each having its own separate and distinct social life. I did not care about the separation after I was told about it, because I never thought all during our childhood association that the girl and the rest of the children of her race were better than I was; in fact, they used to look up to me. So I simply had no regrets.

After my first lesson in race distinction, I never thought of playing with white girls any more, even if they might be next-door neighbors. (Bob Blaisdell, ed., *Selected Writings and Speeches of Marcus Garvey*, New York: Dover Publications, Inc., 2004, 2).

Enlightened by his first encounter with the "Race Card Evil" attitude, in 1914 Garvey founded his Universal Negro Improvement Association (UNIA) at age twenty-seven and thereafter his African Communities Imperial League (ACIL)—organizations with the avowed goal of uniting the world's people of color and creating a universal society of their own. Next, in 1916 Garvey came to America and founded a branch of his UNIA in Harlem. Unfortunately, because Garvey's speeches concerned "Black Self-Reliance Without White Involvement," some of Harlem's "Black" leadership became his political enemies; and within six years of founding his New York based UNIA, Garvey made more enemies by associating with "white racist" groups. Indeed, when speaking about Garvey's 9 July 1922 Liberty Hall speech in New York City—entitled "Honorable Marcus Garvey Tells of [his 25 June 1922] interview with the [Atlanta, GA] Ku Klux Klan"—Mr. Blaisdell noted in his introduction to *Selected Writings and Speeches,*

> It was on his cross-country speaking tour in 1922 that he began his disturbingly close associations with white racist groups. Without apologizing for such dealings, he insisted that white racist organizations were the only honest representatives of American sentiment, and compared the beliefs of the U.N.I.A. with those of such groups: "The Ku Klux Klan is the invisible government of the United States of America. The Ku Klux Klan expresses to a great extent the feeling of every real white American…The attitude of the Universal Negro Improvement Association is in a way similar to the Ku Klux Klan. Whilst the Ku Klux Klan desires to make America absolutely a white man's country, the Universal Negro Improvement Association wants to make Africa absolutely a black man's country."This avowed kinship with the white supremacists dismayed many of his followers and sympathizers and left his opponents in the N.A.A.C.P. and the Communist Party volubly outraged. Garvey tried to make his pow-wows with racists sound simply pragmatic: "So you realize that the Universal Negro Improvement Association is carrying out just what the Ku Klux Klan is carrying out—the purity of the white race down South—and we are going to carry out the purity of the black race not only down South, but all through the world." Garvey's stance on miscegenation and "racial purity" was a position that Garvey's greatest scholar, Robert A. Hill, believes tripped up the momentum of the Universal Negro Improvement Association and kept it from extending beyond what Hill calls the "propaganda stage": that is, "… the disintegration of the U.N.I.A. as a radical political force began the moment Garvey resorted to the ideology of racial purity." (Ibid., p. viii; Mr. Blaisdell directly referring, later at pp. 74–82, to Garvey's 1922 speech)

As 1922 drew to a close, FBI agent J. Edgar Hoover arrested Garvey for allegedly violating federal mail fraud statutes regarding his "Black Star" shipping enterprise. In 1923, he was convicted of the charges and detained until 1926, at which time he received a Presidential pardon and thereafter deported. Garvey's Harlem-based UNIA slowly died out after his deportation. However, that was not the end of his dream.

In 1913, about three years prior to Garvey founding his Harlem-based UNIA branch, a twenty-seven-year-old North Carolinian named Timothy Drew founded a "civic-religious" organization in Newark, New Jersey, variously called rhe Moorish Divine and National Movement and the Canaanite Temple. Viewing Garvey in a "harbinger-prophet" role similar to John the Baptist, Timothy Drew—called "Prophet Noble Drew Ali" by his followers—assumed a "judgment-prophet" role similar to Jesus of Nazareth. Like Garvey, Drew believed that the people called "Negroes" needed to become community-oriented and self-reliant. And like Garvey, Drew believed that those called "Negroes" needed a real sense of "cultural heritage," "national identity" and "race pride." However, Drew also believed that those called "Negroes" had to be taught proper "civic behavior" or "citizenship" to thrive in American society. By 1925, Drew had relocated his organization to Chicago, Illinois, and changed it to a "religious" organization called the Moorish Holy Temple of Science. Finally, in 1928 he changed it to a "civic-fraternal" organization called The Moorish Science Temple of America, Inc.—with the goal of teaching his Moorish-American membership concepts that would make them "better citizens."

Rejecting "ethnic," "national" or "racial" names such as "black," "colored," "Ethiopian," "Negro," and "Nigger," Drew taught his membership that during America's Colonial and Revolutionary War eras the "indentured servant" status of their ancestors was changed to legalize the "Race Card Evil" oriented "African slavery" scheme. He said this was accomplished by stripping them of their "Moorish" identity and substituting the terms "black-a-moor," "black moor," "Ethiopian," and "Negro" in its place.

In effect, Noble Drew Ali taught that the enslaved Africans called "Negro" hailed from a "Moorish" identity. And since their descendants were born in America, then their national identity was "Moorish-American"—meaning that they were "Americans" by nationality with a "Moorish" cultural history, not a people without a cultural or historical identity; and not any of the denigrating names "forced" upon their ancestors during the Spanish and British-American Colonial Eras. Said Mr. Ali in his organization's constitution and by-laws:

> With us all members must proclaim their nationality and we are teaching our people their nationality...that they may know...that they are not Negroes, Colored Folks, Black People or Ethiopians, because these names were given to slaves by slaveholders...(The *Divine Constitution and By-laws of the M.S.T. of A.*, Act 6 passim)

Most importantly, Mr. Ali taught his membership that (1) none of the rejected names were part of the "human family" listed in the *Genesis* 10 "Table of Nations"; (2) it was an insult to the Creator for people to accept slavery-imposed names as a "national" or "racial" identity; and (3) it was a "sin" for one group of people to "force" themselves upon another group that did not wish to associate. Having taught his membership that there was only "one human race" artificially subdivided into "two races" called "Asiatics" (Asians and Africans included) and "Europeans" (Caucasians), Mr. Ali said,

> According to all true and divine records of the human race there is no negro, black, or colored race attached to the human family...The time has come when every nation must worship under its own vine and fig tree, and every tongue must confess his own...We, as a clean and pure nation descended from the inhabitants of Africa, do not

> desire to amalgamate or marry into the families of the
> pale-skinned nations of Europe. Neither serve the gods
> of their religion…Therefore we are returning the Church
> and Christianity back to the European Nations…While
> we, the Moorish Americans, are returning to Islam…
> ("Egypt, The Capital Empire" [47:9, 15] and "The End
> of Time" [48:6–8]; *The Holy Koran of the Moorish Science
> Temple of America*, pp. 58–59 passim)

Understanding the "antisocial" attitude of many "white" Americans (particularly the "1915" KKK) displayed toward "nonwhite" Americans, Nobel Drew Ali, like Marcus Garvey, did not agree with the NAACP's "colored people" and "racial integration" platform. And being well ahead of his time, Mr. Ali felt that the "real problem" did not stem from "white" Americans. Rather, he believed that it stemmed from the low self-esteem and self-destructive behavior demonstrated by so-called "black" or "Negro" Americans—a "self-image" problem that made them "desire" (covet) to date, marry, and socialize with "whites" as opposed to positively interacting with their own ethnic community to uplift it academically, financially, politically, socially, and spiritually.

Interestingly enough, because of his firm stance on self-reliance, non-Christian (WASP) religious orientation (although there existed both Christian and Jewish "Moorish" temples at one time or another), and nonintegration, Mr. Ali made a number of political enemies; and a similar "Garvey-like" fate happened to him (some enemies even stooped to "yellow journalistic" tactics to discredit him). However, Mr. Ali's worst enemies would come from within his own organization—as predicted centuries ago by Jesus of Nazareth (Matt. 10:34–38, KJV).

In 1928, Mr. Ali's leadership was contested by a member named Claude Green-to be safe it is best to use Claude Greene. During the spring of 1929 Mr. Greene was murdered and, on 15 March 1929, Mr. Ali was arrested and charged with complicity in the crime. Unfortunately, Ali never made it to trial to exonerate himself—because after posting bail, he died on 20 July 1929. And although Mr. Ali's membership accused the Cook County, Illinois, Police Department of causing his death (via a beating he allegedly received while incarcerated), the coroner's report cited "pneumonia and pulmonary heart failure" as the cause of the forty-three-year-old Ali's demise.

After Prophet Noble Drew Ali's death his organization fell victim to power struggles, which resulted in rival members claiming ultimate authority over his organization. Out of this factionalism the Nation of Islam (NOI) was born. These events twentieth-century Cuban-American author Prince-A-Cuba recounted in his 1992 *Gnosis Magazine* article entitled "Black Gods of the Inner City." Said he,

> Outsiders have done little in-depth research to trace the NOI's doctrinal predecessors. The NOI itself has denied its connections with previous movements, specifically the Moorish Science Temple of Noble Drew Ali. Ali, who was born as Timothy Drew in North Carolina in 1886, taught, among other things, that Blacks are descended from the ancient Canaanites…Eventually relocating [from Newark, New Jersey] to Chicago, Ali built an organization that numbered perhaps 30,000 adherents at its peak.
>
> On March 15, 1929, Ali was arrested after factional violence resulted in the death of a rival, Sheik Claude Greene. Arrested and held in the county jail, Ali was eventually released on bail, but died on July 20, 1929, under mysterious circumstances.
>
> The story of the NOI itself starts with a man variously known as Wali Farrad, W. D. Fard, Wallace Fard Muhammad, and Farad Muhammad, but who is best known as Mater Fard Muhammad…Master Fard Muhammad is officially noted by the NOI as having arrived in Detroit on July 4, 1930, and departed on June 30, 1934…Prior to Fard's appearance in 1930, Noble

Drew Ali's Moorish Science Temples of America were in decline. After the loss of its founder [Ali] in 1929, the movement had fallen into three separate schisms…But according to scholar Ravanna Bey, W. D. Fard, known at the time as Abdul Wali Farrad Muhammad, and two other Moorish Scientists, Mealy El and Charles Kirkman Bey, contested the authority of [John] Givens El [who publicly claimed in Chicago's Pythian Hall, on 7 August 1929, to be the reincarnation of Noble Drew Ali]. The latter two went on to establish their own independent Moorish Science Temples, while Fard converted a Detroit Moorish Science Temple and renamed it the Temple of the Lost-Found People of Islam…A [12 November 1942 FBI Detroit Field Office Report] wartime memo [file #100–26356] claimed W. D. Fard was one Sheik Davis El from Kansas…While the oral histories of Moorish Science adherents claim Fard as one of their own gone astray, NOI initiates say that Fard, arriving in the "wilderness of North America" as early as 1910, taught Noble Drew Ali, Father Divine, Daddy Grace, and Sufi Abdul-Hamid the concept of Black godhood, though all of these later went on their own way. There is also a tradition that in Egypt Fard taught Duse Muhammad Ali, the mentor of Marcus Garvey…as well as Garvey himself, whom he met in London. (Prince-A-Cuba, "Black Gods of the Inner City," *Gnosis Magazine*, Fall 1992, 57–59 passim)

Although the ideas of "black self-help," "black economic empowerment," "Black nationalism," and "black ethnic separation" were basically the same for the Garveyite, Moorish, and Nation of Islam movements, the NOI's reason for "ethnic separation" differed from the first two. As concerns the Garveyite and Moorish doctrines of "ethnic separation," both Garvey and Drew felt that "whites" or "Europeans" who desired to separate from "blacks" were entitled to make that "social choice"—one that imputed no "evil" to "white" skin color. However, the NOI's doctrine did. As concerns the NOI's "ethnic separation" doctrine, author Cuba said,

> Central to these teachings were the knowledge of self and the Black man's godhood. According to these teachings, the Black man was by nature divine, and in fact was the original man, ancestor of the human race (antedating Louis and Mary Leakey's discoveries of early human remains in Africa by nearly thirty years).
>
> White people, on the other hand, were produced out of Black people by a scientist named Yacub approximately six thousand years ago. Discovering a recessive gene in the Black man, Yacub used a system of [Hitler-like] eugenics on a group of sixty thousand people on an island and, after six hundred years, was able to create a biological mutation: the White man. Of course Yacub did not live to see his creation, but he left behind an infrastructure to propagate his system, as well as the ideological basis of White supremacy. Bleached of the essence of humanity, Whites were "without soul." Nonetheless the [White] race was destined to rule for an allotted period extending to 1914 A.D. though, as Fard's messenger Elijah Muhammad put it, "a few years of grace have been given to complete the resurrection of the Black man, and especially the so-called Negroes whom Allah has chosen for this change (of a new nation and world). They (so-called Negroes) have been made so completely mentally dead…that the extra time is allowed." It was also taught that the supreme god amongst this mighty nation of Black gods commanded the name of Allah. This title was claimed by Master Fard Muhammad himself. (Ibid., 57–58)

Obviously, the NOI's "Yacub" doctrine derived from the biblical story about "Jacob's" experiment with his uncle Laban's livestock—in which story the farm animals' "coat" or "outer skin complexion" was changed to teach a moral point about underhanded business dealings. And obviously, the NOI's association of "evil" with "white" skin color was a reversal of the *Genesis* 9 "Ham cursed" story used to justify enslaving people of "black" or "dark" skin color for profit during the Spanish and British American Colonial Eras.

Ironically, the NOI's "Race Card Evil" oriented "Yacub" doctrine would never have gained the popularity that it did in America had it not been for two significant events—both of which transpired after NOI leader Elijah Muhammad (formerly Paul Robert Poole of Sandersville, Georgia) shaped the group into a powerful force to be reckoned with after World War II's end.

The first significant event to impact both "black" and "white" America was the introduction of Malcolm Little to Elijah Muhammad. Explained author Cuba,

> Born Malcolm Little in Omaha, Nebraska, in 1925, Malcolm X had been introduced to Elijah Muhammad through family members while in prison in Massachusetts. In the early 1950s he converted and took his "X." Upon his release he joined the organization in Detroit and subsequently rose to a position of leadership, eventually moving to New York City, where he was assigned Temple #7. (Ibid., 60)

Being the son of a "dark-skinned" and uneducated Baptist minister-Garveyite father named Reverend Earl Little and "light-skinned" educated Granada-born mother named Mrs. Louise Little, the "Race Card Evil" experiences that Malcolm's parents underwent before and during his formative years played a large part in preparing him for his rise to prominence within the NOI during his latter years.

Although Earl wanted to provide a stable home for his wife and children, he was forced to constantly change localities to protect his family due to his "Garveyite" preachings—the Georgia native Earl having moved to Piladelphia (PA) (where he met and married Louise), then to Omaha (NB), next to Milwaukee (WI), and finally to Lansing (MI) where he was murdered in 1931 when Malcolm was age six. In his *Autobiography of Malcolm X*, Malcolm recounted his parents' pilgrimage and the contradictory "Race Card Evil" events that plagued the Little family along the way:

> When my mother was pregnant with me, she told me later, a party of hooded Ku Klux Klan riders galloped up to our home in Omaha, Nebraska, one night. Surrounding the house, brandishing their shotguns and rifles, they shouted for my father to come out. My mother went to the front door and opened it. Standing where they could see her pregnant condition, she told them that she was alone with her three small children, and that my father was away, preaching, in Milwaukee. The Klansmen shouted threats and warnings at her that we had better get out of town because "the good Christian white people" were not going to stand for my father's "spreading trouble" among the "good" Negroes of Omaha with the "back to Africa" preachings of Marcus Garvey…Still shouting threats, the Klansmen finally spurred their horses and galloped around the house, shattering every window pane with their gun butts. Then they rode off into the night, their torches flaring, as suddenly as they had come.
>
> My father was enraged when he returned. He decided to wait until I was born—which would be soon—and then the family would move…My mother was twenty-eight when I was born on May 19, 1925, in an Omaha hospital. Then we moved to Milwaukee…Our family stayed only briefly in Milwaukee…(Malcolm X and Alex Haley, *The Autobiography of Malcolm X*, New York: Ballantine Books, 1992 ed., 3–5 passim)

And Malcolm recalled that when he was about four years old:

> We went next to…to Lansing, Michigan. My father bought a house and soon, as had been his pattern, he was

doing freelance Christian preaching in local Negro Baptist churches, and during the week he was roaming about spreading word of Marcus Garvey…when, as always, some stupid local Uncle Tom Negroes began to funnel stories about his revolutionary beliefs to the local white people. This time, the get-out-of-town threats came from a local hate society called The Black Legion. They wore black robes instead of white. Soon, nearly everywhere my father went, Black Legionaires were reviling him as an "uppity nigger" for wanting to own a store, for living outside the Lansing Negro district, for spreading unrest and dissention among "the good niggers."

As in Omaha, my mother was pregnant again, this time with my youngest sister. Shortly after Yvonne was born came the nightmare night in 1929, my earliest vivid memory. I remember being suddenly snatched awake into a frightening confusion of pistol shots and shouting and smoke and flames. My father had shouted and shot at the two white men who had set the fire and were running away. Our home was burning down around us. We were lunging and bumping and tumbling all over each other trying to escape. My mother, with the baby in her arms, just made it into the yard before the house crashed in, showering sparks. I remember we were outside in the night in our underwear, crying and yelling our heads off. The white police and firemen came and stood around watching as the house burned down to the ground. (Ibid., 5–6)

In 1929 Malcolm's parents moved to the outskirts of East Lansing. There, Earl continued to hold Garveyite meetings in various homes and receive threats from the Black Legion. Two years later, when Malcolm was age six, his father was murdered one night in 1931. Although no in-depth investigation followed, or arrests made, people sympathetic to Louise blamed her husband's murder on the Black Legion.

Curiously enough, the "Race Card Evil" oriented events that Malcolm's family experienced in Nebraska and Michigan contradicted "white supremacists'" goals. Indeed, given the fact that Marcus Garvey drew fire from the "black" sector for his associations (and similar views) with "white supremacist" groups, given the fact that Malcolm's "Garveyite" father preached the "black self-sufficiency, back-to-Africa, racial purity" doctrine, and given the fact that the Klan or any other true "white racist" group would have "popularized" and not "demonized" Garvey's views, then it is highly suspect that the "genuine" Klan or Black Legion said what Malcolm recounted about the Nebraska and Michigan events. Said he,

> The Klansmen shouted…"the good Christian white people" were not going to stand for my father's "spreading trouble" among the "good" Negroes of Omaha with the "back to Africa" preachings of Marcus Garvey.
>
> Soon…Black Legionaires were reviling him as an "uppity nigger" for wanting to own a store, for living outside the Lansing Negro district, for spreading unrest and dissention among "the good niggers." (Ibid., 3, 5)

Clearly, such statements do not reflect the "white racist" views expressed to and by Garvey during his nationwide tour—since all such groups agreed with him. Rather, the statements sound more like "anti-Garvey whites" fueled by "anti-Garvey blacks"; for as Malcolm himself said, "As always, some stupid local Uncle Tom Negroes began to funnel stories about his [Earl's] revolutionary beliefs to the local white people." Regardless of the real deal, the "genuine" Ku Klux Klan and Black Legionaires became the "fall guys" for the events Malcolm's family underwent before and after Earl's murder.

In any event, the things Malcolm heard or witnessed during his formative years did not make him a "racist." Grappling with events such as Louise's father being a "white" man whom she was ashamed of and glad to have never known (probably because her mom was a rape victim; hence Malcolm's allusion to "the white rapist" in his speeches), and four of his father's six brothers being killed by "white" men (with Earl becoming the fifth statistic) could have made Malcolm "antiwhite." Instead, he accepted the things he could not change and kept moving forward.

For instance, in 1937 twelve-year-old Malcolm saw his forty-year-old mom suffer a mental breakdown from which she never recovered. Already in "survival mode" prior to Louise's institutionalization, he stole food to help his siblings survive. This "hustler" trait followed Malcolm to Boston (where he lived with his half-sister Ella), and then to New York—being known in both cities by the street name "Detroit Red." In 1946, this "street" lifestyle got twenty-one-year-old Malcolm a ten-year sentence in Massachusetts' Charlestown State Prison. After serving two years Malcolm was transferred to Concord Prison and, with Ella's assistance, then to the Norfolk Prison Colony rehabilitation facility. During this second leg of his prison journey, Malcolm learned that most of his siblings lived in either Chicago or Detroit and had joined the Nation of Islam (NOI). Encouraged by his siblings Malcolm joined the NOI and, unfortunately, was sent back to the Charlestown facility where he remained until notified in the spring of 1952 that he was being paroled. Urged by his siblings to move to Detroit, Malcolm did so once paroled and joined the NOI there. Having upgraded his education while incarcerated, Malcolm X rose to prominence in the Detroit Temple and became Elijah Muhammad's national spokesman.

The second significant event to impact both "black" and "white" America occurred after Malcolm joined the NOI. During the early part of 1959, TV journalist Louis Lomax informed colleague Mike Wallace about the Nation of Islam's doctrine. By July 1959 the Wallace-Lomax team produced a TV documentary on the NOI entitled "The Hate That Hate Produced." This documentary catapulted both the NOI and Malcolm X into the national and international spotlights. *Wikipedia* article entitled the same recounted,

> *The Hate That Hate Produced* is a television documentary about the Nation of Islam. It was produced in 1959 by Mike Wallace and Louis Lomax.
>
> In 1959, Wallace and Lomax were television journalists for *News Beat*, a program on WNTA-TV in New York. Lomax told Wallace about the Nation of Islam, and Wallace became interested in the group. Lomax, who was African American, was given rare access to the organization. Accompanied by two white camera operators, Lomax conducted interviews with the Nation's leaders and filmed some of its events. *The Hate That Hate Produced* was broadcast in five parts during the week of July 13–17, 1959, and was repeated several days later. *(Wikipedia*, s.v. "The Hate That Hate Produced," http://en.wikipedia.org/wiki/The_Hate_That_Hate_Produced, p. 1. Retrieved 22 October 2012)

Narrator Mike Wallace opened the TV documentary by stating, "While city officials, state agencies, white liberals, and sober-minded Negroes stand idly by, a group of Negro dissenters is taking to street-corner step ladders…across the United States, to preach a gospel of hate that would set off a federal investigation if it were preached by Southern whites." Mr. Wallace then put the camera on NOI Minister Louis X (later known as Minister Louis Farrakhan) and his all-encompassing indictment of the "white" man during one of his speeches:

> I charge the white man with being the greatest liar on earth! I charge the white man with being the greatest drunkard on earth…the greatest gambler on earth. I charge the white man, ladies and gentlemen of the jury, with being the greatest murderer on earth…the greatest peace-breaker on earth…the greatest robber on earth…the greatest deceiver on earth…the greatest trouble-maker on

> earth. So therefore, ladies and gentlemen of the jury, I ask
> you, bring back a verdict of guilty as charged! (Ibid., p. 2)

Informing his viewers that Mr. Farrakhan's "indictment" was an excerpt taken from a morality play, sponsored and produced by a "Negro religious group who call themselves 'The Muslims,'" Mr. Wallace then described the NOI as "the most powerful of the Black Supremacist groups." Thereafter, the documentary shifted to Louis Lomax's interviews of NOI leader Elijah Muhammad and its national spokesman Malcolm X.

On interviewing Mr. Muhammad, Mr. Lomax asked whether the NOI leader was "preaching hate." Mr. Muhammad answered that he was "just teaching truth," that "he believed black people were divine and white people were devils," and that "Allah was a black man." And on interviewing Malcolm, Mr. Lomax asked whether the National Spokesman believed that "all white people were evil." Malcolm said that "white people were collectively evil" and added: "History is best qualified to reward all research, and we don't have any historic example where we have found that they have, collectively, as a people, done good."

When the documentary ended, many Americans realized that something was seriously wrong in America. And the public's reaction to the documentary was varied, as *Wikipedia's* article "The Hate That Hate Produced" recounted.

> *The Hate That Hate Produced* shocked many of the millions of people who watched it. Most white people had never heard of the Nation of Islam before, and many were stunned to learn that some black people had such strong feelings toward white people. For many white viewers, it was the first time they learned there was a radical black alternative to the Civil Rights Movement.
>
> Some African Americans could not believe that black people were saying such things out loud, but more than a few agreed with it. The number of people attending Nation of Islam meetings increased significantly, and the

group's membership doubled to 60,000 within weeks after the broadcast.

*The Hate That Hate Produced* catapulted Malcolm X to national attention. Although he had rarely been mentioned in the mainstream press before the program went on, Malcolm X soon became a frequent participant in television debates on race-related issues and one of the most sought-after speakers on college campuses across the United States. (Ibid., pp. 2–3)

Interestingly enough, modern scholars say that *The Hate That Hate Produced* documentary was a product of "yellow journalism," biased against the Nation of Islam, and thus "Race Card" oriented from the start—a fact implied by the *Wikipedia* article's summary of it:

Recent commentators generally feel that *The Hate That Hate Produced* was biased against the Nation of Islam… One of the first things Wallace said about Muhammad and Malcolm X was that they had served time in prison, a statement that seemed designed to call their leadership credentials into question and suggest the organization itself was criminal…In his book *White Violence* [*and*] *Black Response* [*:From Reconstruction to Montgomery*] [1988], Herbert Shapiro criticizes Wallace's opening comments that the Nation of Islam "preach[es] a gospel of hate that would set off a federal investigation if it were preached by Southern whites." He noted that some Southern whites— including state and local elected officials—did in fact preach such a gospel of hate, but the federal government had done almost nothing to stop their hate propaganda. Shapiro also argues that Wallace confused the Nation's rhetoric that condemned white people with a specific plan for violence against white people. (Ibid., p. 3, brackets partly ours)

Whatever the public's reaction, the 1959 documentary took Malcolm X on a wonderful journey in search of enlightenment and truth. Malcolm remained committed to the NOI and Mr. Muhammad for approximately four years after the documentary aired. However, during 1962–1963—while in charge of the NOI's Harlem Temple number 7—Malcolm discovered serious flaws in both Mr. Muhammad's moral behavior and philosophical doctrine. Using the 22 November 1963 assassination of President John F. Kenedy as an excuse to break with the NOI, Malcolm purposely violated Mr. Muhammad's gag order about Kenedy's murder. Consequently, the NOI "banned" (distanced itself from) him. In the face of reputed death threats from members in his own Temple—because some saw an irreparable rift developing between Malcolm and Mr. Muhammad—and doubting the correctness of the NOI's "white man equals the devil" equation, Malcolm sought the help of his siter Ella and United Nations advisor Dr. Mahmoud Youssef Shaw in order to make a trip to Mecca in search of the "truth" about Islam.

During the spring of 1964 Malcolm embarked on his journey and, all along the way, what he saw opened up new horizons of enlightenment for him—an awareness that would bring him into mortal combat with "the Race Card Evil." Indeed, from the time *The Hate That Hate Produced* aired Malcolm, being NOI National Spokesman, was on the defensive combating media questions about his organization's "black racism." His defense of NOI doctrine was honest and based on numerous historical examples of tolerated "white racism"—both inside and outside of America. However, his (or rather the NOI's) "all-encompassing" conclusion that "all people of a particular skin color or ethnicity" were "evil" was fatally flawed and in need of revision. Hence, his trip to Mecca was the appropriate antidote for his erroneous thinking.

One of Malcolm's first horizon-broadening encounters occurred when his Saudi, Arabia bound plane stopped over at Frankfurt, Germany. Said he,

The brother Muslim and I both were struck by the cordial hospitality of the people in Frankfurt. We went into a lot of shops and stores…and it would be Hello! People who never saw you before, and knew you were strangers. And the same cordiality when we left…In America, you walk in a store and spend a hundred dollars, and leave, and you're still a stranger. Both you and the clerks act as though you're doing each other a favor. Europeans act more human, or humane, whichever the right word is… and I saw something I had already experienced when I was looked upon as a Muslim and not as a Negro, right in America. People seeing you as a Muslim saw you as a human being and they had a different look, different talk, everything. (*Autobiography of Malcolm X*, 369)

And on landing at Cairo, Egypt Malcolm encountered another event that altered his one-dimensional "color-coded" thinking. Said he,

Back at the Frankfurt airport, we took a United Arab Airlines plane on to Cairo. Throngs of people, obviously Muslims from everywhere, bound on the pilgrimage, were hugging and embracing. They were of all complexions, the whole atmosphere was of warmth and friendliness. The feeling hit me that there really wasn't any color problem here. The effect was as though I had just stepped out of a prison. (Ibid., 369–70)

Next, on boarding a plane enroute to Jeddah, Saudi Arabia, Malcolm encountered yet another eye-opener. He stated:

Packed in the plane were white, black, brown, red, and yellow people, blue eyes and blond hair, and my kinky red hair—all together, brothers! All honoring the same God Allah, all in turn giving equal honor to each other…The captain of the plane came back to meet me. He was an Egyptian, his complexion was darker than mine…The co-pilot was darker than he was…Both of the pilots were smiling at me, treating me with the same honor and respect I had received ever since I left America. (Ibid., 372)

On reaching Jeddah, Malcolm ran into a technicality that required him to appear before an examination board to verify that he was a genuine Muslim. He was escorted to a dormitory to await examination. And while en route to the dorm, he encountered yet another revelation. Malcolm said,

Right outside the airport was a mosque, and above the airport was a huge, dormitory-like building…Pilgrims from Ghana, Indonesia, Japan, and Russia, to mention some, were moving to and from the dormitory where I was being taken. I don't believe that motion picture cameras ever have filmed a human spectacle more colorful than my eyes took in. We reached the dormitory and began climbing, up to the fourth, top, tier, passing members of every race on earth. Chinese, Indonesians, Afghanistanians. Many, not yet changed into the *Ihram* garb [white skull cap, long white nightshirt gown, and white slippers], still wore their national dress. It was like pages out of the *National Geographic* magazine. (Ibid., 375)

And just when Malcolm thought that what he had experienced could not be outdone, on contacting Dr. Omar Azzam (son of Adb-Al-Rahman Azzam) and being taken to his home, he encountered genuine hospitality. Said Malcolm,

Dr. Omar Azzam came straight to the airport. With the four officials beaming, he wrung my hand in welcome, a young, tall, powerfully built man. I'd say he was six foot three. He had an extremely polished manner. In America, he would have been called a white man, but—it struck me, hard and instantly—from the way he acted, I had no *feeling* of him being a white man…It was early in the morning when we reached Dr. Azzam's home. His father was there, his father's brother, a chemist, and another friend—all up that early, waiting. Each of them embraced me as though I were a long-lost child. I had never seen these men before in my life, and they treated me so good! I am going to tell you that I had never been so honored in my life, nor had I ever received such true hospitality…"You must rest," Dr. Azzam said. He went to use the telephone.

I didn't know what this distinguished man was doing. I had no dream. When I was told that I would be brought back for dinner that evening, and that, meanwhile, I should get back in the car, how could I have realized that I was about to see the epitome of Muslim hospitality?

Abd-Al-Rahman Azzam, when at home, lived in a suite at the Jedda Palace Hotel. Because I had come to them with a letter from a friend, he was going to stay at his son's home, and let me use his suite, until I could get on to Mecca.

When I found out, there was no use protesting: I was in the suite; young Dr. Azzam was gone; there was no one to protest to. The three-room suite had a bathroom that was as big as a double at the New York Hilton. It was suite number 214. There was even a porch outside, affording a beautiful view of the ancient Red Sea city.

There had never before been in my emotions such an impulse to pray—and I did, prostrating myself on the living-room rug. (Ibid., 381–82 passim)

This encounter forced Malcolm to seriously reflect on the real deal about the 'Race Card Evil." Said he,

Nothing in either of my two careers [criminal and minister] as a black man in America had served to give me any idealistic tendencies. My instincts automatically examined the reasons, the motives, of anyone who did anything they didn't have to do for me. Always in my life, if it was any white person, I could see a selfish motive.

But there in that hotel that morning, a telephone call and a few hours away from the cot on the fourth-floor tier of the dormitory, was one of the few times I had been so awed that I was totally without resistance. That white man—at least he would have been considered "white" in America—related to Arabia's ruler, to whom he was a close advisor, truly an international man, with nothing in the world to gain, had given up his suite to me, for my transient comfort. He had *nothing* to gain. He didn't need me. He had everything. In fact, he had more to lose than gain. He had followed the American press about me. If he did that, he knew there was only stigma attached to me. I was supposed to have horns. I was a "racist." I was "anti-white"—and he from all appearances was white. I was supposed to be a criminal; not only that, but everyone was even accusing me of using his religion of Islam as a cloak for my criminal practices and philosophies...I had no job. I had no money. Just to get over there, I had had to borrow money from my sister [Ella].

That morning was when I first began to reappraise the "white man." It was when I first began to perceive that "white man," as commonly used, means complexion only secondarily; primarily it described attitudes and actions. In America, "white man" meant specific attitudes and actions toward the black man, and toward all other non-white men. But in the Muslim world, I had seen that men with white complexions were more genuinely brotherly than anyone else had ever been.

That morning was the start of a radical alteration in my whole outlook about "white" men. (Ibid., 383)

After the Hajj ended, Malcolm and about twenty Muslims were sitting in a tent on Mount Arafat. On being asked what impressed him most about the the Hajj, he answered, "The *brotherhood!* The people of all races, colors, from all over the world coming together as *one*! It has proved to me the power of the One God." Then Malcolm said,

It may have been out of taste, but that gave me an opportunity, and I used it, to preach them a quick little sermon on America's racism, and its evils...And in everything I said to them, as long as we talked, they were aware of the yardstick that I was using to measure everything—that to me the earth's most explosive and pernicious evil is racism, the inability of God's creatures to live as One, especially in the Western world...The *color-blindness* of the Muslim world's religious society and the *color-blindness* of the Muslim world's human society: these two influences had each day been making a greater impact [on me], and an increasing persuasion against my previous [NOI] way of thinking...in the land of [Prophet] Muhammad and the land of [Prophet] Abraham, I had been blessed by Allah with a new insight into *the true religion of Islam*, and a better understanding of America's entire racial dilemma. (Ibid., 388–89, italics partly ours)

What was so remarkable about Malcolm X was the courage he displayed by admitting to Americans of all colors, creeds, and ethnicities that his former NOI view was wrong. Seeking to enlighten the members of his newly formed Muslim Mosque, Inc., and the American press, Malcolm wrote an honest letter to his organization and requested that it be sent to the press for publication. Said he,

Never have I witnessed such sincere hospitality and the overwhelming spirit of true brotherhood as is practiced by people of all colors and races here in this Ancient Holy Land, the home of Abraham, Muhammad, and all the other prophets of the Holy Scriptures. For the past week, I have been utterly speechless and spellbound by the graciousness I see displayed all around me by people *of all colors*.

I have been blessed to visit the Holy City of Mecca... There were tens of thousands of pilgrims, from all over the world. They were of all colors, from blue-eyed blonds to black-skinned Africans. But we were all participating in the same ritual, displaying a spirit of unity and brotherhood that my experiences in America had led me to believe never could exist between the white and the non-white.

America needs to understand Islam, because this is the one religion that erases from its society the race problem. Throughout my travels in the Muslim world, I have met, talked to, and even eaten with people who in America would have been considered 'white'—but the 'white' attitude was removed from their minds by the religion of Islam. I have never before seen *sincere* and *true* brotherhood practiced by all colors together, irrespective of their color.

You may be shocked by these words coming from me. But on this pilgrimage, what I have seen, and experienced, has forced me to *re-arrange* much of my thought-patterns previously held, and to *toss aside* some of my previous conclusions...I have been always a man who tries to face facts, and to accept the reality of life as new experience and new knowledge unfolds it. I have always kept an open mind, which is necessary to the flexibility that must go hand in hand with every form of intelligent search for truth.

During the past eleven days here in the Muslim world, I have eaten from the same plate, drunk from the same glass, and slept in the same bed (or on the same rug)—while praying to the *same* God—with fellow Muslims, whose eyes were the bluest of blue, whose hair was the blondest of blond, and whose skin was the whitest of white. And in the *words* and in the *actions* and in the *deeds* of the "white" Muslims, I felt the same sincerity that I felt among the black African Muslims of Nigeria, Sudan, and Ghana.

We were *truly* all the same (brothers)—because their belief in one God had removed the "white" from their *minds*, the "white" from their *behavior*, and the "white" from their *attitude*.

I could see from this, that perhaps if white Americans could accept the Oneness of God, then perhaps, too, they could accept *in reality* the Oneness of Man—and cease to measure, and hinder, and harm others in terms of their "differences" in color.

With racism plaguing America like an incurable cancer, the so-called "Christian" white American heart should be more receptive to a proven solution to such a destructive problem. Perhaps it could be in time to save America from imminent disaster—the same destruction brought upon Germany by racism that eventually destroyed the Germans themselves. (Ibid., 390–92)

On 21 May 1964, Malcolm returned to America and was met by news reporters with an onslaught of questions about a number of events—some of which he had knowledge of and some of which he did not. Eventually, one reporter asked him about his letter from Mecca and was it correct to quote him as saying that he now accepted "white" men as brothers. Malcolm replied,

> Yes—I wrote a letter from Mecca...My pilgrimage broadened my scope. It blessed me with a new insight. In two weeks in the Holy Land, I saw all *races*, all *colors*—blue-eyed blonds to black-skinned Africans—in *true* brotherhood! In unity! Living as one! Worshipping as one! No segregationists—no liberals; they would not have known how to interpret the meaning of those words.
>
> In the past, yes, I have made sweeping indictments of *all* white people. I never will be guilty of that again—as I know now that some white people are truly sincere, that some truly are capable of being brotherly toward a black man. The true Islam has shown me that a blanket indictment of all white people is as wrong as when whites make blanket indictments against blacks.
>
> Yes, I have been convinced that *some* American whites do want to help cure the rampant racism which is on the path to *destroying* this country!
>
> It was in the Holy World that my attitude was changed, by what I experienced there...And now that I am back in America, my attitude here concerning white people has to

be governed by what my black brothers and I experience here, and what we witness here—in terms of brotherhood. The *problem* here in America is that we meet such a small minority of individual so-called "good," or "brotherly" white people. Here in the United States, notwithstanding those few "good" white people, it is the *collective*...white people whom the *collective*...black people have to deal with!

Why, here in America, the seeds of racism are so deeply rooted in the white people collectively, their belief that they are "superior" in some way is so deeply rooted, that these things are in the national white subconsciousness. Many whites are even actually unaware of their own racism, until they face some test, and then their racism emerges in one form or another.

Listen! The white man's racism toward the black man here in America is what has got him in such trouble all over this world, with other non-white peoples. The white man can't separate himself from the stigma that he automatically feels about anyone, no matter who, who is not his color. And the non-white peoples of the world are sick of the condescending white man! That's why you've got all of this trouble in places like Viet Nam. Or right here in the Western Hemisphere...On the African continent, even, the white man has maneuvered to divide the black African from the brown Arab, to divide the so-called "Christian African" from the Muslim African. (*Autobiography of Malcolm X*, 416–17)

Undoubtedly, some Americans were skeptical that any religion could so immediately and drastically change a person's perspective—especially such a controversial person as Malcolm X. Yet, those enlightened enough to know simple honesty when spoken readily saw that his transformation was genuine. And his sincerity flared more brightly when it came to reevaluating the people and events that shaped his former "limited view" of Humanity. Said Malcolm,

In Mecca, too, I had played back for myself the twelve years I had spent with Elijah Muhammad as if it were a motion picture. I guess it would be impossible for anyone ever to realize fully how complete was my belief in Elijah Muhammad. I believed in him not only as a leader in the ordinary *human* sense, but also I believed in him as a *divine* leader. I believed he had no human weaknesses or faults, and that, therefore, he could make no mistakes and that he could do no wrong. There on a Holy World hilltop, I realized how very dangerous it is for people to hold any human being in such esteem, especially to consider anyone some sort of "divinely guided" and "protected" person.

My thinking had been opened up wide in Mecca. In the long letters I wrote to friends, I tried to convey to them my new insights into the American black man's struggle and his problems, as well as the depths of my search for truth and justice.

"I've had enough of someone else's propaganda," I had written to these friends. "I'm for truth, no matter who tells it. I'm for justice, no matter who it is for or against. I'm a human being first and foremost, and as such I'm for whoever and whatever benefits humanity *as a whole*." (Ibid., 420–21)

Although Malcolm retained his position on the hypocrisy demonstrated in America's history, he was perfectly clear about why he was steadfast in his view. Said he,

White society *hates* to hear anybody, especially a black man, talk about the crime the white man has perpetrated on the black man…When the white man came into this country, he certainly wasn't demonstrating any "non-violence." In fact, the very man [Dr. Martin Luther King, Jr.] whose name symbolizes non-violence here today has stated:

"Our nation was born in genocide when it embraced the doctrine that the original American, the Indian, was an inferior race. Even before there were large numbers of Negroes on our shores, the scar of racial hatred had already disfigured colonial society. From the sixteenth century forward, blood flowed in battles over racial supremacy. We are perhaps the only nation which tried as a matter of national policy to wipe out its indigenous population. Moreover, we elevated that tragic experience into a noble crusade. Indeed, even today we have not permitted ourselves to reject or to feel remorse for this shameful episode. Our literature, our films, our drama, our folklore all exalt it. Our children are still taught to repect the violence which reduced a red-skinned people of an earlier culture into a few fragmented groups herded into impoverished reservations." (Ibid., 423–24 passim)

And Malcolm retained his disapproval of what came to be called the "Christian" religion. Said he,

You can go right back to the very beginning of Christianity. Catholicism, the genesis of Christianity as we know it to be presently constituted, with its hierarchy, was conceived in Africa—by those whom the Christian church calls the "Desert Fathers." The Christian church became infected with racism when it entered white Europe. The Christian church returned to Africa under the banner of the Cross—conquering, killing, exploiting, pillaging, raping, bullying, beating—and teaching white supremacy. This is how the white man thrust himself into the position of leadership of the world—through the use of naked physical power… Well, if this is so—if the so-called "Christianity" now being practiced in America displays the best that world Christianity has left to offer—no one in his right mind should need any much greater proof that very close at hand is the *end* of Christianity…And what is the greatest single reason for this Christian church's failure? It is its failure to combat racism. It is the old "You sow, you reap" story. The Christian church sowed racism—blasphemously; now it reaps racism.

> Sunday mornings in this year of grace 1965, imagine the "Christian conscience" of congregations guarded by deacons barring the door to black would-be worshippers, telling them "You can't enter *this* House of God!" (Ibid., 424–25 passim)

And Malcolm retained his disapproval of the professed "Jewish black" Civil Rights Alliance. Said he to a suspected government agent he met on one occasion,

> I told him [the suspected agent] I'd had so much experience with how Jews would attack me that I usually could identify them. I told him all I held against the Jew was that so many Jews actually were hypocrites in their claim to be friends of the American black man, and it burned me up to be so often called "anti-Semitic" when I spoke things I knew to be the absolute truth about Jews. I told him that, yes, I gave the Jew credit for being among all other whites the most active, and the most vocal…in the Negro civil rights movement. But I said at the same time I knew that the Jew played these roles for a very careful strategic reason: the more prejudice in America could be focused upon the Negro, then the more the white Gentiles' prejudice would keep diverted off the Jew. I said that to me, one proof that all the civil rights posturing of so many Jews wasn't sincere was that so often in the North the quickest segregationists were Jews themselves. Look at practically everything the black man is trying to "integrate" into for instance; if Jews are not the actual owners, or are not in controlling positions, then they have major stockholdings or they are otherwise in powerful leverage positions—and do they really sincerely exert these influences? No!
>
> And an even clearer proof for me of how Jews truly regard Negroes, I said, was what invariably happened wherever a Negro moved into any white residential neighborhood that was thickly Jewish. Who would always lead the whites' exodus? The Jews! Generally in these

situations, some whites stay put—you just notice who they are: they're Irish Catholics, they're Italians; they're rarely ever any Jews. And, ironically, the Jews themselves often still have trouble being "accepted."

Saying this, I know I'll hear "anti-Semitic" from every direction again. Oh, yes! But truth is truth. (Ibid., 428–29)

Significantly, Malcolm (like Marcus Garvey, Noble Drew Ali, and Elijah Muhammad) agreed with the "white separatist" doctrine—holding that no governmental law could force brotherhood between citizens. This point the *American Jurisprudence* [*Legal*] *Encyclopedia* (second edition) agreed with by stating,

> Natural rights, as distinguished from civil rights, exist regardless of municipal or other law, if not repealed by legal fiat. They are those rights which appertain originally and essentially to each person as a human being and are inherent in his nature, as contrasted to civil rights, which are given, defined, and circumscribed by such positive laws, enacted by civilized communities, as are necessary to the maintenance of organized government...Civil rights have also been distinguished from social rights or privileges, and it has been pointed out in this connection that the purely social intercourse and relations of individuals cannot be enforced by law and are not guaranteed by any constitutional provision. (*American Jurisprudence 2d*, s.v. "Natural, political, and social rights distinguished," section 2, pp . 282–83)

And in a note under the same heading it further stated,

> An individual has the right "to pick his own associates so as to express his preferences and dislikes, and to fashion his private life by joining such clubs and groups as he chooses...But a municipal golf course that serves only one race is state activity indicating a preference on a matter as

to which the State must be neutral. What is 'private' action and what is 'state' action is not always easy to determine [cf. *Evans v. Newton*, 382 US 296 (1966)]." (Ibid., p. 283, n. 25)

Significantly, both Malcolm and an American Abassador he met in Africa agreed that the American "white" man was "not racist." Rather, they concluded that the real "racist" was America's economic, political, and social infrastructure. Said Malcolm,

> An American white ambassador in one African country was Africa's most respected American ambassador: I'm glad to say that this was told to me by one ranking African leader. We talked for an entire afternoon. Based on what I had heard of him, I had to believe him when he told me that as long as he was on the African continent, he never thought in terms of race, that he dealt with human beings, never noticing their color. He said he was more aware of language differences than of color differences. He said that only when he returned to America would he become aware of color differences.
>
> I told him, "What you are telling me is that it isn't the American *white* man who is a racist, but it's the American political, economic, and social *atmosphere* that automatically nourishes racist psychology in the *white* man." He agreed.
>
> We both agreed that American society makes it next to impossible for humans to meet in America and not be conscious of their color differences. And we both agreed that if racism could be removed, America could offer a society where rich and poor could truly live like human beings.
>
> That discussion with the Ambassador gave me a new insight—one which I like: that the *white* man is *not* inherently evil, but America's racist society influences him to act evilly. The society has produced and nourishes a

psychology which brings out the lowest, most base part of human beings. (Ibid., 427, italics partly ours).

Significantly, Malcolm recognized the true connection between religion (church) and government (state)—and he tried to clarify the relationship regarding religion and government working together to combat the "Race Card Evil." Said he,

Every free moment I could find, I did a lot of talking to key people whom I knew around Harlem, and I made a lot of speeches, saying, "True Islam taught me that it takes *all* of the religious, political, economic, psychological, and racial ingredients, or characteristics, to make the Human Family and the Human Society complete.

"Since I learned the *truth* in Mecca, my dearest friends have come to include *all* kinds—some Christians, Jews, Buddhists, Hindus, agnostics, and even atheists! I have friends who are called Capitalists, Socialists, and Communists! Some of my friends are moderates, conservatives, extremists—some are even Uncle Toms! My friends today are black, brown, red, yellow, and *white*!"... I said that on the American racial level, we had to approach the black man's struggle against the white man's racism as a human problem, that we had to forget hypocritical politics and propaganda. I said that both races, as human beings, had the obligation, the responsibility, of helping to correct America's human problem. The well-meaning white people, I said, had to combat, actively and directly, the racism in other white people. And the black people had to build within themselves much greater awareness that along with equal rights there had to be the bearing of equal responsibilities. (Ibid., 431–32)

Significantly, Malcolm (like Marcus Garvey, Noble Drew Ali, and Elijah Muhammad) pointed out that combating the "Race Card Evil" did not mean doing so from an "integrationist" standpoint—that is to say, by "forcing" one's self and lifestyle upon another. Rather, the best way to combat the evil was for people to work within their own communities enlightening their members about it—while teaching them "self-help" ethics. Said he,

> I tell sincere white people, "Work in conjunction with us—each of us working among our own kind." Let sincere white individuals find all other white people they can who feel as they do—and let them form their own all-white groups, to work trying to convert other white people who are thinking and acting so racist. Let sincere whites go and teach non-violence to white people!
>
> We will completely respect our white co-workers. They will deserve every credit. We will give them every credit. We will meanwhile be working among our own kind, in our own black communities—showing and teaching black men in ways that only other black men can—that the black man has got to help himself. Working separately, the sincere white people and sincere black people actually will be working together. (Ibid., 434)

Most significantly, Malcolm's views reflected the broadened horizon he received by making a pilgrimage in search of the truth needed to combat the "Race Card Evil"—an enlightenment he demonstrated on the day after his return to the United States. Said he,

> The next day I was in my car driving along the freeway when at a red light another car pulled alongside. A white woman was driving and on the passenger's side, next to me, was a white man. "*Malcolm X!*" he called out—and when I looked, he stuck his hand out of his car, across at me, grinning. "Do you mind shaking hands with a white man?" Imagine that! Just as the traffic light turned green, I told him, "I don't mind shaking hands with human beings. Are you one?" (Ibid., 418)

As should be expected, Malcolm's decision to contest the "Race Card Evil" would not go unpunished—and he had no delusions about it. Rather, he faced the inevitable result by stating,

> Sometimes, I have dared to dream to myself that one day, history may even say that my voice—which disturbed the white man's smugness, and his arrogance, and his complacency—that my voice helped to save America from a grave, possible even a fatal catastrophe.
>
> The goal has always been the same, with the approaches to it as different as mine and Dr. Martin Luther King's nonviolent marching, that dramatizes the brutality and the evil of the white man against defenseless blacks. And in the racial climate of this country today, it is anybody's guess which of the "extremes" in approach to the black man's problems might *personally* meet a fatal catastrophe first—"nonviolent" Dr. King, or so-called "violent" me. (Ibid., 434–35)

History recounted that Malcolm X's foreboding was correct. On Sunday afternoon, 21 February 1965, thirty-nine-year-old Muslim Minister Malcolm X—more correctly Mr. El-Hajj Malik El-Shabazz—was assassinated in upper Manhattan's Audubon Ballroom prior to making his speech. Malcolm's assassins were the same ethnicity as he, but they flew the "Race Card Evil's" colors. And as for Dr. Martin Luther King Jr., on Thursday evening, 4 April 1968, an assassin's bullet ended the thirty-nine-year-old Christian Minister's life as he stood on the Lorraine Motel balcony in Memphis, Tennessee. Martin's assassins were not the same ethnicity as he, but they flew the "Race Card Evil's" colors. In either case of these two ministers, one Muslim and one Christian, their assassins proved to be "the same color"—neither "black" nor "white," but the "Race Card Evil's" color.

## 12

# Things that Sink Deep in the Heart: "Which Are You?"

### (Concluding Thoughts by Haywood Isaac)

> Who hath [has] believed our report? [A]nd to whom is
> the arm of the LORD [Creator] revealed?
>
> —Isaiah 53:1 (KJV)

MALCOLM X'S JOURNEY from "limited" to "unlimited" brotherhood is a journey that each of us should take sooner or later. Being dissatisfied with the "selective" brotherhood displayed by Jews, Christians, his own Nation Of Islam members, and other American groups Malcolm believed that he found "unlimited" or "universal" brotherhood in Islam as practiced in the East. However, did he? Indeed, how would he feel had he lived to see our twenty-first century "religious" world? For instance, when covering the great humanitarian works that the American Anti-Slavery Group and Christian Solidarity International were undertaking to end modern-world slavery in the Sudan, *Washington Times* columnist Nat Hentoff revealed in his 31 January 2000 article entitled "Where was Jesse [Jackson]":

> Celebrating the birthday of Martin Luther King Jr. on Jan. 17, Newark's Paradise Baptist Church [in New Jersey] joined the American Anti-Slavery Group in a special service to call urgent attention to the mass slavery of black Christians and animists in southern Sudan by the Arab Islamic government in the north.
>
> Nat Hentoff, "Where was Jesse? The reverend's silence on slavery," *The Washington Times*, 31 January 2000, Op-Ed, p. A15.

Significantly, Mr. Hentoff recounted the 27 May 1999 testimony of Ms. Victoria Ajang to the US Congress. When speaking about the Arab-Islamic government's raid on her village, Ms. Ajang, an escaped slave, testified,

> Against the dark sky, we saw flames from the houses the [government's] soldiers had set on fire. The cries of the people forced inside filled our ears as they were burned to death. Our people were being turned into ash…
>
> "My neighbor, Batul Adam, was captured as well. Her beautiful daughters were taken captive and given to northern masters. There is a *powerful ideology* that drives these slave raids. In the government's mentality, all blacks are bad—slaves. Whether *Christian*, *Muslim*, or *animist*, we should be slaves forever. We are inferior beings who must submit or be killed…I still see the bones of starved people, who lack even the energy to bury the dead around them. (Ibid., p. A15, italics mine)

Surely such "antisocial" and "unbrotherly" Muslim behavior would shock Malcolm X. Yet, neither he nor we should be "shocked"—given the "Arab-Muslim" role in the "international slave trade" and the reality cited by Ms. Ella Wheeler Wilcox, the nineteenth-century American poetess, in her poem entitled "Which Are You?" Therein she said,

There are two kinds of people on earth to-day;
Just two kinds of people, no more, I say.

Not the sinner and saint, for it's well understood,
[That] the good are half bad, and the bad are half good.

Not the rich and the poor, for to rate a man's wealth,
You must first know the state of his conscience and health.
Not the humble and proud, for in life's little span, he who
puts on vain airs, is not counted a man.
Not the happy and sad, for the swift flying years,
Bring each man his laughter and each man his tears.

No; the two kinds of people on earth I mean,
Are the people who lift, and the people who lean.

Wherever you go, you will find the earth's masses,
Are always divided in just these two classes.

And oddly enough, you will find too, I ween,
[That] there's only one lifter to twenty who lean.

In which class are you? Are you easing the load,
Of overtaxed lifters, who toil down the road?

Or are you a leaner, who lets others share [bare],
Your portion of labor, and worry and care?

Ella Wheeler Wilcox, "Which Are You," *Custer and Other Poems* (Chicago: W.B. Conkey Co., 1896); see also, "The American Verse Project," http://quod.lib.umich.educ/ cgi/t/text/text-idx?c=amverse;idno=BAC5729.0001.001. Retrieved 10 February 2014.

The point Ms. Wilcox raised is modernly validated by the fact that Ms. Ajang's "powerful ideology," better known as the Race Card Evil, is alive and well in this twenty-first-century world—and not just in America! Moreover, her testimony to Congress proved that the "Ancient Serpent" is an "equal-opportunity employer-oppressor" that does not discriminate because of age, financial position, educational level, ethnic heritage, gender orientation, political affiliation, religious preference, or social status! This truth twentieth-century American Chaplain Levi H. Dowling hinted at in his *Aquarian Gospel*. When speaking about sixteen-year-old Jesus of Nazareth's view on the Brahmic religion's "caste" doctrine, Chaplain Dowling recounted,

> One day he [Jesus] sat among the [Brahmic] priests and said to them, "Pray [please], tell me all about your views of castes; why do you say that all men are not equal in the sight of God?"
>
> A master of their laws stood forth and said, "The Holy One whom we call Brahm, made men to suit himself, and men should not complain.
>
> "In the beginning days of human life Brahm spoke, and four men stood before his face…the first man…was *white*…a brahman he was called… he had no need of toil [labor, work]…he was called the priest…to act for Brahm in all affairs of earth.
>
> "The second man was *red*… was called [a] shatriya… he was made to be the king, the ruler and the warrior, whose highest ordained duty was protection of the priest.
>
> "And… the third man came; and he was called a visya…a *yellow* man, and his it was to till the soil, and keep the flocks and herds.
>
> "And…the fourth man came; and he was *black*…was called the sudras, one of low estate…he has no rights that others need respect [cf. *Dred Scott v. Sandford*]; he may not hear the Vedas [Holy Book] read, and it means death to

him to look into the face of priest, or king, and naught but death can free him from his state of servitude."

And Jesus said, "Then Parabrahm is not a God of justice and of right; for with his own strong hand he has exalted one and brought another low...My Father-God... Who in the boundlessness of love has made all men to equal be. The *white*, the *black*, the *yellow* and the *red* can look up in thy face say, Our Father-God...Father of *the human race*, I praise thy name."

And all the priests were angered by the words which Jesus spoke; they rushed upon him, seized him, and would have done him harm...then Lamaas raised his hand and said, "You priests of Brahm, beware! You know not what you do; wait till you know the God this youth adores."

Levi H. Dowling, *The Aquarian Gospel of Jesus the Christ* (Marina Del Rey, CA: DeVorss and Co., 1985 [originally 1907], 42–43 passim, "The Brahmic doctrine of castes. Jesus repudiates it and teaches human equality." Italics and quotation marks mine)

And when addressing the connection between the Emancipation Proclamation, Thirteenth Amendment, Congress's post-Civil War legislation, and America's intended destiny, John Ballou added in his *Oahspe's* section entitled "Jehovih Overthroweth Slavery in Guatama [America],"

In the olden times, and *in the eastern countries*, Jehovih [The Creator] began His revelations. *The western continent* He left for the finishing thereof...Jehovih said: "Let this be a testimony, that this [Western] land [America] is the place of the beginning of the *kosmon era* [universal enlightenment, freedom, and brotherhood era]. There shall be *no caste* amongst my people...in this era I come not to an exclusive [separate] people, but to the combination of all peoples commingled together as one [united] people. Hence, I have called this, the *Kosmon*

*Era*...My chosen shall be of the amalgamated [melting pot] races [ethnicities], who choose Me. And these shall become the best, most perfect of all peoples on the earth... *they shall not consider race or color*, but health and nobleness as to the mortal part; and as to the spirit [part], peace, love, wisdom and good works, and *one Great Spirit* [Creator] *only*."

*Oahspe*, "Jehovih Overthroweth Slavery in Guatama," 770–72 passim (brackets, italics, and quotation marks mine).

And in agreement with Mr. Ballou's assessment *The First Book of Adam and Eve*—an ancient undated work of unknown Egyptian authorship (with parts of it found in both the *Talmud* and *Qur'an*)—in a chapter entitled "The Prophecy of the Western Lands" stated,

And Adam said unto Eve, "Since we know not what there is *to the westward* of this cave, let us go forth and see it to-day." Then they came forth and went towards *the western border*...And God said unto Adam, "O Adam, what seekest thou *on the western border*? And why hast thou left of thine own accord *the eastern border*, in which was thy dwelling-place?

"Now, then, turn back to thy cave, and remain in it...

"For *in this western border*, O Adam, there will go from thee a seed [descendants], that shall replenish it; and that will defile themselves with their sins, and with their yielding to the behests of Satan, and by following his works.

"Therefore will I bring upon them the waters of a flood, and overwhelm them all. But I will deliver what is left of the righteous among them; *and I will bring them to a distant land*, and the land in which thou dwellest now shall remain desolate and without one inhabitant in it." (Rutherford H. Platt, Jr., and J. Alden Brett, Eds., and Rev. S. C. Malan, D. D. (Vicar of Broadwindsor) Trans., *The*

*Forgotten Books of Eden,* USA: Alpha House, Inc., 1927, England, 1882), pp. 34–35, brackets and italics mine).

Despite the real American history covered herein that points to America's destiny, most "modern" Americans are unaware of what the founders intended when they established our Republic. This "unawareness" stems from two chief causes: (1) the willful failure of our academic, fraternal, and religious institutions to teach America's history from an honest standpoint regardless of "embarrassing" people (the truth is what it is); and (2) the willful failure of many "modern" Americans to research our country's history in order to accurately teach our children what "citizenship" entails—its "privileges, immunities, and rights," as well as its "duties, obligations, and responsibilities." Thus, before ending our journey, a few more things need be said that should sink deep in our hearts (minds).

*First,* despite both the Leakey Family's 1948–1960 archaeological findings and 2009 National Geographic "Human Family Tree" TV documentary tracing humanity's birthplace back to "Africa," we still hear so-called "black" and "white" Americans talk of "black" and "white" races (so why should Ms. Rachel Dolezal apologize for lying about her "race" when many of us are lying about ours?). Indeed, in volume one of *Ancient Lights* we showed that "color," "ethnicity," and "race" were not the same thing—our "colors" varying because of our "melanin" pigmentation concentration, our "ethnicities" stemming from Noah's "seventy post-flood nations," and our "race" originating from our "Adamite" or "human" ancestors (although some of us are suspect of being "inhuman").

*Second,* in 2015 a young "white" American male named Dylann Roof fell victim to the "Race Card Evil" by shooting "black" Americans holding a night church service. He said that he did so in an attempt to start a "race war" (unrealistic because we live in a nuclear age; impractical because the economies of most of the Club Nuke members are tied in to each other). Although one may agree with his statement that some "blacks" complain and cry "racism" too much, one cannot agree that "murder" is the solution for "crying" (I wonder what his solution would be for crying babies?). Sadly, Mr. Roof fell victim to "hate" propaganda and misused the Confederate battle flag as a "hate-separatist" symbol to perpetrate a "criminal act" (wrong choice of symbolism). Unfortunately, Mr. Roof (and those who subscribe to his "race war" view—black, white, other) erred by thinking that "skin color" or "ethnicity" made "allies." This "myth" historian J. A. Rogers' refuted in volume two of his *Sex and Race*. Therein he recounted,

> Rich Negroes, as was said, bought white people...Some of these rich Negroes had white wives and married their mulatto daughters to white men...Ham[m]et Achmet, who was famed for being the servant of George Washington...married a young white girl, who had been reared by himself and his first wife, acolored woman. The girl, so as not to excite comment when she went out with Hamet, "washed her face and hands in a decoction [concoction] of mahogany chips" to look colored. At Hamet's death...she married a white sailor...named Folio, whereupon she allowed the stain on her face to wear off and became white again.
>
> Charles Bowles, an unmixed Negro, a hero of the Revolutionary War, born inBoston [in] 1761, married the white daughter of Colonel Morgan, of the Rifle Corps of the American Army.
>
> Lemuel Haynes, noted divine, pastor of white churches in Vermont, Connecticut, and New York, and minute-man of the [1776] Revolution, married "Elizabeth Babbett, a young and well-educated white woman of excellent family" on September 23, 1783. This was evidently done with full approval of his white flock because it was three years after he had begun to preach. Haynes' mother was a white woman who deserted him at birth.
>
> "Rich Negroes With White Wives And Concubines" (*Sex and Race*, vol. 2, 246–47; Rogers citing E. T. Stedman, *Hammet Achmet* (1920); W. C. Nell, *Colored Patriots of the American Revolution*, 1855, p. 28; T. T Cooley, *Lemuel*

*Haynes* (1837) and *National Cyclopedia of American Biography*, vol. 12, 1904, p. 256.)

*Third*, Mr. Roof's misuse of the battle flag sparked what amounts to a modern "witch hunt" by some attention-seeking political activists—one that now includes statues of notables such as Supreme Court Chief Justice Roger B. Taney and General Robert E. Lee to name a few (have we become idol woshippers?). While some may not "like" the political or military positions these men occupied, that has nothing to do with what they actually stood for (we addressed this earlier)!

*Fourth*, this flag-statue "witch hunt" has confused many Americans. How can one "condemn" the battle flag, but not the Union Jack (or flags flown by African, Islamic, or other countries involved in the international slave trade)? How can one "protest" Taney and Lee, but not Grant—since they were all slaveowners? And then there's the fact that Congress's "Statuary Hall" has statues of Henry Clay (1850 Fugitive Slave Law), Jefferson Davis (the Confederacy president), Robert E. Lee, and George Washington to name a few? Does one propose that Congress "remove" them? Thus this modern "witch hunt" reeks of "bullyism," "discrimination," "inquisition," and a violation of the Old Testament warning against "removing a neighbor's landmark" (see Lev. 19:15, 18, 35–36; Deut. 19:14; Matt. 6:9–15; 7:1–2) (KJV).

*Fifth*, we should consider the fact that: "Jewish" Americans have no standing to complain about anyone being "anti-Semitic," because their ancestors formulated the "Chosen Superior One" doctrine that Adolph Hitler's Nazi Party used against them; "white" Americans have no standing to complain about not being "separate," because their ancestors were "separate" until they left England or Europe and migrated to countries inhabited by "people of color" (Lincoln hinted at this when debating Douglas about "squatter's rights"); "Native" Americans have no standing to complain about being "annihilated" and "displaced," because their ancestors helped the "whites" who migrated to the Americas survive so that they could be "annihilated" and "squatted on."; "black" Americans have no standing to complain about "not getting an apology" from "whites" (American or European), because their "black" ancestors (Christian, Jewish, Moorish, Muslim, or tribal) introduced Europe's "whites" to the international slave trade—then participated in, and helped further, the evil (we covered this in volume one); and of course people coming or fleeing to America from other countries have no standing to complain about not "liking"American culture, and then trying to impose their "Old World" ways on the "New World" they came or fled to (see Rev. 21:1) (KJV).

You see, there lies the problem in America and the world—we want the world to be made in our "image and likeness." But as Ms. Wilcox rightly said, the world only has two kinds of people— those whom "religion" call "good" or evil," but more accurately are "lifters" or "leaners" (see Matt. 7:6–12, KJV). Because of this reality James Monroe, in *The Federalist Papers* number 51, said regarding government and the governed,

> "[i]f men were angels, no government would be necessary. If angels were to govern men, neither external nor internal controls on government would be necessary. In framing a government which is to be administered by men over men, the great difficulty lies in this: you must first enable the government to control the governed; and in the next place oblige it to control itself. A dependence on the people is, no doubt, the primary control on the government; but experience has taught mankind the necessity of auxiliary precautions."
>
> Laurence H. Tribe and Michael C. Dorf, *On Reading the Constitution* (Cambridge, MA: Harvard University Press, 1991, 6, "How Not to Read the Constitution"; Tribe and Dorf quoting from James Madison, "The Federalist No. 51," *The Federalist Papers* New York: Random House, 1937, 337)

That Mr. Madison's observation was and is correct is shown by modern adherents of the "three sisters"—Judaism, Christianity, and Islam. All over the world many of their adherents are enslaving or oppressing people, suppressing intellectual advancement (via doctrines and cults), invading and occupying other people's lands, preventing indigenous people from governing themselves, spreading hatred and racism, burning sacred books, destroying livelihoods or property, and shooting or bombing people because they don't "like" what someone said or printed (thus committing murder)—all of this done "in *God's* name." This needs to stop—because such behavior reeked of "The Race Card Evil" in the past, reeks of it today, and is uncharacteristic of the demeanor of Abraham, Jesus of Nazareth, and Muhammad Ibn Abdullah (Surah 3:59, 65–68, *The Glorious Qur'an*, John 8:31–44, KJV). Having said this, it is time to end our journey by reminding Americans of a few important points.

First are the replies by Americans to Dear Abby's "Racism is many-sided problem," who said,

> "Teaching to hate because others hate only shows [a] willingness to sink to someone else's level and to conform to racist policies, which only fuels racism."—Citizens for an equal America, Paxton, Ill[inois]
>
> "When our society gets to the point where…we begin to describe ourselves as "Americans," and not "something-Americans," then and only then can we make the statement that there is no racism."—Hoping for a non-racist America.
>
> "Hatred and bigotry should be condemned as strongly when they come from a minority as when they came from the majority."—D. L. in S[outh] C[arolina]
> "Dear Abby," *Chicago Tribune*, 27 October 1999: 9.

Next, there is the song, "Choice of Colors," that summed up the problem in America and the world by stating,

> People must prove to the people,
> A better day is coming, for you and for me.
> With just a little bit more education,
> And love for our nation,
> Would make a better society.
> Now some of us would rather cuss and make a fuss,
> Than to bring about a little trust.
> But we shall overcome our beliefs someday,
> If you'll only listen to what I have to say.
> And how long have you hated your white teacher, Who told you, you [should] love your black preacher[?] (Curtis Mayfield and the Impressions)

And finally, here are some parting shots that also need to sink deep in the heart.

For people, domestic or foreign, who would try to "address" or "change" things by violence—bombing, shooting, child-elderly-spousal-animal abuse-murder (gangs, drug dealers, disgruntled employees or students, police officers, military personnel, and ordinary citizens)—it is best to heed that nineteenth-century American essayist, who said,

> "We may not always be responsible for the things that happen to us, but we are responsible for how we behave when they do." (Ralph Waldo Emerson)

For people who believe that some great conspiracy exists to prevent them from achieving, it is best to heed that enlightened twenty-first-century African American president, who said,

> "Our destiny is not written for us, but by us." (Barack H. Obama)

For people who believe they can waste time on trivial pursuits, it is best to heed the incomparable El-Hajj Malik El-Shabazz who, at page 435 of his *Autobiography*, said,

"Anything I do today, I regard as urgent. No man is given but so much time to accomplish whatever is his life's work…I am only facing the facts when I know that any moment of any day, or any night, could bring me death." (Malcolm X )

And for people who willfully fail to understand what Malcolm meant, and believe that they'll always be around to do as they please with impunity, it is best to heed that enlightened "preacher" who added,

"Remember your Creator in the days of your youth… Because man goes to his lasting home, and mourners go about the streets…And the dust returns to the earth as it once was, and the life breath returns to God who gave it." (Ecclesiates 12:1–7 passim, NAB)

Oh, by the way, we"ll be back to reveal the connection between the "Race Card Evil" and the beast bearing the number "six hundred threescore and six"—cited in *Revelation* 13:18 (KJV). *God* willing, see you soon!

# Bibliography

Ali, Timothy Drew. *The Holy Koran of the Moorish Science Temple of America*. Chicago: Self-published, 1928.

Bancroft, George. *The History of the United States of America from the Discovery of the Continent*. Abridged and edited by Russel B. Nye. Chicago: The University of Chicago Press, 1966 (originally 1876–79).

Blumenbach, Johann F. *The Anthropological Treatises of Johann Friedrich Blumenbach*. London: Longman, Green, Roberts, et. al., 1865 (reprint 1969).

Chisolm, N. Jamilya. "Imitation of Life." (October 2002).

Commager, Henry S., and Milton Cantor. *Documents of American History: Volume 1, 1898*, tenth ed. Englewoods Cliffs, NJ: Prentice Hall, Inc., 1988.

Congressional Globe,</i>38th Congress, 1st Session, 1864.

Cuba-A, Prince. "Black Gods of the Inner City." *Gnosis* (Fall 1992).

Dunston, Jr., Alfred G. *The Black Man in The Old Testament and Its World*. Trenton, NJ: Africa World Press, Inc., 1994.

Franklin, John H., and Loren Schweninger. *Runaway Slaves: Rebels on the Plantation*. New York: Oxford University Press, 1999.

Frederickson, George M. *White Supremacy: A Comparative Study in American and South African History*. New York: Oxford University Press, 1981.

Gladstone, John, and George Perpich. *The HPAC and V Contractor's Reference Book and Lincense Review*, 2d ed. Coral Gables, FL: Engineer's Press, 1991.

Harris, Clarissa M. "Against All Odds." *Smithsonian* 33, no. 4 (July 2002).

Hinchliff, Peter. "Africa." *The Oxford Illustrated History of Christianity*. Edited by John McManners. New York: Oxford University Press, 1990.

Helper, Hinton R. *Nojoque: A Question For A Continent*. New York: George W. Carleton and Co., Publishers, 1867.

Huxley, Thomas H. *Man's Place in Nature and other [Anthropological] Essays*. New York: E.P. Dutton and Co., 1927. New York: D. Appleton and Co., 1929.

Koger, Sr., Earl. *Jocko: A Legend of the American Revolution*. Englewoods Cliffs, NJ: Prentice-Hall, 1976.

Logan, John A. *The Great Conspiracy: Its Origin and History*. New York: A.R. Hart and Co., 1886. Freeport, NY: Books for Libraries Press, 1971.

McPherson, Edward. *The Political History of the United States of America During the Period of Reconstruction* (from April 15, 1865, to July 15, 1870,), 2d ed. New York: Negro University Press, 1969 reprint (originally 1871).

Rayback, Joseph G. "The American Workingman and the Antislavery Crusade." *Journal of Economic History* 3, (1943).

Rogers, Joel A. *Sex and Race: A History of White, Negro, and Indian Miscegenation in the Two Americas*. Vol. II (The New World), 6th printing (1970), 9th printing (1989). St. Petersburg, FL: Helga M. Rogers, 1989 (originally 1942).

Rogers, Joel A. *Sex and Race*. Vol. III (Why White and Black Mix in Spite of Opposition), 5th ed. St. Petersburg, FL: Helga M. Rogers, 1972 (originally 1944).

*Selected Writings and Speeches of Marcus Garvey.* Edited by Bob Blaisdell. New York: Dover Publications, Inc., 2004.

Shenk, Joshua W. *Lincoln's Melancholy.* New York: Houghton Mifflin, 2005.

Stowe, Harriet B. *Uncle Tom's Cabin or Life Among the Lowly.* New York: Random House, Inc., 1996 (originally 1852).

*The Constitution Of The United States Of America As Amended.* Presented by Chairman Robert Ney. Washington, DC: United States Government Printing Office, 2003.

*The Forgotten Books of Eden.* Edited by Rutherford H. Platt, Jr., and J. Alden Brett. USA: Alpha House, Inc., 1927 (originally England, 1882).

*The Holy Bible: King James Version.* New York: American Bible Society, 1611.

*The Meaning of the Glorious Qur'an.* Translated by Abdullah Yusuf Ali. Istanbul: Asir Media, 2002.

*The New American Bible, Revised Edition.* Washington, DC: Confraternity of Christian Doctrine, Inc., 2010.

*The Oahspe: A New Bible in The Words Of Jehovih And His Angel Embassadors.* Transcribed by John Ballou Newbrough. New York: Oahspe Publishing Association, 1882.

*The Universal History of the World.* 16 Volumes. Edited by Irwin Shapiro and Jonathan Bartlett. New York: Golden Press, Inc., 1966.

Tribe, Laurence H., and Michael C. *On Reading the Constitution.* Cambridge, MA: Harvard University Press, 1991.

Tsesis, Alexander, "Interpreting the Thirteenth Amendment," *University of Pennsylvania Journal of Constitutional Law* 11, no. 5 (2009).

Wilcox, Ella W. "Which Are You?" *Custer and Other Poems.* Chicago: W.B. Conkey Co., 1896.

Wright, Carroll D., and William O. Hunt. *The History and Growth of the United States Census*. Washington, DC: United States Government Printing Office, 1900.

X, Malcolm, and Alex Haley. *The Autobiography of Malcolm X*. New York: Ballantine Books, 1973–92 (originally New York: Grove Press, Inc., 1964–65).

# Authors' Biographies

**Haywood Isaac**

A Baltimore (MD) resident and alumni of Baltimore's Coppin State University (mathematics, magna cum laude; Alpha Kappa Mu), with over forty years of historical research background in the Western world's three major religions (Judaism, Christianity, and Islam) and American political history, Mr. Isaac is the author of the two-volume work entitled *Ancient Lights: The Real Deal about the Race Card Evil* and *Ancient Lights: The Real Deal about the Birth of the American Nation.*

**Christine Isaac**

A Baltimore (MD) resident and alumni of Fort Collins Colorado's US Career Institute (accounting, magna cum laud), with over seven years of historical research background in the Western world's three major religions, American political history, and how they impact female equality in worldwide society, Mrs. Isaac is coauthor of the two-volume Ancient Lights work.